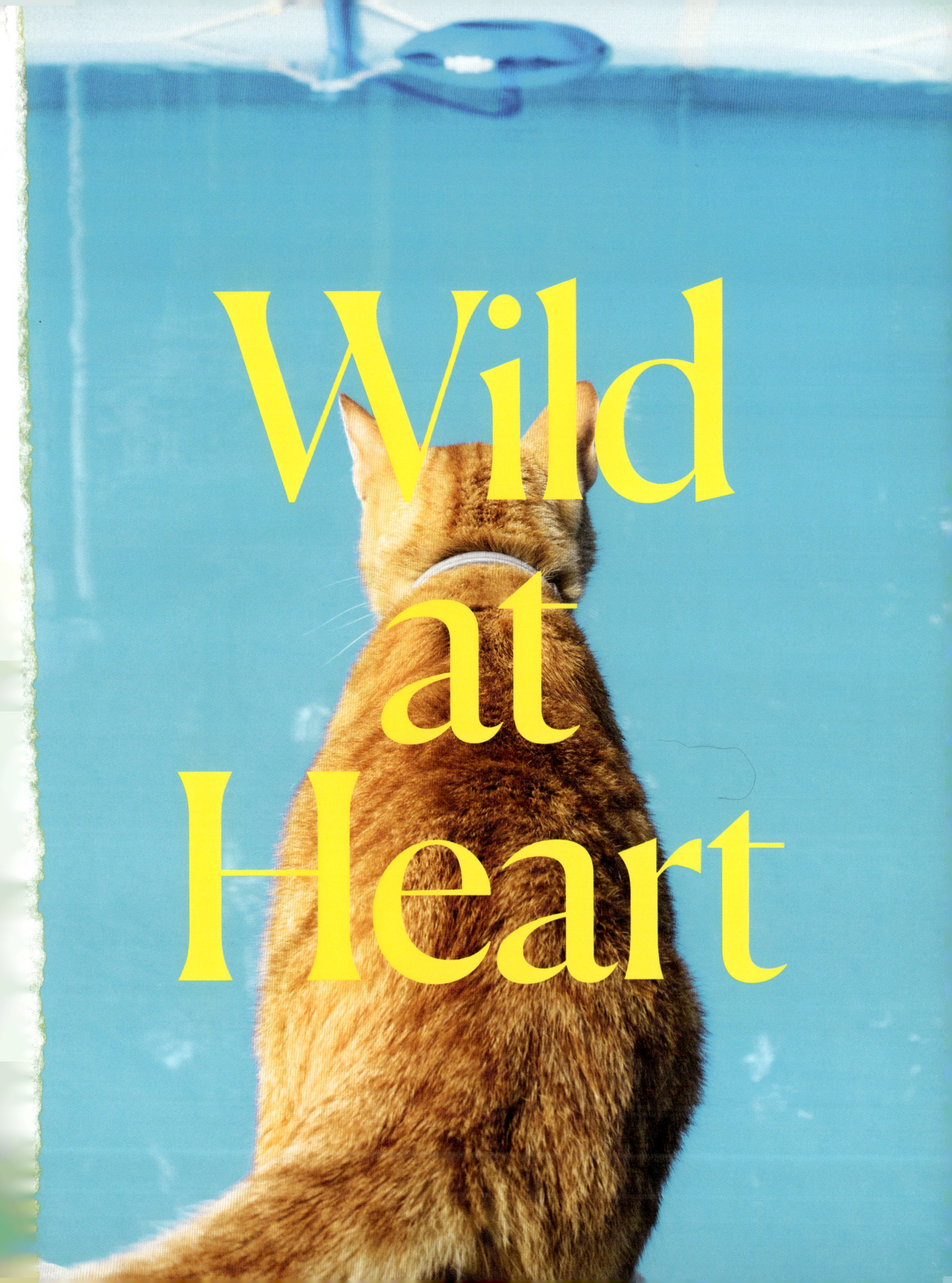

Wild
at
Heart

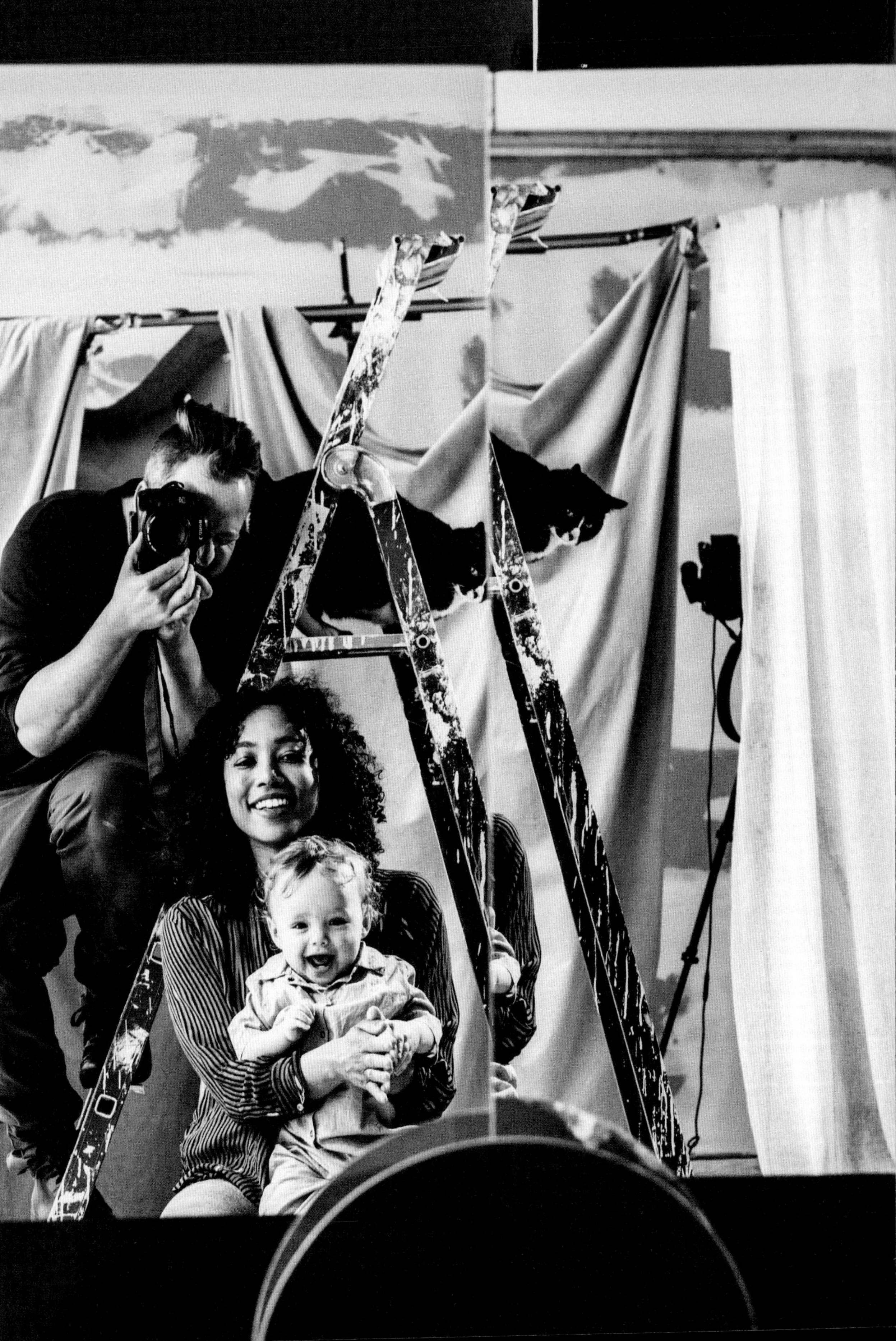

Pets and people, it's a family affair

Pets, people, their inspiring homes, and personal stories. How can you not love this combination? This book is intended as a tribute to the connection between people and animals and a wild lifestyle, which is totally linked with the special relationship we have with pets. For 'Wild at Heart' Bart Kiggen - my husband, photographer and designer of this book - and I visited fifteen families in the city and in the countryside, that are passionate about animals.

We both have a soft spot for animals, having been raised with pets around the house. The same applies to our son Nolan Ayo, who is completely fascinated with our three cats, Tealc, Kostuum, and Sottsass. While the felines cause chaos and destroy our stuff, they also liven up the house and are a source of warmth. They have become part of our family. Our attitude towards them teaches us a lot about ourselves. As animal love is such an emotional topic, we looked for kindred spirits to share their stories and their beautiful homes. This and a passion for beauty inspired us to make this book.

The homes in Bart's analog and digital photos are complex and messy, imperfect and magnificent, but always perfectly framed. Through the use of light and shadow, his images are illuminated in a manner that gives life and adds a layer of poetry to the interiors he shows - almost painterly, thus revealing the souls of these gems, and of the people and animals inhabiting them.

We both really enjoyed working on 'Wild at Heart', the many stimulating conversations and the patient waiting together for that magical instant, the genuine emotions and interaction and the sky's ever-changing colours at sunrise and sunset.

Magali Elali

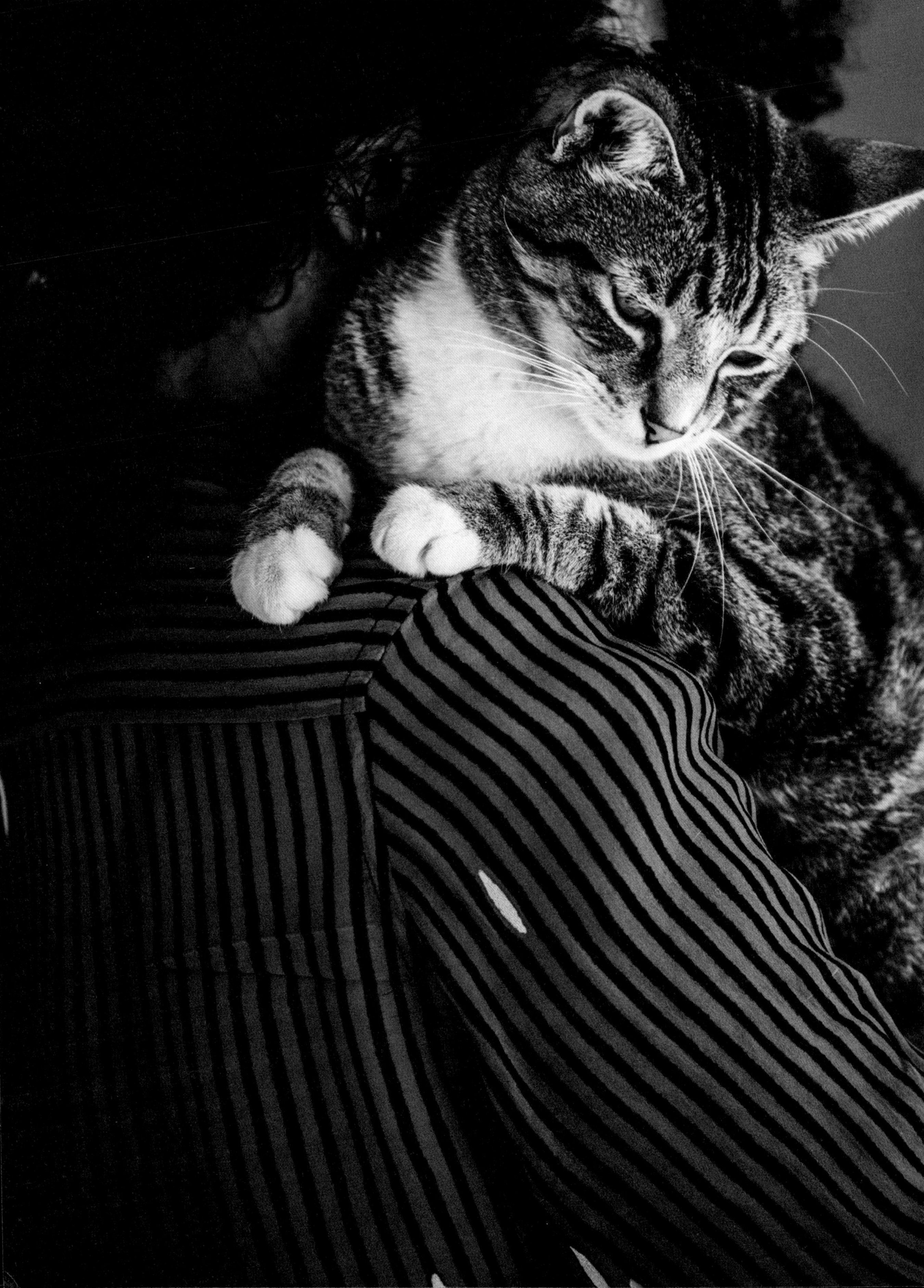

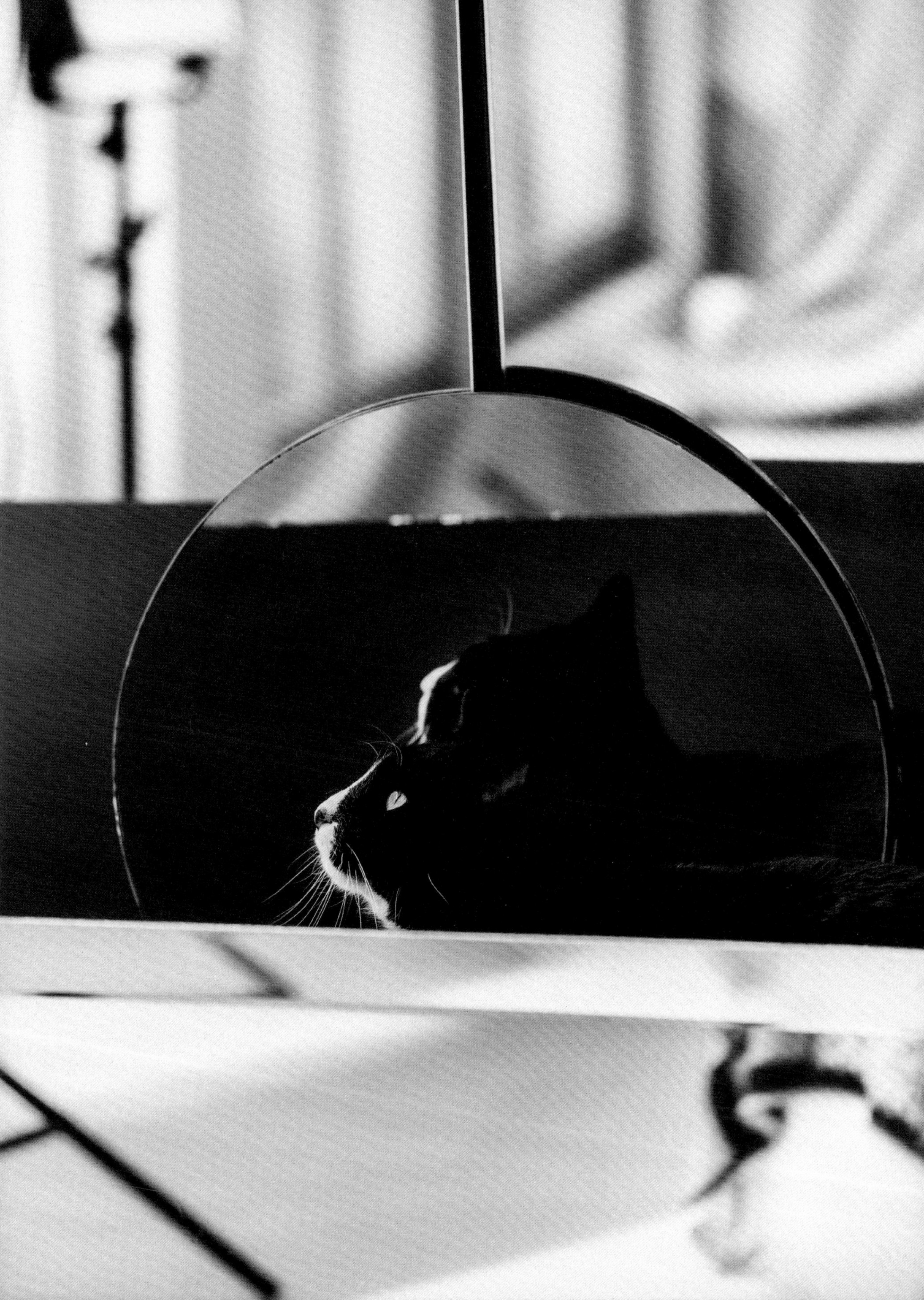

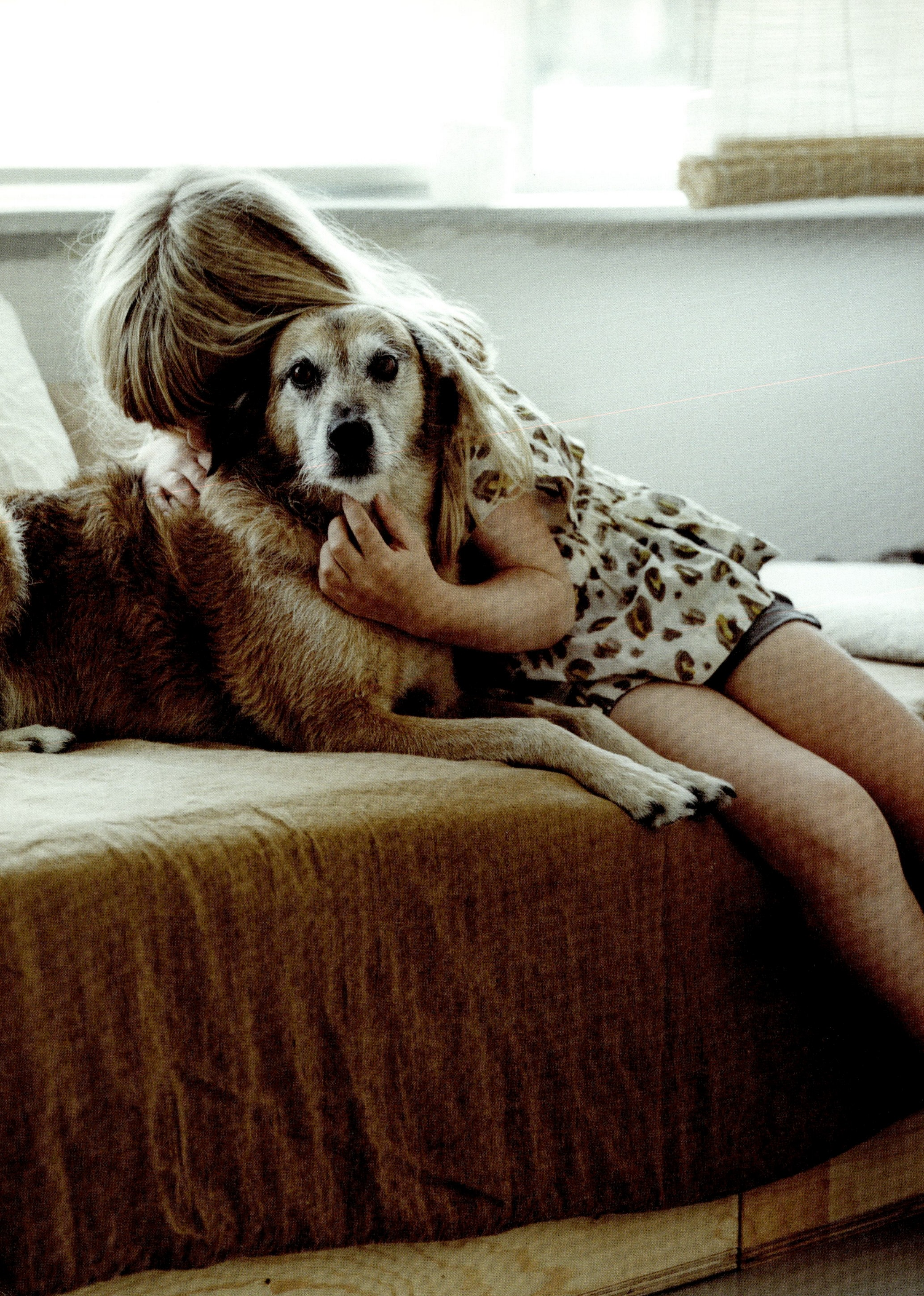

Contents

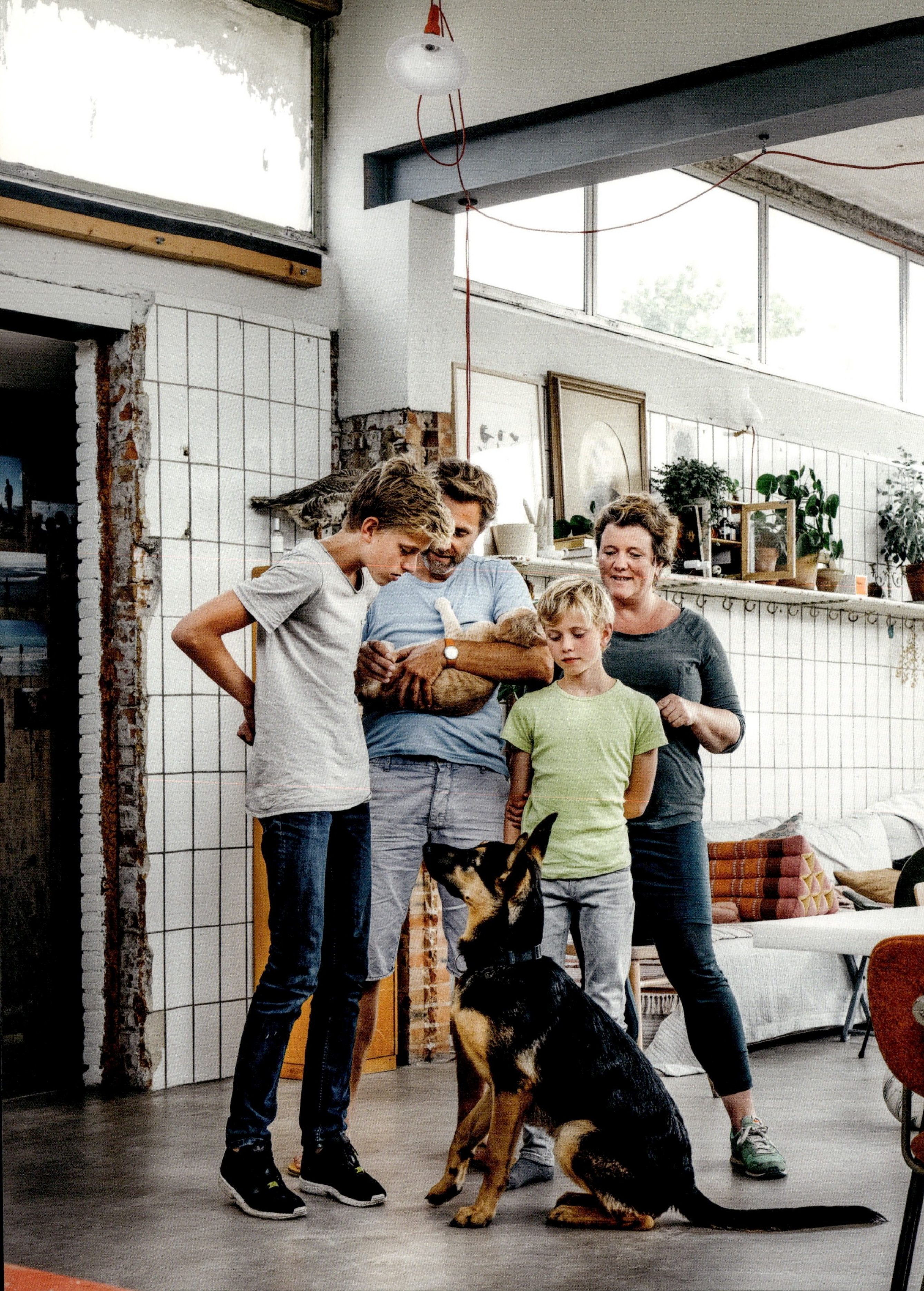

A former slaughterhouse is not exactly the kind of home you'd associate with people who love animals. But Françoise and Jack succeeded in transforming it into the perfect home for their sons and pets. The couple, whose studio is called 'Een Paar Ontwerpers' (a couple of designers), has an eye for special projects and locations that combine living with working. But the proximity of nature is also a valuable asset. The family can take long walks with their dog, while the cats can roam around freely.

Traces of the past
After Jack Brandsma and Françoise de Thouars lived in a barn and a caravan, they fell under the spell of a former slaughterhouse. They ended up buying it and transforming it into a contemporary family home. 'It was our dream to renovate a place that did not originally have a residential function. You can design very freely when you are not influenced by your predecessor's legacy or style,' says Jack, who is a designer and an interior architect. They added on a volume, which is clad with wooden planks on the outside. The interior was completely stripped. Here and there you still see traces of the building's morbid past, such as the meat hooks on the ceiling and the white wall tiles. 'What you see now is a real mish-mash of materials and textures, which we like. But there is still plenty of work to do,' says Françoise. The pastel hues and the large window with a view of the stunning nature have helped convert this slaughterhouse into a warm and cosy nest.

Slow pace, more time
The location is also unusual, near a lake and a forest. One of the main reasons for leaving the city was the nature around the building. 'But the location has plenty of other advantages,' Jack explains. 'Currently, the countryside is contending with a brain drain, with young people moving to the big cities. While urban areas provide more stimuli and energy, you also feel more rushed, and there is more competition. Here, the pace is much slower. The air is clean. Life is cheaper. You have plenty of space. And you make more time for your family.' Instead of taking the car, they bike, swim, or walk. And their dog goes everywhere with them. Including to the workshop and studio, in the nearby old renovated fire station and school.

A friend for life
Françoise, who grew up with animals, thinks of their dog as part of the family. Beer is a seven-month-old puppy, which they adopted locally. He is a German shepherd/Rottweiler mix. This breed should be given obedience training at a young age, and get used to having people around them all the time, to prevent them from becoming too protective or aggressive. Jack says punishing him doesn't work and that they have achieved more in terms of training when they reward him for good behaviour. While we sip our coffee, Beer goes completely bonkers when the dishwasher is opened. 'He thinks he will get to lick something clean,' Jack explains. 'We really need to unteach him this.' Beer feels entirely at home here, and he gets on like a house on fire with their sons Pelle (14 years) and Sil (10 years). He is a real family dog.

He goes everywhere they go and follows them like a shadow. 'When you decide to get a pet, you have a friend for life. A dog will never shun you and looks forward every day to the time you come home. Their love is unconditional, and they can't live without you. It does make you feel happier,' Françoise laughs.

A trio of cats
The family also has three cats, which Beer adores. 'He always wants to cuddle them, but because he has such awkward motor skills, their head sometimes ends up in his mouth,' Jack explains. The ginger cat, Muis, is the oldest cat, and the boss. He behaves like a king. One day, after a visit to the butcher's, Françoise came home with a kilo of meat and a kitten they called Chuckie. He has lovely, beige fur, and blends in with the interior. He is very gentle and friendly and can roam the house freely. Whereas Chuckie tends to seek out the boys, Muis likes to crawl into bed with Jack and Françoise. Muis likes to sit on their lap, Chuckie doesn't. Muis meows, while Chuckie talks. Jostie is the neighbours' cat and always follows Chuckie inside. 'I have tried to chase him away with water plenty of times, but he always returns. In the end, cats like to choose their homes, and we don't really have a say in this,' says Françoise.

No scratching posts or litter trays
Three cats, and yet there are no scratching posts or litter trays in the house. 'We don't have any. We prefer aesthetics over functionality,' says Jack. 'They don't scratch the furniture that much. And we don't have expensive furniture either,' adds Françoise. They pee and poo outside. They walk in and out. Now and then they'll bring in some dead mice or bids, which they like to leave on the bathroom floors. But mice are better than rats, which the family had to contend with when they installed a chicken coop in the garden. 'We briefly tried to raise chickens. But as you can see, we have our hands full with the boys, the dog and the cats,' Jack laughs, while he holds Chuckie in his arms. After a few minutes, the cat indicates he's had enough. Time to go outside, in the garden, to play with his friends.

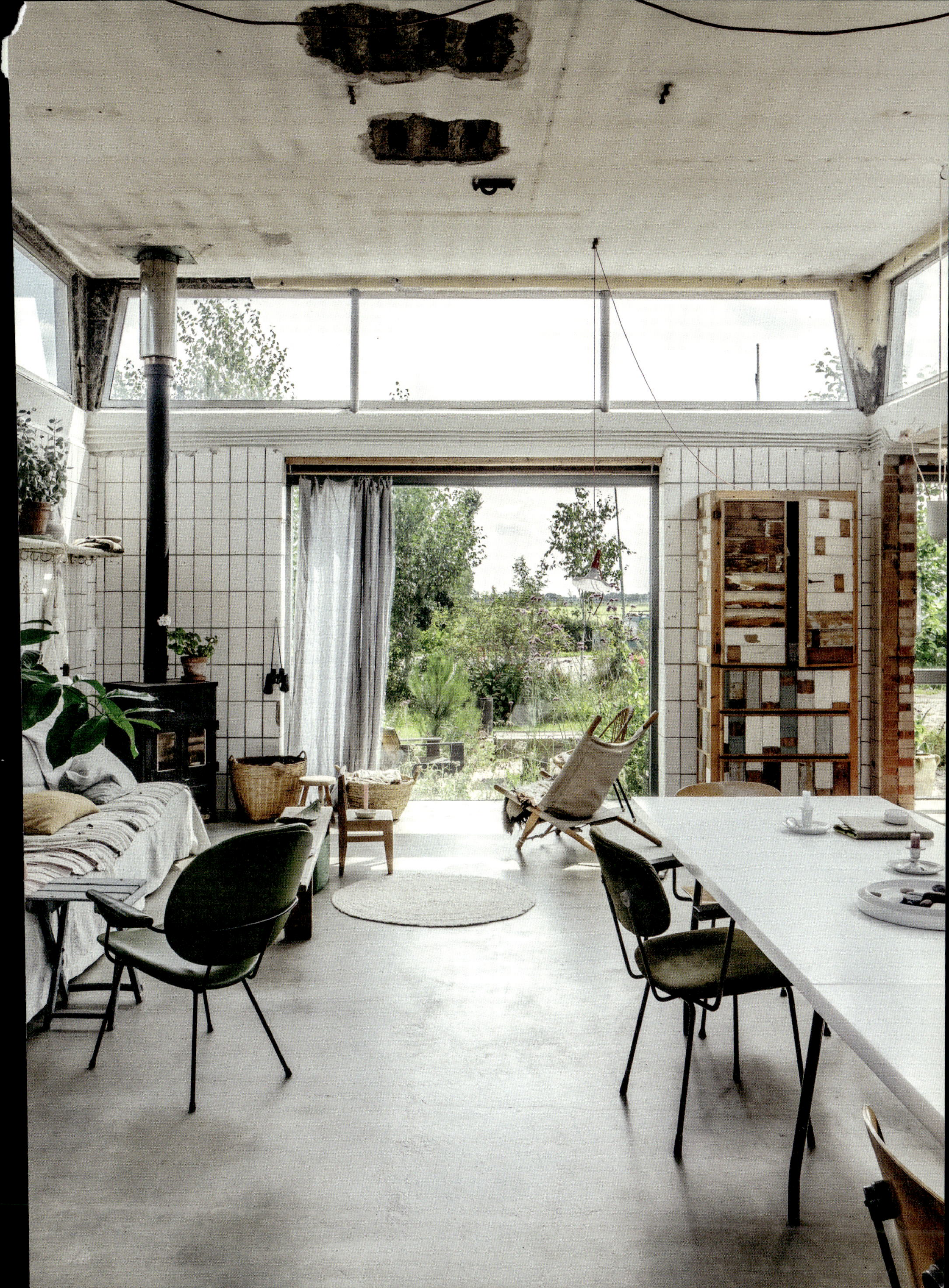

Jack and Françoise live in an old slaughterhouse. The renovation
is an excellent, multiannual project, which allows them to flex
their skills and talent as product and interior designers.

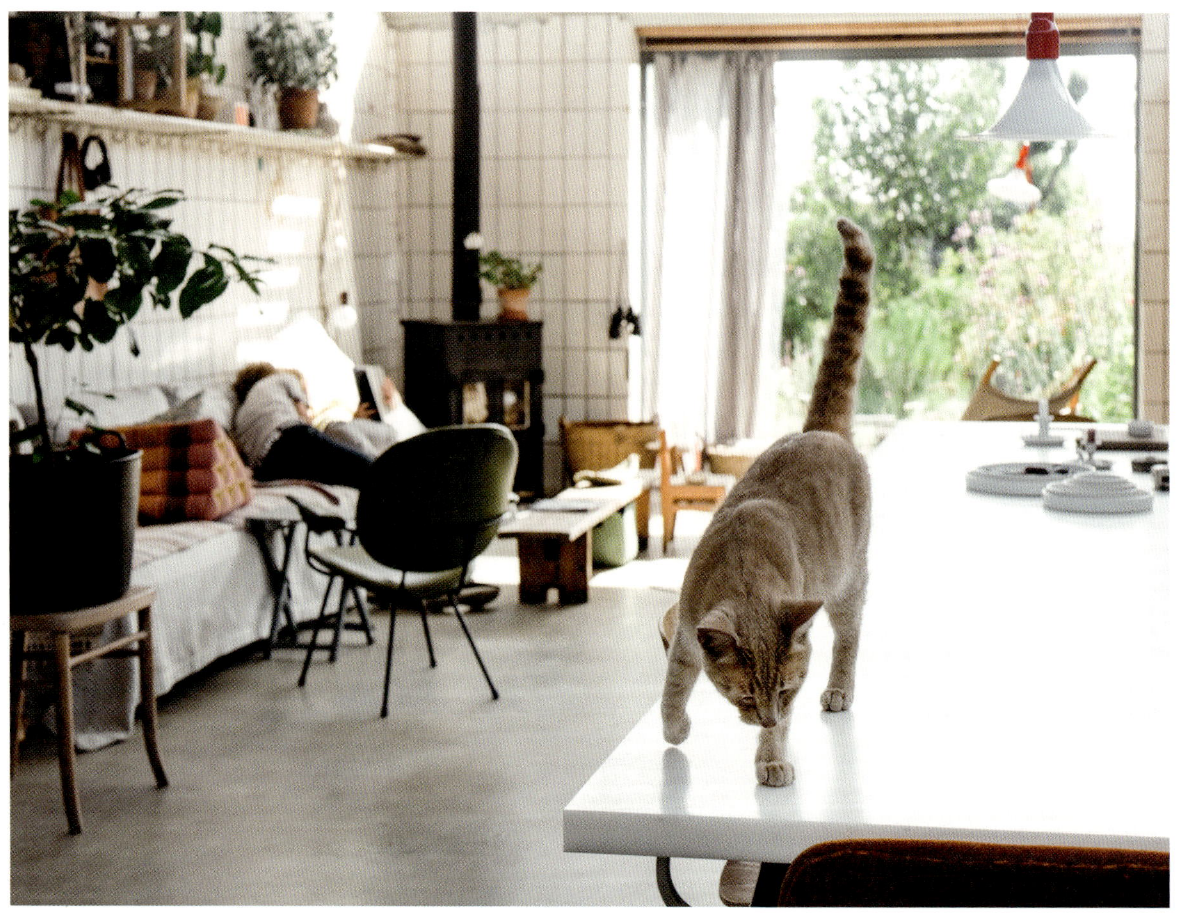

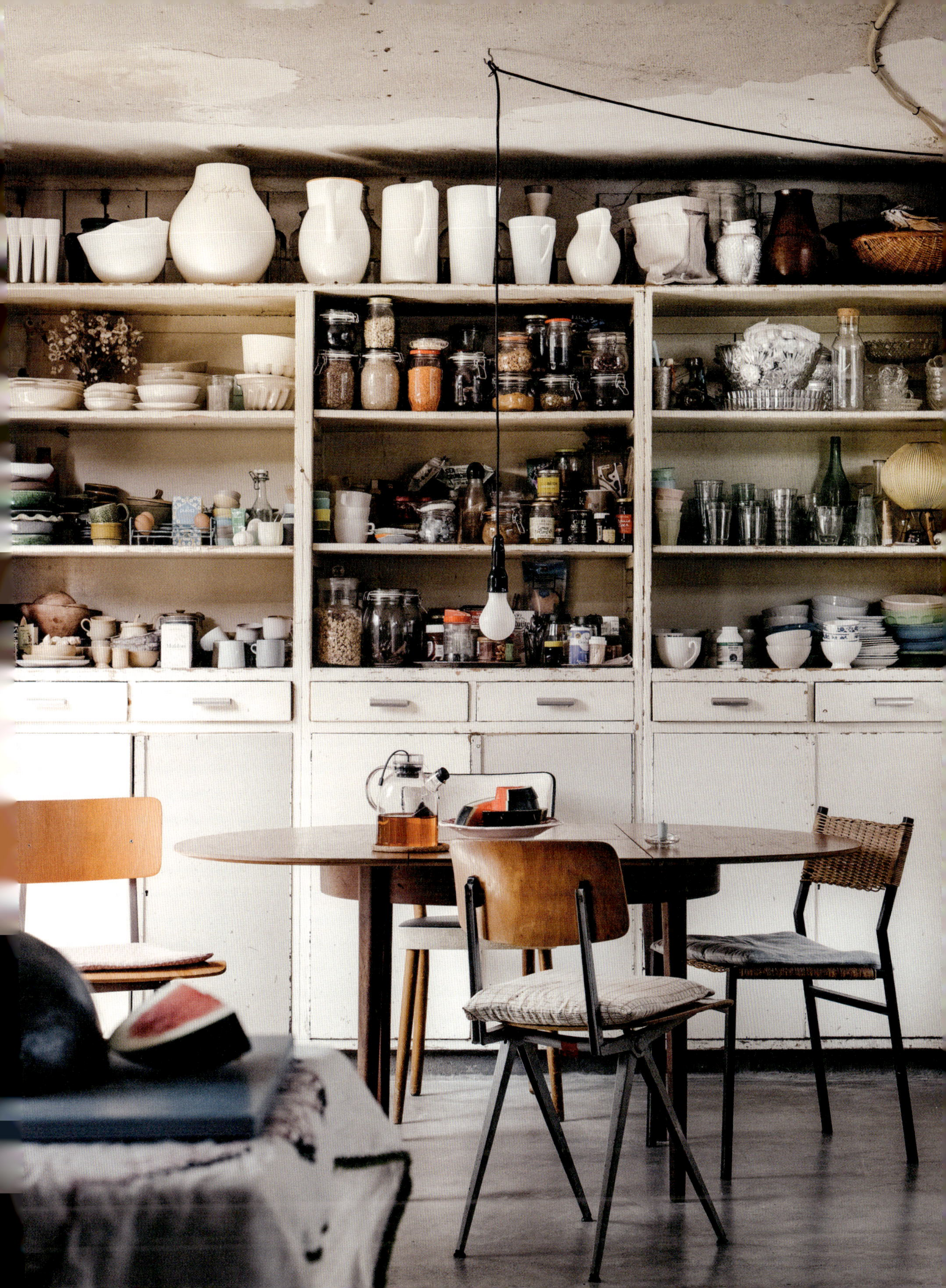

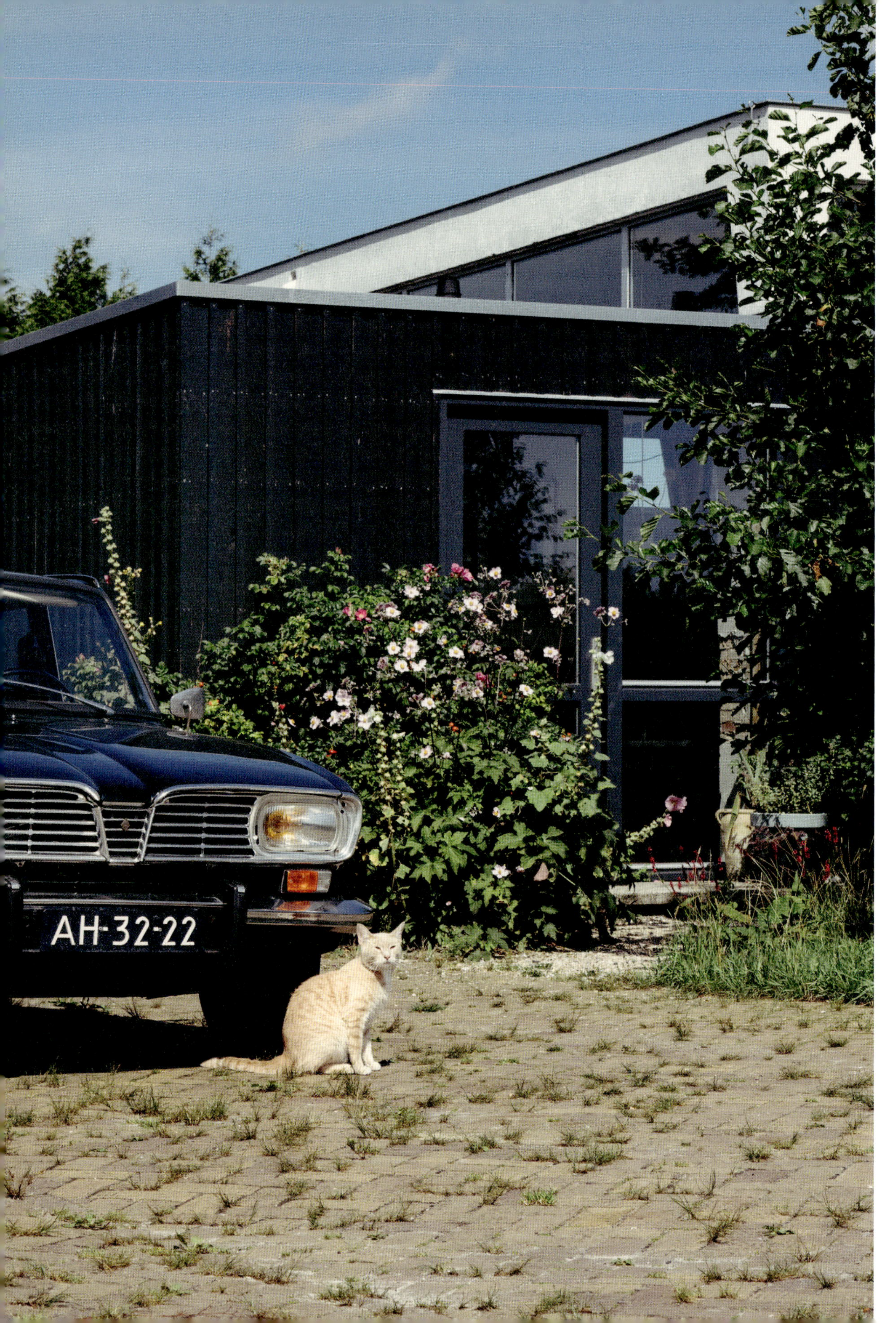
AH-32-22

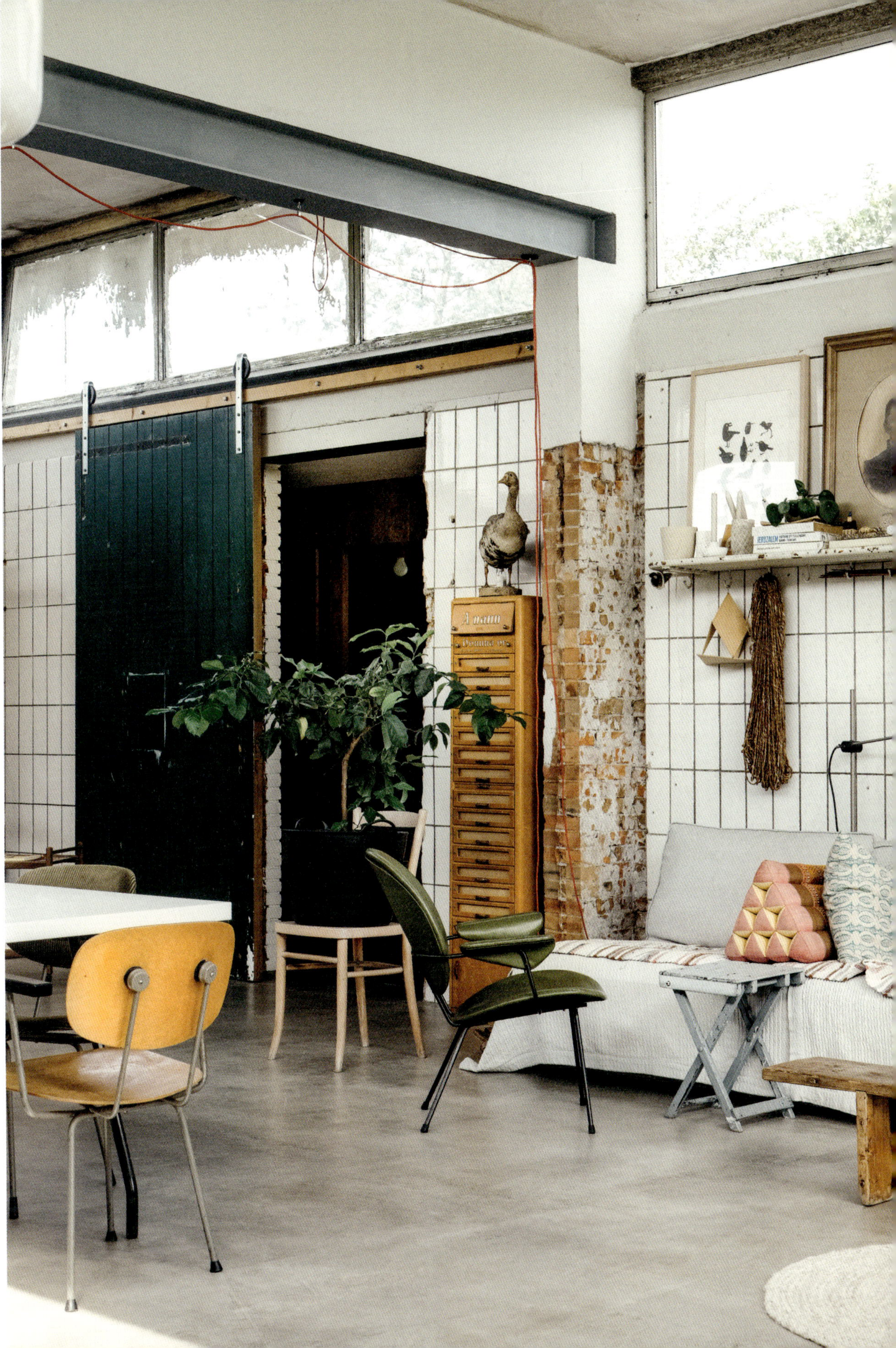

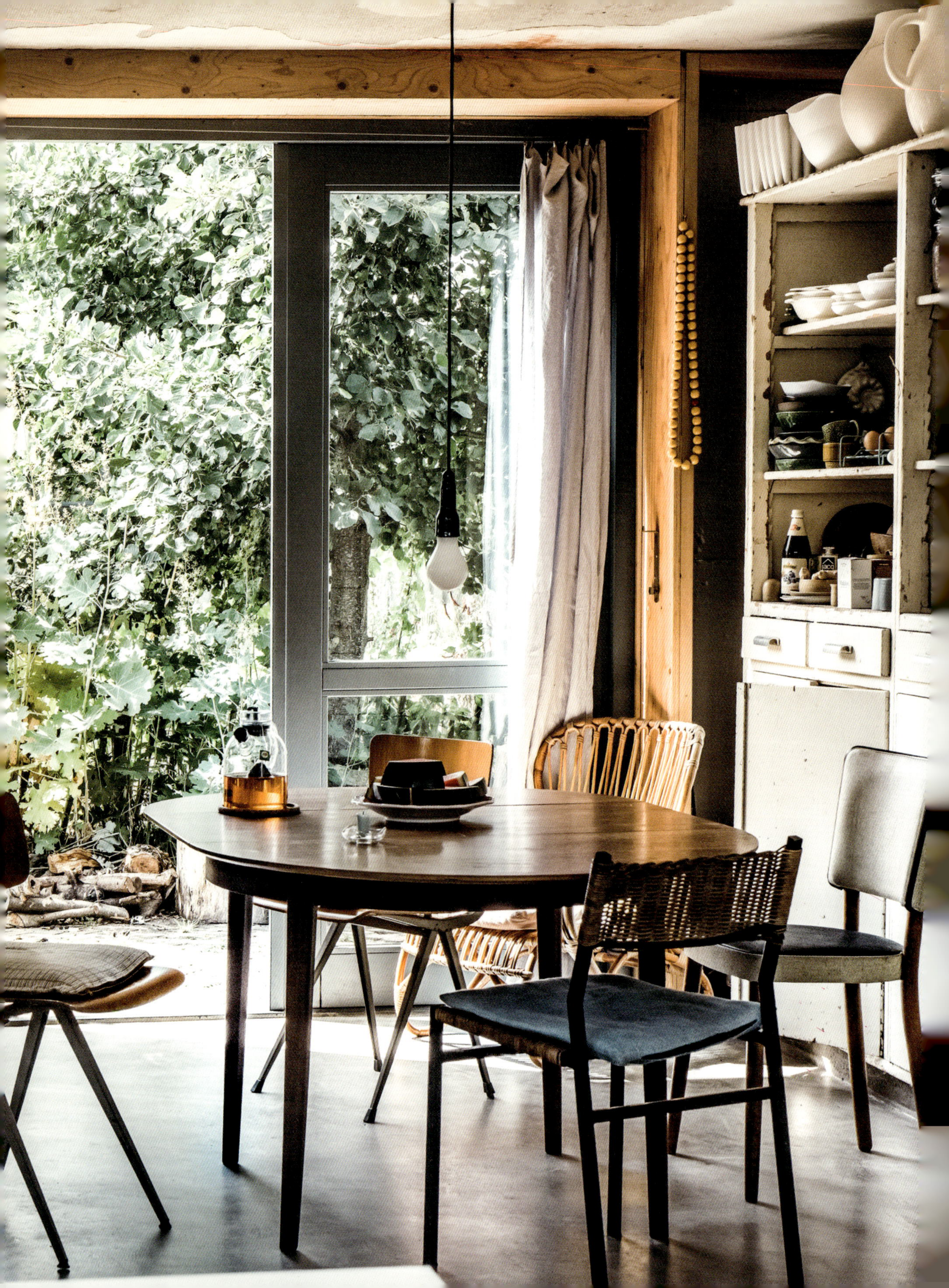

Living and working at the same place has enabled the duo to spend
more time with their kids and their pets.

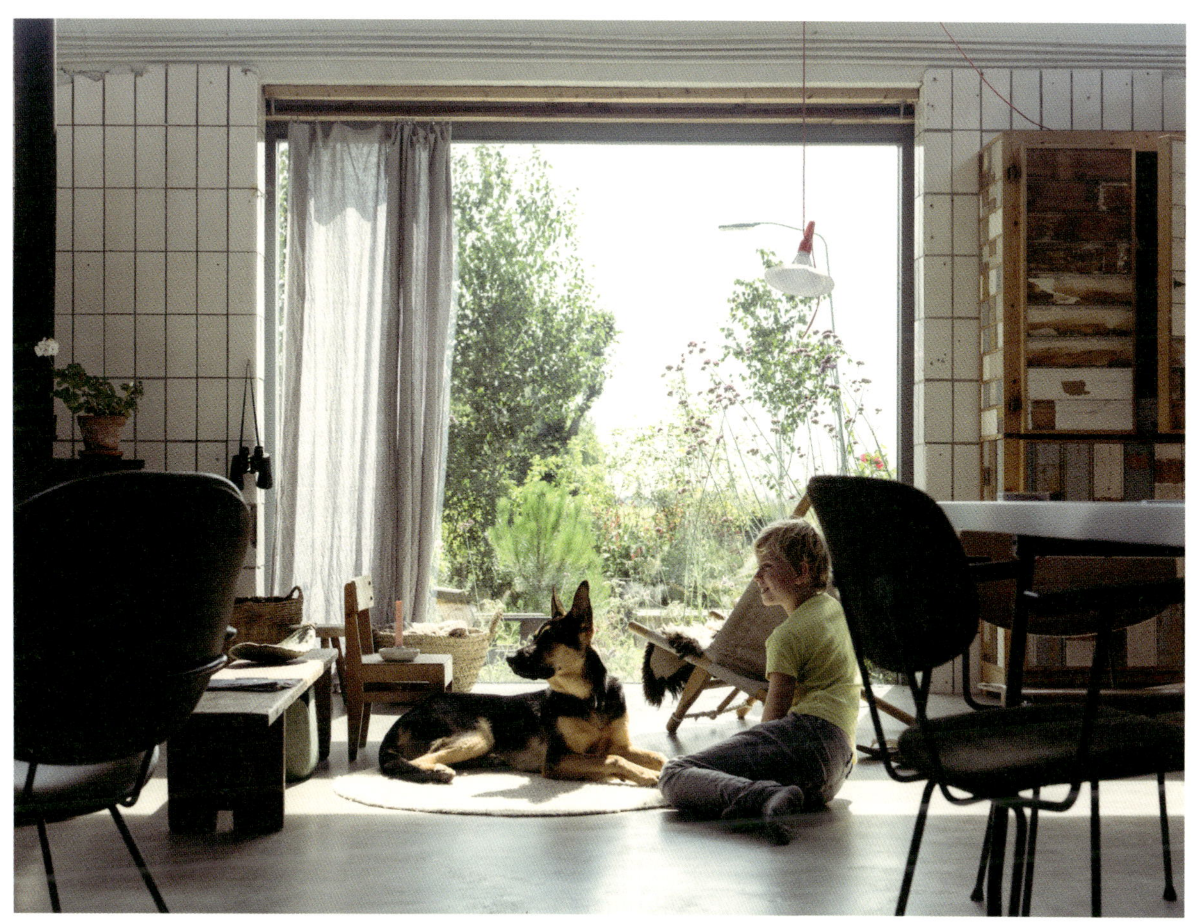

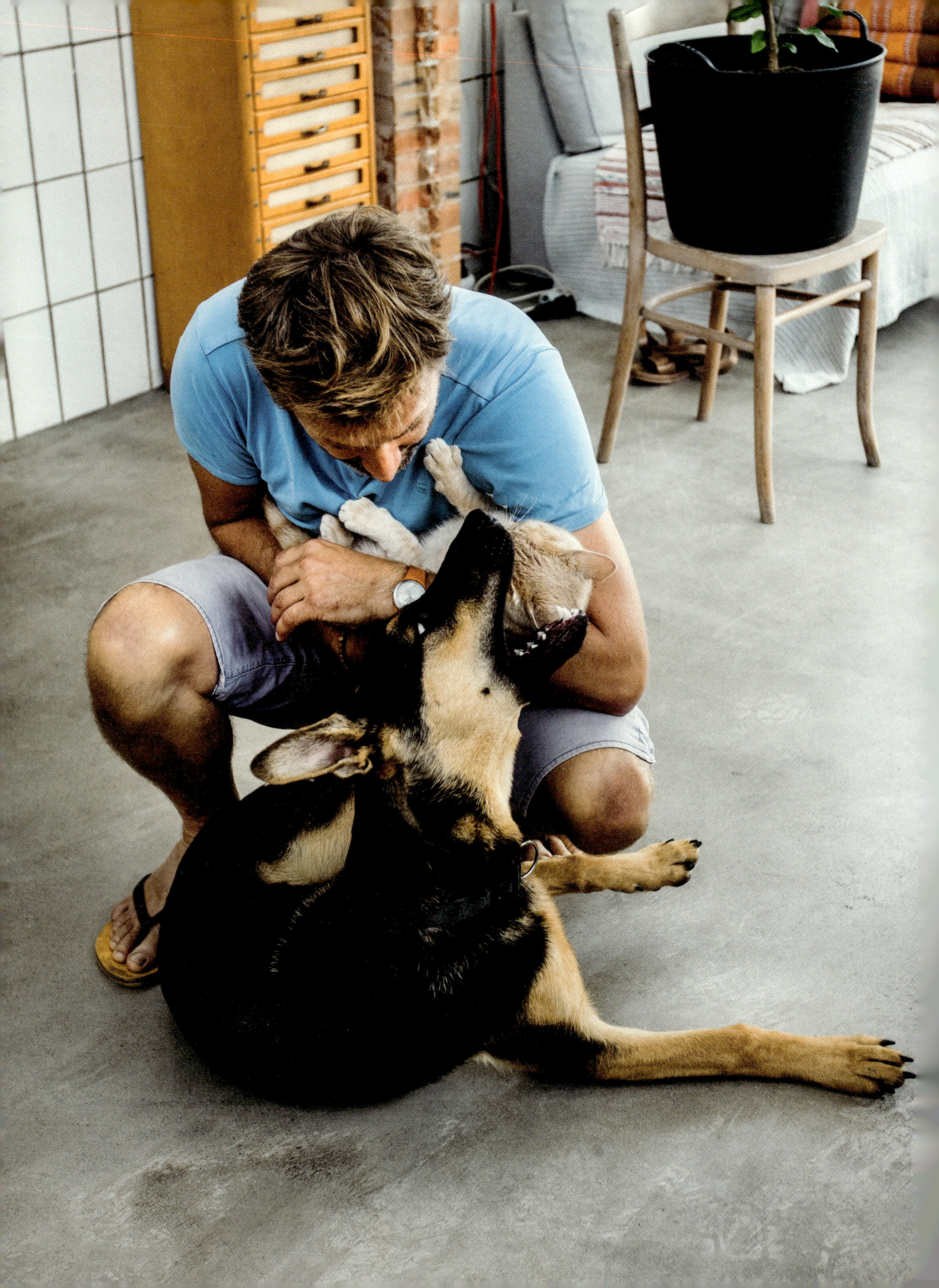

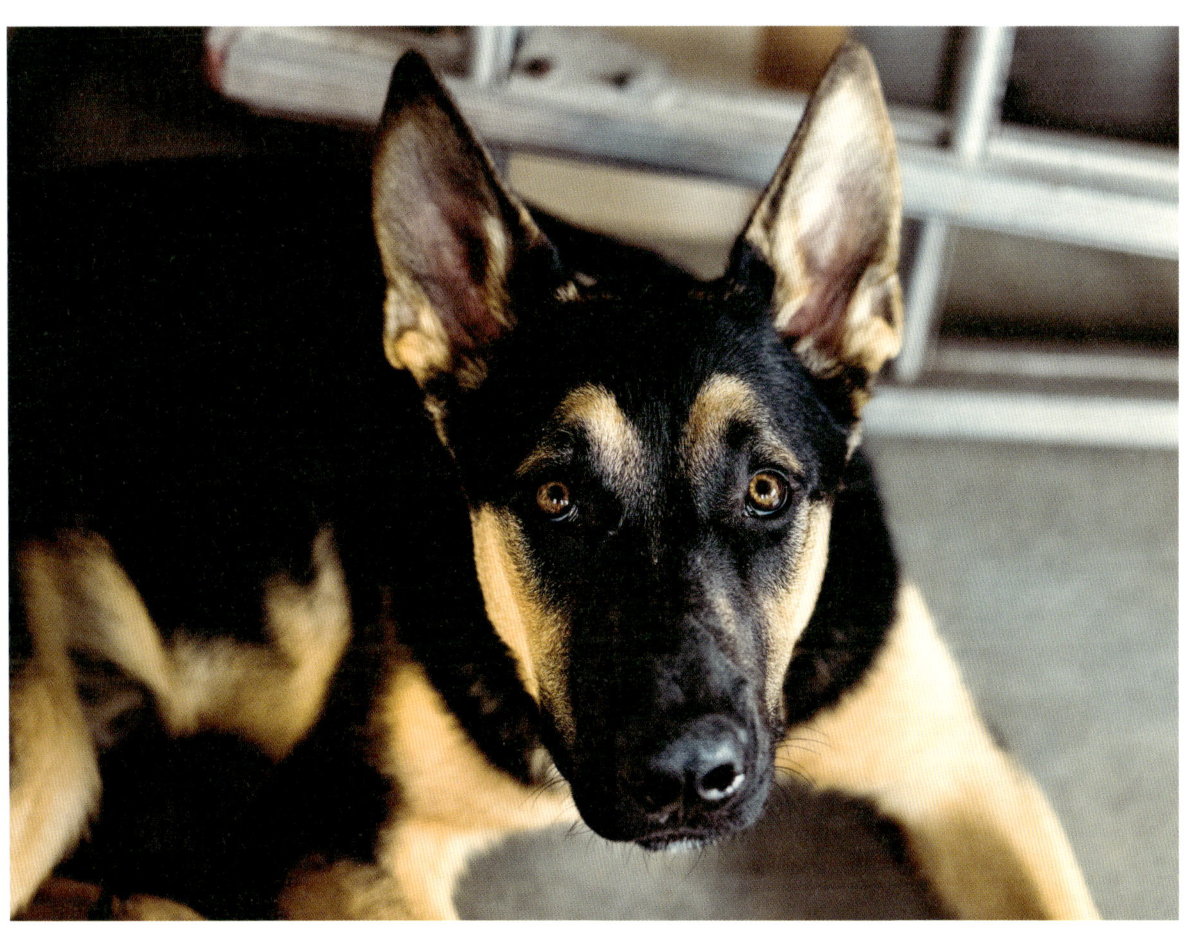

Beer is a German shepherd/Rottweiler mix. He goes out of his
mind when he hears the dishwasher or sees one of the cats.

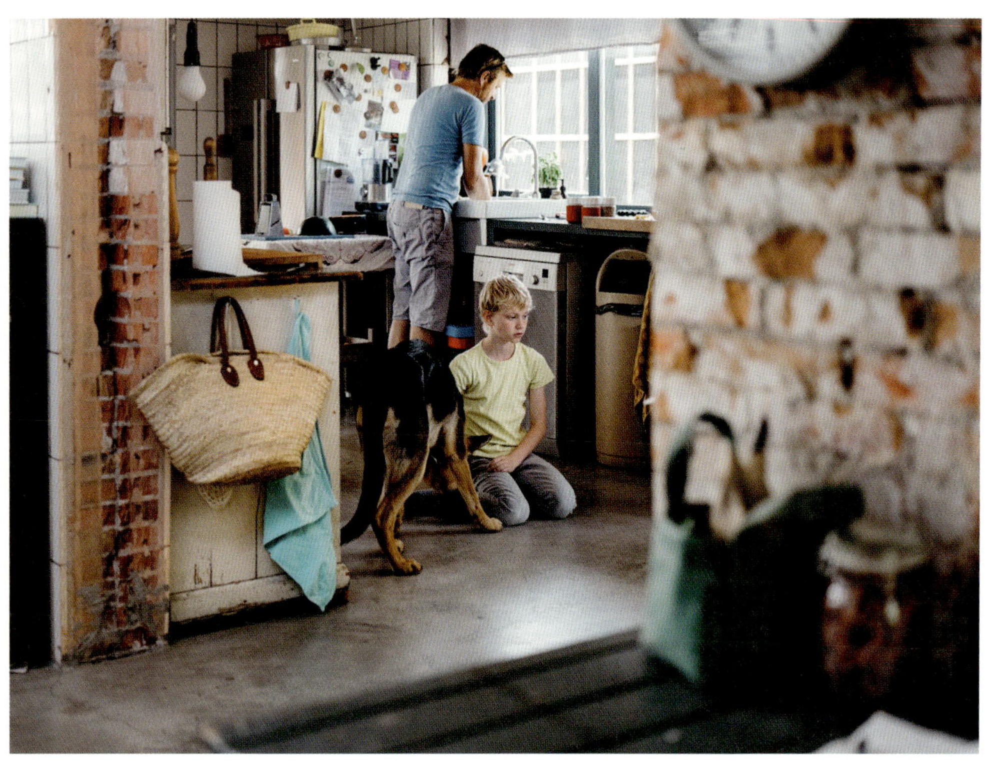

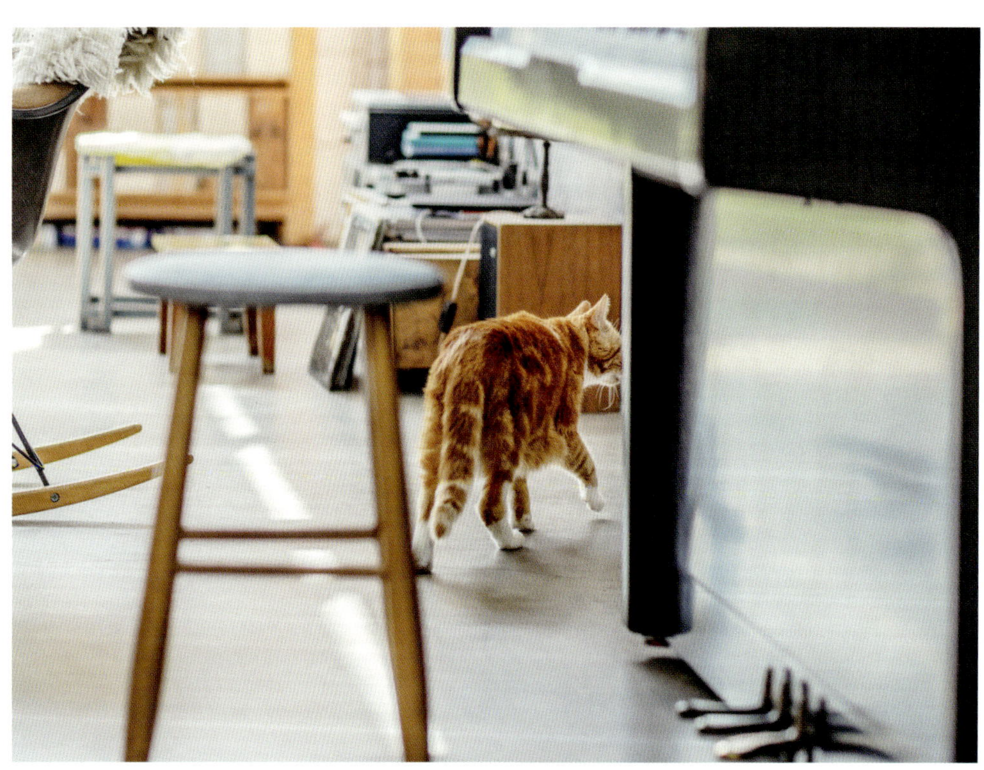

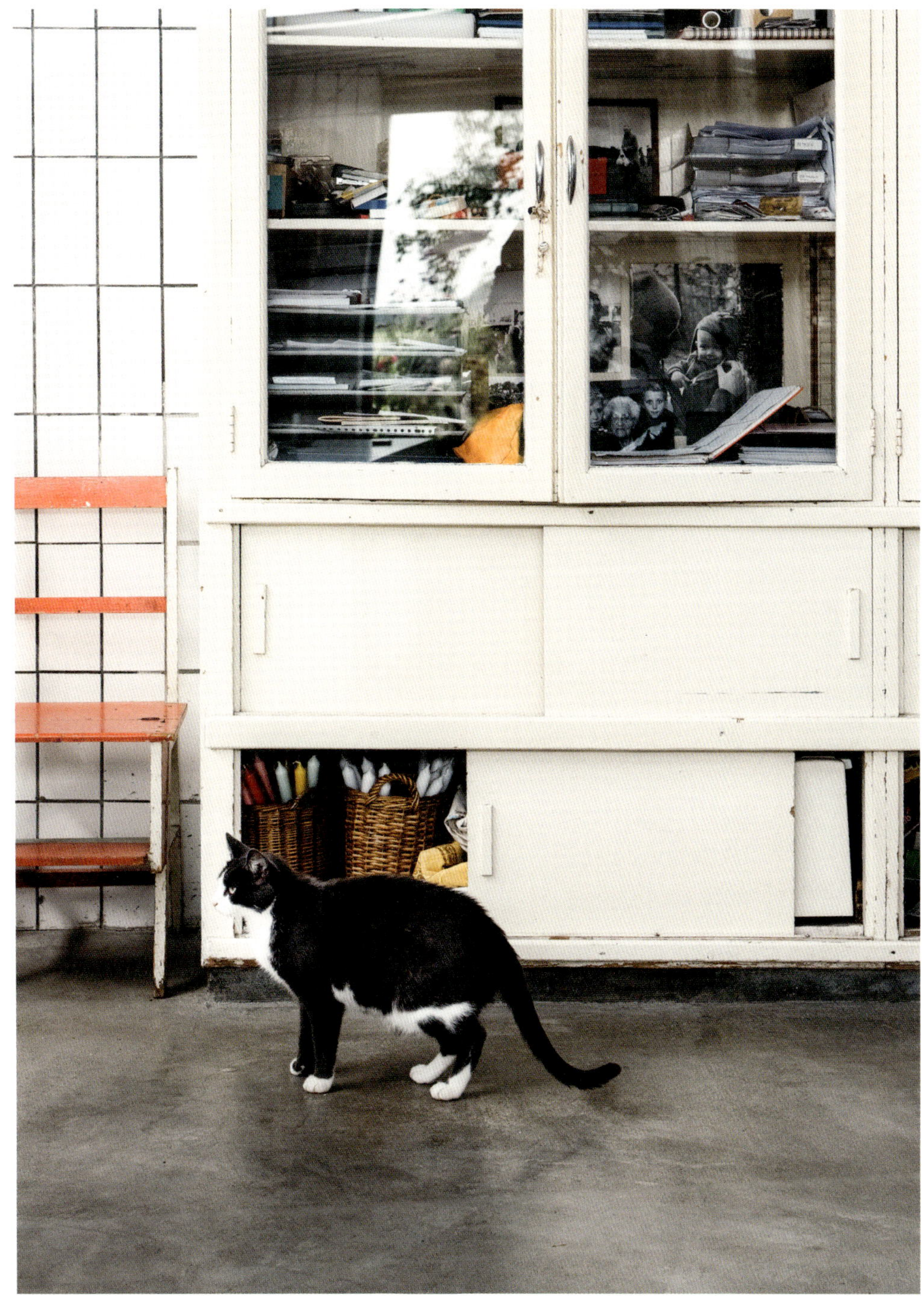

One day, after a visit to the butcher's, Françoise came home with
a kilo of meat and a kitten they called Chuckie. The cat roams
around the house, the garden, or naps in the old caravan.

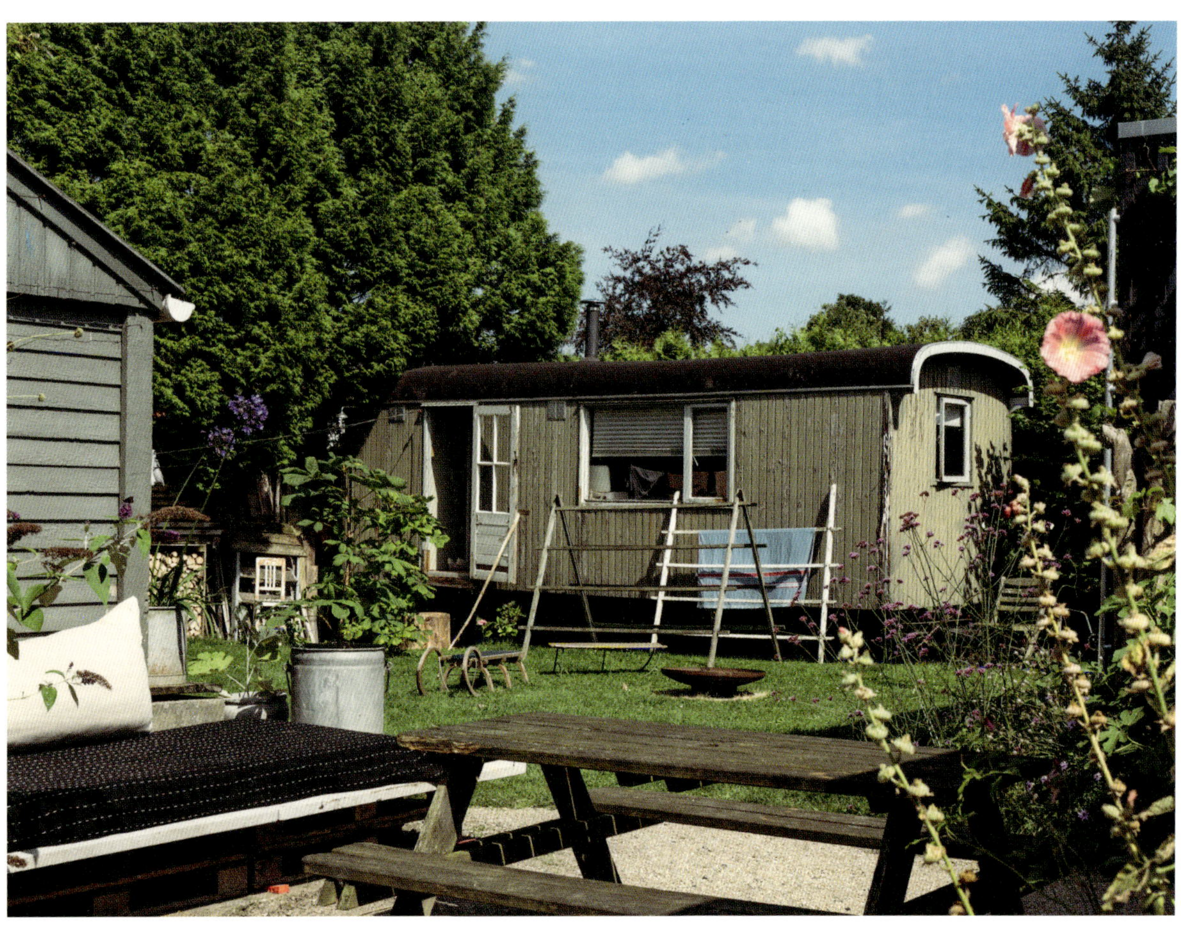

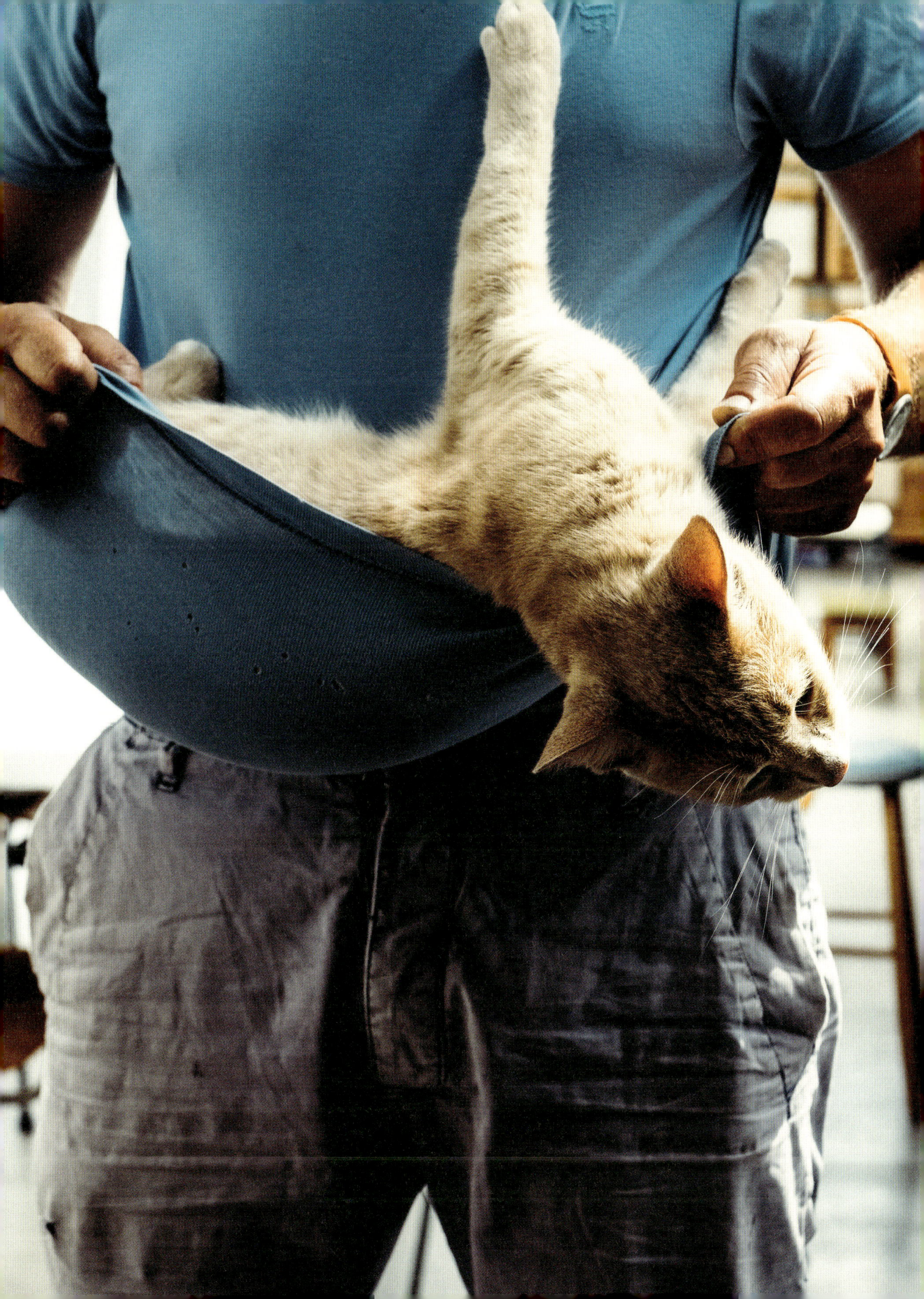

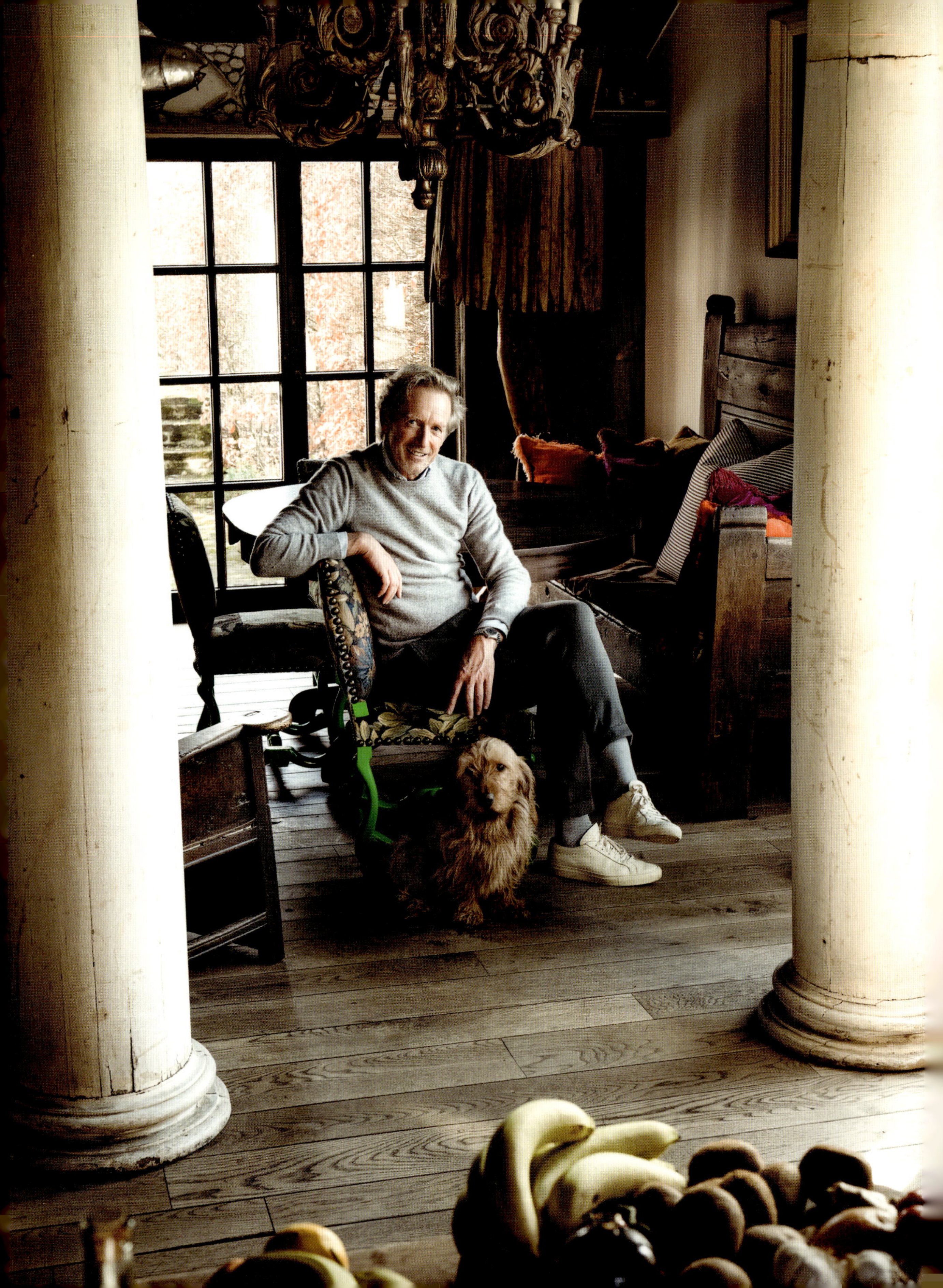

A brown dog, a yellow canary and black chickens: florist Johan Gryp surrounds himself with some colourful company, both at home and at work. And it perfectly matches the ambience and interior of his house and flower shop. The mix of tones, patterns, styles and textures is breath-taking. His dog Omer, a basset fauve de Bretagne, follows him everywhere he goes. In the greenhouse, when he's out making deliveries, in the orangerie and in the garden. The two are inseparable and very popular with flower lovers.

Beloved and patient

The old greenhouse on Johan Gryp's land is covered in foliage. He uses it as a flower shop, which is filled to the rafters with house plants, brightly-coloured vases and pots and an impressive arsenal of seasonal flowers. We gaze around open-mouthed, taking in the beauty until Omer comes running towards us to welcome us. Johan appears just a few minutes later. 'Omer is like a living bell. He always lets me know when there are customers in the shop,' Johan says. The dog loves his owner. When he's not sniffing around the shop or sleeping under the counter, you'll find him outside in the garden. There he patiently waits until Johan leaves on his flower delivery rounds. The dog is Johan's shadow.

A hunting dog and chickens

Before Omer, Johan had a vizsla, a Hungarian standing dog. After it died, he had no intention of getting another dog. Until he met Ludo, the basset fauve de Bretagne of interior decorator Jean-Philippe Demeyer. 'When I saw him, I said to myself: I wouldn't mind one of those. They're compact. Gentle. The perfect friend for me.' A few months later, the florist travelled to Normandy to collect his new puppy. Omer is a hunting dog, and his instinctive behaviour is to chase any fox he spots in the garden. He doesn't go near the neighbours' horses in the field that adjoins the garden. And he's not a fan of the chickens that Johan's mother gave him. Johan keeps them for practical reasons. 'I didn't name the chickens, and I don't pet them either. But they do gather around me when I feed them. They lay three to four eggs a day, which is too much for one person. That's why I like to give them to customers and friends.'

Flowers on the ceiling

Johan has one hectare of land, which he planted with shrubs, trees, and hedges of his own choice. He also has a large cutting garden, with plenty of greenery, which he uses in his natural flower arrangements. He finds manipulating flowers a waste of time, preferring to enhance their simplicity instead. He has surrounded himself with lavish flowers, both in the shop as well as in his home. You can even spot them on the orangerie's ceiling. The striking paintings were inspired by Henri Matisse's work and were made by Pablo Piatti. The interior decorator Jean-Philippe Demeyer, whose exuberant signature style is apparent throughout the house, came up with the idea. While the residence looks as it has a long and rich history, it is actually a new-build. When Johan bought the land thirty years ago, there was nothing there except for the rundown greenhouse.

A cathedral-like cage

The orangerie is Johan's favourite space. It's also where his yellow canary lives in a cathedral-like cage, which Demeyer found for him. Originally the birdcage was installed in the greenhouse, with four birds, which the florist received from a breeder who lives nearby. After they died, the cage was moved to the orangerie and became the new home of a yellow canary. But it didn't stay long either because one day the cleaning lady forgot to close the door and so it escaped. She was so embarrassed that she bought exactly the same bird. During our visit, we listen as it sings its little heart out. We ask Johan whether he doesn't feel lonely in his large cage. 'Canaries can live on their own on condition that you give them plenty of attention. They like toys and a daily bath. Besides seeds, they enjoy green food, such as lettuce and dandelion leaves and apples.' Omer watches the canary from a distance, enjoying his birdsong.

Social animal

The dog leaves the bird and the furniture alone. You'll never catch him crawling into an armchair, jumping on the table, going up the stairs or getting into another mischief. He's always in his basket in the orangerie or under the counter in the greenhouse. Johan took him to dog school, where he received basic obedience training because he wanted him to be able to get along with other visiting animals. 'I had no idea that he'd become such a social creature,' Johan laughs. 'He'll sniff anything and everyone if I give him free rein.' Suddenly Omer jumps up, heading in the direction of the flower shop where customers are waiting. Time to stop chatting and get to work.

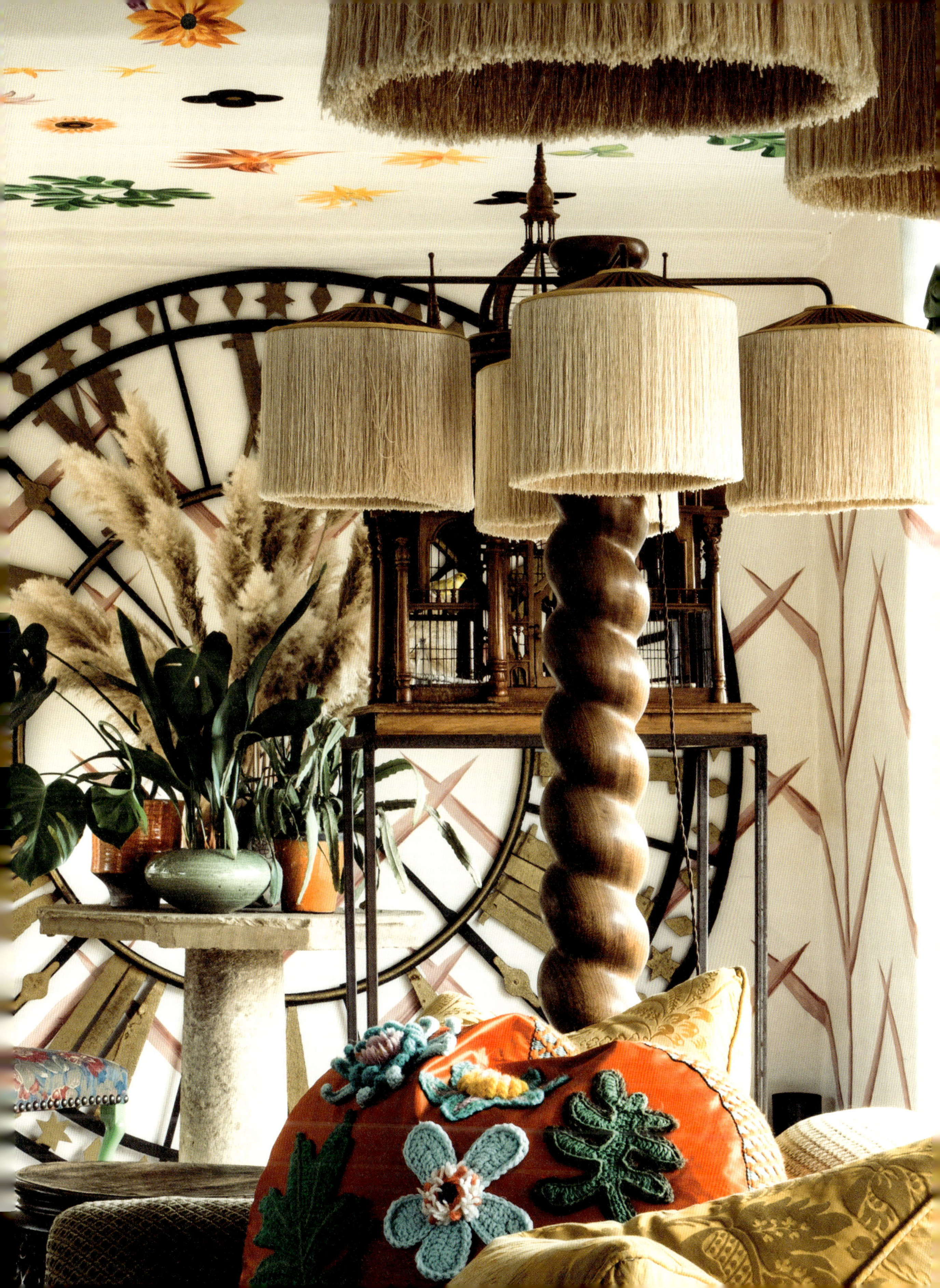

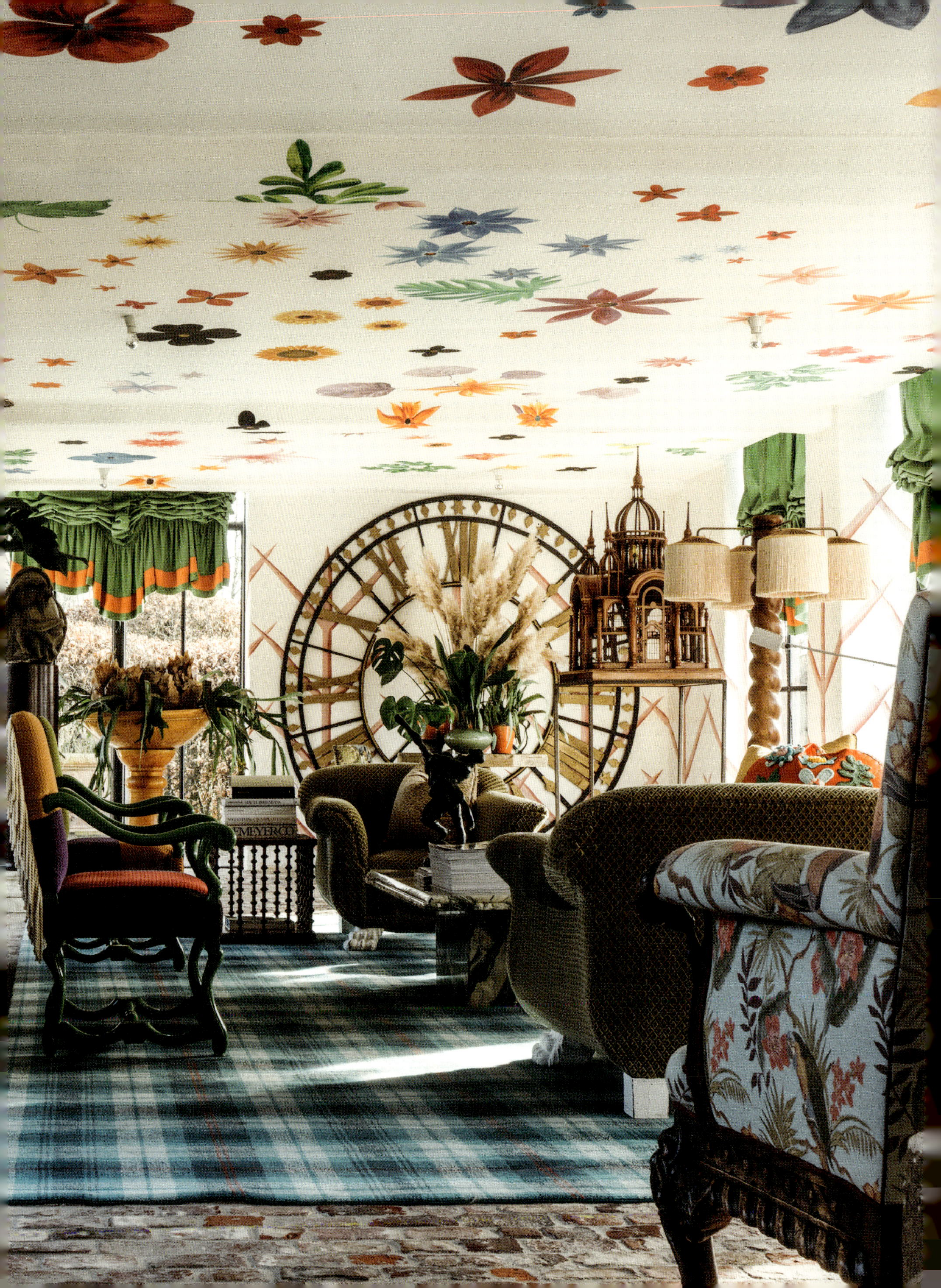

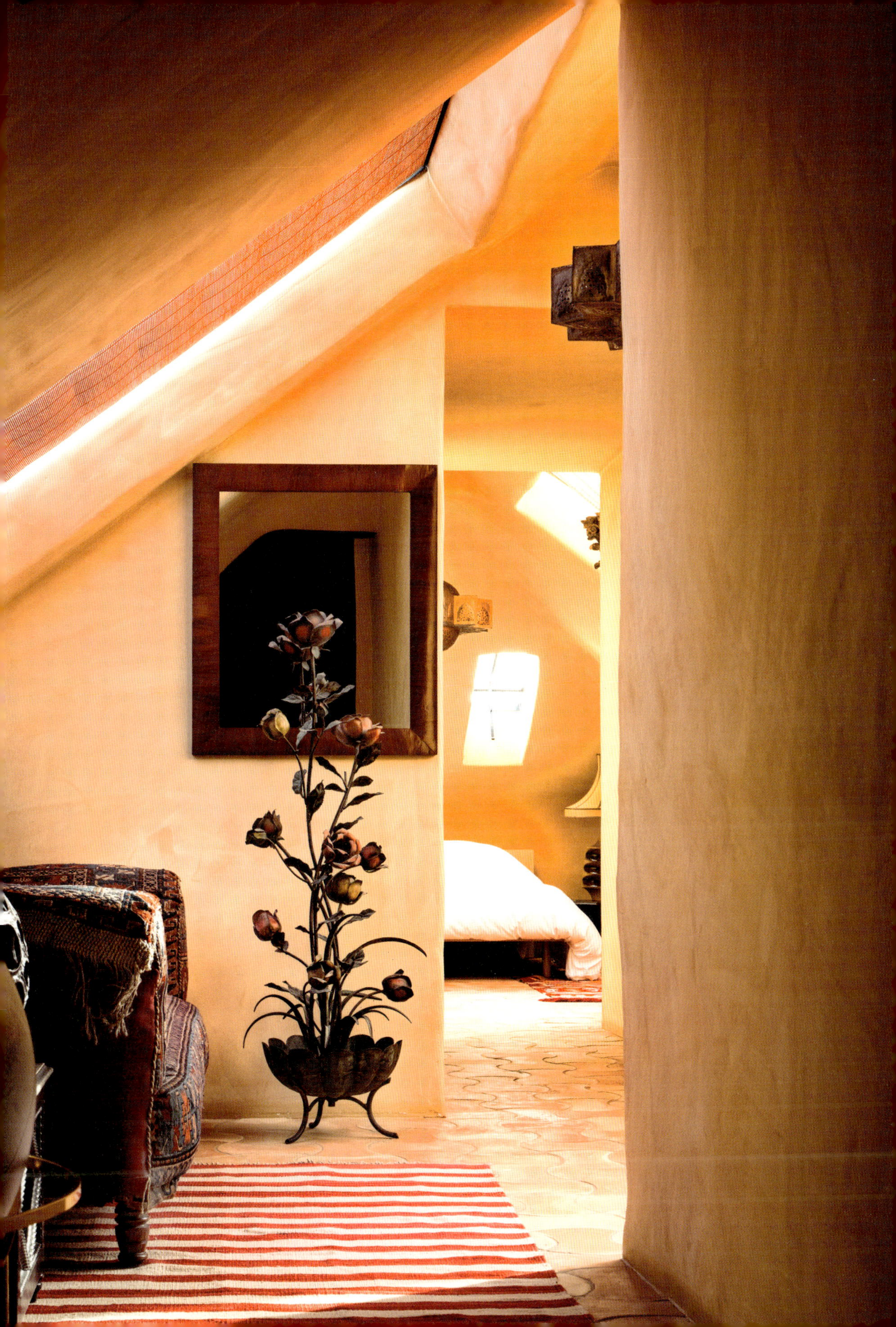

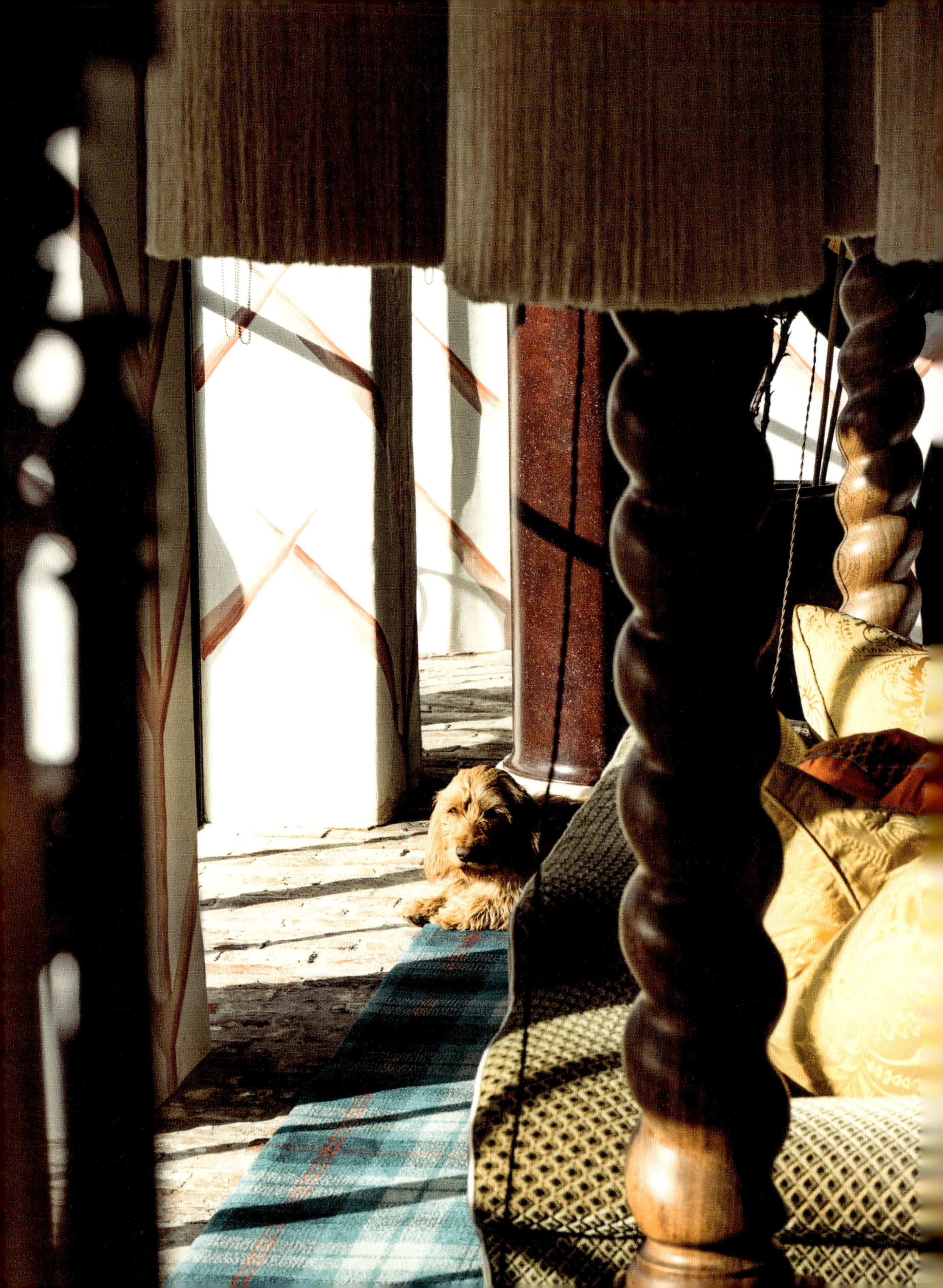

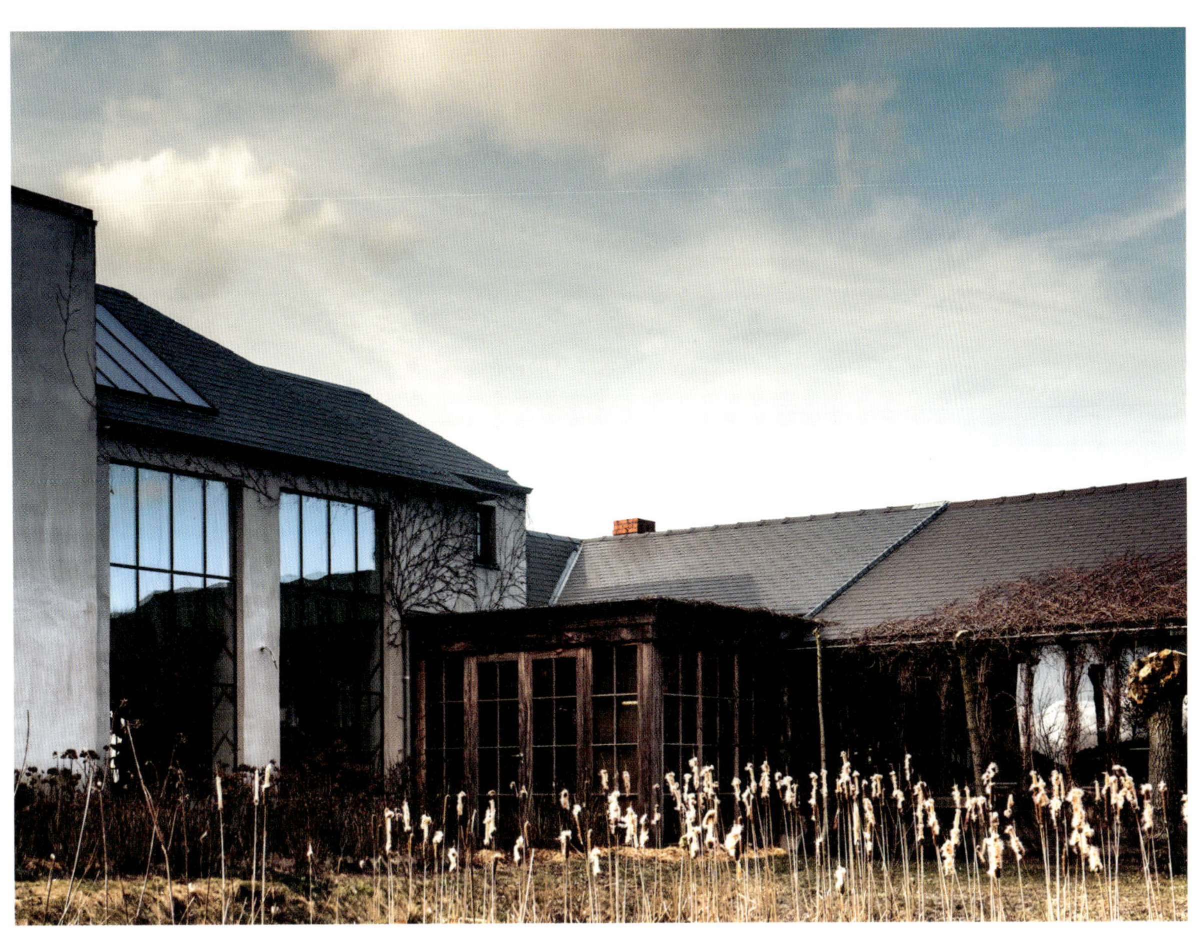

The greenhouse, which is used as a flower shop, adjoins the
new-build, which was renovated by the extravagant designer
Jean-Philippe Demeyer.

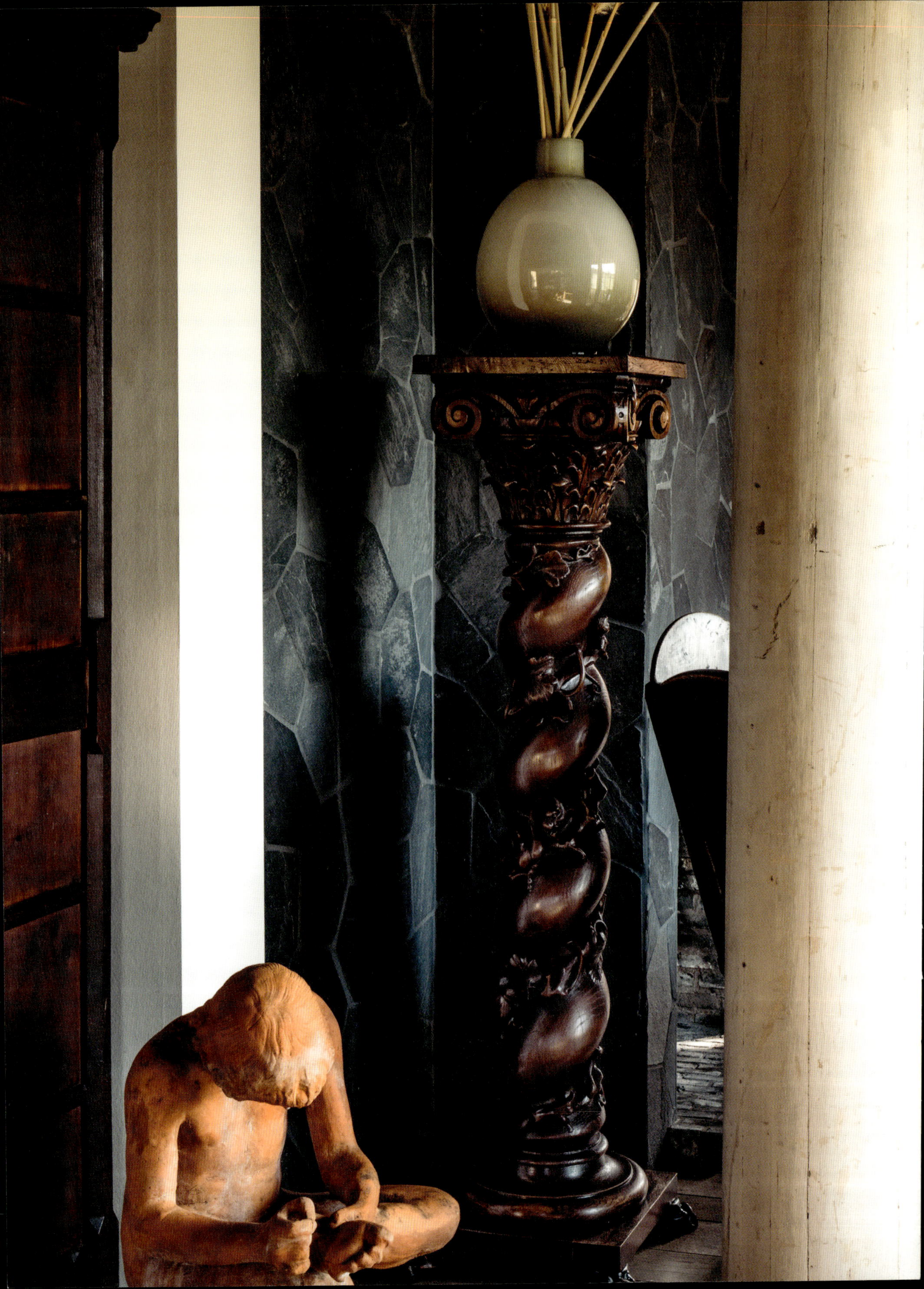

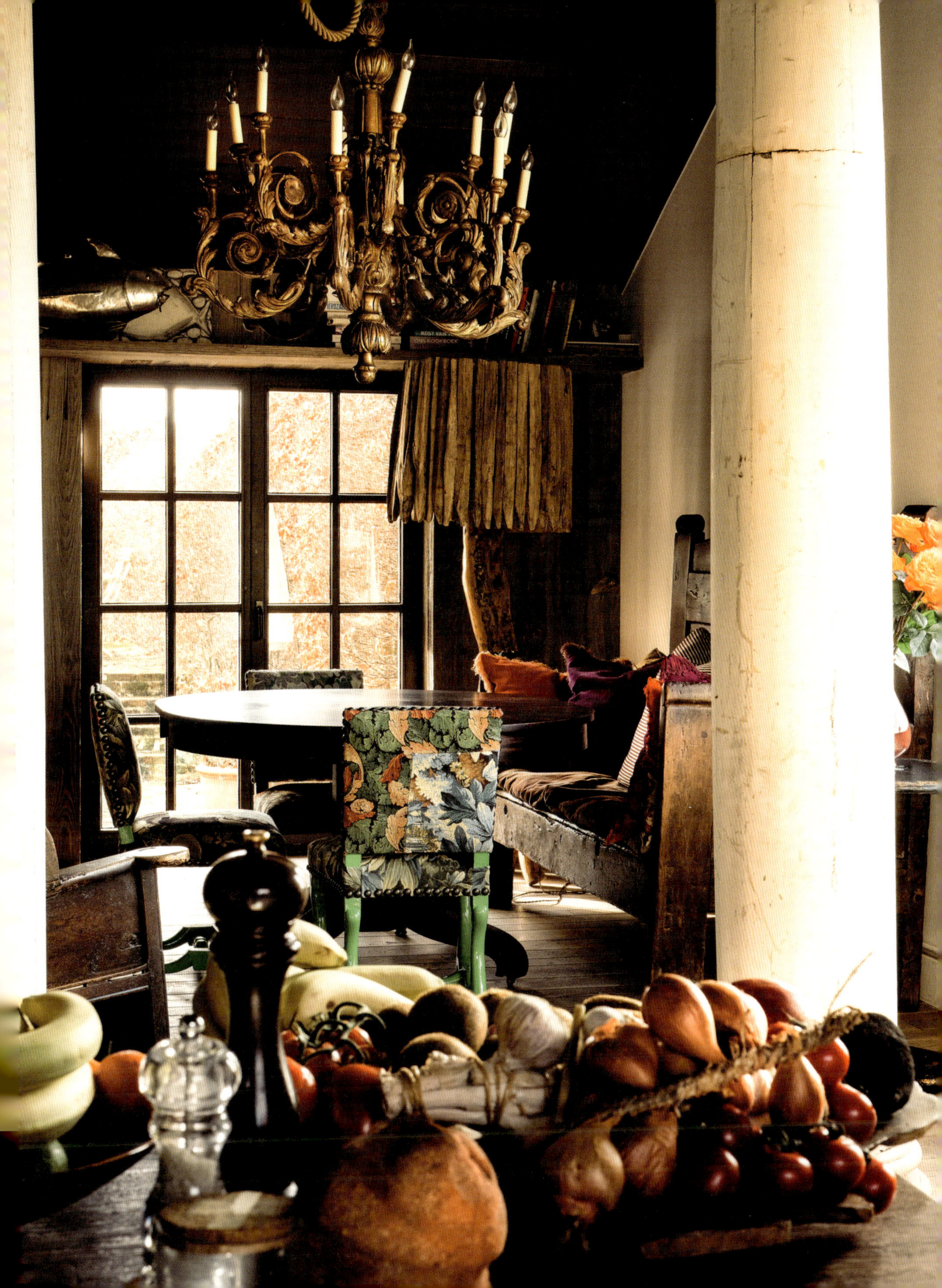

In addition to his dog, Johan also has a canary in a majestic cage
and chickens in the garden.

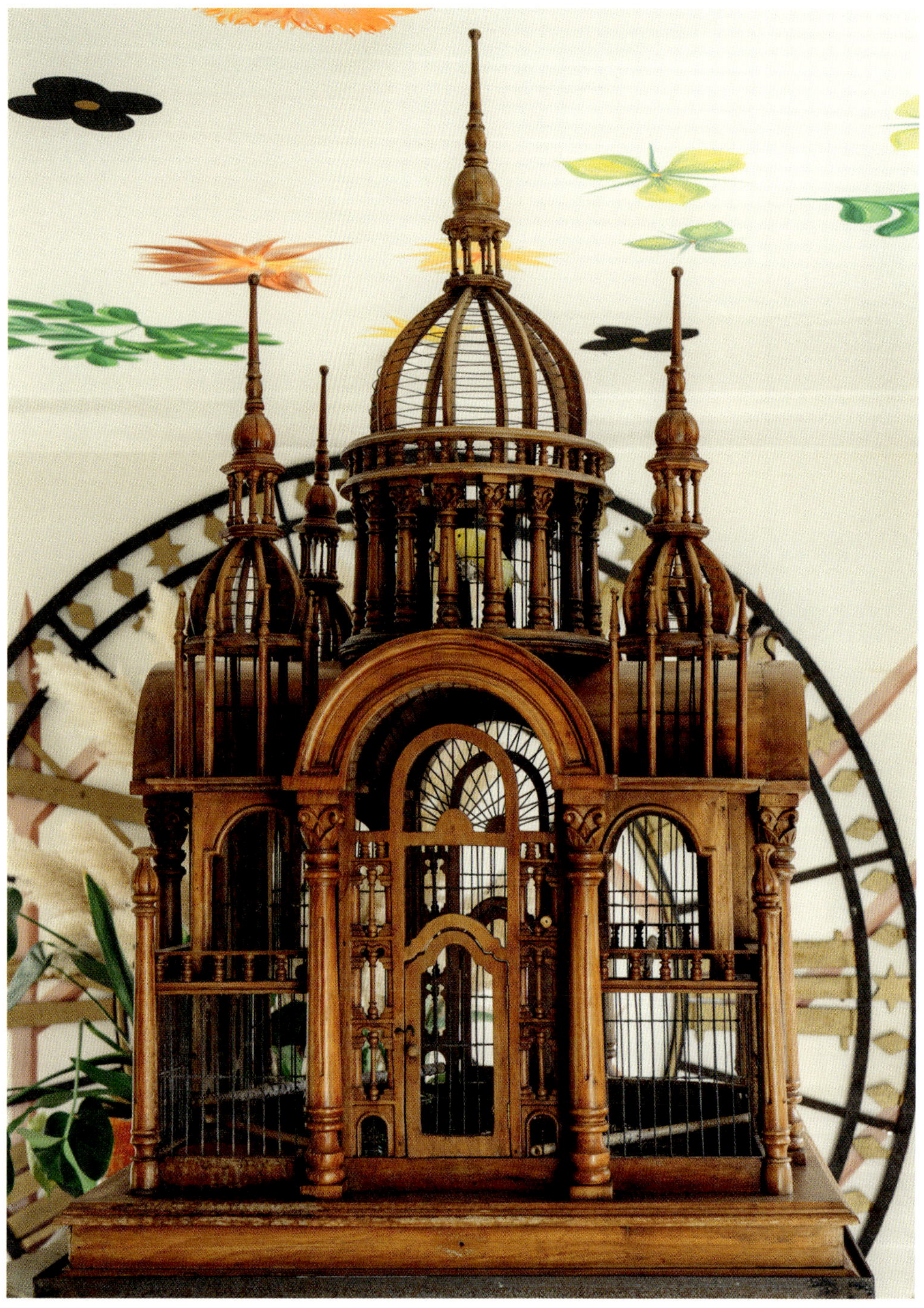

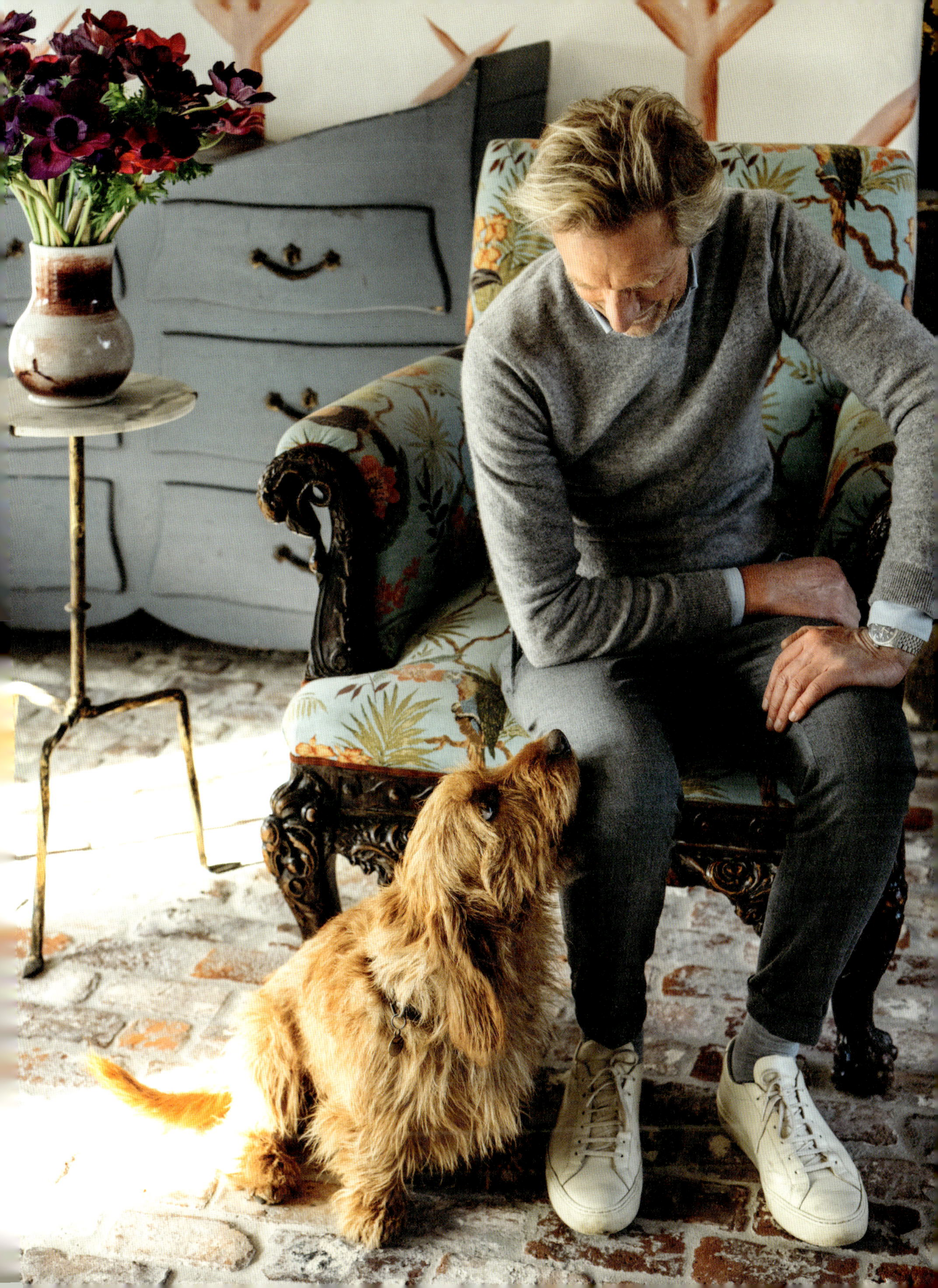

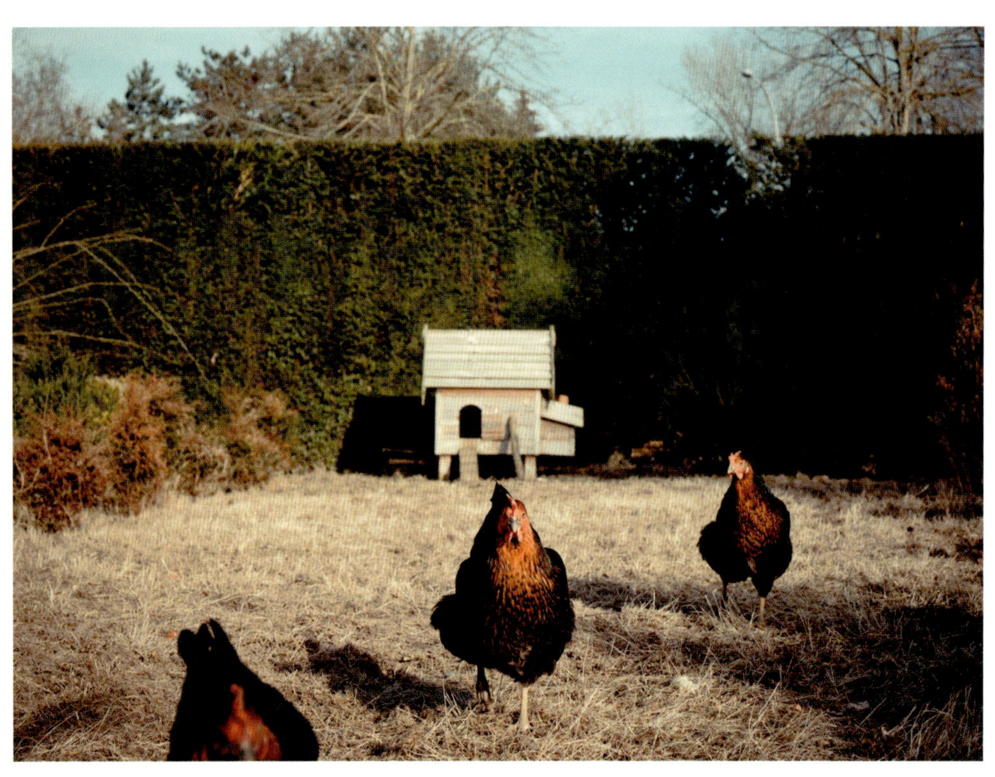

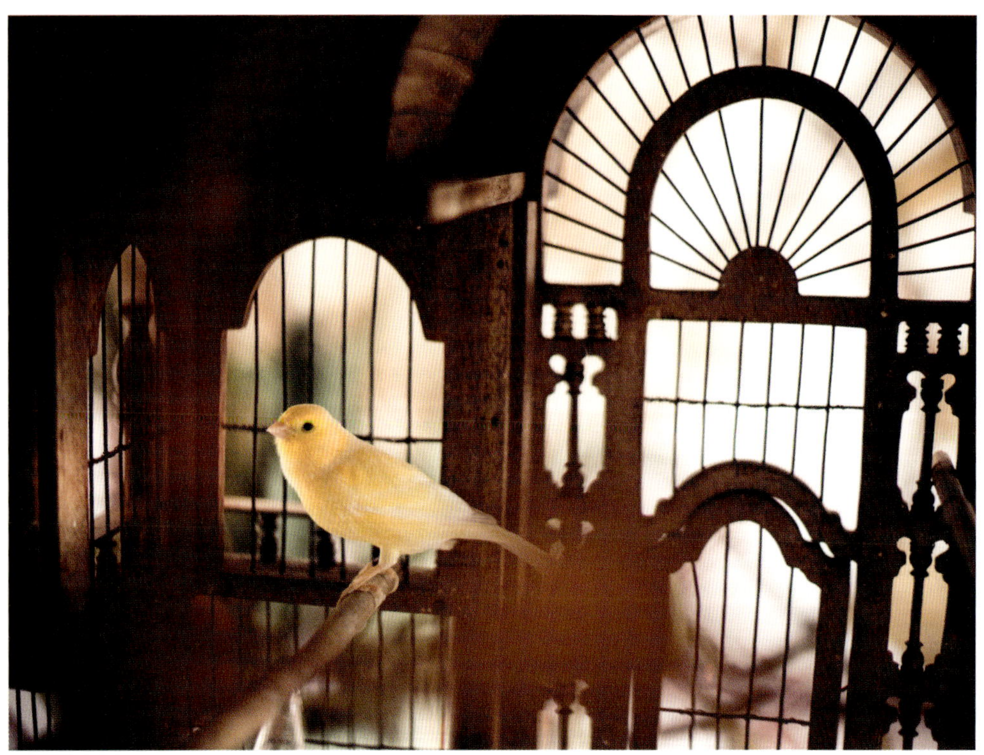

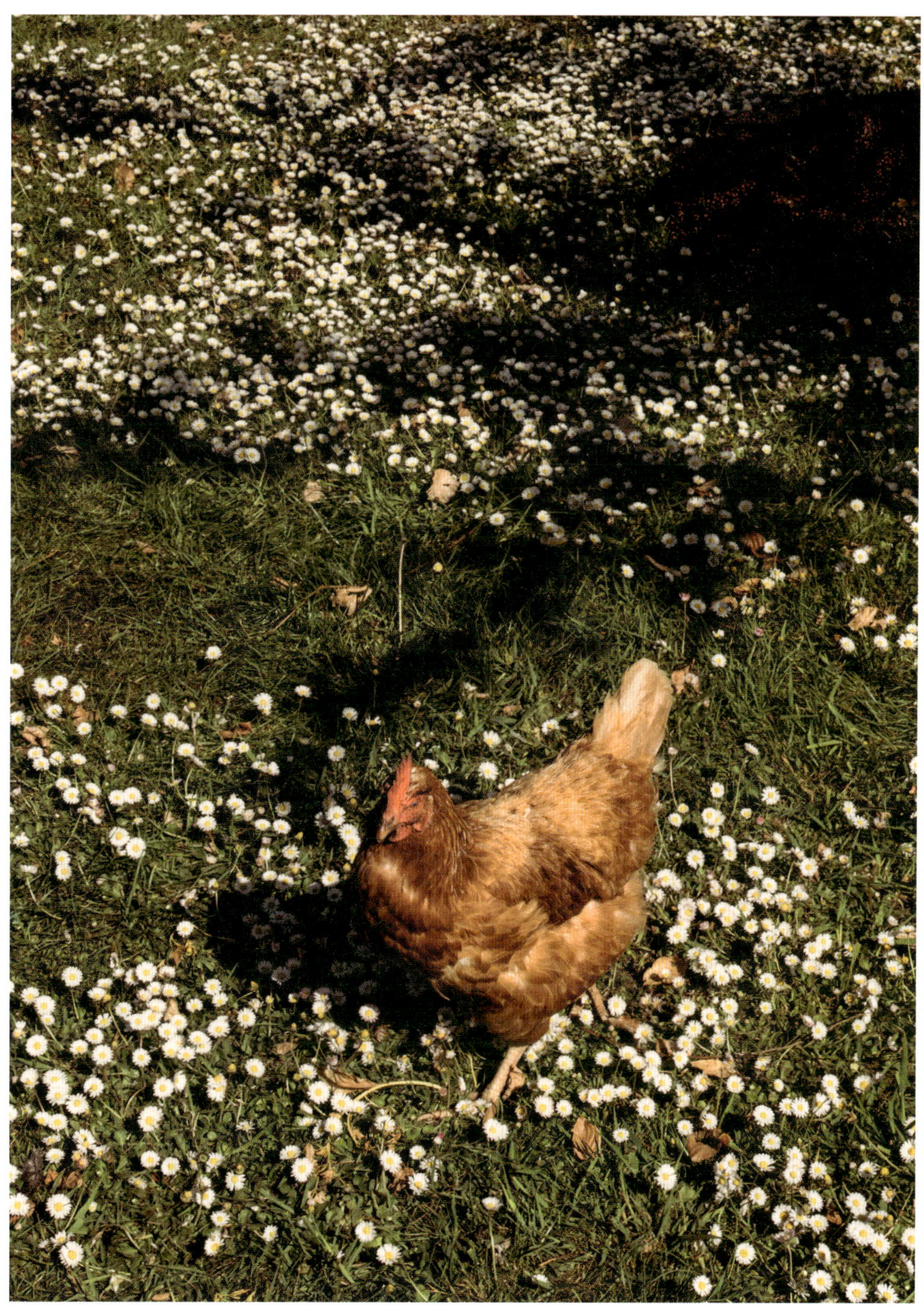

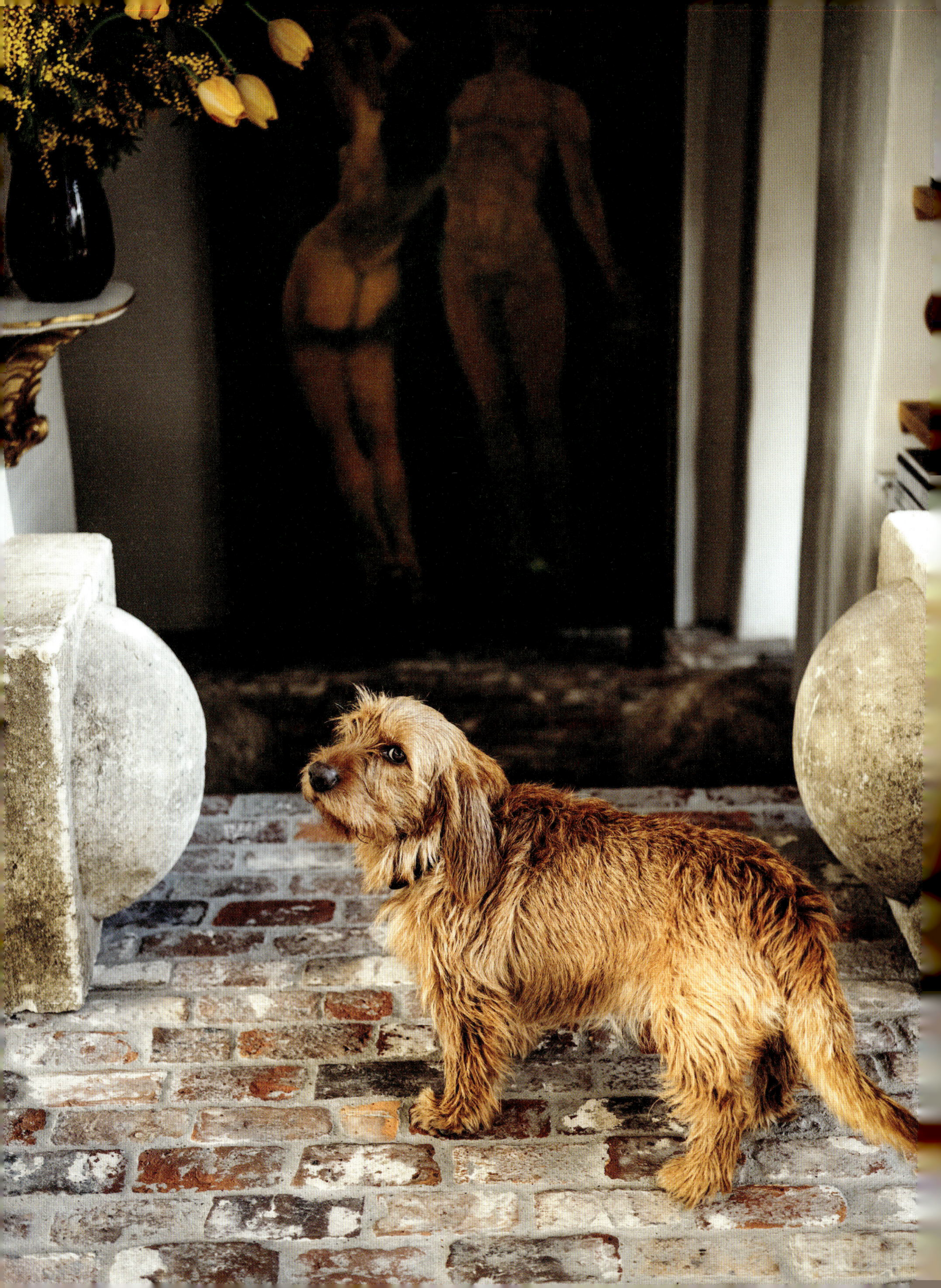

Johan's flower arrangements are lavish and natural, and never
look artificial. He succeeds in bringing out the simplicity and
beauty of flowers.

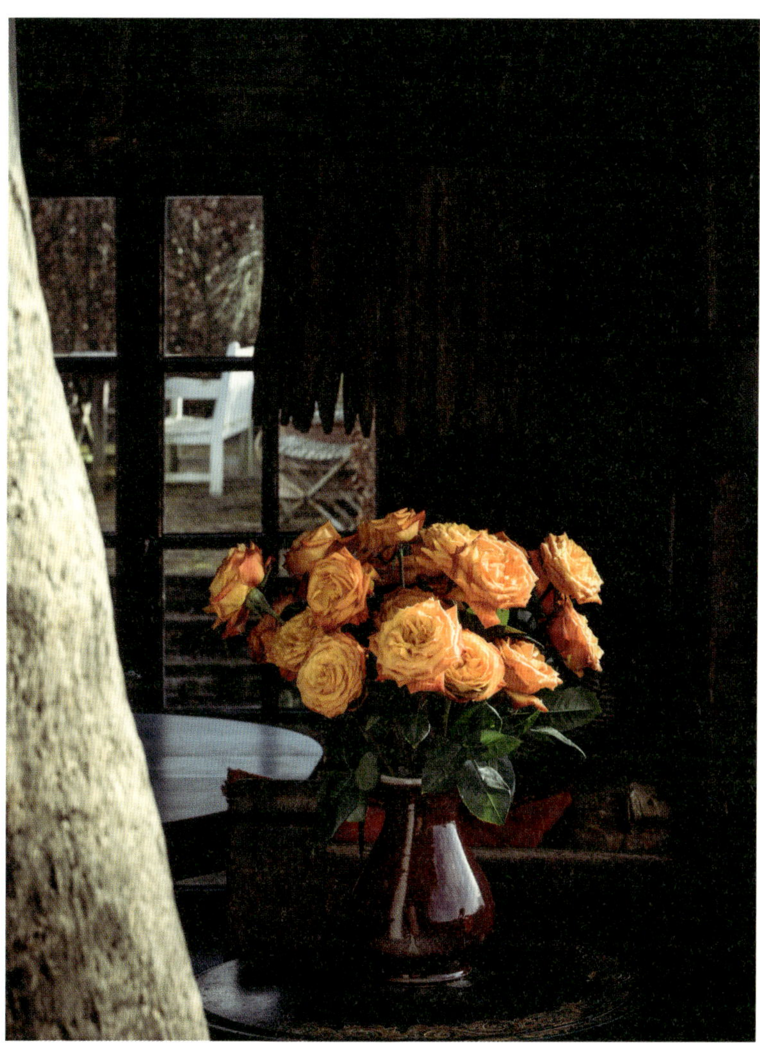

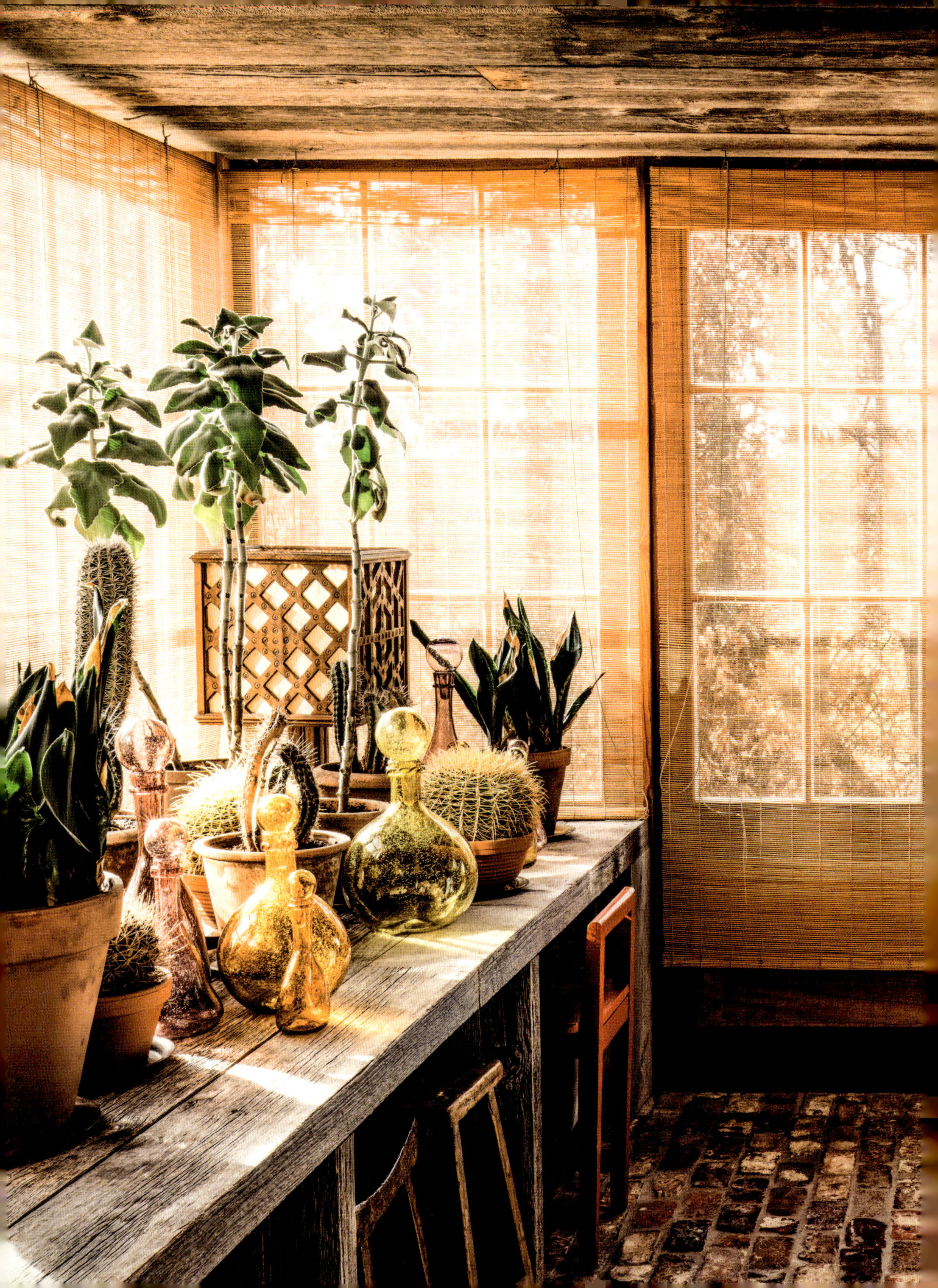

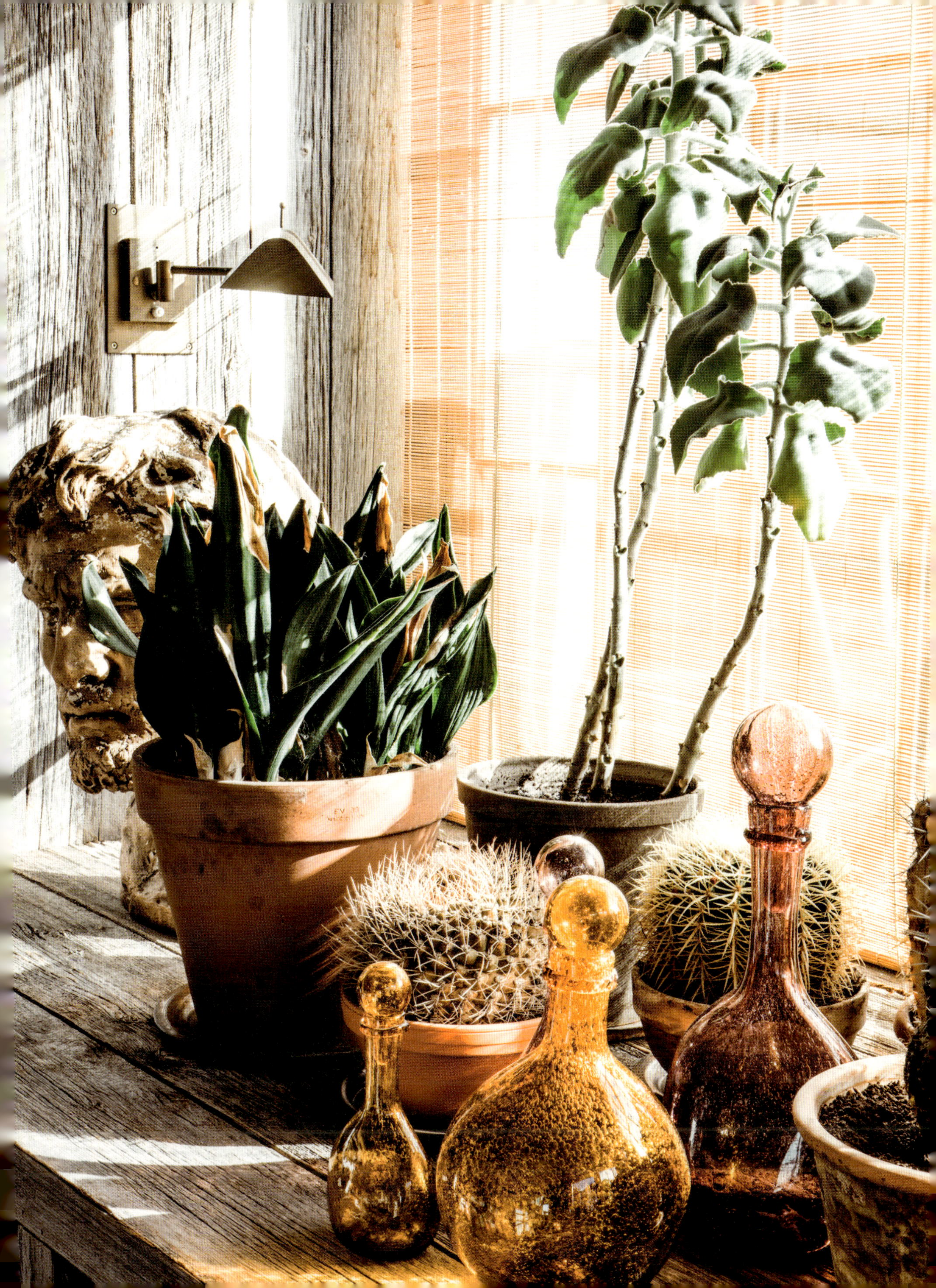

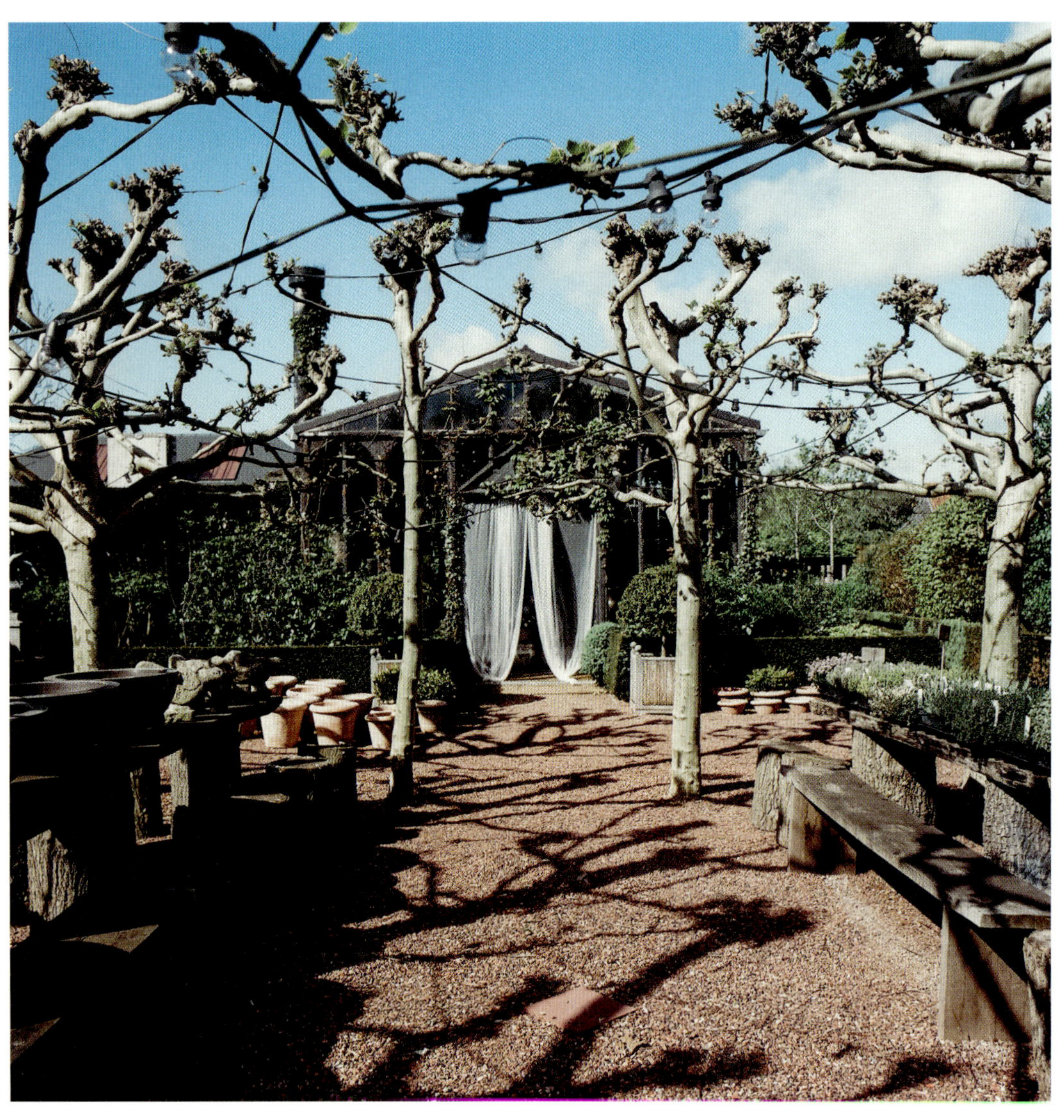

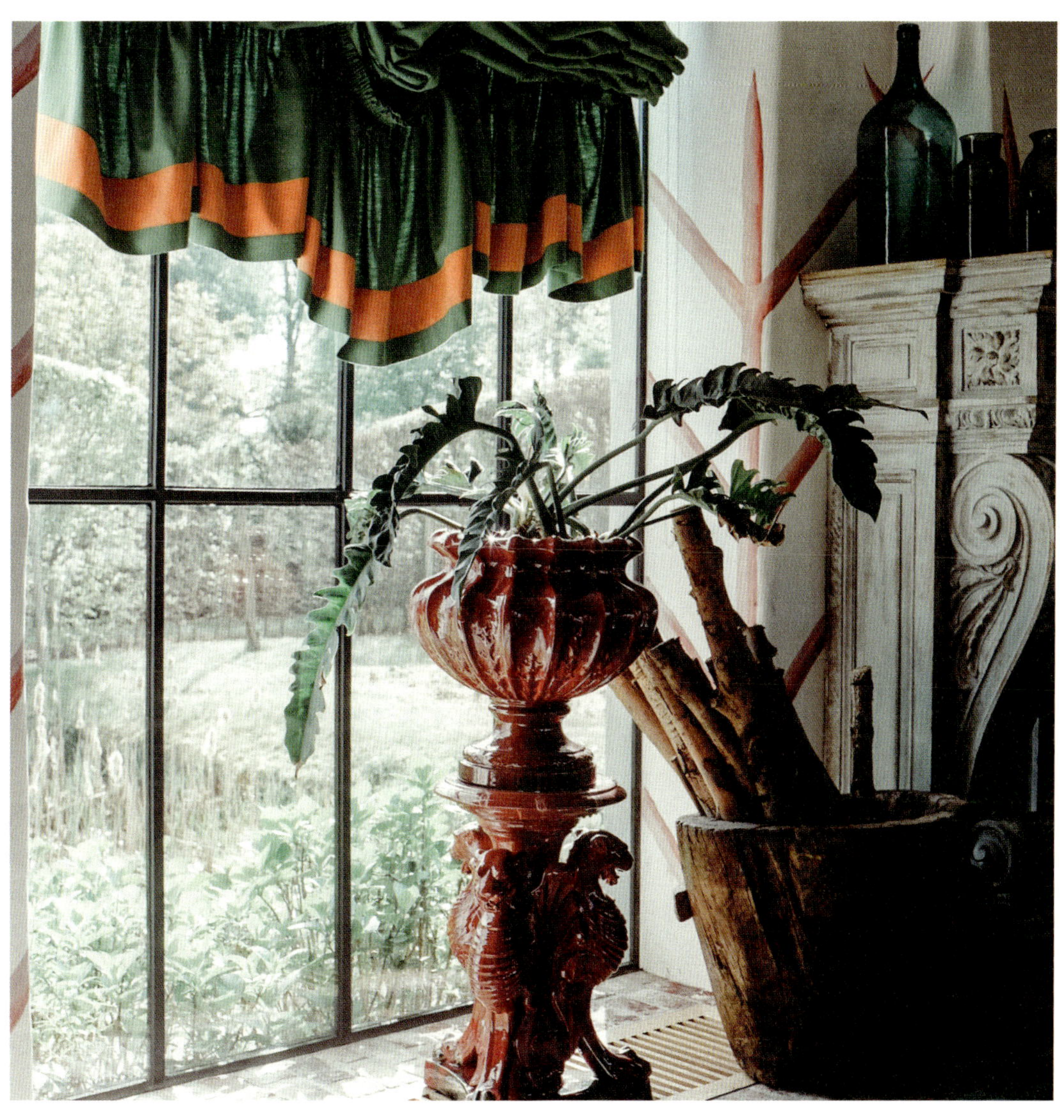

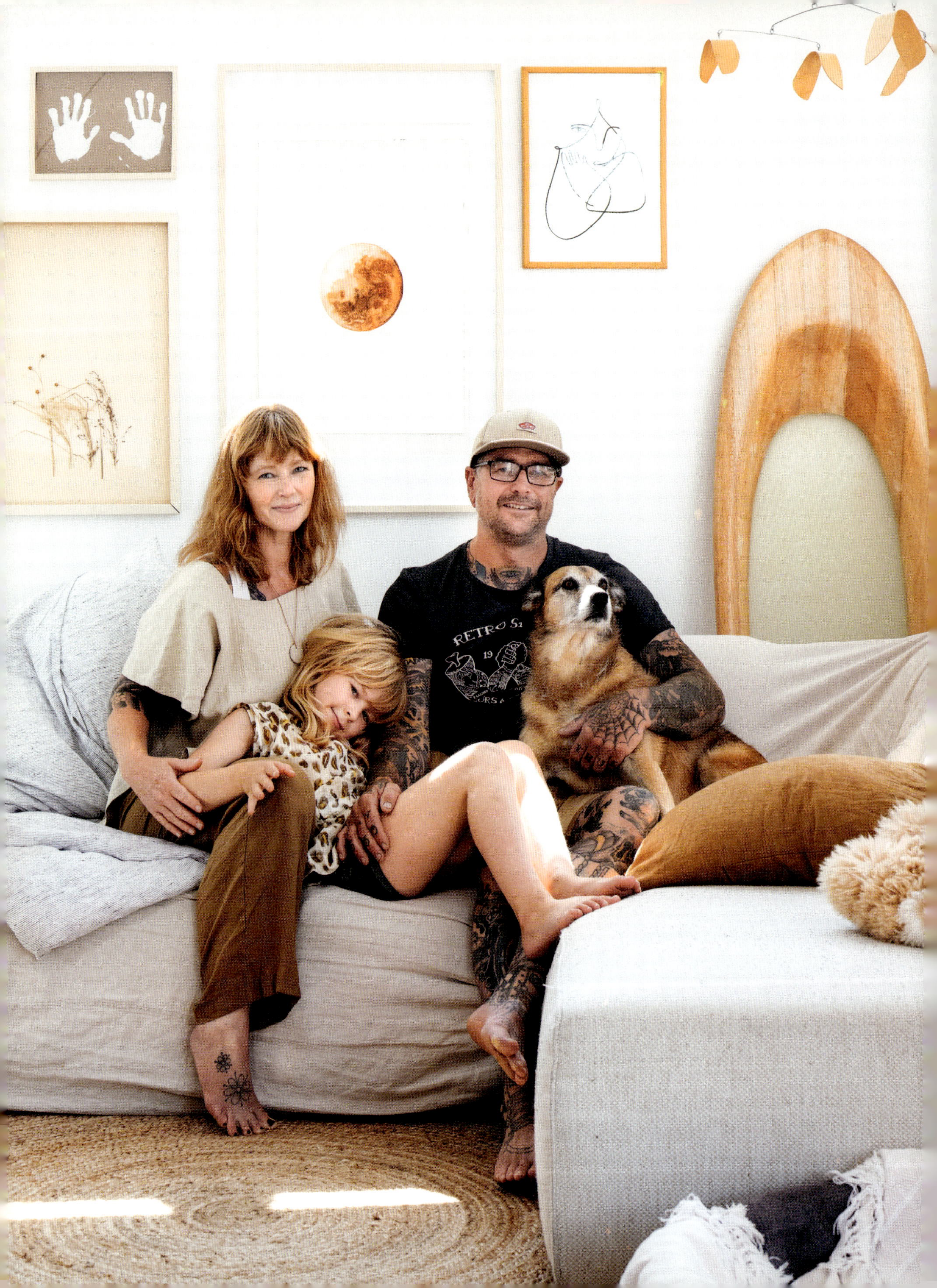

The home of Tinta and Rutger of Woodchuck and their daughter Dieuwertje looks like a beach house. The sea is just a stone's throw away, and the interior design is dominated by natural materials and airy colours. The spirit is laid-back. They share their 'Live and let live' philosophy with Pax, the stray they rescued. The dog has become part of the family and follows them everywhere they go. If he's not on the beach or in his basket, you can always find him in Dieuwertje's room. The two are best friends.

Strong as a bear but oh so sweet
While Pax may not be much to look at, he is 'the
sweetest pet ever,' according to Dieuwertje (8 years).
Tinta Luhrman and Rutger de Ruiter saved this stray
from a life in a Portuguese rehoming centre, when
he was just a puppy. They immediately knew 'this is
the one' when they gazed into his large, round eyes,
with black eyeliner. Pax is a very social animal, he
gets on very well with the other dogs that live nearby.
Rutger explains that strays are usually very strong,
compared with pedigree dogs, that are only bred for
profit. And while so many sweet strays are looking
for a forever home, they couldn't help but notice that
a growing number of pedigree dogs are also ending
up in rehoming centres. Tinta points out that people
often don't know what they are letting themselves
in for when they decide to get a pet. 'If you grew up
with dogs, you know that it's like taking on the care
for another child. A dog can't spend a lot of time
alone, so you need to take it everywhere you go,
even on holiday.' Both their transportation and holiday
destinations are now geared towards Pax. During the
summer vacation, they pack up their camper van and
venture out into nature.

Dogs welcome
Every day starts out with a tour of the surroundings.
The family lives within walking distance of the beach
and dunes, where Pax can run around as much as he
wants, off the leash, and chase rabbits and sheep.
The beach is really popular with dogs and their owners.
But the number of beaches where they are both
welcome is dwindling. 'I don't get it,' Rutger responds
furiously. 'A dog needs to be able to run around freely
and explore nature. Cats can stroll around your garden
without a care in the world, while dogs are immediately
categorised as a nuisance. Live and let live is my motto.
Everyone will be bothered by something.' Rutger
obviously loves dogs but he and Dieuwertje are allergic
to felines. 'A dog is always happy to see you, unlike a
cat, which treats you like you're the help.' Wherever
we go during our visit, Pax is never far away. He has
become Rutger's shadow. Fortunately, his job allows
him to keep the pet with him. Rutger and Tinta run a
workshop called Woodchuck, which produces wooden
objects and furniture, and offers interior design
services. And Pax always joins them when they visit
clients.

A child's love of animals
Pax is Dieuwertje's best friend. As we enter the house,
they are rolling around on the floor. 'I like to cuddle
him a lot because I think he needs it,' Dieuwertje
laughs. She hopes to become a vet one day for she
loves animals so much. 'Pax and I often play together.
I have an old cuddly toy, which I let him bite into.
And then I drag him around on the carpet, while he
holds it in his muzzle. It's such a funny sight.' They
only discovered each other recently because when she
was just born, the dog was not at all interested in her.
Over time, he even became jealous of her. 'But then
they became best friends,' Tinta says. There are plenty
of tricks to introduce your pooch to your baby. You
can let it smell a used diaper or clothes. Pax is now 10
years older. And although they know he still has many
years to go, they sometimes stop to think about the
time when he will no longer be there with them. 'One
day the time will come. Dying is part of life. I have no
idea whether we'll get another pet,' Rutger confesses.

A pet that blends in with the interior
Living with a dog only works, according to Rutger, if
you respect the following rule: 'He thinks of a family as
his pack, but before you know it, he'll take over. We are
the boss, and Pax has to learn that he always comes
last.' There are no other rules. The dog can go roam
where he wants. He opens doors with his nose, which
means he can get into every room. Even the bedrooms.
He regularly seeks out Dieuwertje in the attic and sleeps
on her cuddly toys. During our visit, he walks in and out,
into the garden, lies down in his basket and jumps onto
the white sofa. Tinta laughs: 'It's already full of stains,
so what.' They vacuum every day however, because Pax
loses loads of hair. 'Our home is very pet-friendly even
though this was not a conscious choice.' The dog has
become part of the household. Even better: he seems to
blend in with the interior, with his brown coat. This can
be no coincidence. Pax just happens to belong here, he's
become part of the scenery.

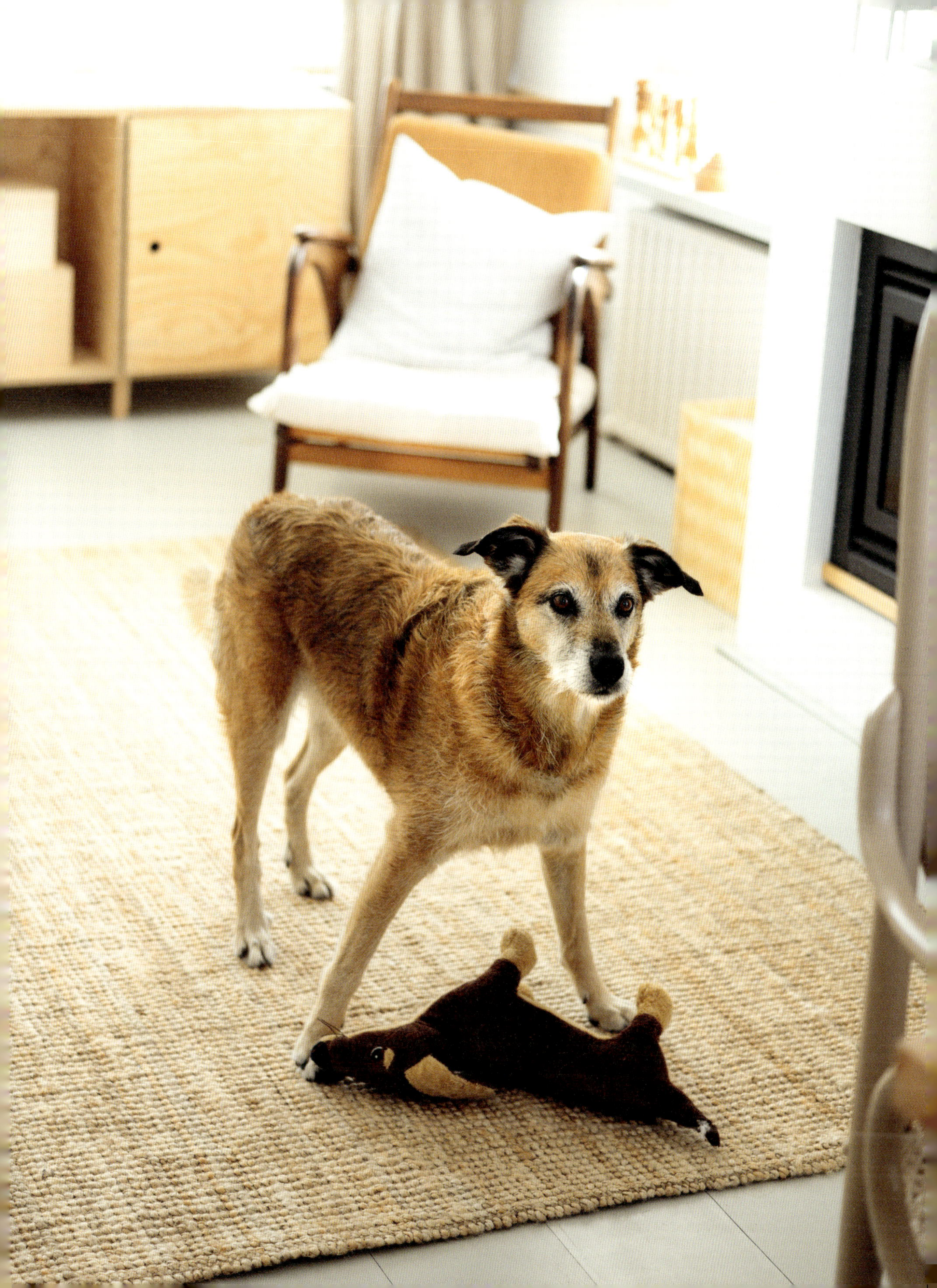

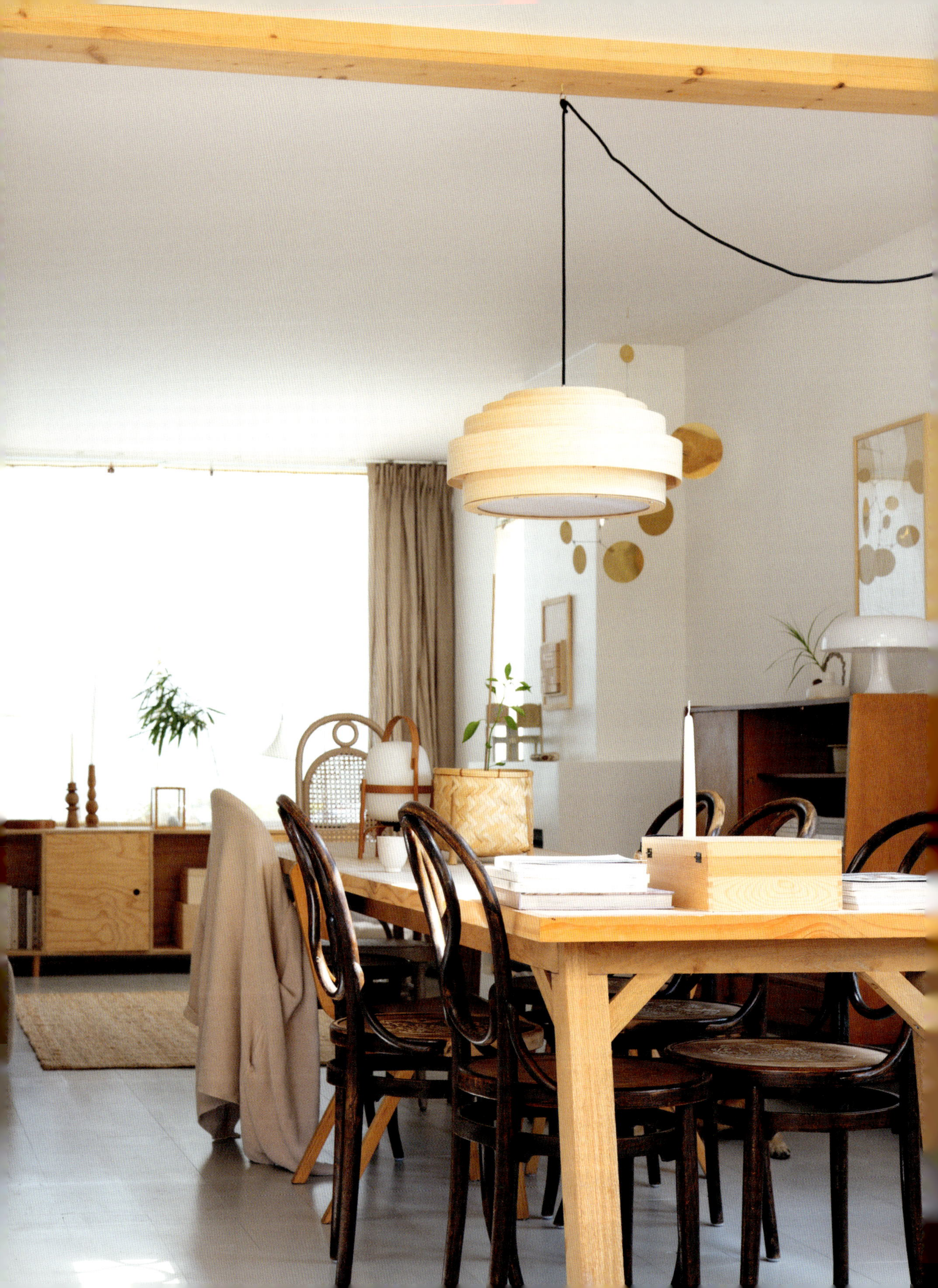

After Tinta had meningitis, they decided to search for a home
without too much environmental noise. They found it near the
beach, in a house from the sixties.

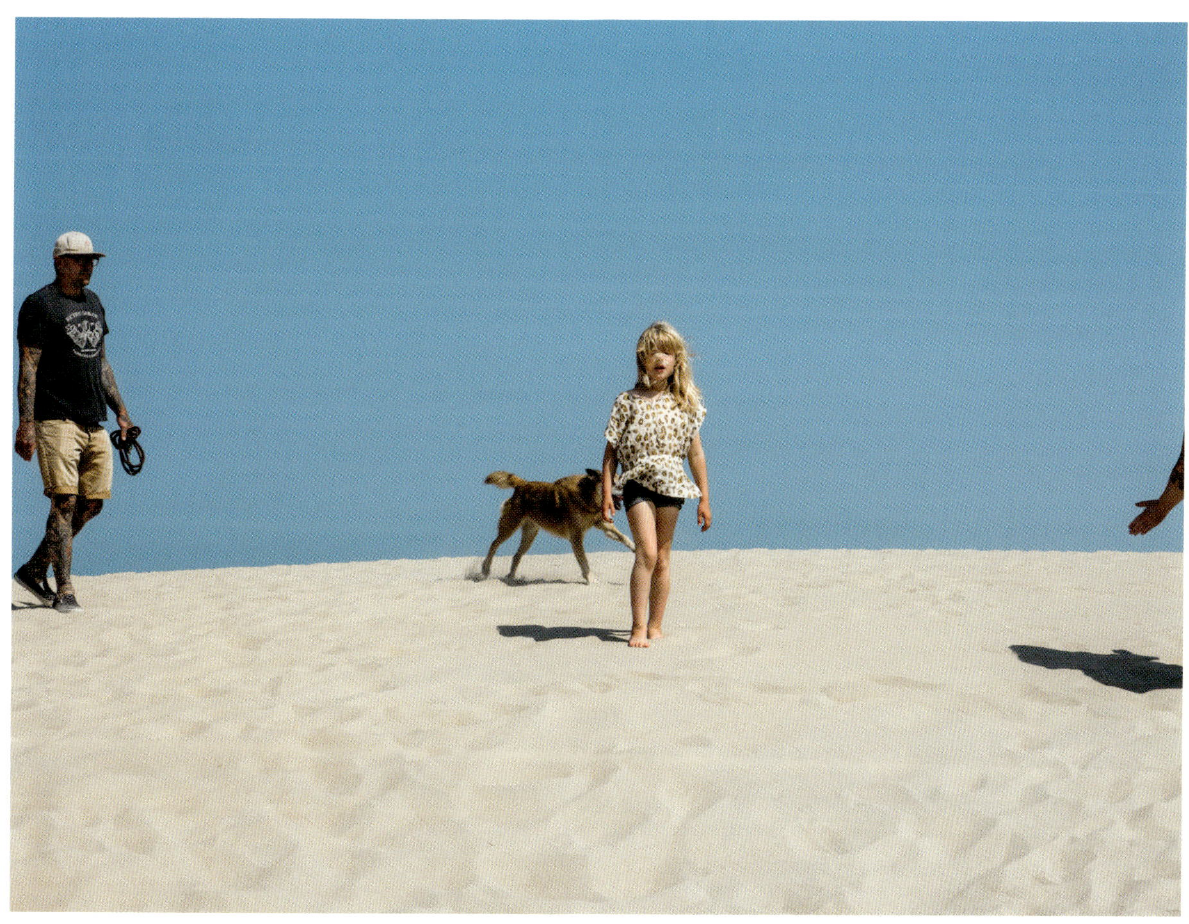

Tinta always works with light, shapes, and colour, as you can
tell by the timeless interior she created for her family home,
with plenty of natural materials and earthy hues.

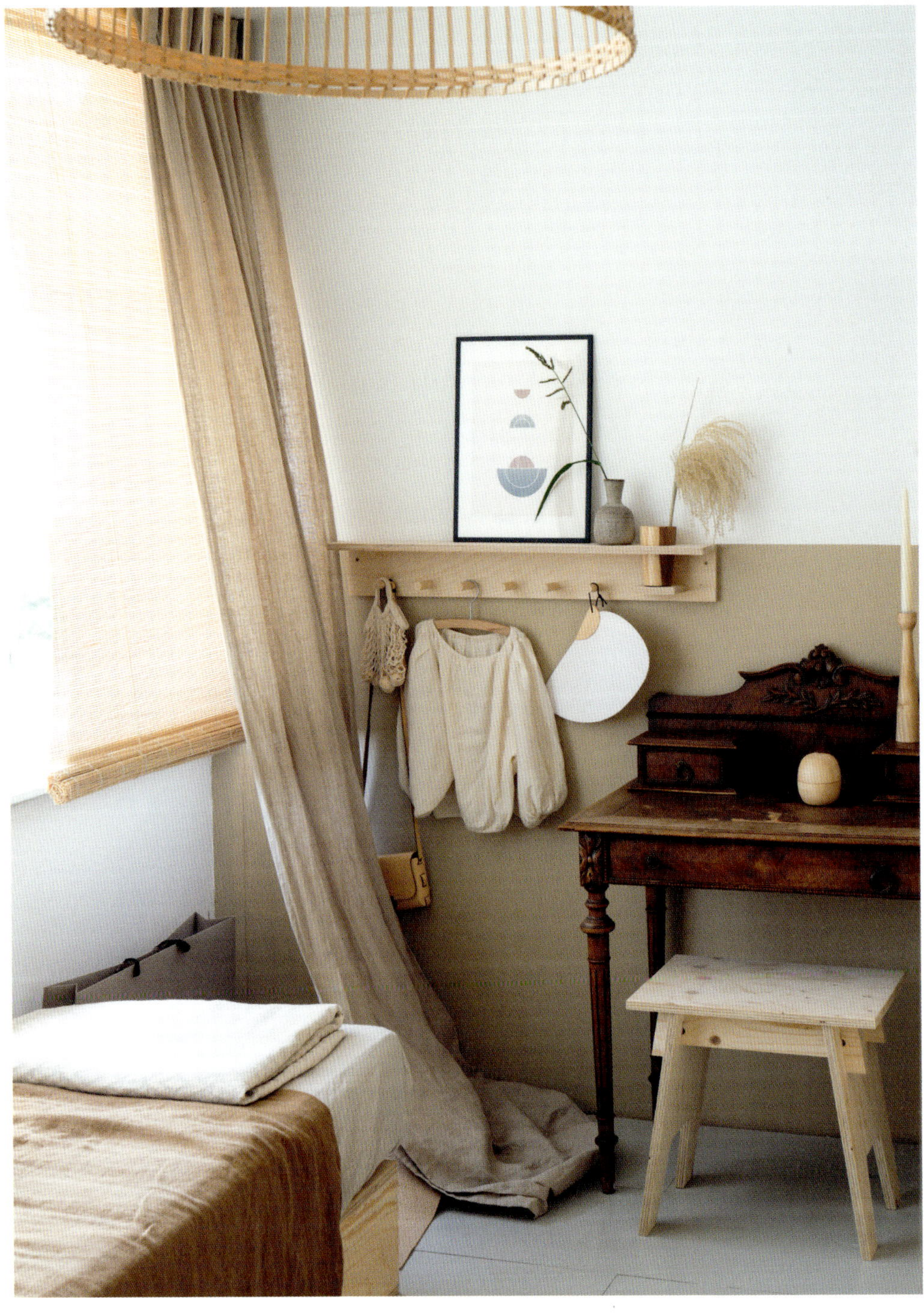

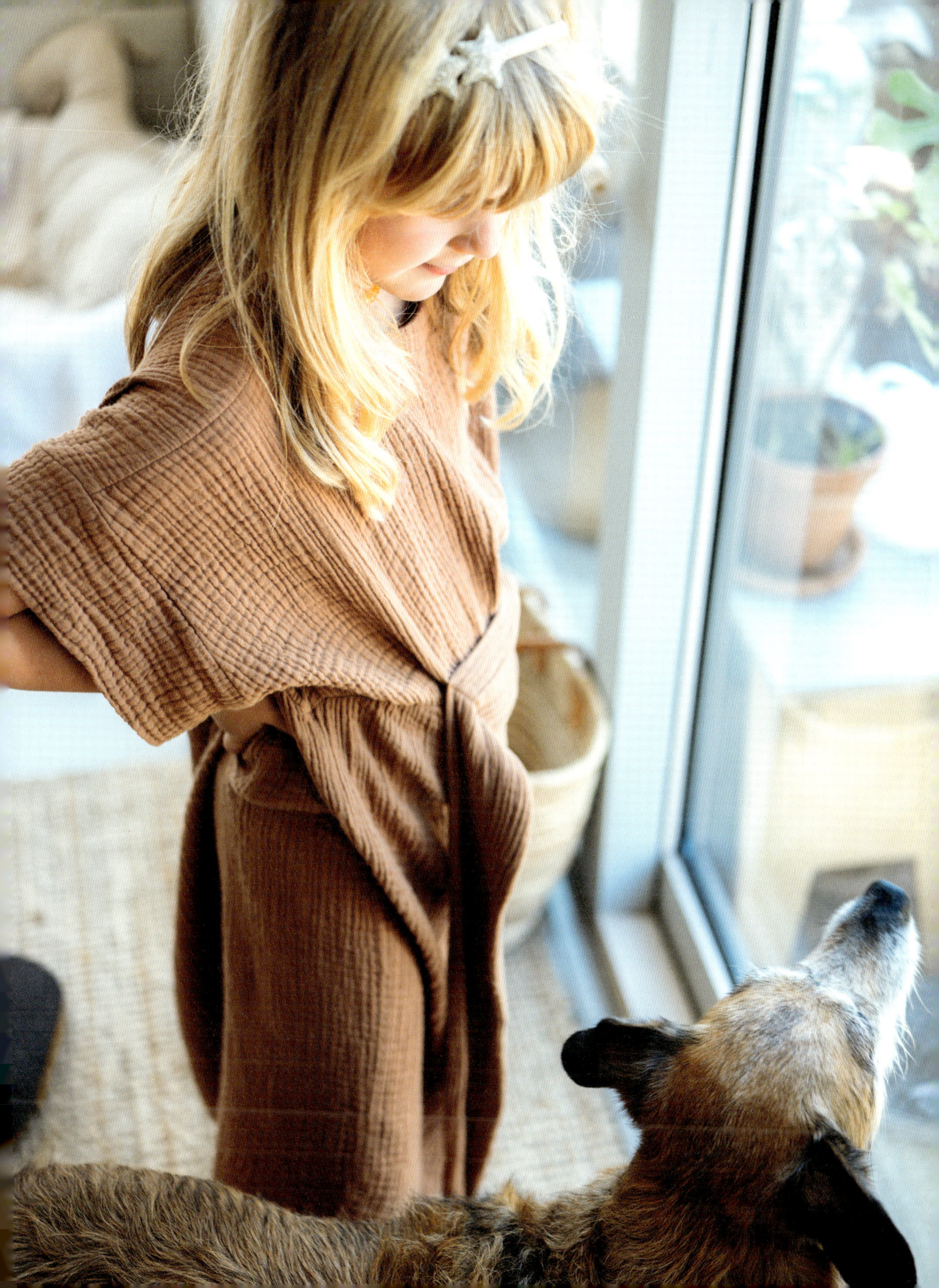

Pax is a rescue dog from Portugal. They take him everywhere
they go: to the beach, to the studio and when travelling in their
camper van.

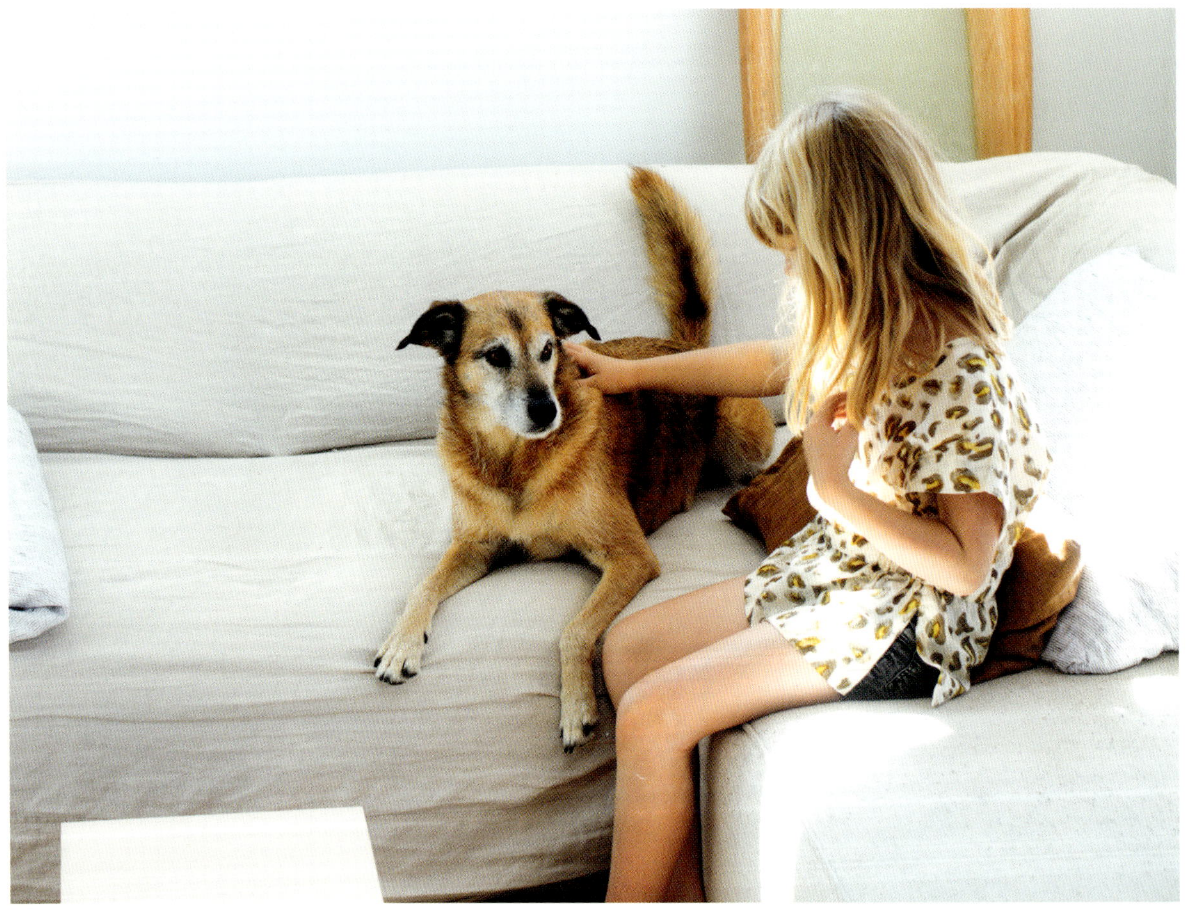

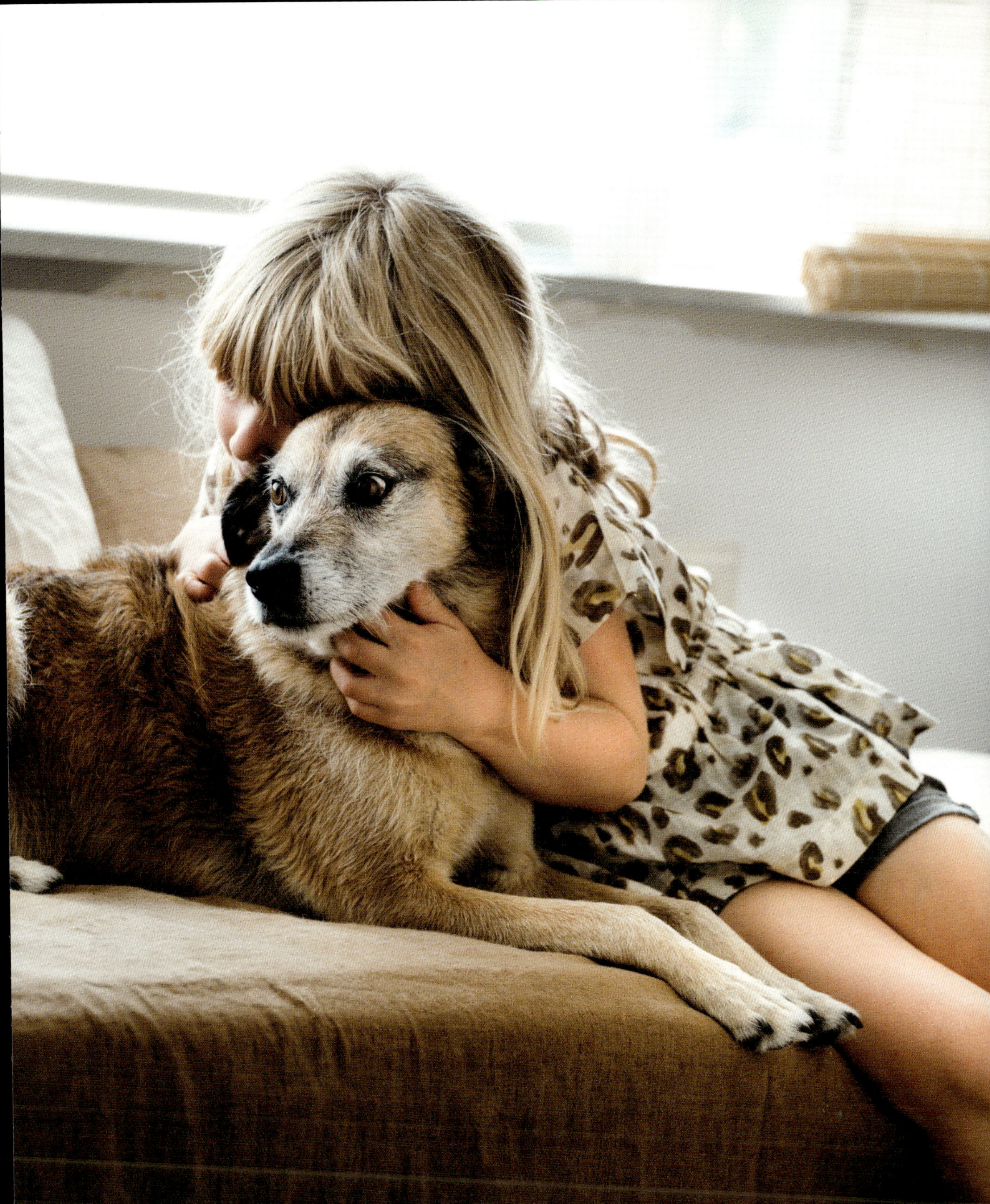

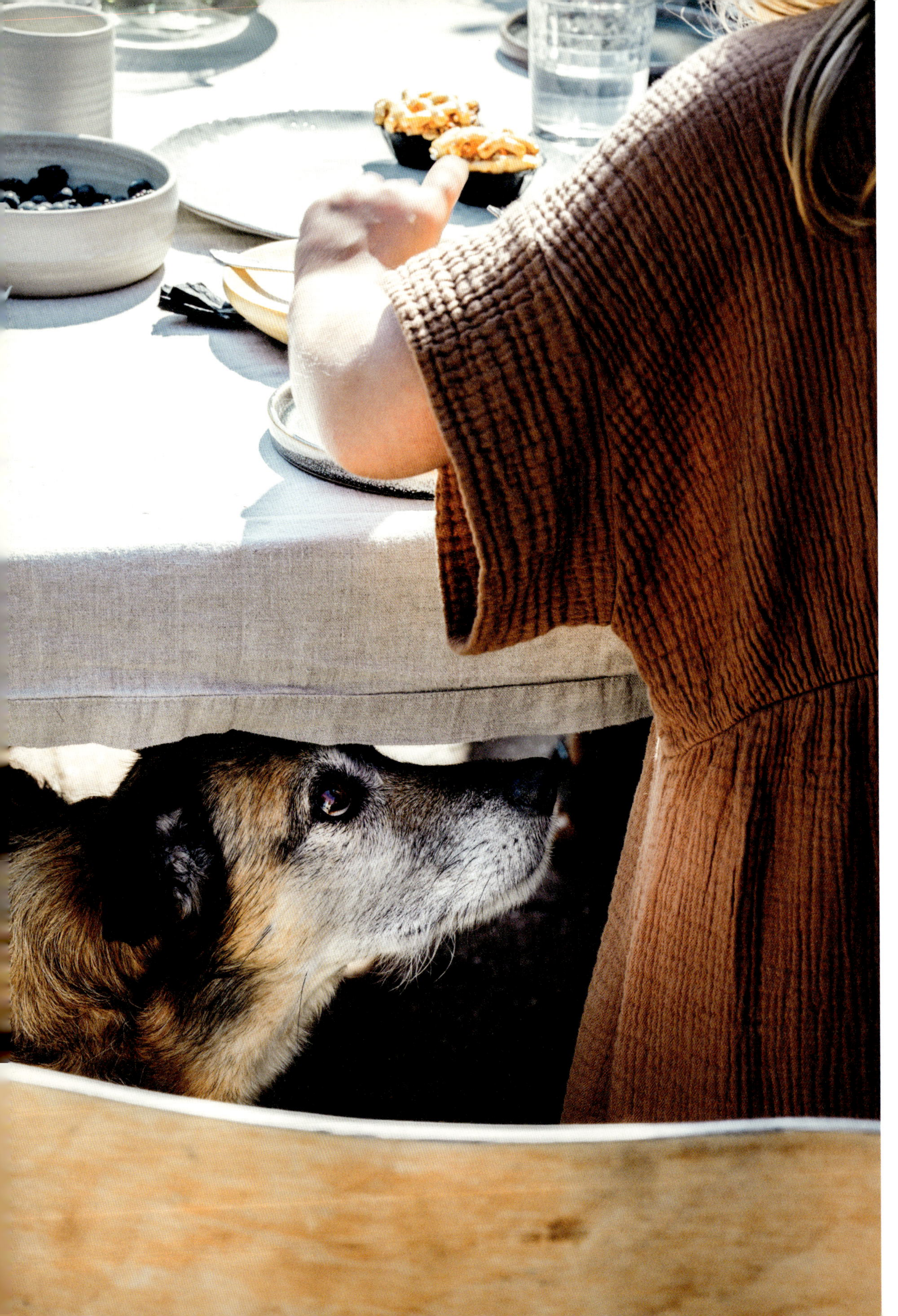

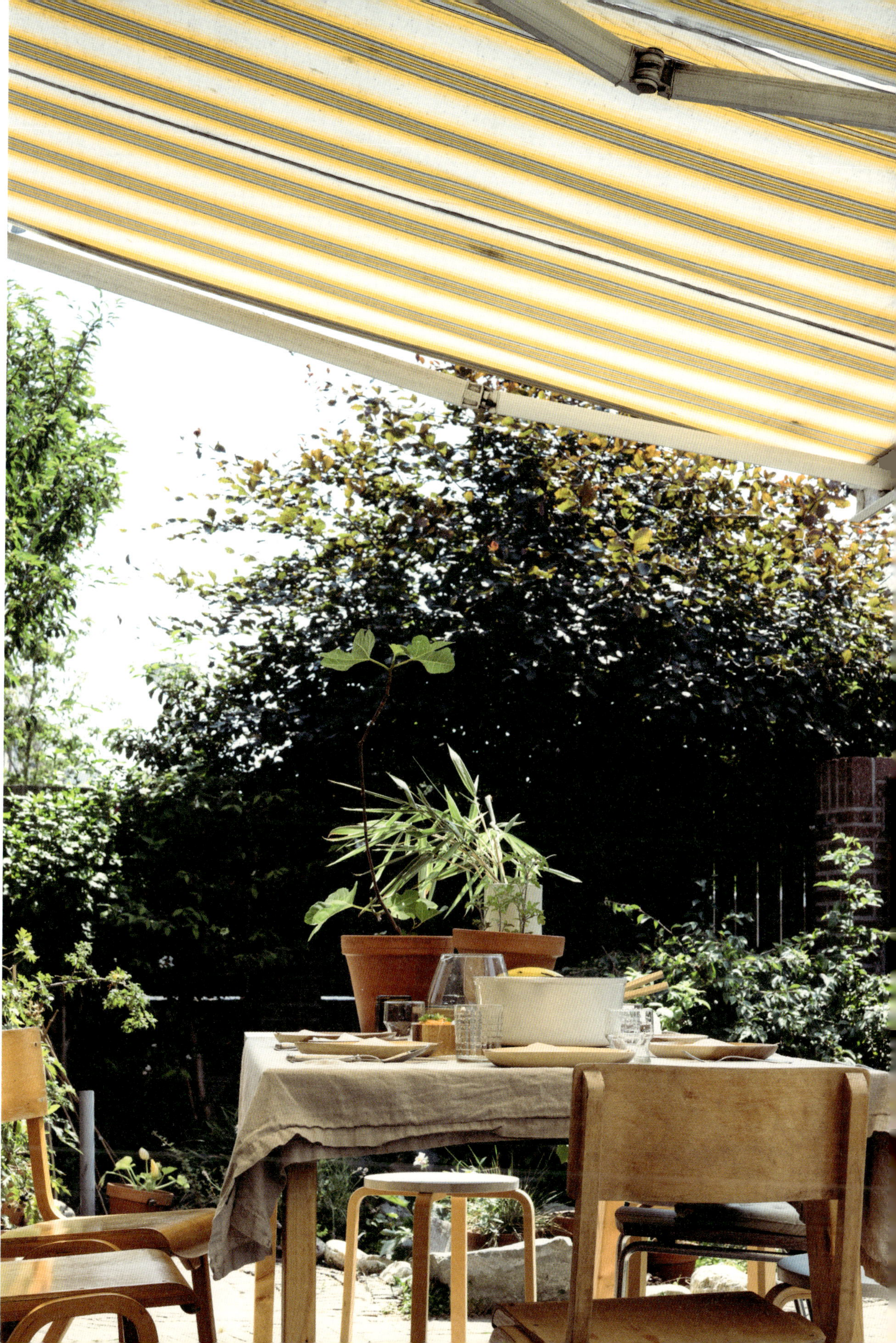

One and a half years ago, the couple founded Woodchuck,
a workshop that produces wooden objects, furniture, and interiors.

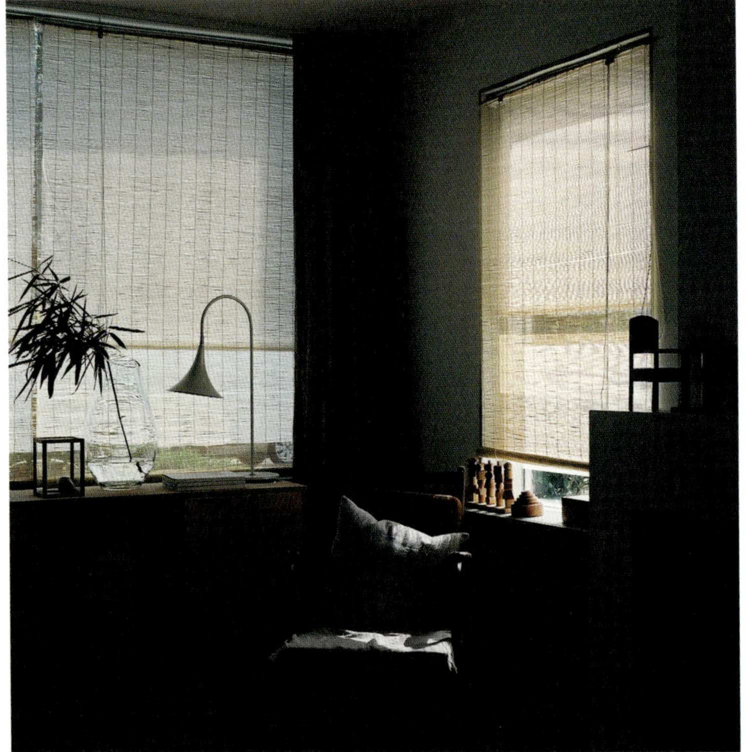

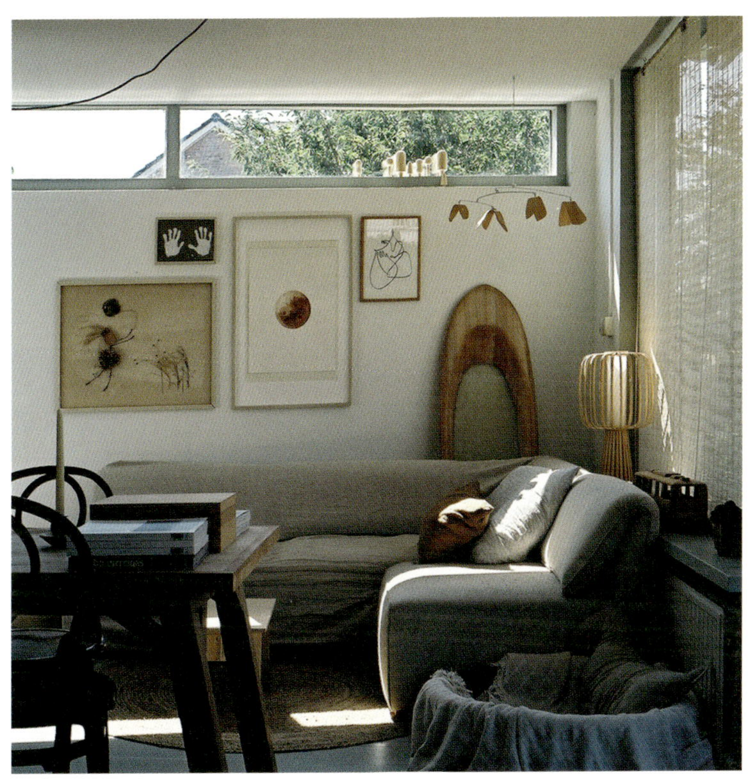

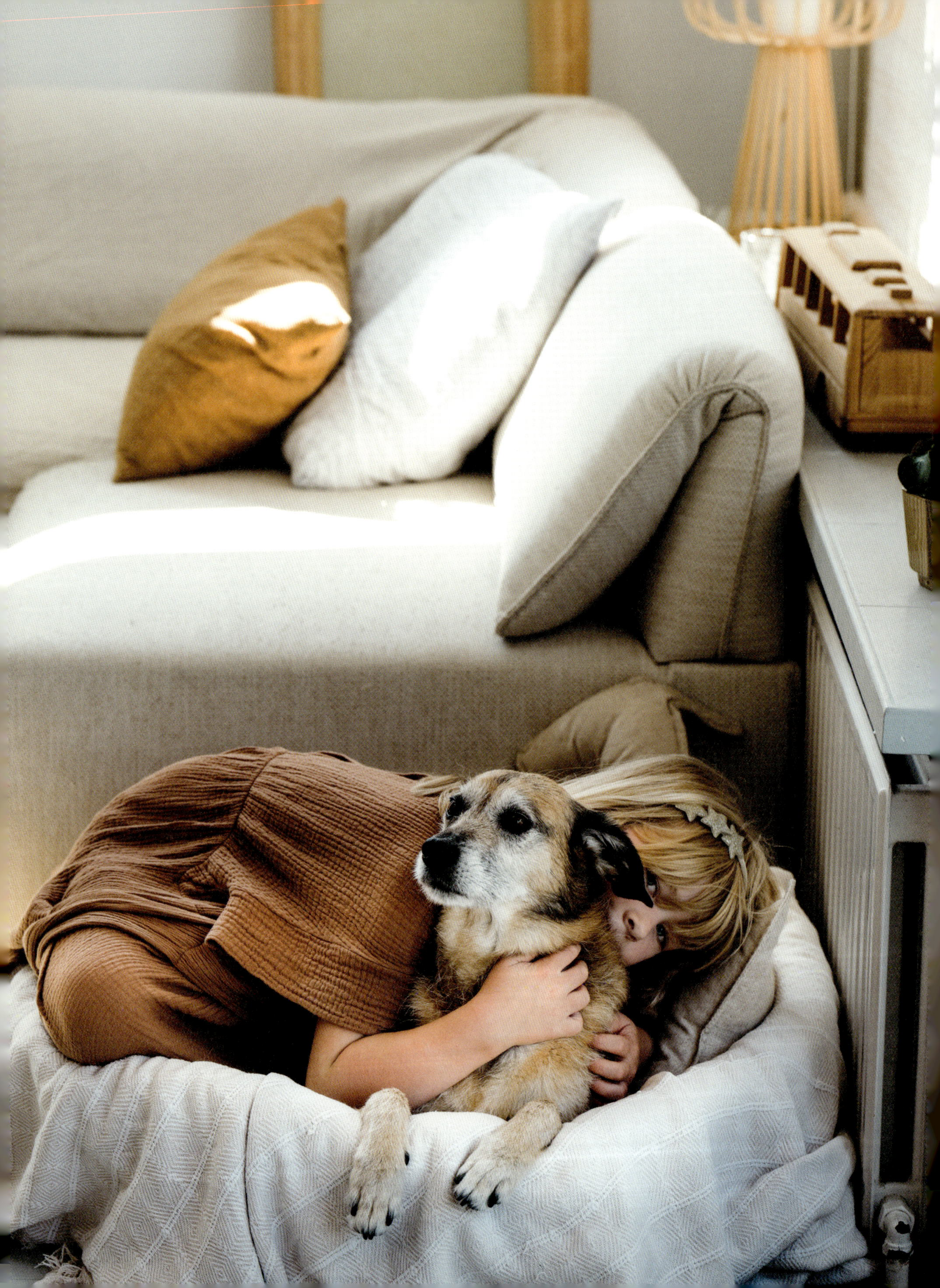

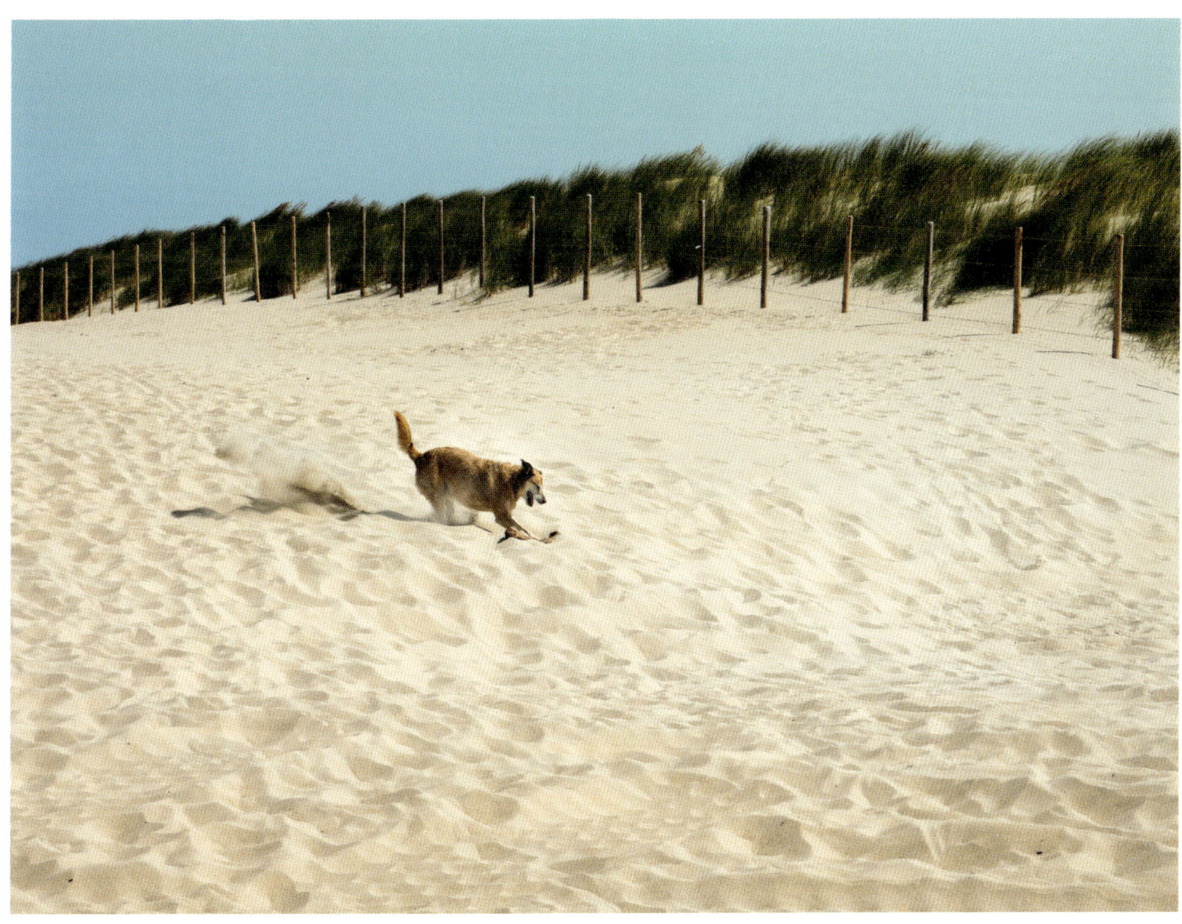

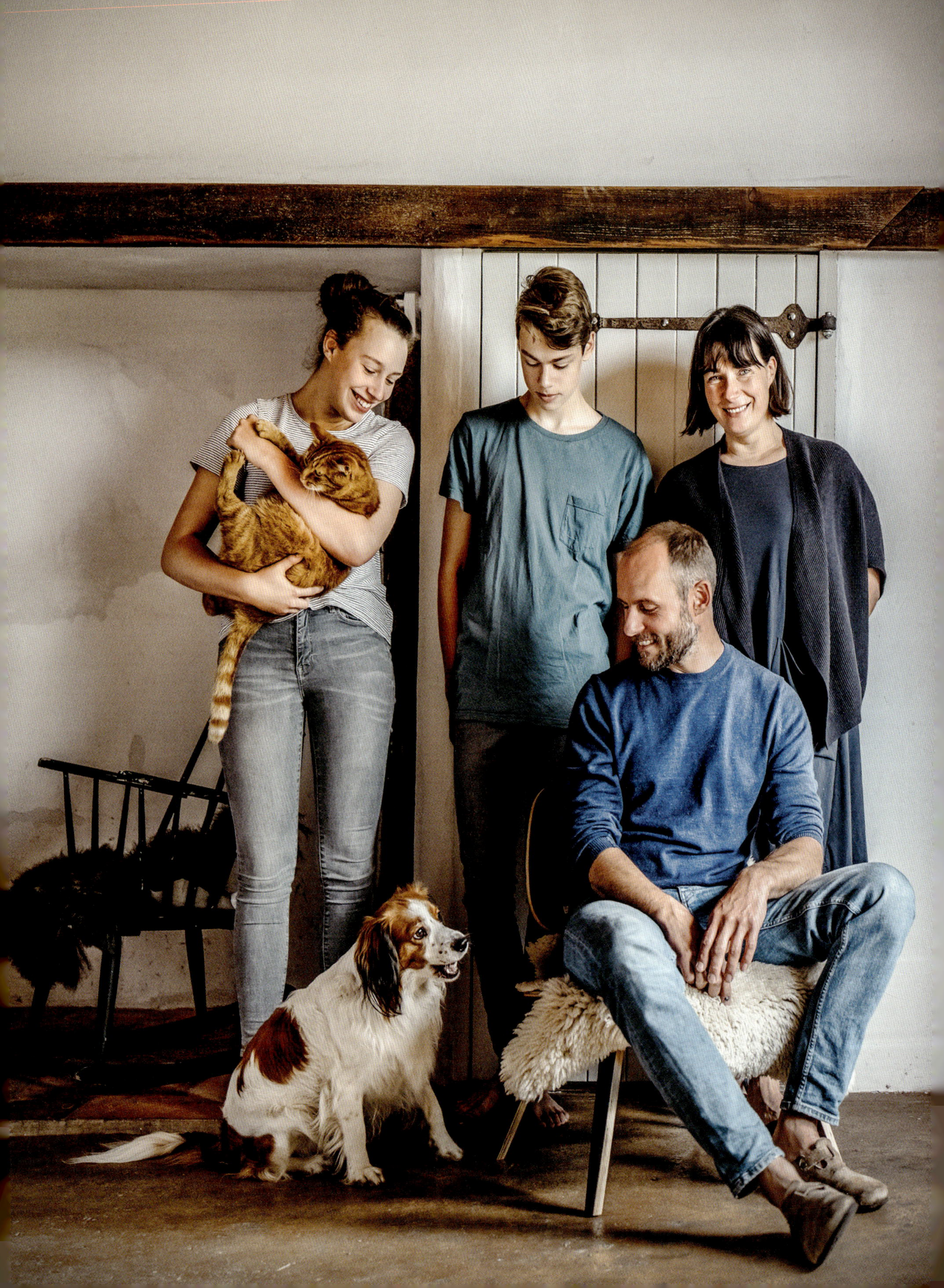

Ann and Jeroen of Studio Simple love simplicity, as you can tell from their designs and their rural lifestyle. Their life, however, is anything but simple when you realise how much work goes on behind the scenes. Everything they do is part of a greater whole, in which living and working become one, and a connection is established between family life, nature, and the animals. Their back to basics mentality has contributed to creating a unique lifestyle, that fuels their creativity.

Giving and sharing

As we walk out, we are rewarded with a crate full of
fresh vegetables from their garden. Ann Vereecken,
Jeroen Worst and their children Lotje (17 years) and
Kamiel (15 years) wave us off. Their dog Thor chases
the car. This final scene is a good summary of the
generous and welcoming atmosphere at Studio Simple.
They like to share the gifts of the land with the guests
that visit them. And as they live on a twelve-acre plot
of land, there is plenty to share. The family lives in
a beautifully-renovated country house surrounded
by fields and forests. The estate looks as if someone
has never stopped tending to it. 'And yet we had to
work very hard to return it to a more or less pristine
state. Everything was overgrown,' Ann confesses. The
property belongs to a foundation, from which they rent
the house and the land. The idea of renting and leasing
ties in with their vision on life, of immaterial pleasures,
of not becoming attached to objects, matter or a place.

A nomadic lifestyle

The couple lives like travellers or nomads. They
examine the potential of a place, ensures it provides
them with what they need, and then leave to go in
search of new adventures. As a family, they share
a unique lifestyle, which inspires them to design
objects and furniture, dictated by their immediate
surroundings. 'When we need something, we use the
materials we have to make it,' Jeroen explains. Their
creations, which include lamps, coat hangers, kitchen
accessories, and smaller furniture are harmoniously
combined with prototypes and secondhand objects
in the country house. Before they ended up here,
they lived in a living group, a farm and a city home
with an annex. What makes this new place so special
is the combination of living and working, and living in
harmony with nature and with the animals in the yard.

A vigilant dog, a lazy cat

Ann and Jeroen are designers first and foremost,
not farmers. Their approach to design is much the
same as their approach to the country estate on
which they live. They continuously respond to needs
as they arise. Which is also how they decided which
animals to include in their family. Thor is a kooiker, a
vigilant working dog. But he is also a real family pet,
and he loves to play. It is he who welcomes us and
accompanies us to the guest room. He who cuddles
with us before we go to sleep and wakes us up when
breakfast is served. Boris, the baron, a fat ginger cat,
is much less on the ball. He spends most of his day
snoozing on his throne, being catered to at every turn.
'It took a while before he and Thor got on with each
other, but now they are best friends,' says Ann.

Clucking in your ears

The estate now also has a flock of tiny chickens, called
chabos, a Japanese bantam chicken. In anticipation of
the arrival of the chicken coop, they have withdrawn
to the hedge around the house. Jeroen thinks the birds
which he got from his friends are good fun. 'Chabos
are small, and they are superb laying hens. They're not
very strong, so they don't ruin a lot, which is why we let
them stay so close to us.' And we have to admit that it
is quite lovely to wake up in the morning to the sound
of clucking and an egg on your plate. The couple
believes in living from the land, and we definitely don't
say no to that.

Smart sheep

In addition to the chickens, the dog and the cat, the
couple also has a dozen sheep, that mow the grass and
fertilise the field. 'We got them for practical reasons,'
Jeroen confesses. He purposefully chose Wiltshire
horns, a very independent and strong breed. They are
smart, attentive, manage well in winter, and rarely
fall ill. What's more, they naturally moult their wool
and coat, so they never have to be shorn. They are
considered 'easy to care for' because of these many
positive characteristics. When Jeroen walks out towards
the sheep with a tray, indicating that it is feeding time,
the animals run towards him, beautifully circling the
yard. It is quite a fantastic sight to experience nature up
from this close.

The cycle of nature

You may expect Wiltshire horns to be rather
aggressive because of their horns and their solid
demeanour, but they are not. Jeroen pets them and
says: 'We currently have two rams and they may
fight as they grow older, in which case we will have
to give up one of them.' In a year, they went from five
to eleven sheep. Jeroen is thinking about removing
a few, but his daughter Lotje disagrees. He thinks
slaughtering is part of the cycle of nature, which is
only allowed if you know the animals had a good
life.' Ann takes us on a tour of the vegetable garden.
'You go back to basics by sowing, harvesting and
sharing vegetables, and also contribute to the cycle.'
It is an understatement to say that the family leads a
simple life when you see how much work it takes to
keep on top of this estate. In a sense, they actually lead
a good and full life.

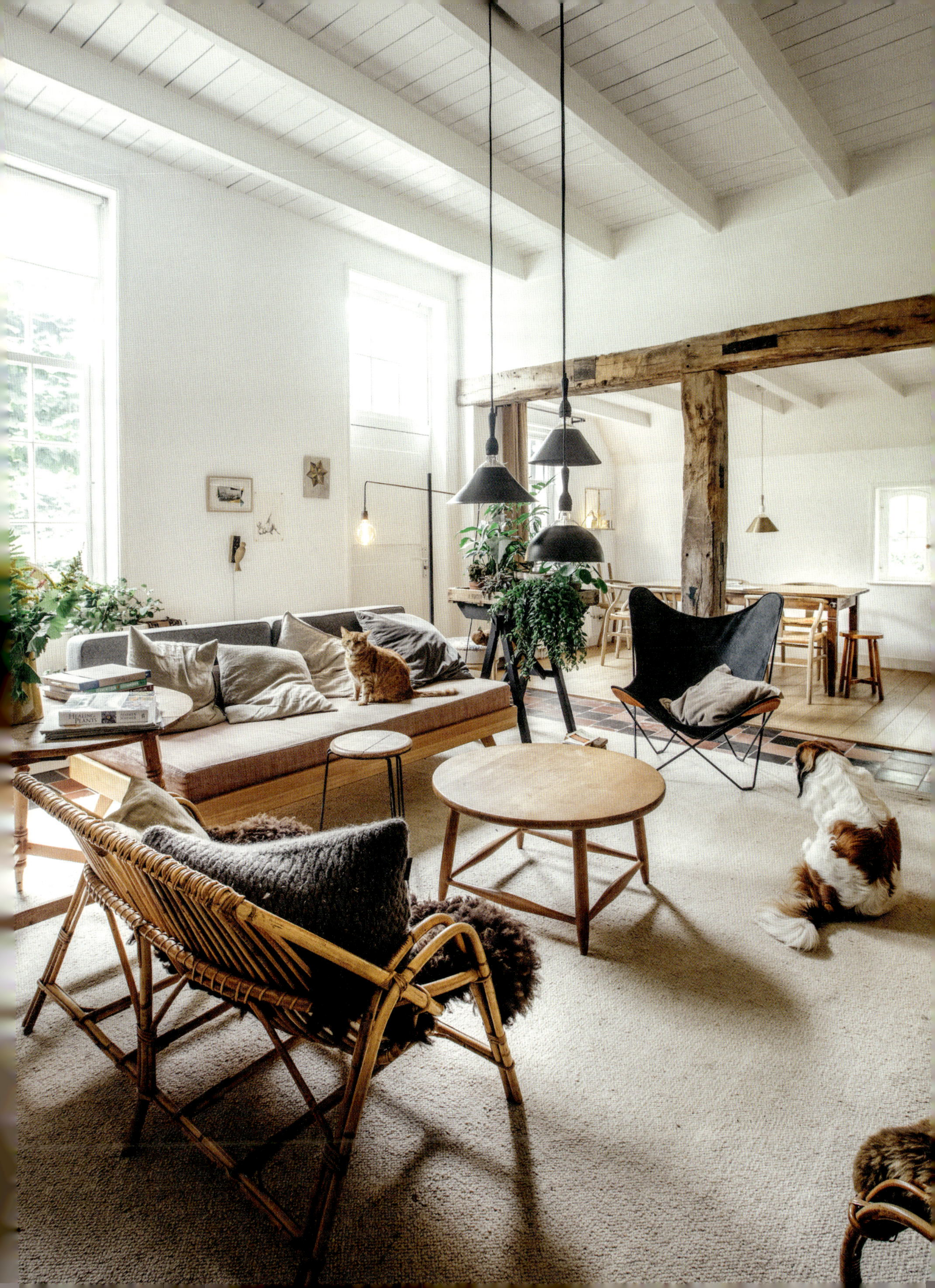

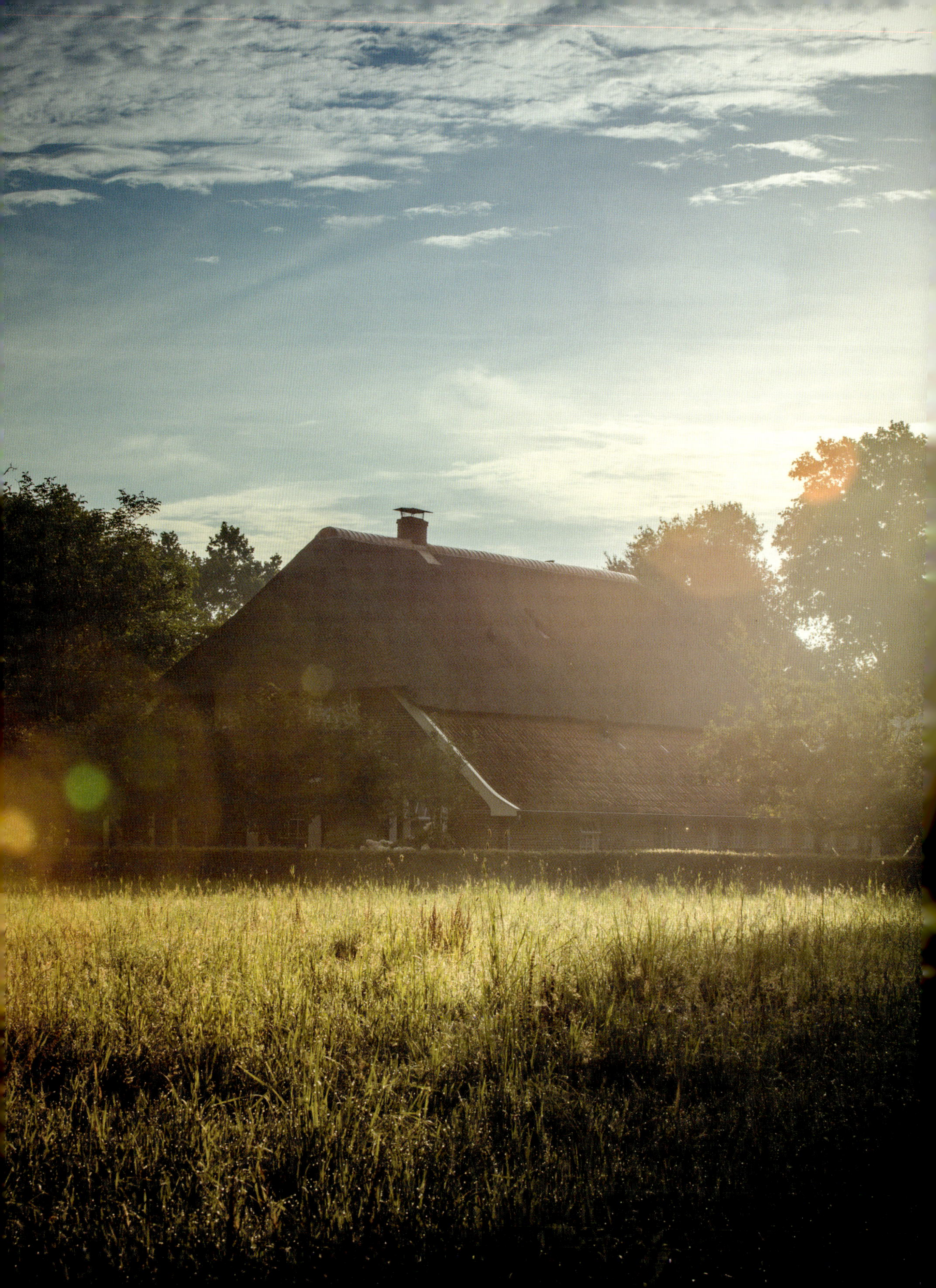

Renting a house and the land ties in with Studio Simple's vision
on life, of immaterial pleasures, of not becoming attached to
objects or a place.

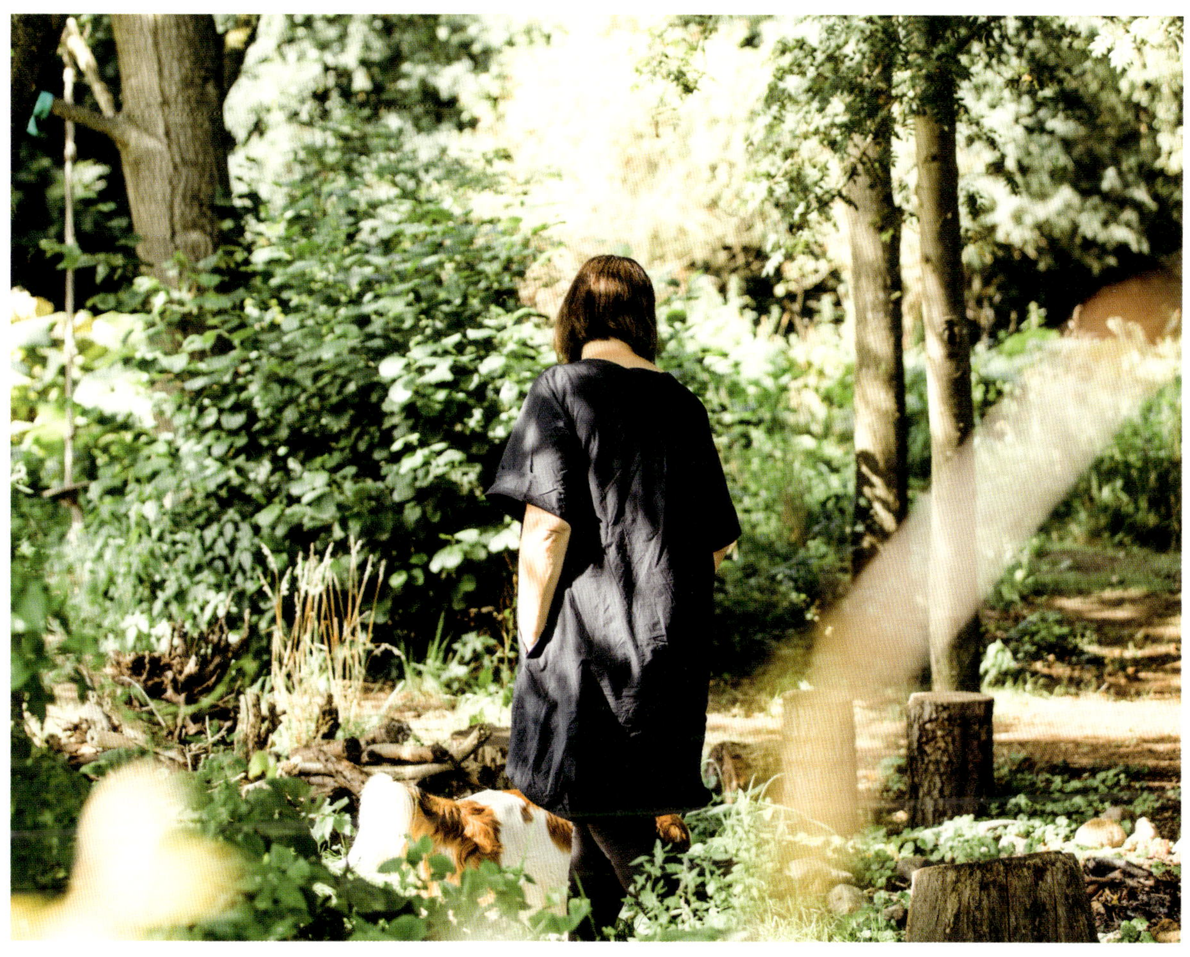

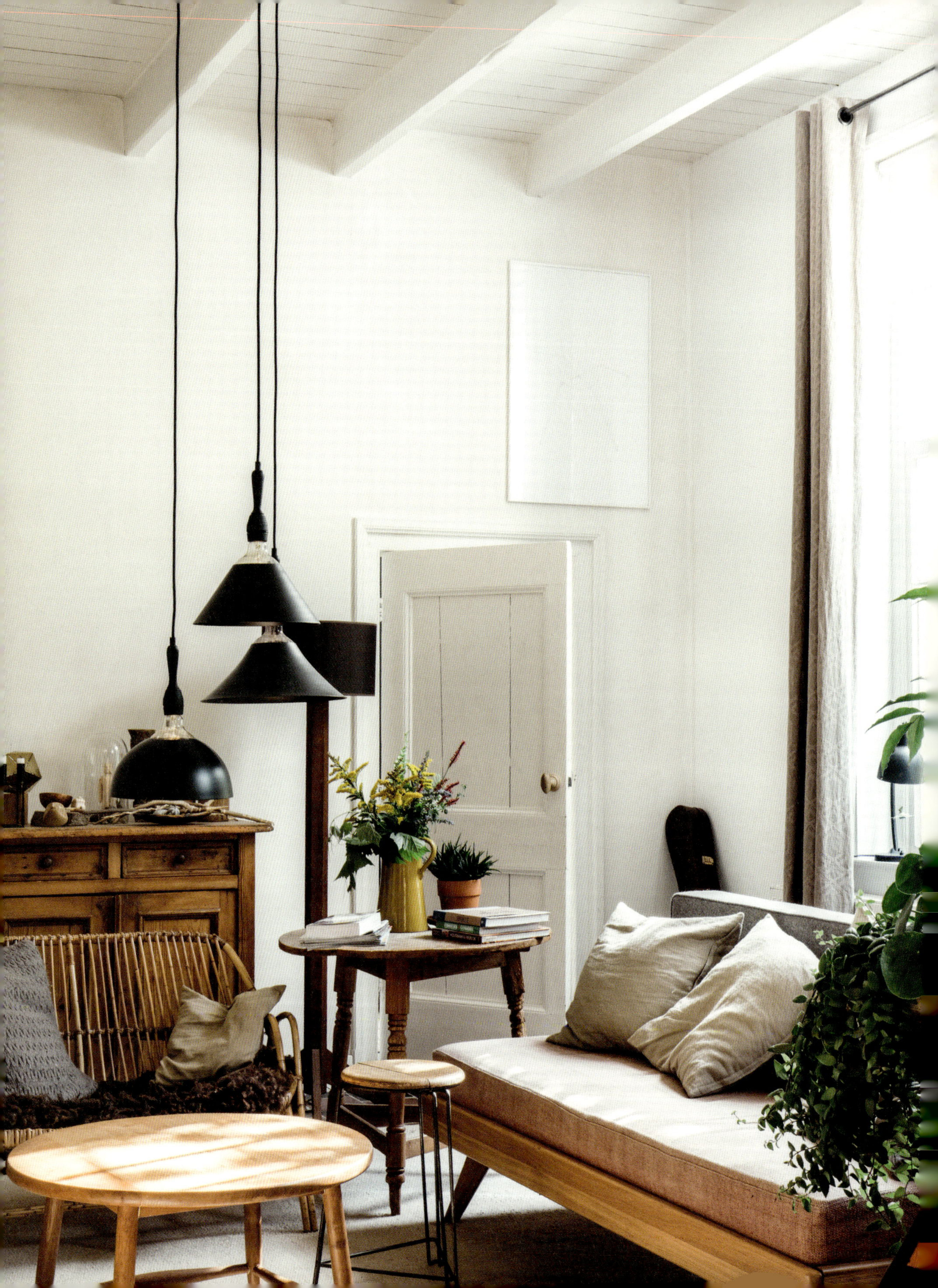

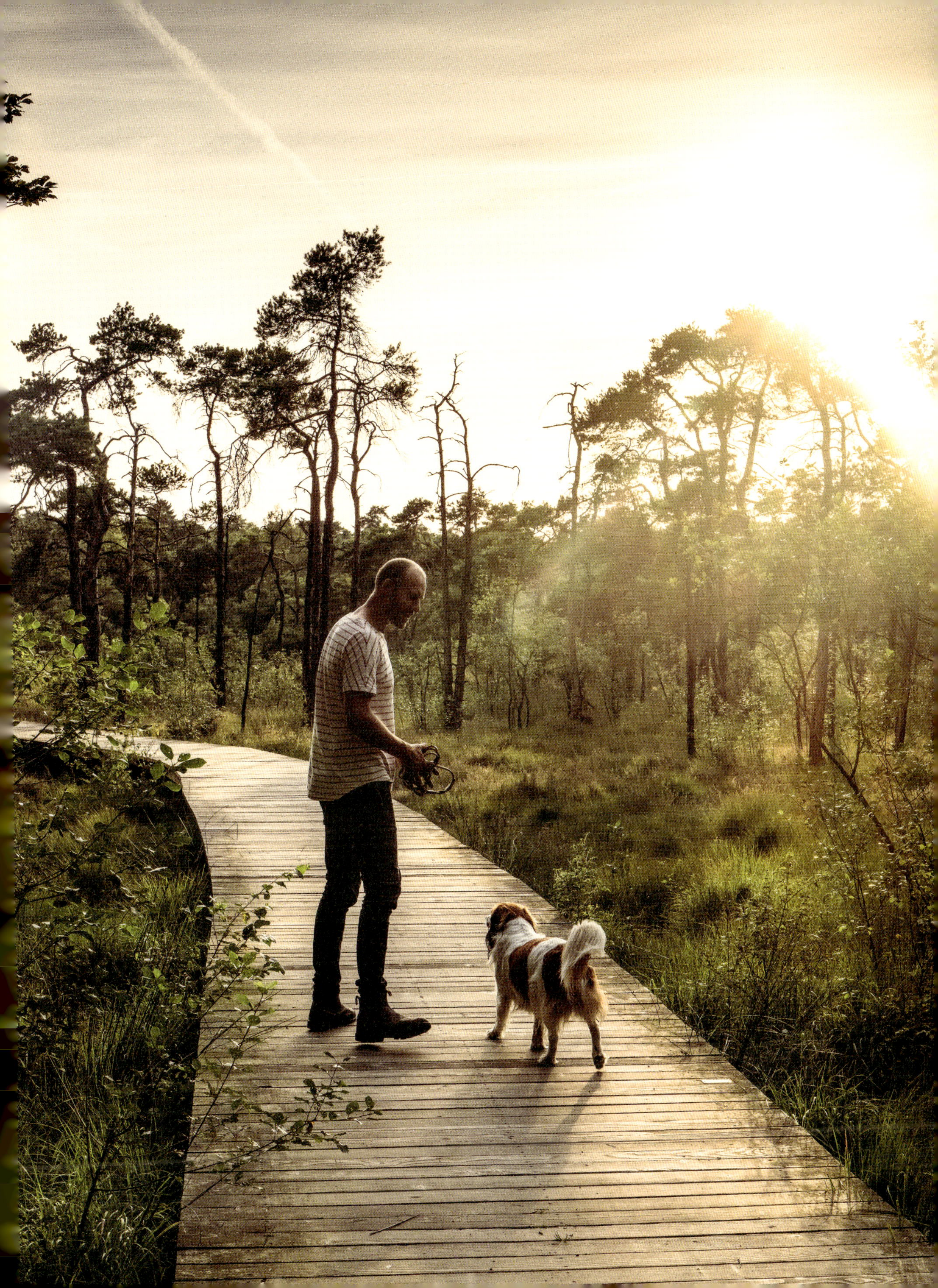

They chose their farm animals based on what the land needs.
The sheep are in charge of lawn maintenance, while the dog
guards the farmyard. The chickens lay eggs, while the cat
lounges in the garden.

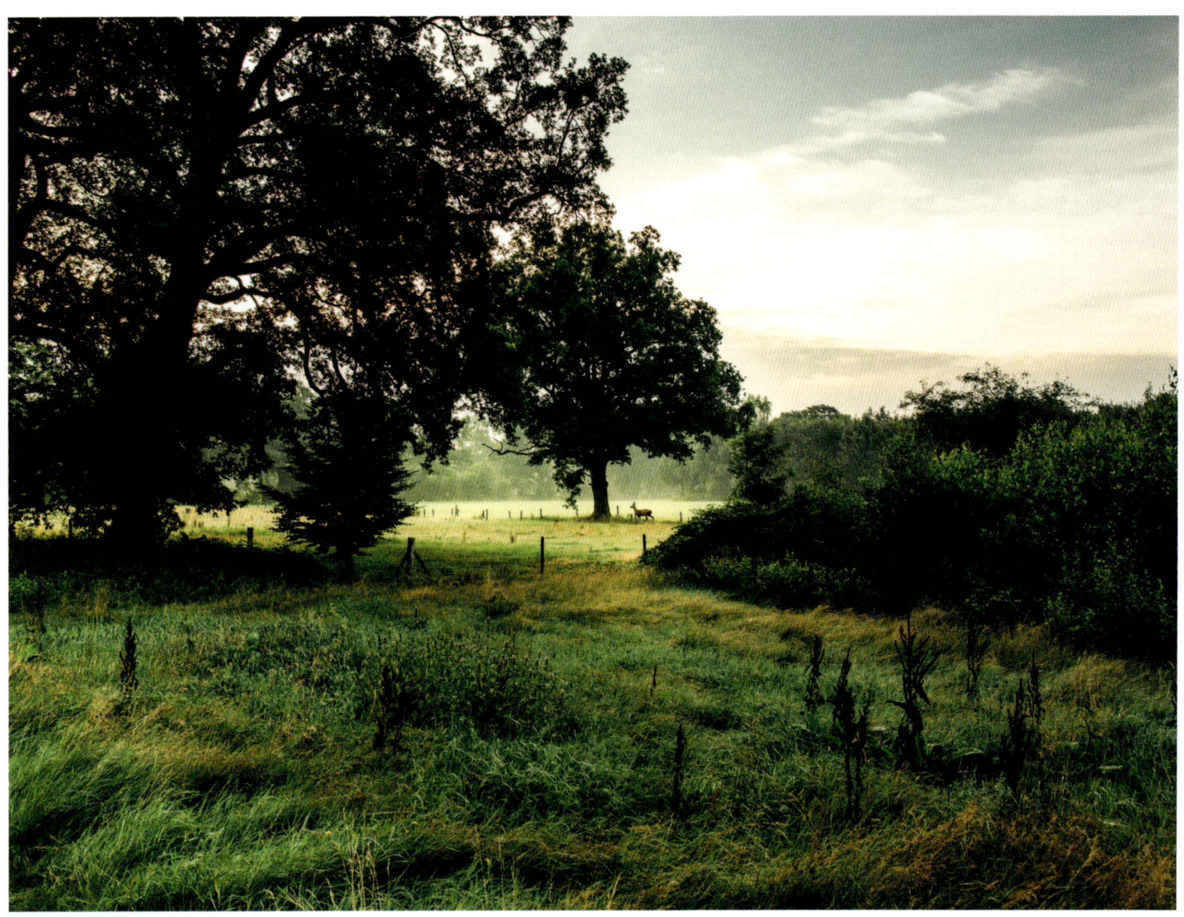

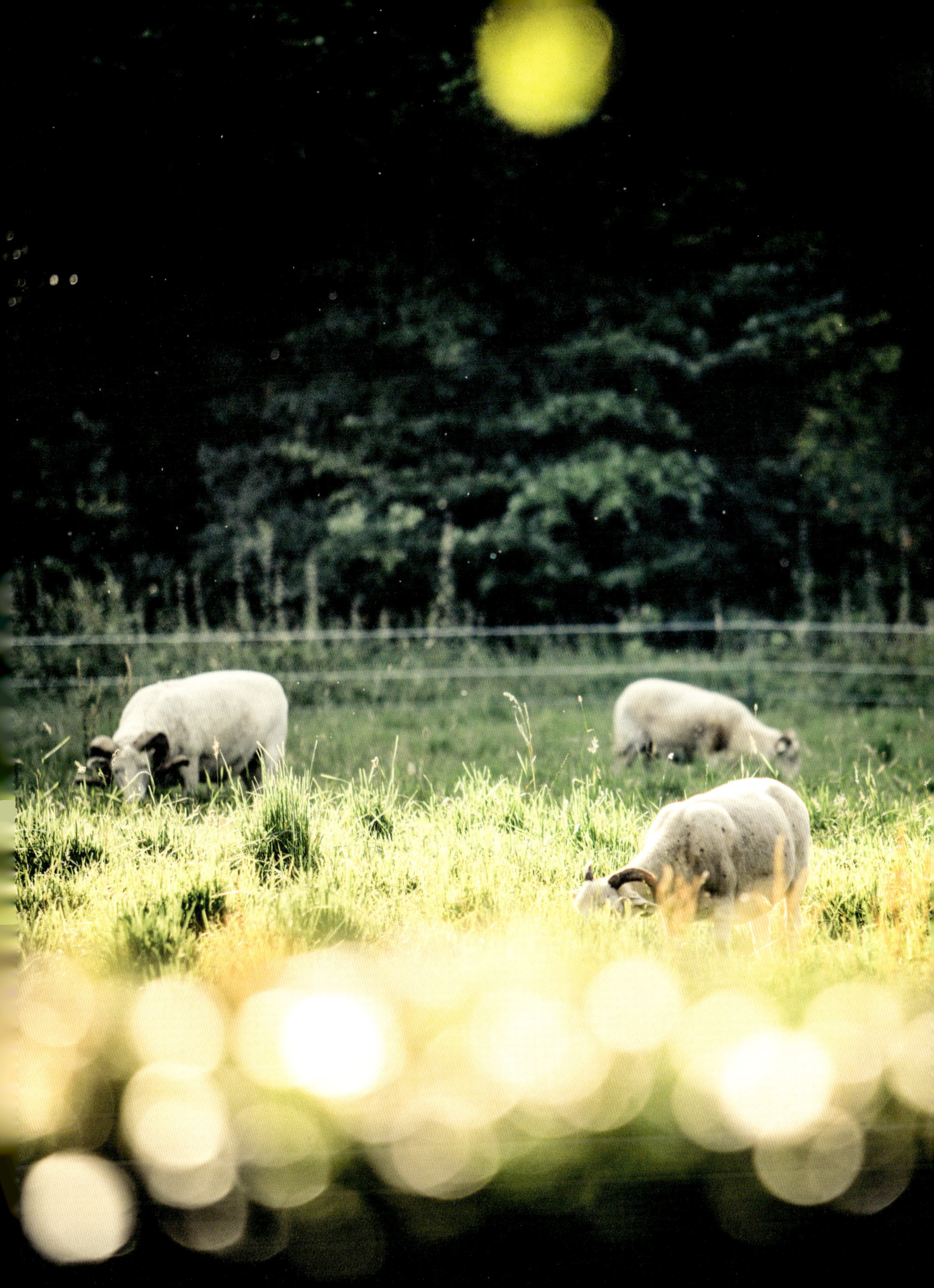

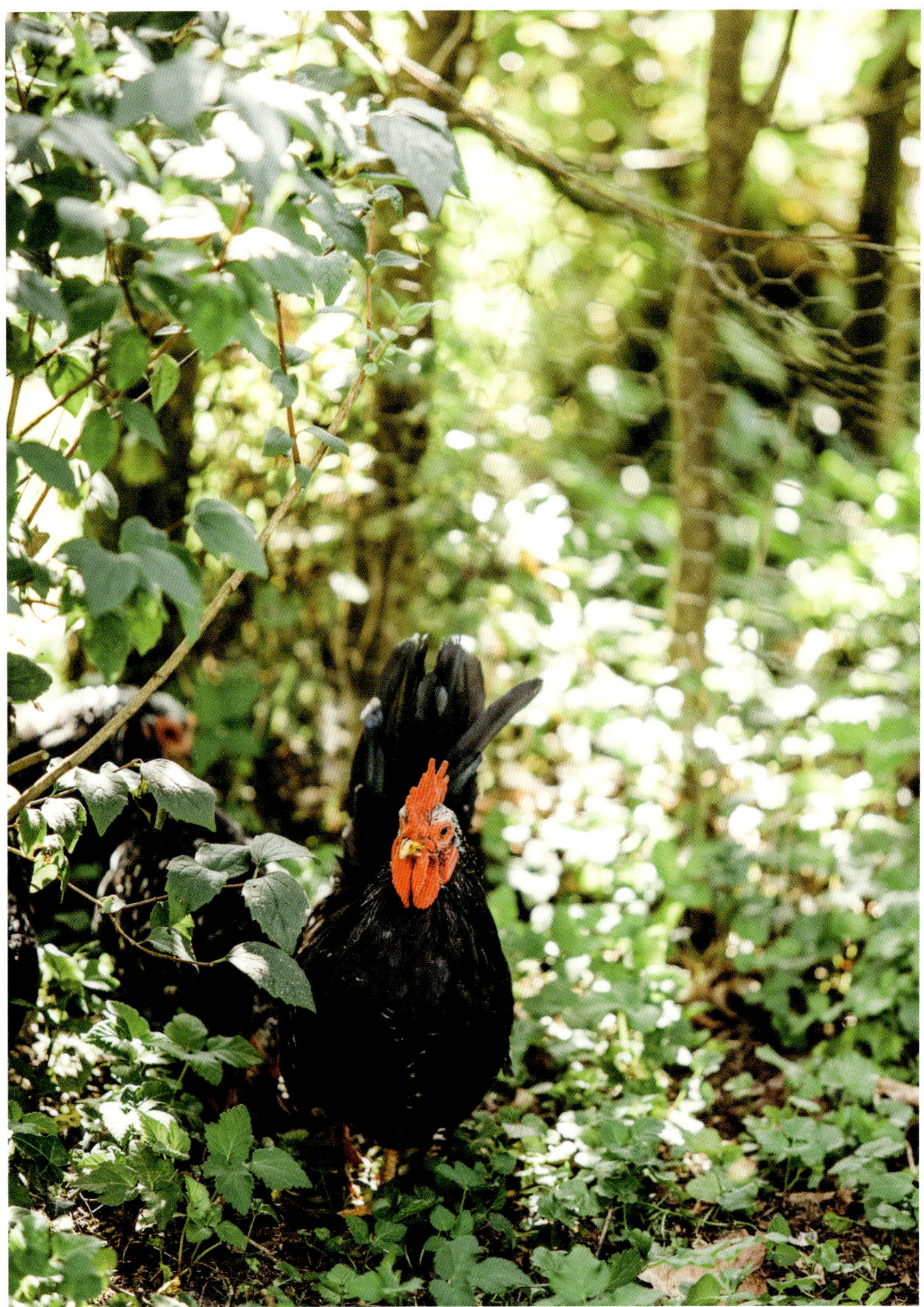

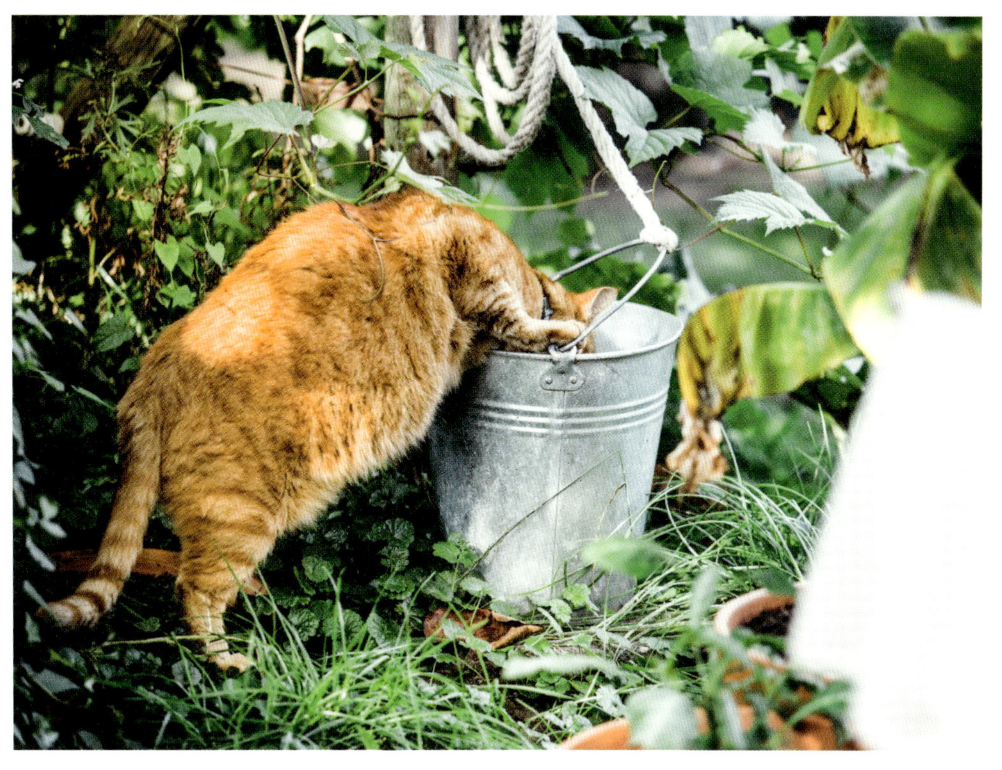

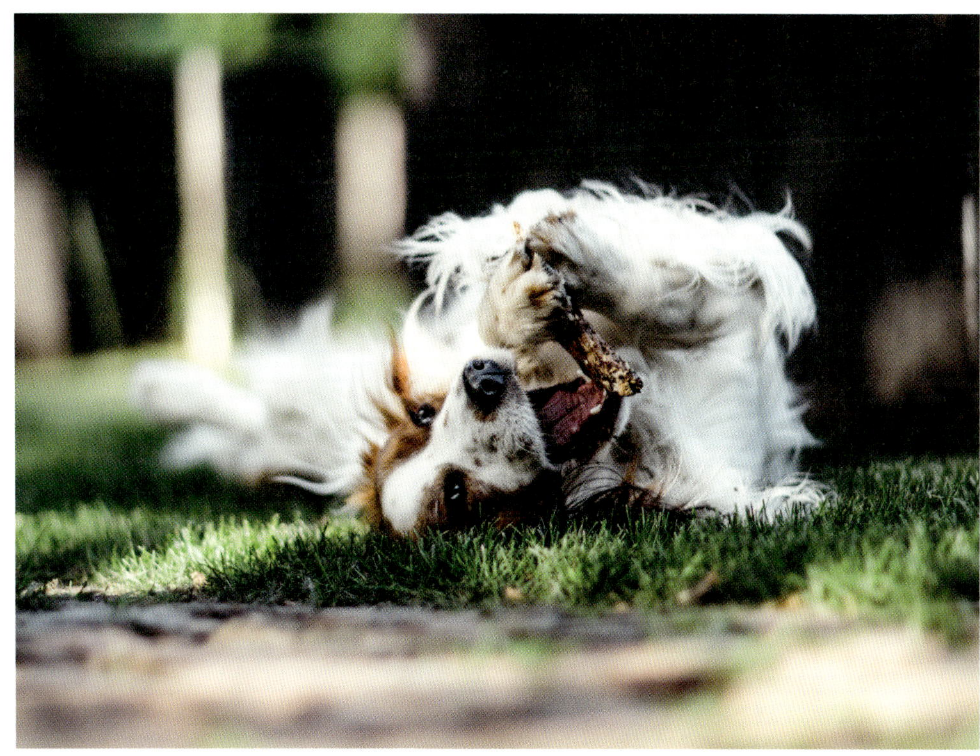

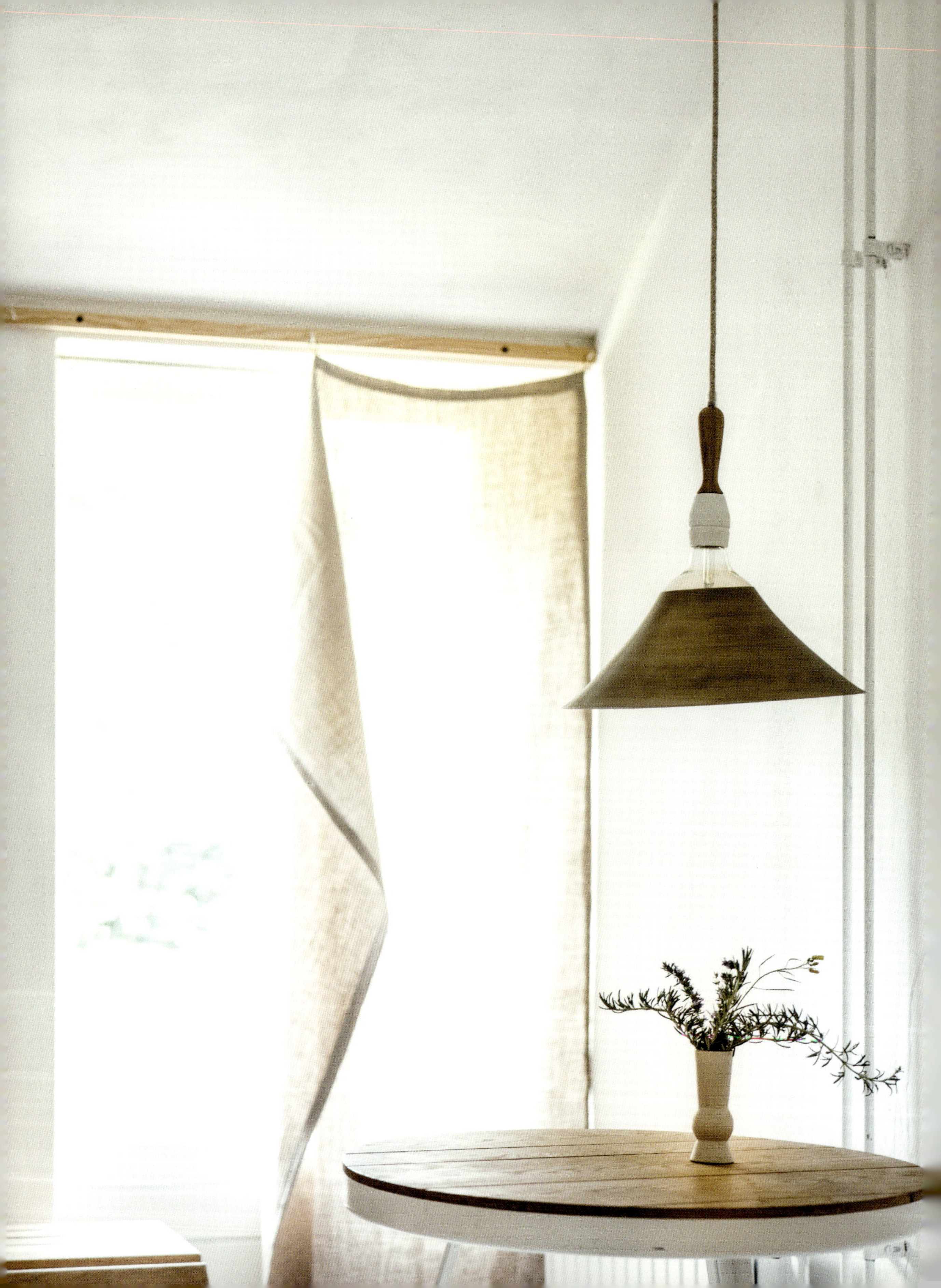

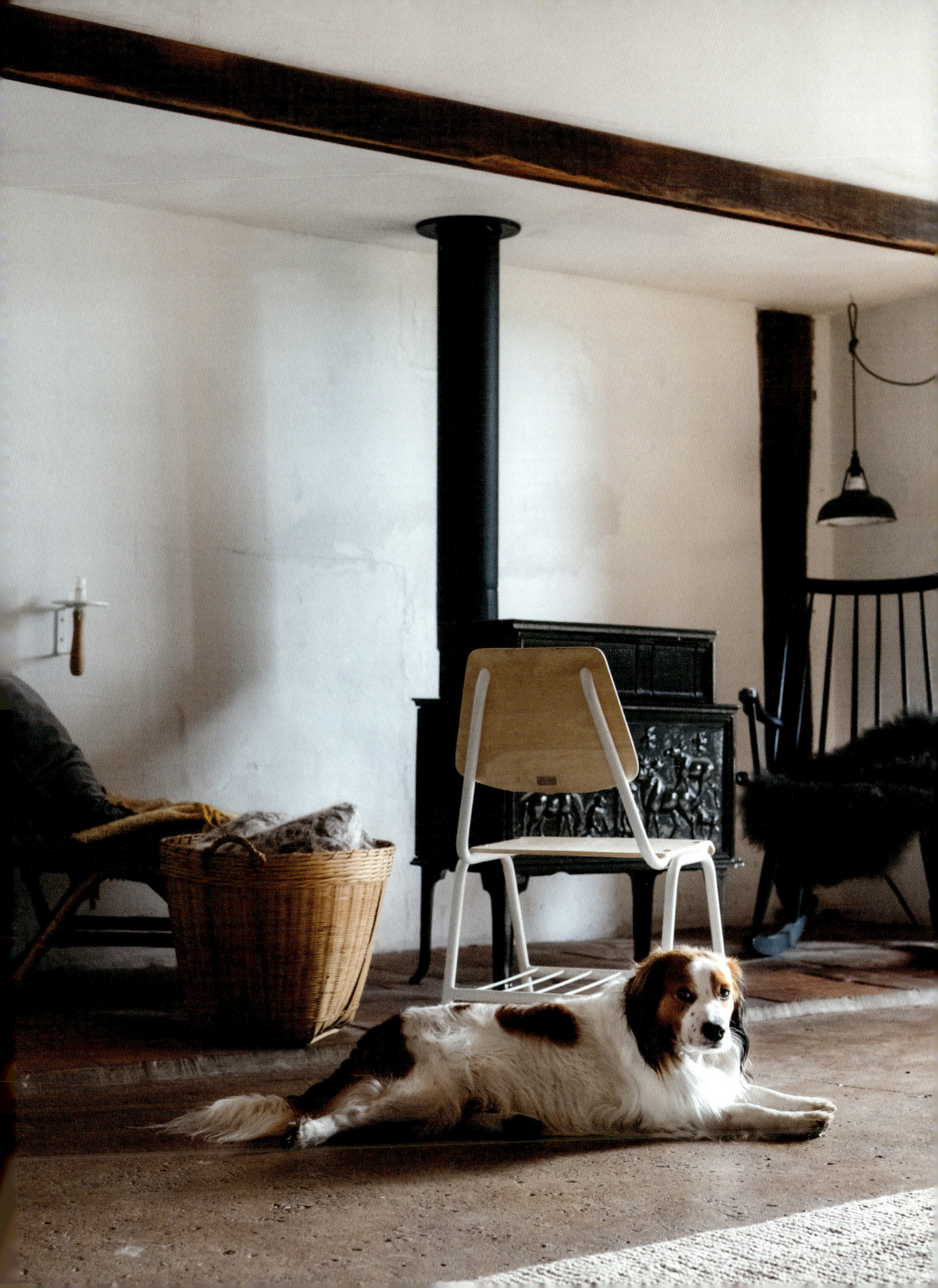

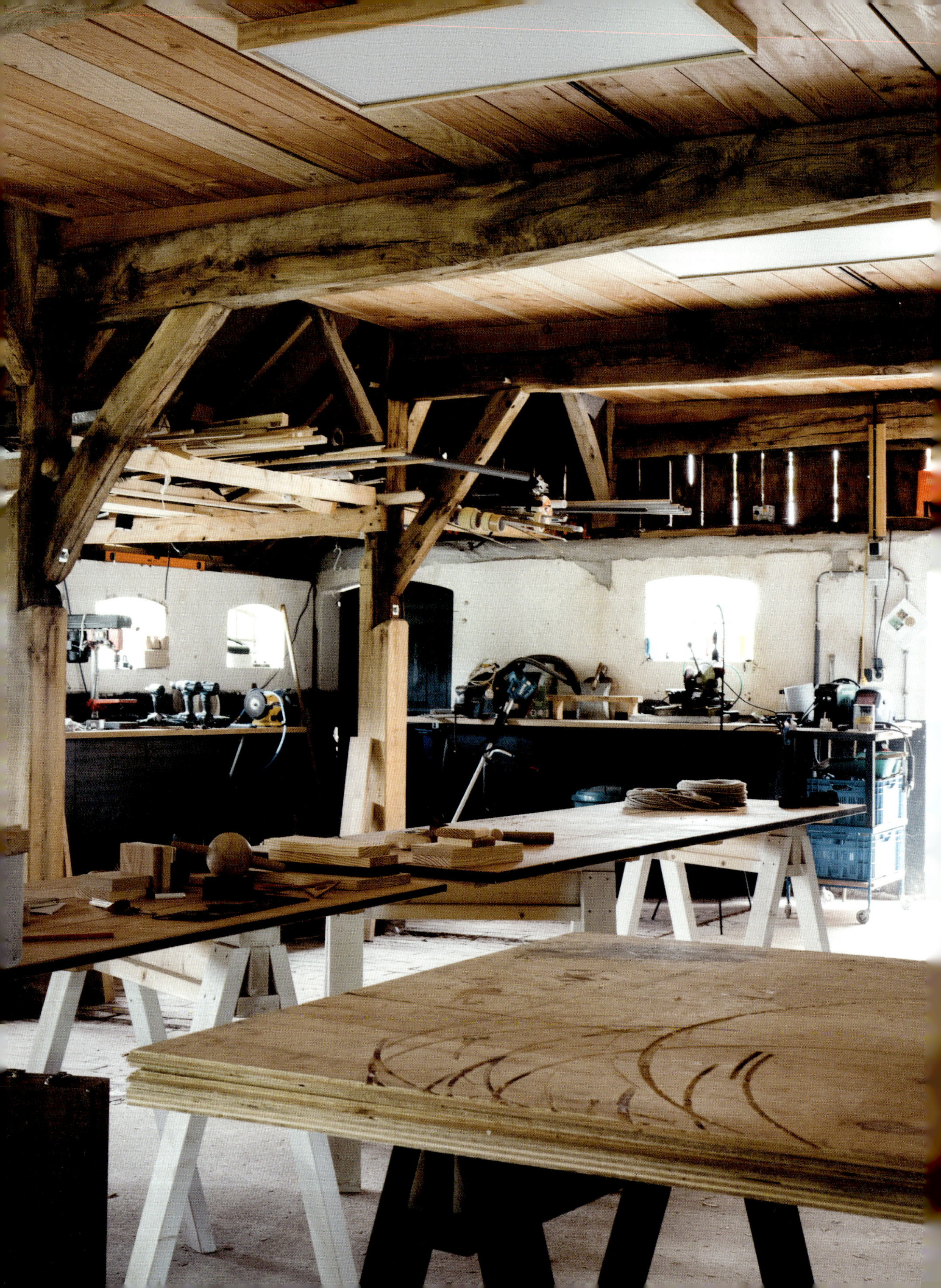

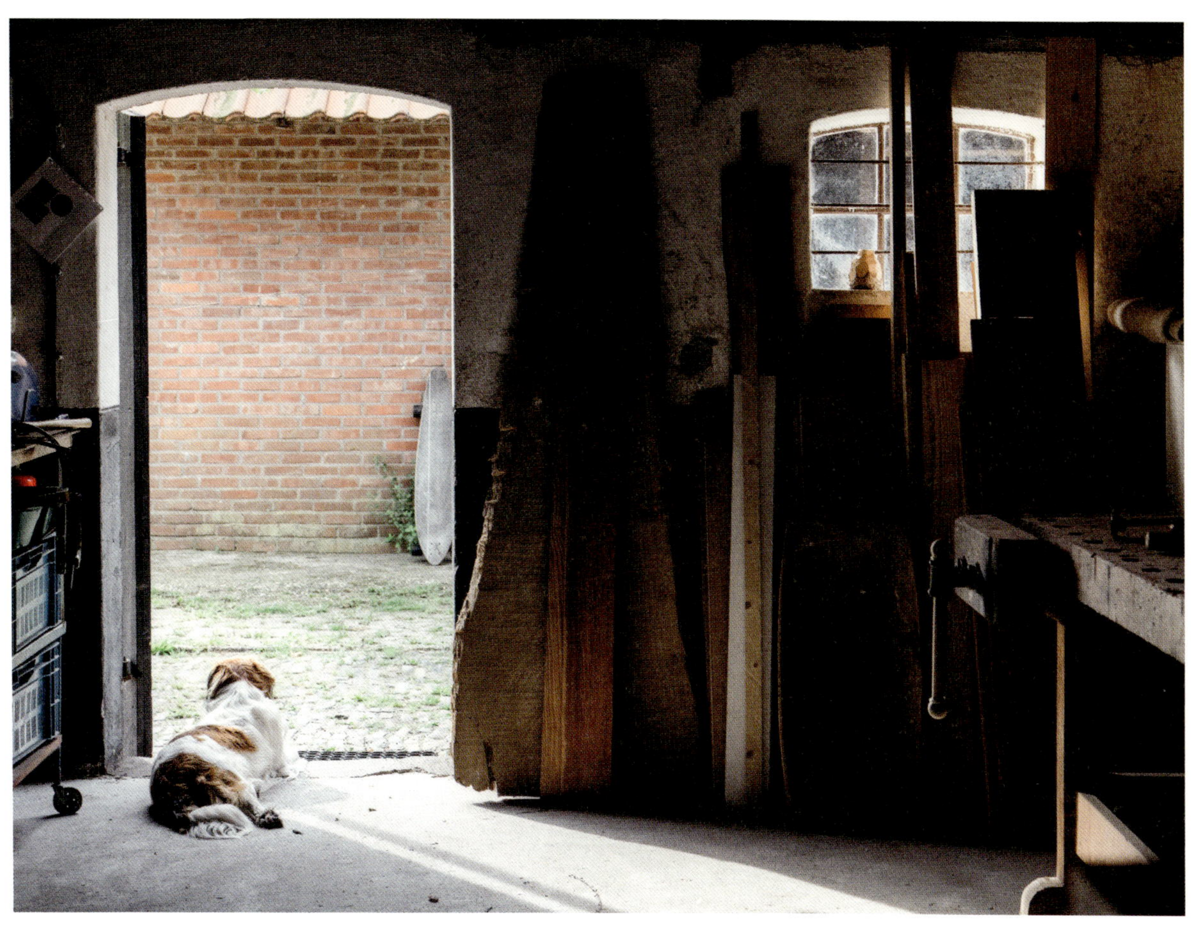

This family shares a unique lifestyle, which inspires them to design objects and furniture. When they need something, they just make it themselves from the materials at hand.

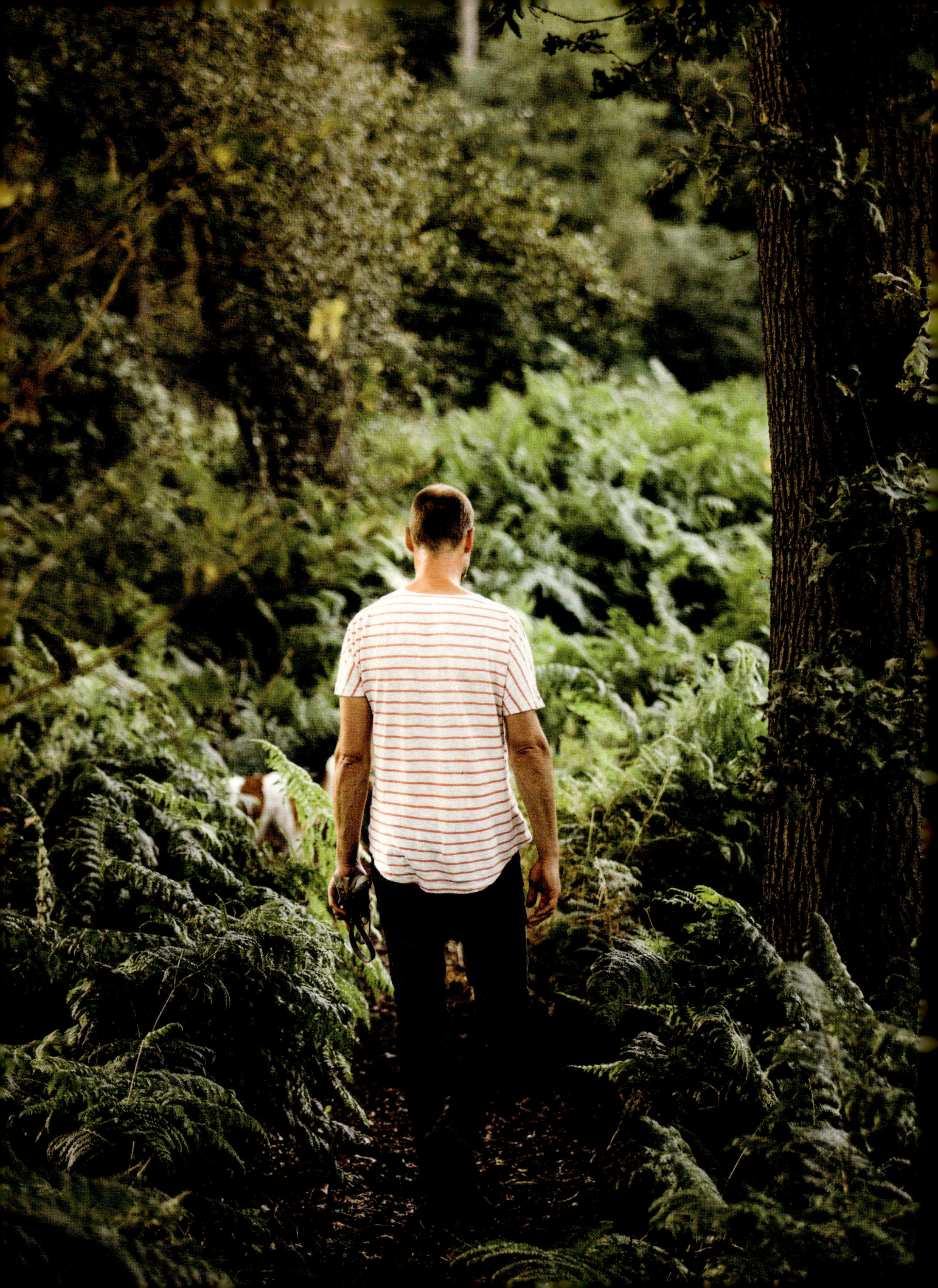

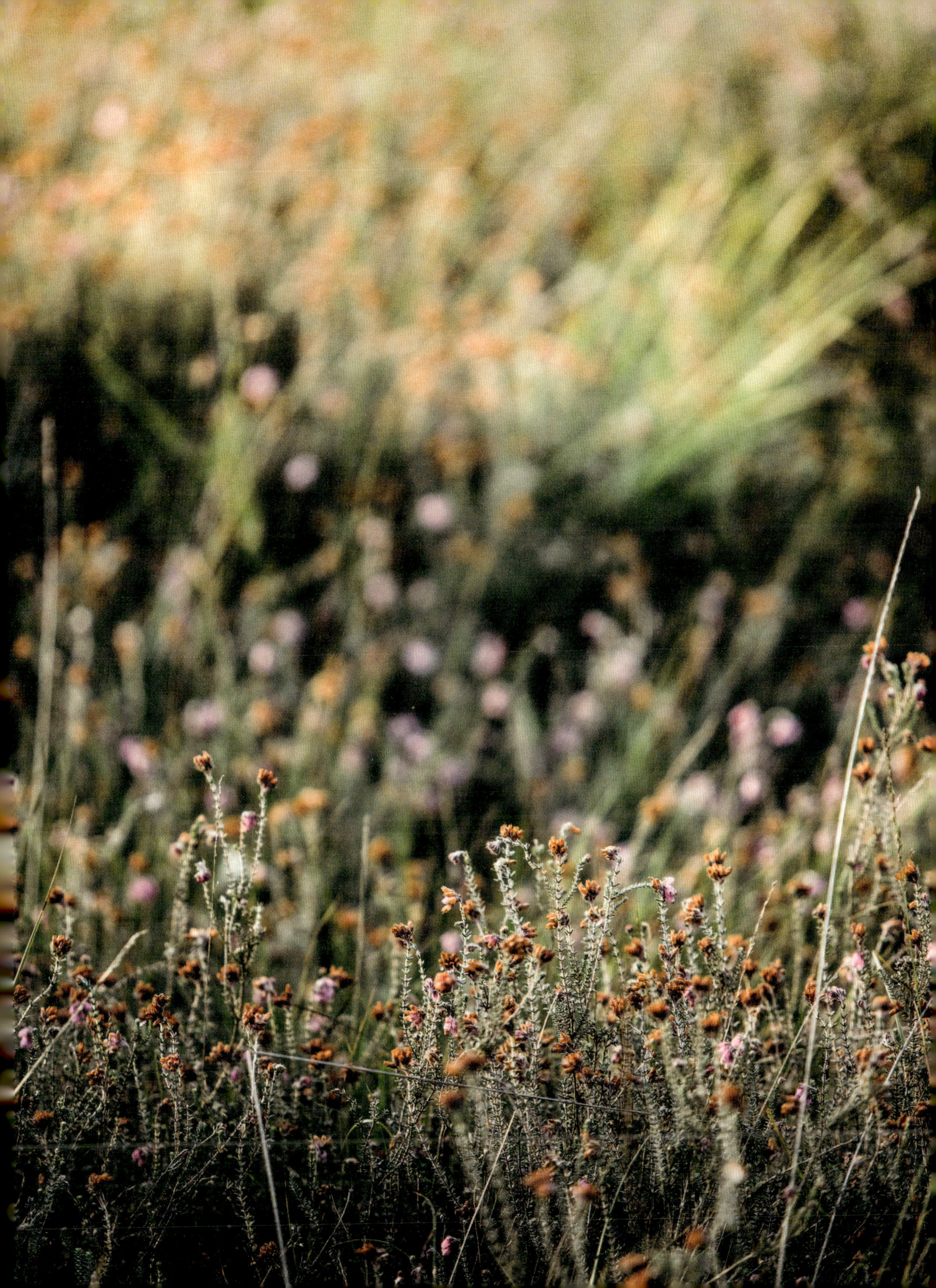

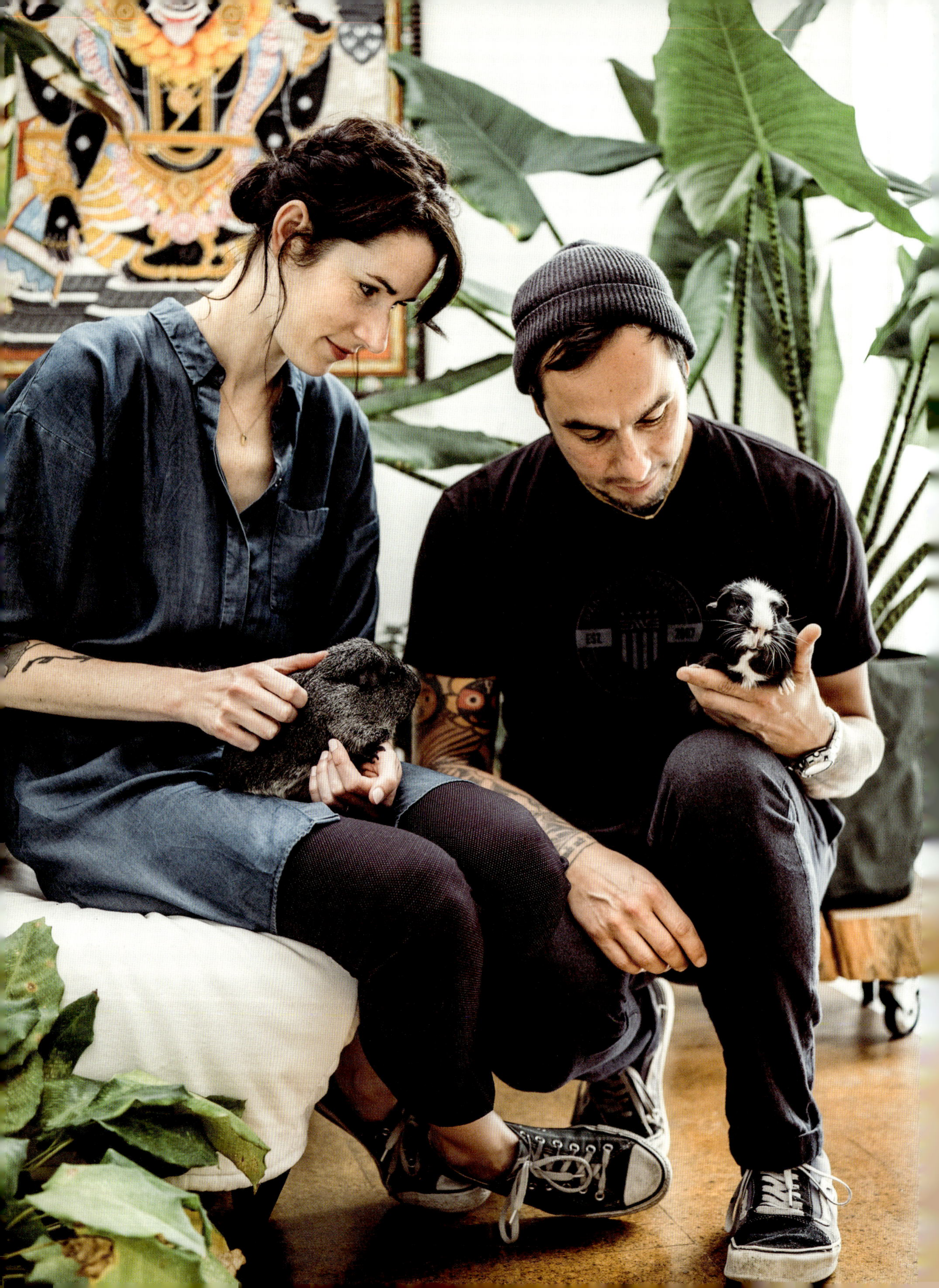

Rena, Sam, and their four guinea pigs live just a stone's throw from Amsterdam. The couple purposefully decided to move to the country, in search of a quieter lifestyle, without neighbours, in green surroundings, with sheep and cows. Here they work at their own pace, which is much slower than that of the rushed lifestyle in the city. The occupants love nature and animals, which is also reflected in their lifestyle and in what they eat. They are both vegetarians and believe in a world without animal cruelty.

Underappreciated guinea pigs

Guinea pigs are sweet, cute creatures, but you don't immediately associate them with adults. They are the perfect pets for teaching children a sense of responsibility. That is why Rena had them from such a young age. And she always loved them, mainly because she is allergic to most other pets. Rodents are small, and before our interview, we are convinced that they don't interact that much with you. Why would you keep them, we ask ourselves. But Rena defends them passionately: 'Guinea pigs are often underestimated as pets. They are adorable, funny, and react to people. Rabbits can be quite grumpy. I also had mice and rats. They are too tiny, they're always moving around making them difficult to caress. But a guinea pig loves to cuddle.' Rena produces ceramics under her own label, called 'Studio Hear Hear'. Sam, 'The Endeavorist', is a software product manager. They both work in the studio. When it's time for a break, they like to pet their tiny friends. The creatures seem to enjoy it. The males get out in the garden regularly to play or dominate each other.

Online pets

Rena happened to stumble upon two of the four guinea pigs on a secondhand website, where they found the studio and most of their vintage furniture. 'A little boy had received them as a present but was unable to keep them. He let us have them for free and gave us the toys and the cage.' Such a deal is not really an exception because when we check out online, we realise that people offer anything from rodents to dogs, cats, turtles, parrots, fish, and other pets. Rena and Sam find it difficult to exercise restraint. They would love to find a new home for all unwanted animals.

A short-lived but good life

Every guinea pig is different. Ben is Rena's favourite and comes from a pet store. He seems to blend in with the sofa, with his mixed grey fur. At-At (all animals are named after Star Wars characters) is Sam's front-runner. 'He's sweet but a bit on the heavy side. We call him 'Patatje' and 'Petoetie'. The couple has more nicknames for their pets than for each other. Ben, At-At, Finn and Lasse are the third group of animals that has the privilege of living with Sam and Rena. Guinea pigs as a rule like to live with others, which is why they recommend you get at least two of them. They usually live six to seven years. 'They love company. They're quite unique. When one of them dies, we're always very sad,' Sam says. 'It's quite pitiful, but a rodent generally doesn't live very long. You get used to it after a while,' Rena adds. 'I can imagine that it must be terrible to lose a cat or a dog because they live much longer.'

Animal lovers don't eat meat

When Sam opens the door to the fridge, the guinea pigs start to squeak loudly. 'They know they're about to get their veggies, it's the only time they make this sound,' Sam laughs. After they have eaten, it's our turn to lunch. We eat outside and enjoy the unique view of the field with the sheep and the cows. 'You're animal lovers. Are you also vegetarians?' Rena asks, who stopped eating meat 15 years ago. 'When I have friends that visit and that like the sheep, I never understand how they can eat lamb.' She reminds us that all animals are equal. 'People don't eat horse meat, but they do eat chicken. What is the difference between the two? And who am I to judge? I really can't live with the fact that a piece of dead animal passes through my body simply because I like it. It makes me sad because I really do love all creatures great and small.' She hates the meat industry, which kills animals daily on a large scale and has an environmental impact.

Organic food for everyone

Although Sam is also a vegetarian, he nuances her statements: 'If you look at how the world is evolving, everyone will become a vegetarian sooner or later. In the old days, they used to call you a hippy if you shopped at the nature store. But now everyone does. I find the growing awareness important, but it doesn't mean that I want to convert everyone to my radical lifestyle.' He points out a large number of tasty alternatives that is available nowadays, but also thinks the price is too high and needs to be reduced urgently. All too often, organic food is just for the happy few. If you want to stop people from eating meat, a lot more needs to happen. Sam and Rena are very serious animal lovers. It is a commitment and an attitude, as you can tell by what's on their plate. Their conviction makes us think: how can you love pets but still consent to killing them? Is it true that real animal lovers don't eat meat?

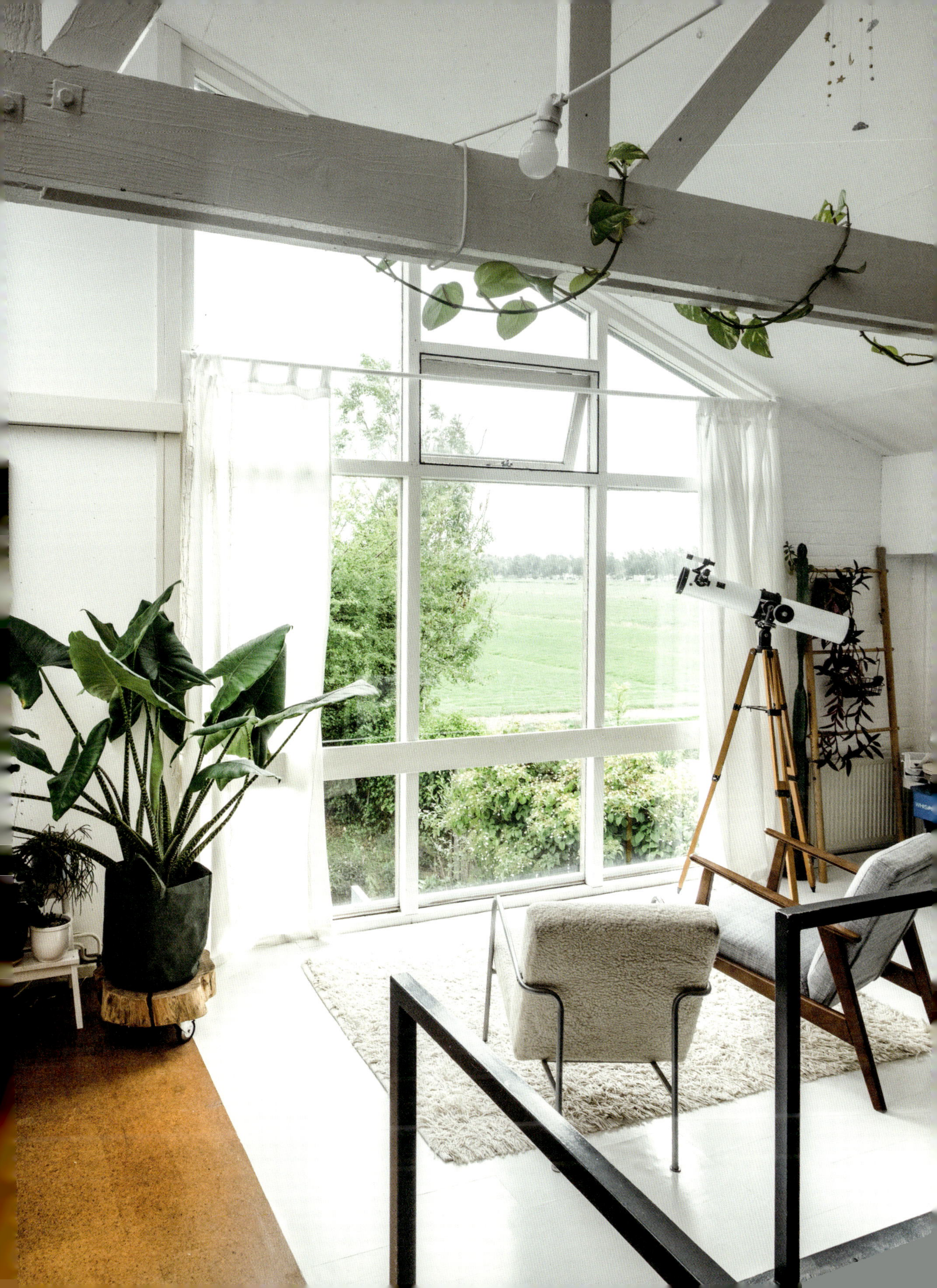

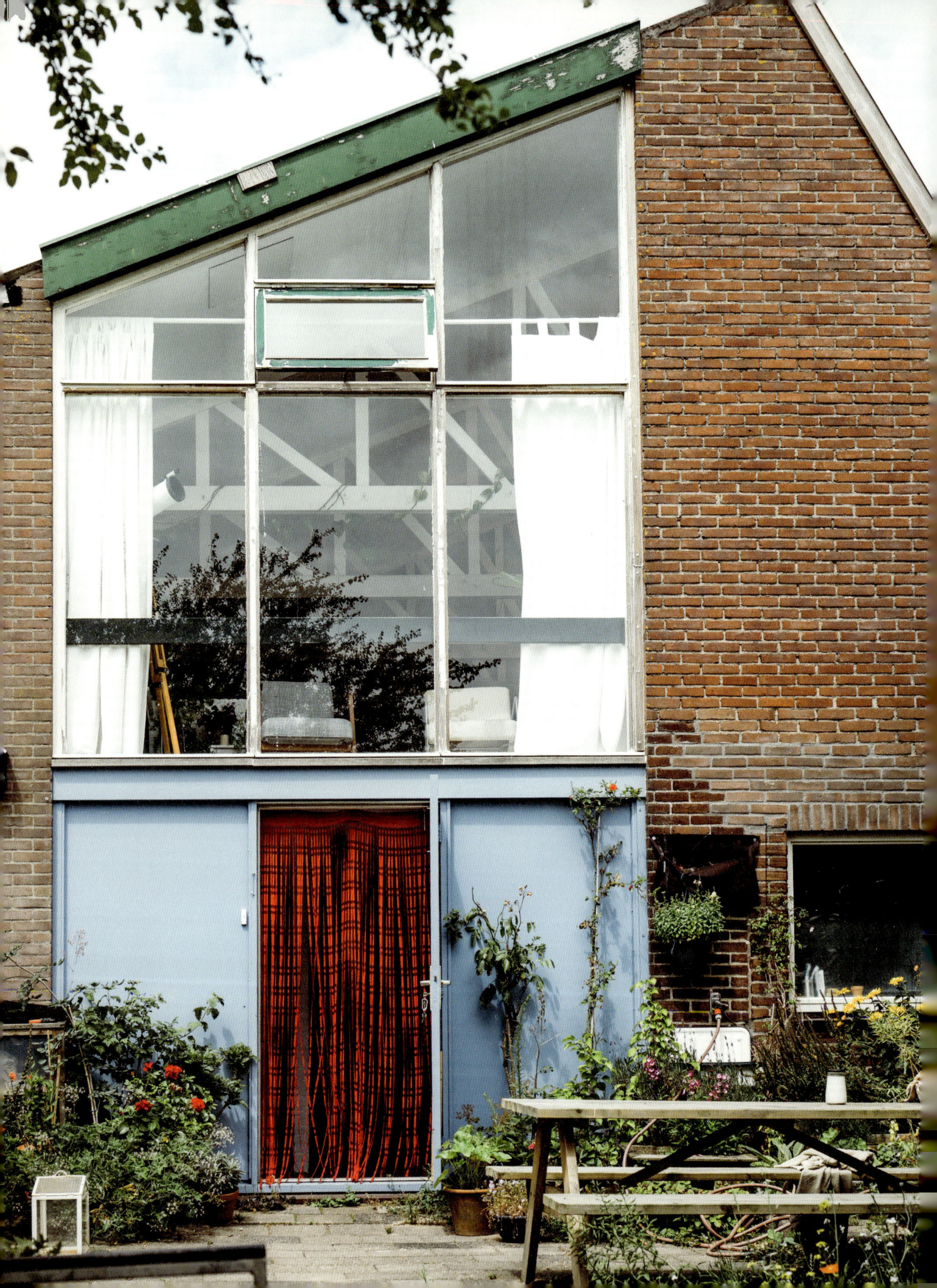

Sam and Rena rent a studio with a view of a field with cows
and sheep.

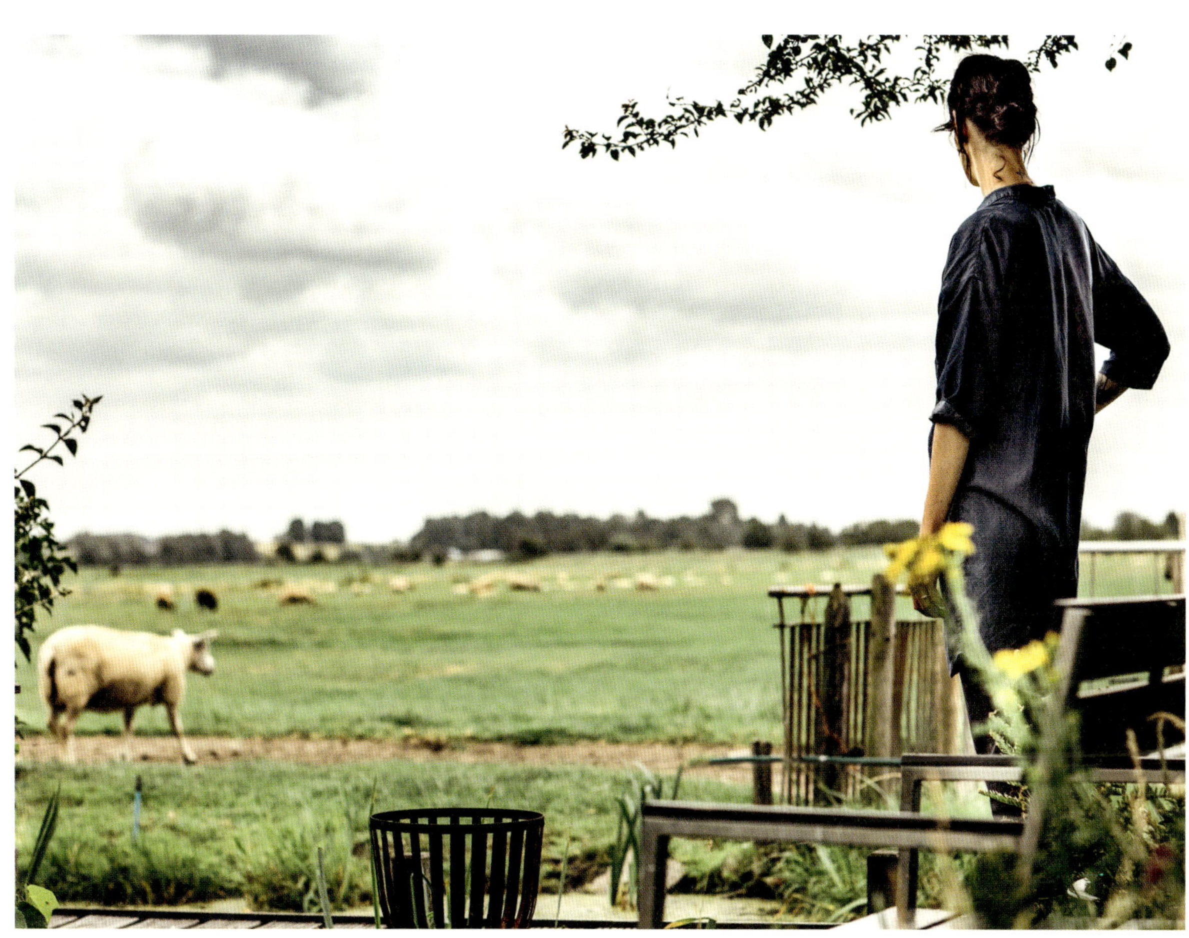

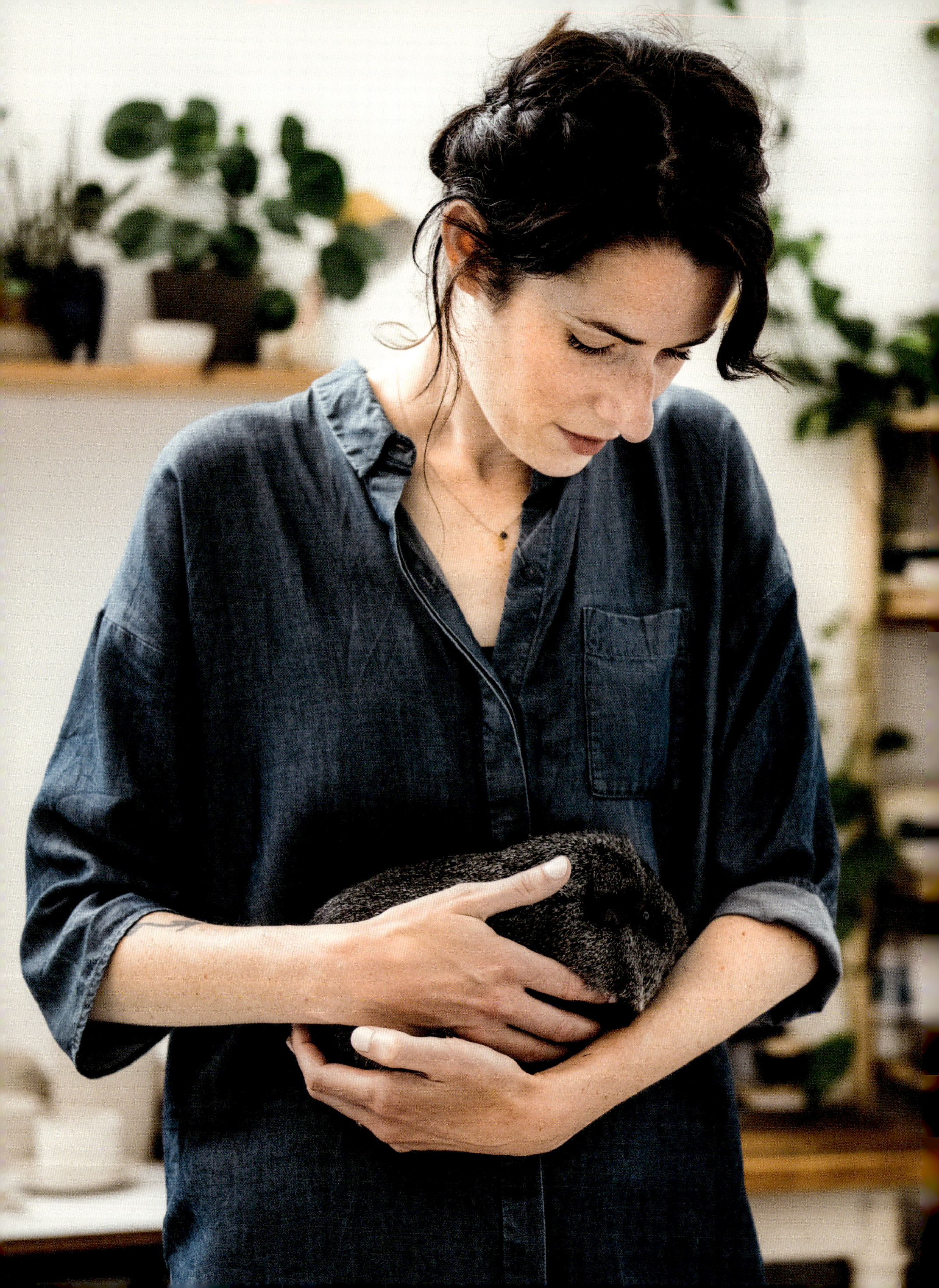

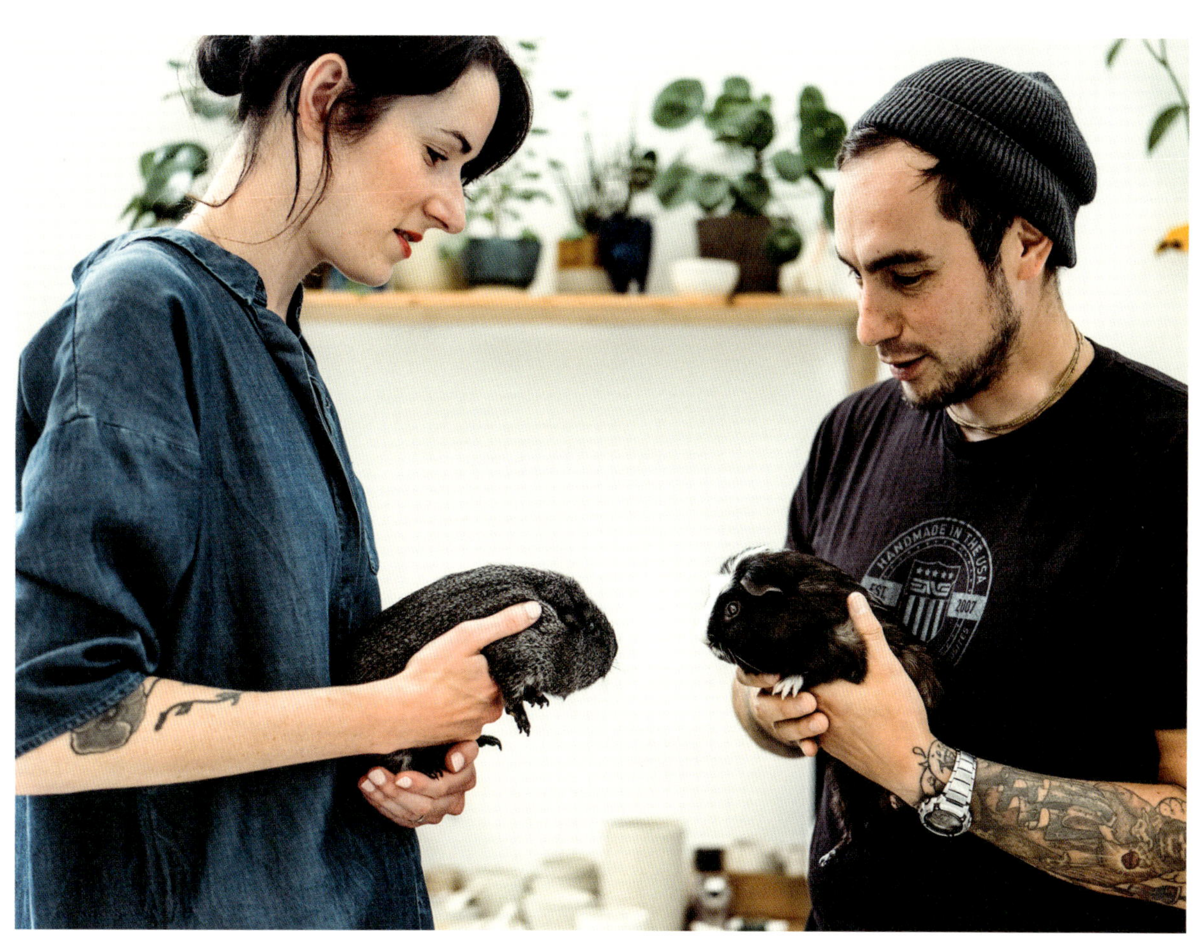

Guinea pigs are cuddly, cute creatures, with which you can enjoy a lot of interaction. They like companionship and usually live six to seven years.

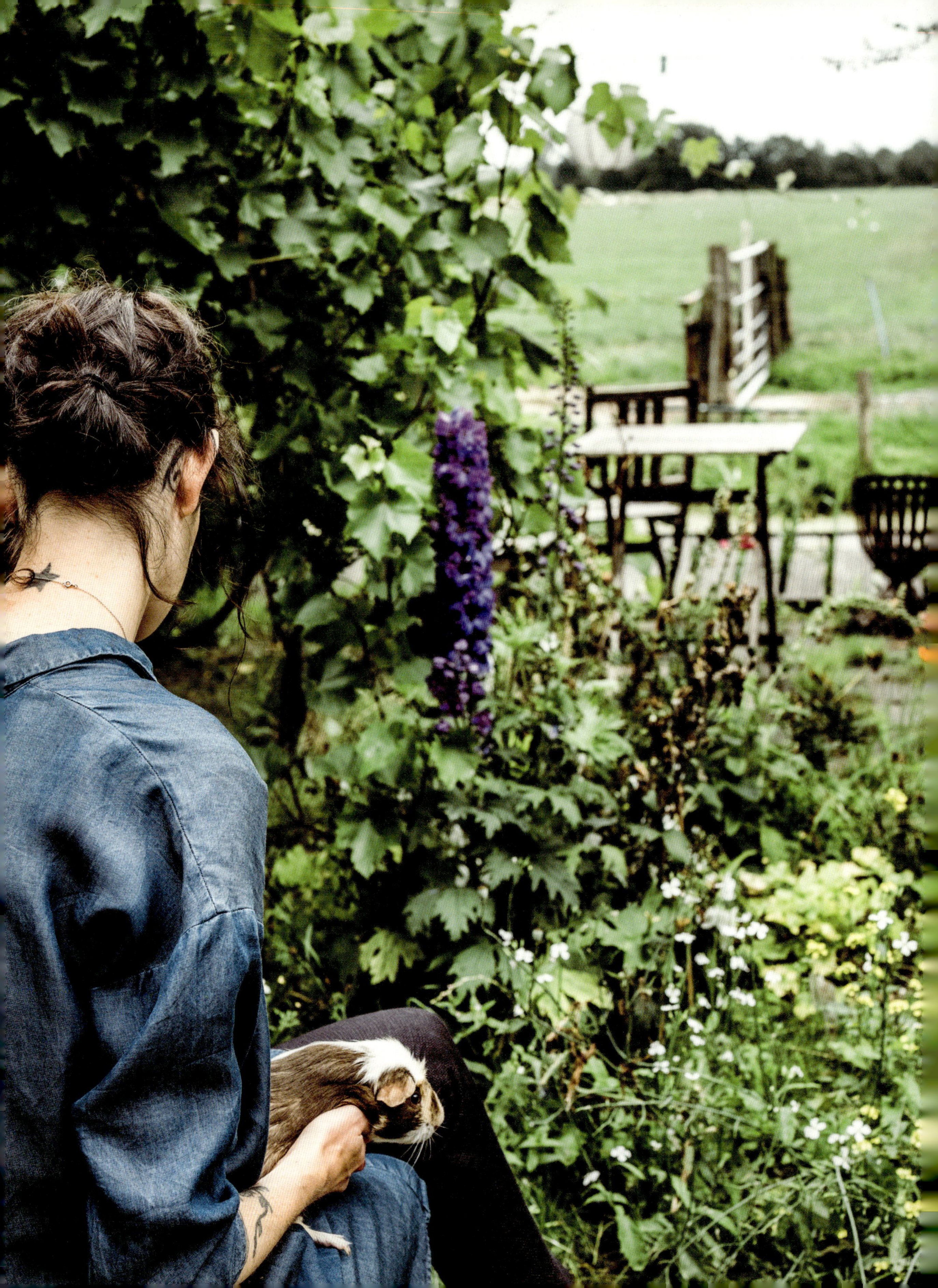

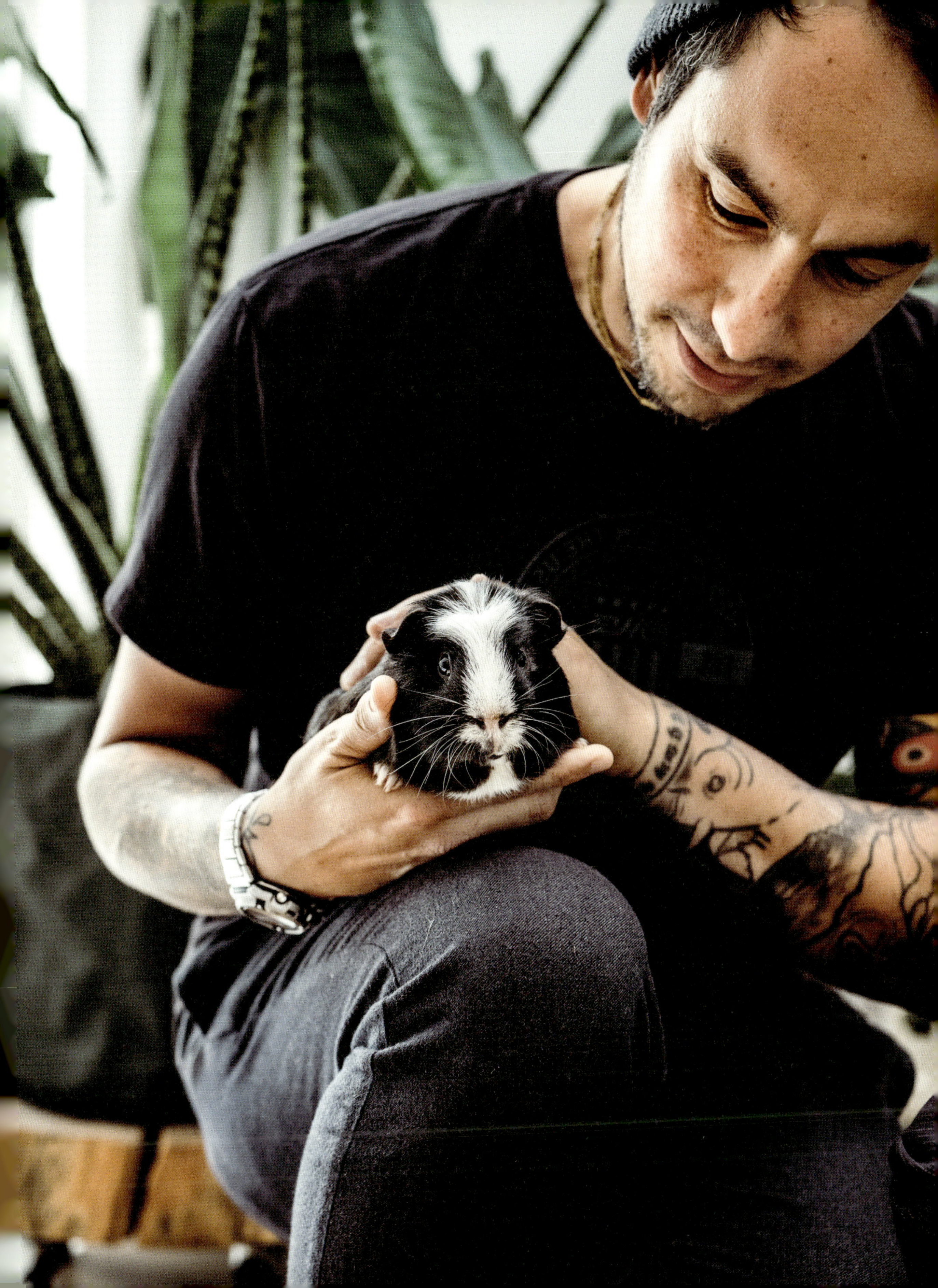

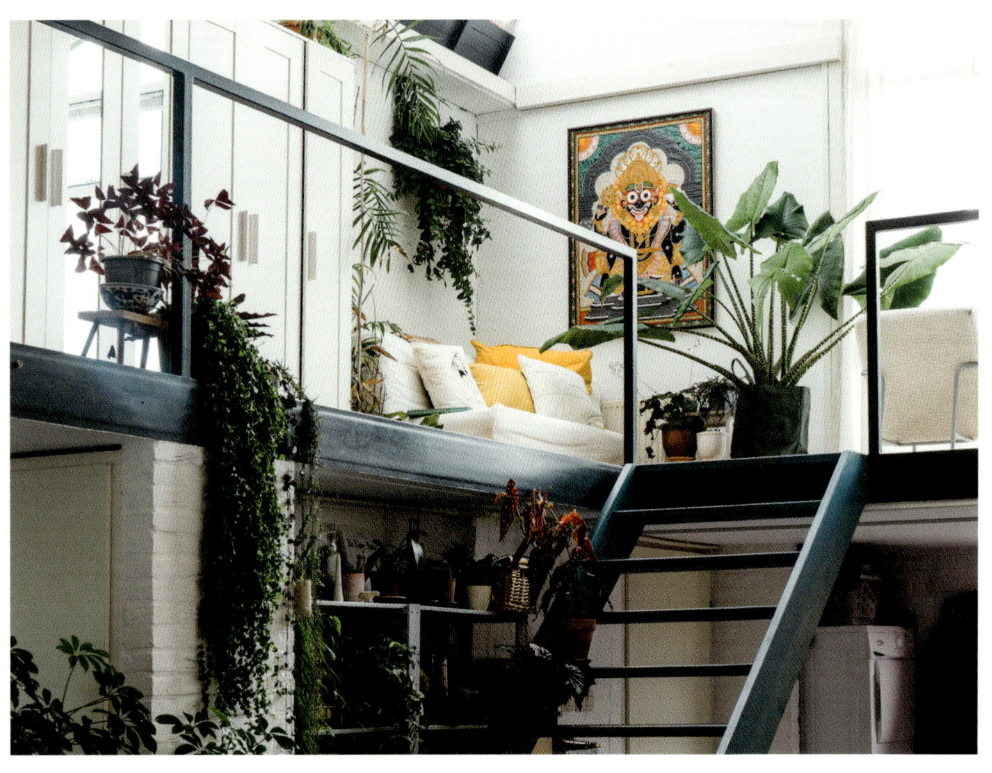

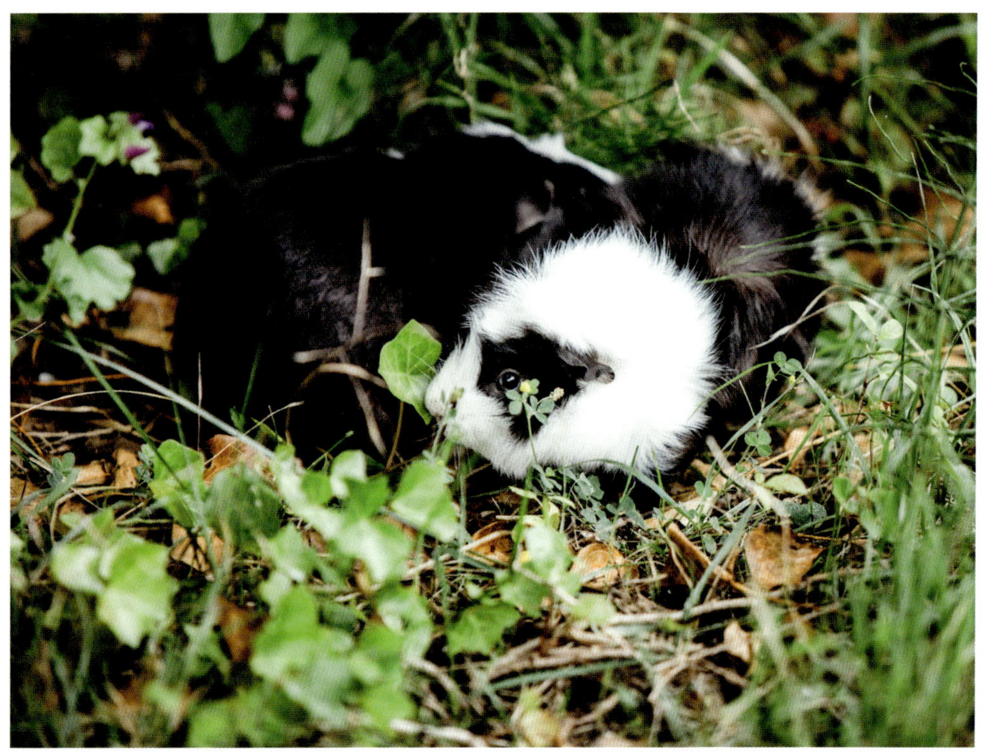

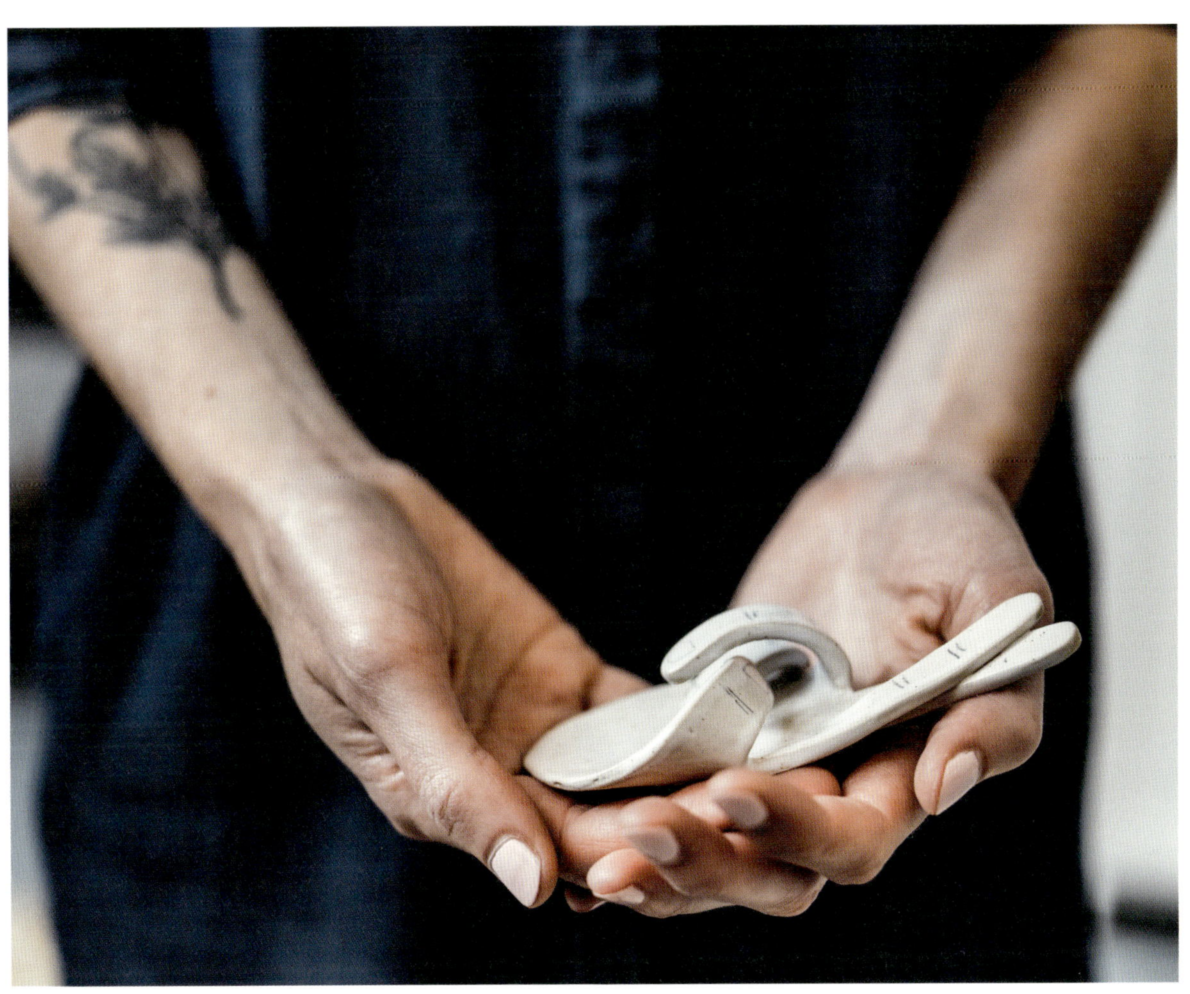

Rena produces ceramics. Sam is a software product manager
and woodcarver. The guinea pigs usually sit on their lap or like
to hop around in the garden.

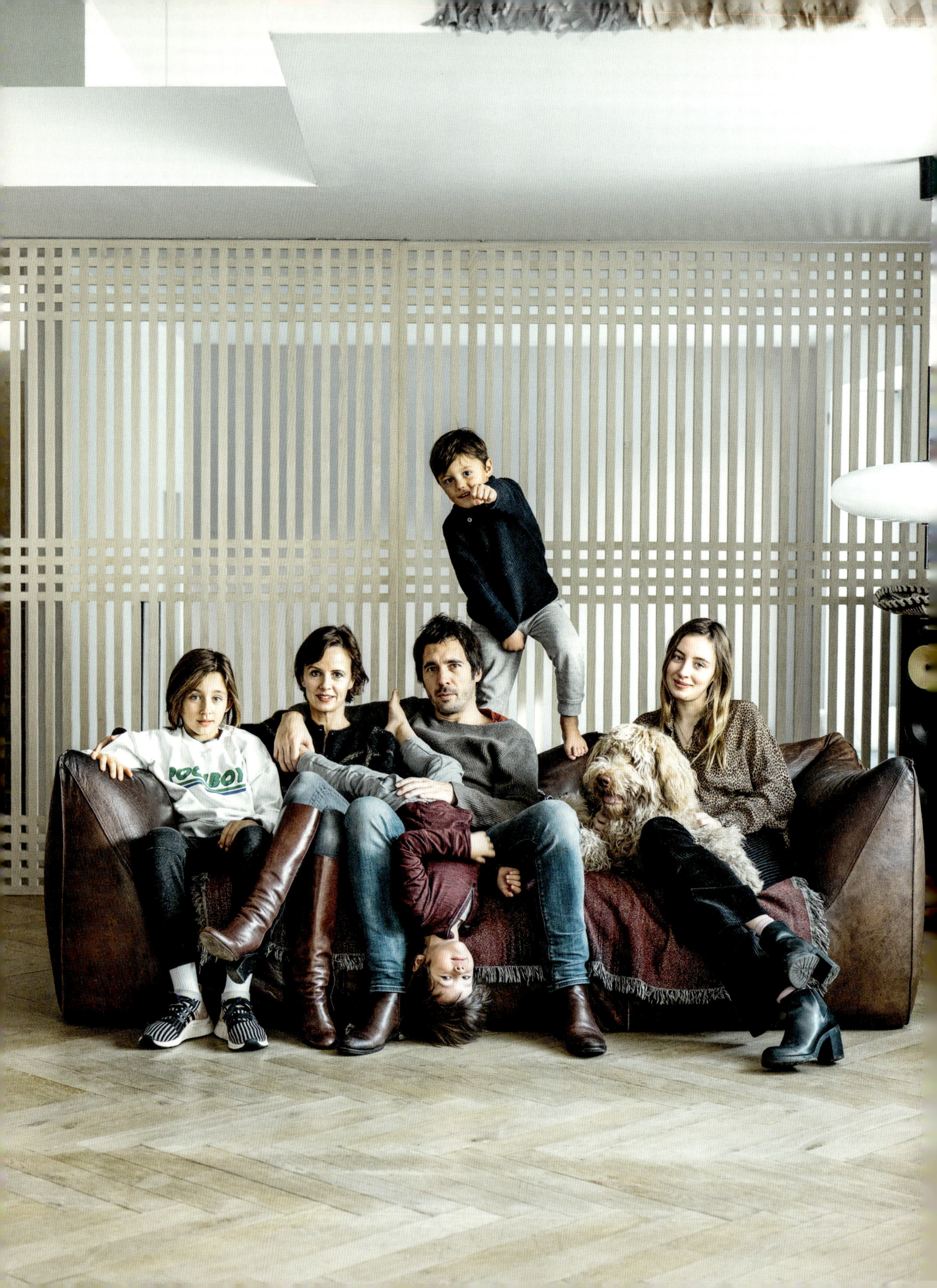

Dogs in the city. Initially, Veva and Jan had their doubts. But because the children begged them to get a pet, Barra Joe, the gold-coloured dog, joined the big family. There is no lack of space for the Australian cobberdog. It can run around in the nearby park and the communal garden and feels completely at home in the renovated school chapel, with a house, online shop, B&B and cafe. Customers love him. And he loves them, being the friendly designer dog and social animal he is.

Lush curls

Before the door is completely opened, we are welcomed by a boisterous dog muzzle. He is clearly ecstatic while he sniffs us and forces us to put everything we are holding down to pet him. Barra Joe, who is named after the Mexican architect Luis Barragán, is an Australian cobberdog and a real cuddle monster. He resembles a mix of a labrador with a poodle. But he also has something of the Irish water spaniel, a curly-coated retriever and a cocker spaniel about him. The result is a lovely curly dog, with a silky, flowing coat, that is just as soft as his gentle nature. His motto 'born to serve' means he is really good, likes to learn, and is a fast learner. He is the perfect family pet for Veva van Sloun, Jan Wauters and their children, Farah (17 years), Idriss (11 years), and Isaac and Noah, the twins (5 years).

The quest for an original playmate

Veva and Jan both grew up with dogs. And yet they hadn't planned on getting one of their own. 'Dogs should be able to roam free, without a leash, which is not that obvious in a city,' says Veva. 'What's more, it's a lot of responsibility. Who's going to walk the pup? What do you do with him when you go on holiday?' In spite of all their reservations, Idriss and Farrah wore them down. As an interior designer and shop owner, Veva has an eye for particular objects and new brands. She went in search of an original pet, that would like to play, with a known history, not too large and not too small. And because he also had to be able to live with small children, she decided not to adopt. She did contact a breeder instead, having fallen in love with a cobberdog. Cobber is a colloquial way of saying friend in Australia.

A residential project in a chapel

Clouds 9000 is the name of the B&B, cafe, and online shop with design furniture and interior accessories, which Veva manages with her husband. Nine other families live in this unique, large-scale residential project. While the result looks very natural, the renovation itself was anything but easy. Veva was also pregnant with the twins during the works. There's always something going on at Clouds 9000, with four children romping around the house and the intricate combination of home and work. And Barra, of course, is part of the mix, with his uncontrolled chaos and boundless enthusiasm. He is so attached to Veva, that he follows her everywhere she goes, including into the cafe, where he entertains the staff and welcomes customers.

Walks as a source of inspiration

There is a park near the chapel, where Veva and Barra take a walk every day. She has come to enjoy this daily routine. 'I really love the long walks. They energise and inspire me. 'Another ritual is the brushing and trimming of the dog's long, fluffy coat. While cobbers don't shed, they need a proper brushing once a week to avoid matting and to remove any loose hair from his fur. It's quite an undertaking and Veva and her daughter take turns doing it. Barra undergoes it without too much fuss and doesn't mind taking a bath or being lathered. He also enjoys going for a regular trim, which completely transforms him.

Designer dog

The appearance of the rest of the house also changes continually. Every time we visit Clouds 9000, we discover something new, or something surprising catches our eye. Veva's sense of colour and a keen interest in original design is constant. Another continual is the question 'how much does it cost?' as all the products are also sold in the couple's online shop. Because everything looks so picture perfect, we ask her what Barra is like inside the house. 'He's actually okay. I didn't have to change much. He loves shoes, sticks, and woollen pillows. And as he just wouldn't leave the twins' cuddly toys alone, he now has his own,' Veva laughs. The dog likes to lay on the sofa, crawl in bed with Jan and seeks out company, which is why he almost seems to blend in with the interior.

Fighting for attention

Everyone loves Barra. And he loves them right back. Sometimes he gets a little jealous however and tries to get in between Veva and the twins by putting his paws on her shoulders. The boys love him and like to tussle with him. 'When Barra sees children run, he thinks that they want to play with him. It's a bad habit, and we urgently need to unlearn it,' Veva confesses, who only took him for dog training a few times. But Barra does listen. During the photo shoot, he also displays model behaviour until he suddenly plops down on his back. His way of showing that he feels at ease and needs a nap. It's been a long day.

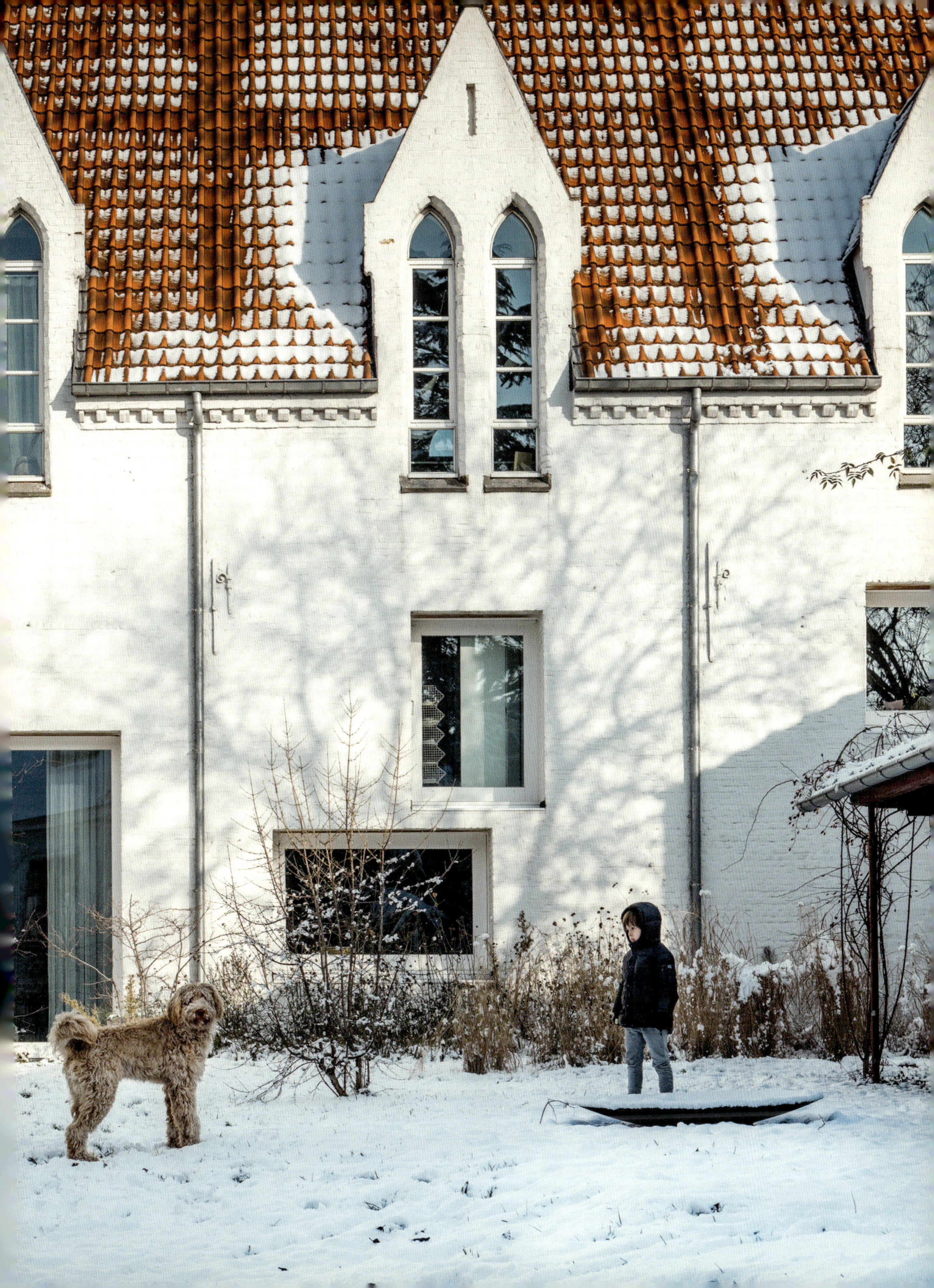

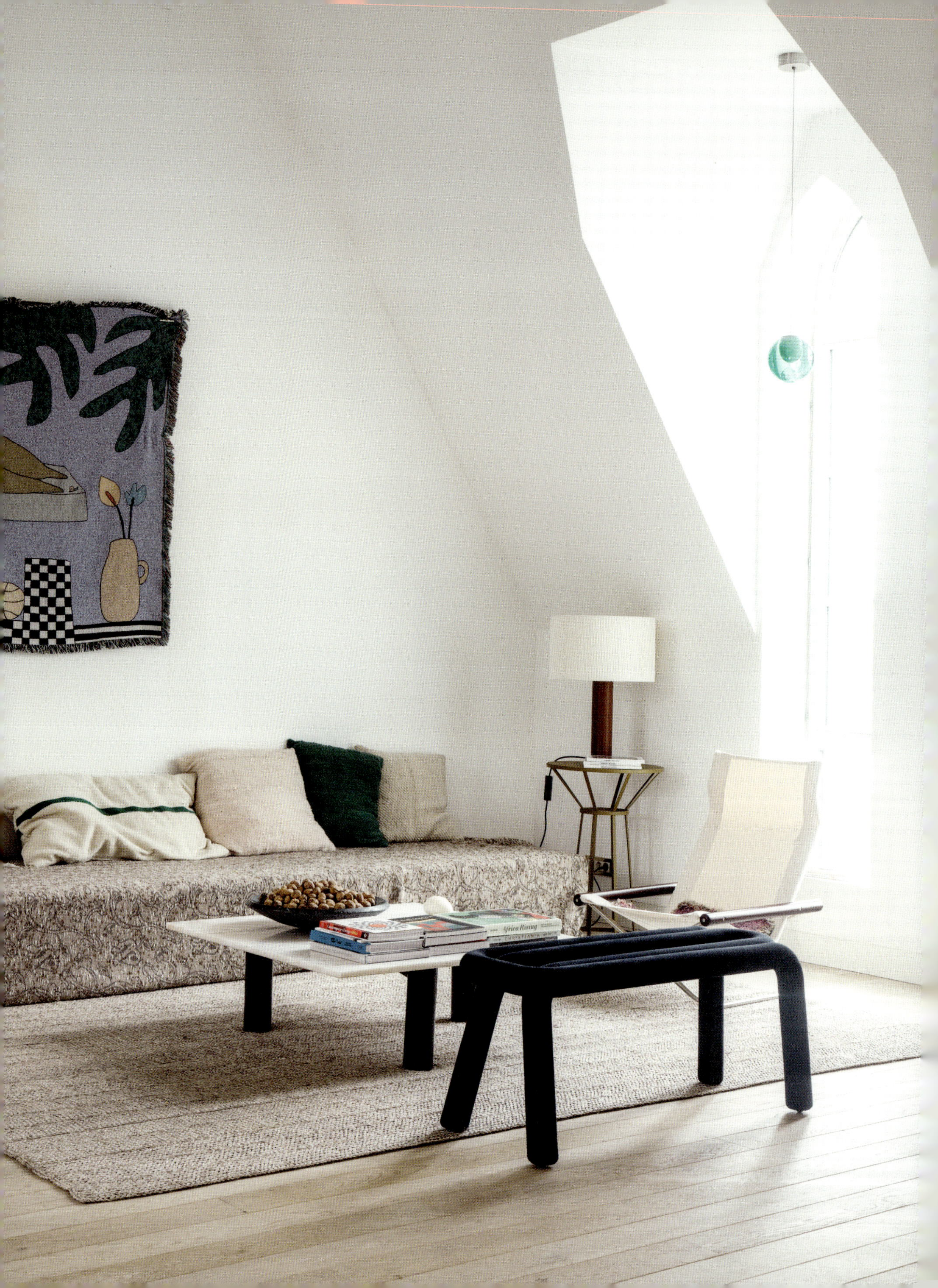

Veva and Jan transformed an old school and chapel into a
charming hotspot with a home, a cafe, a B&B, an online shop
and multifunctional spaces.

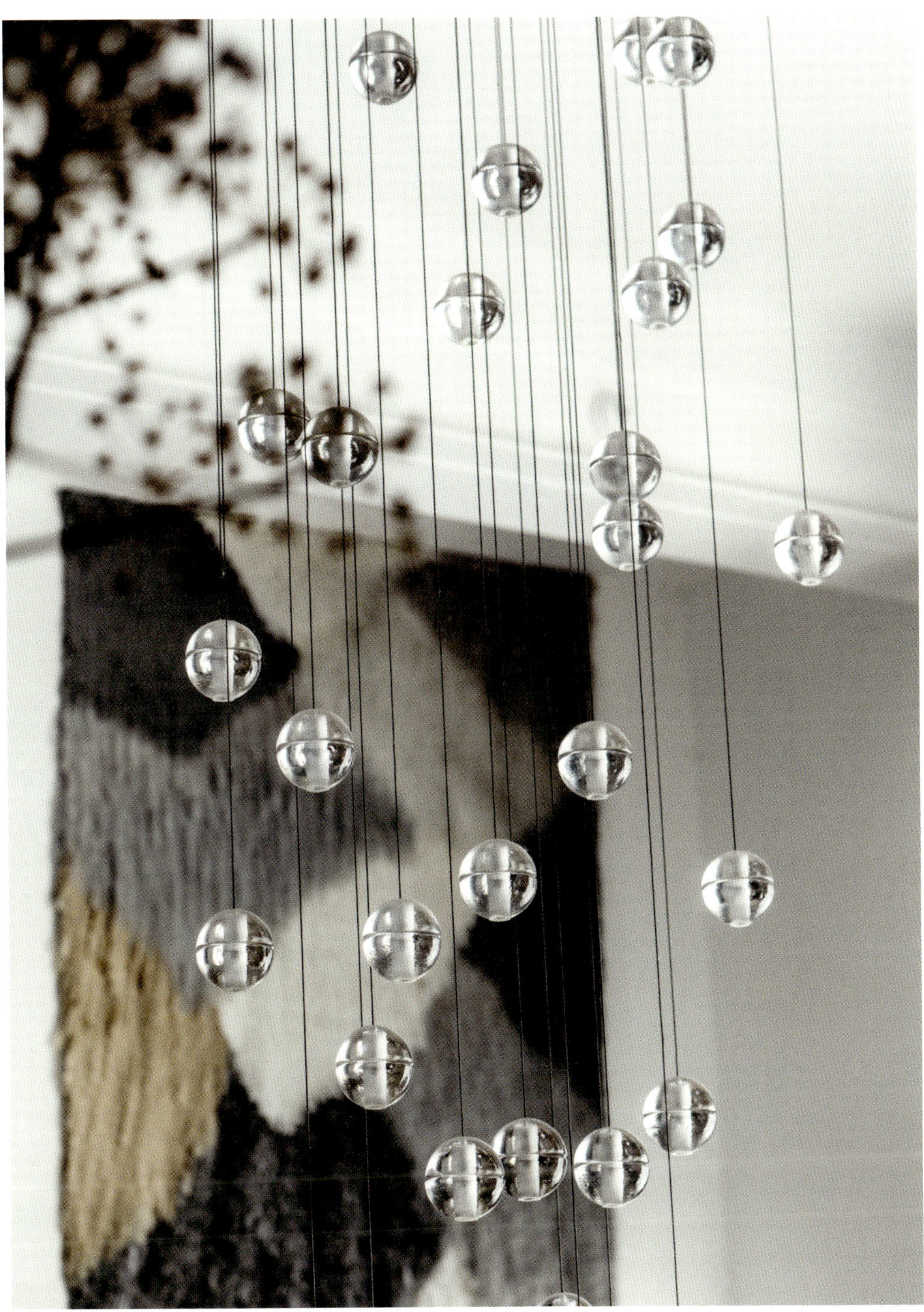

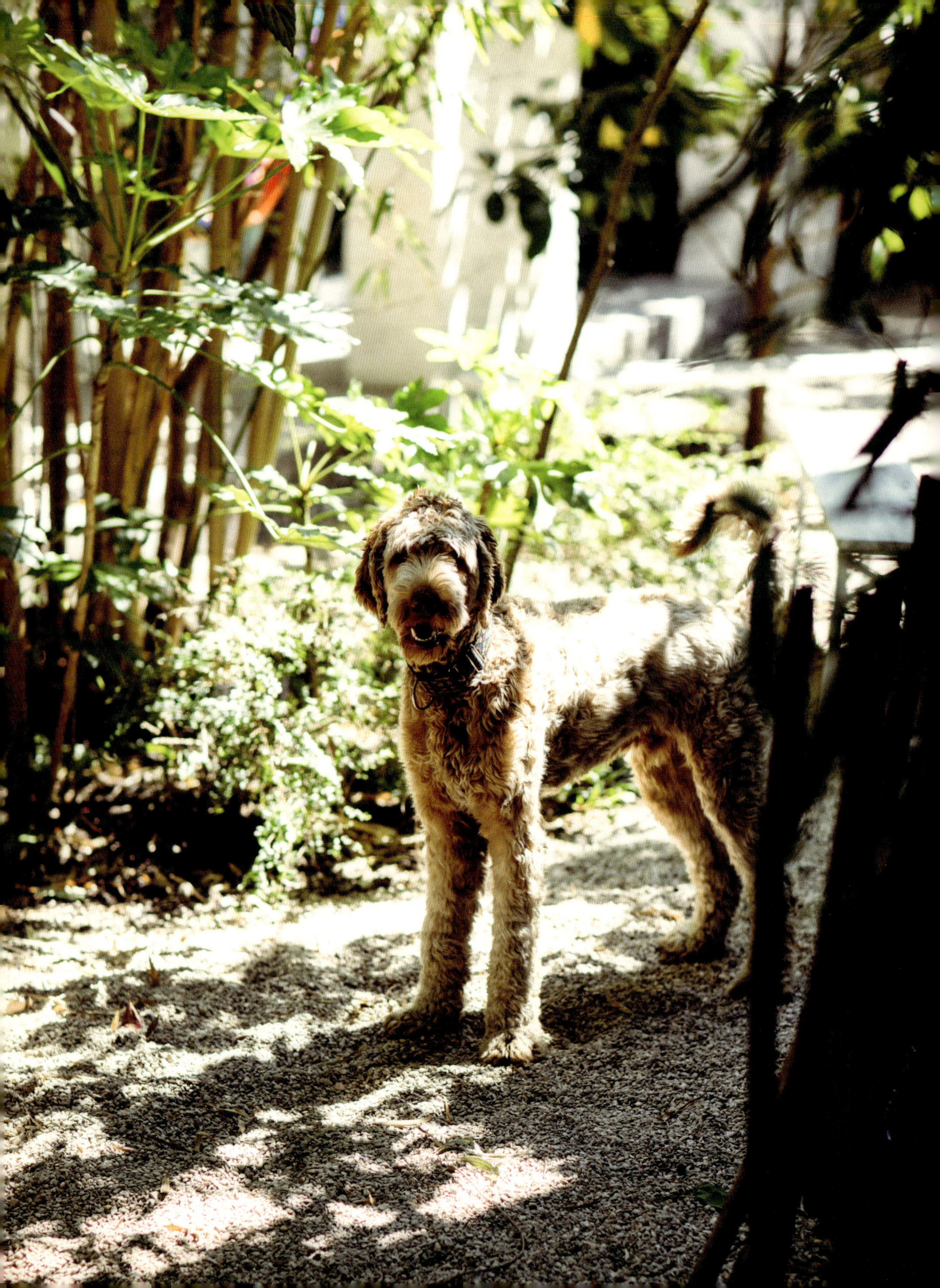

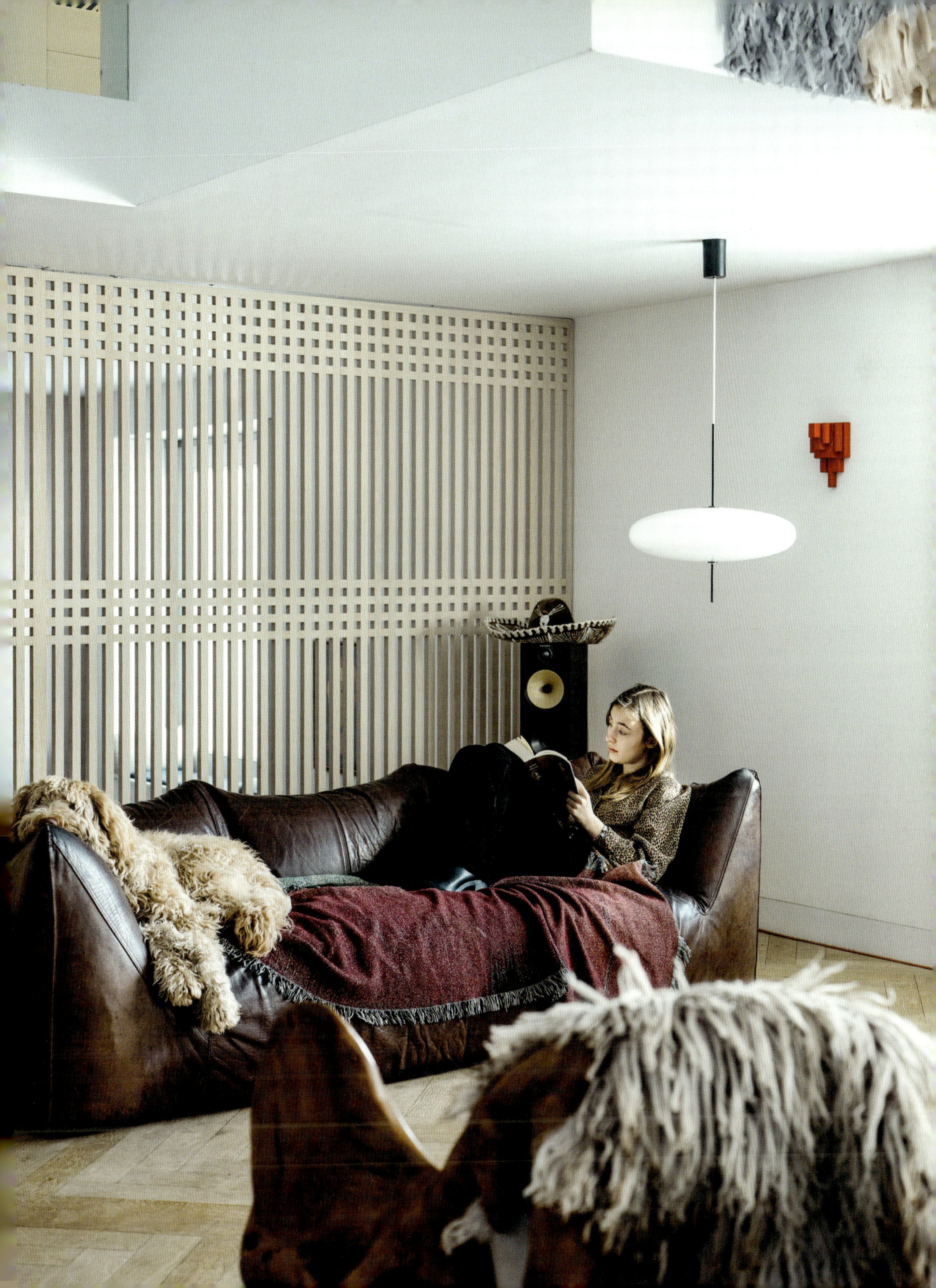

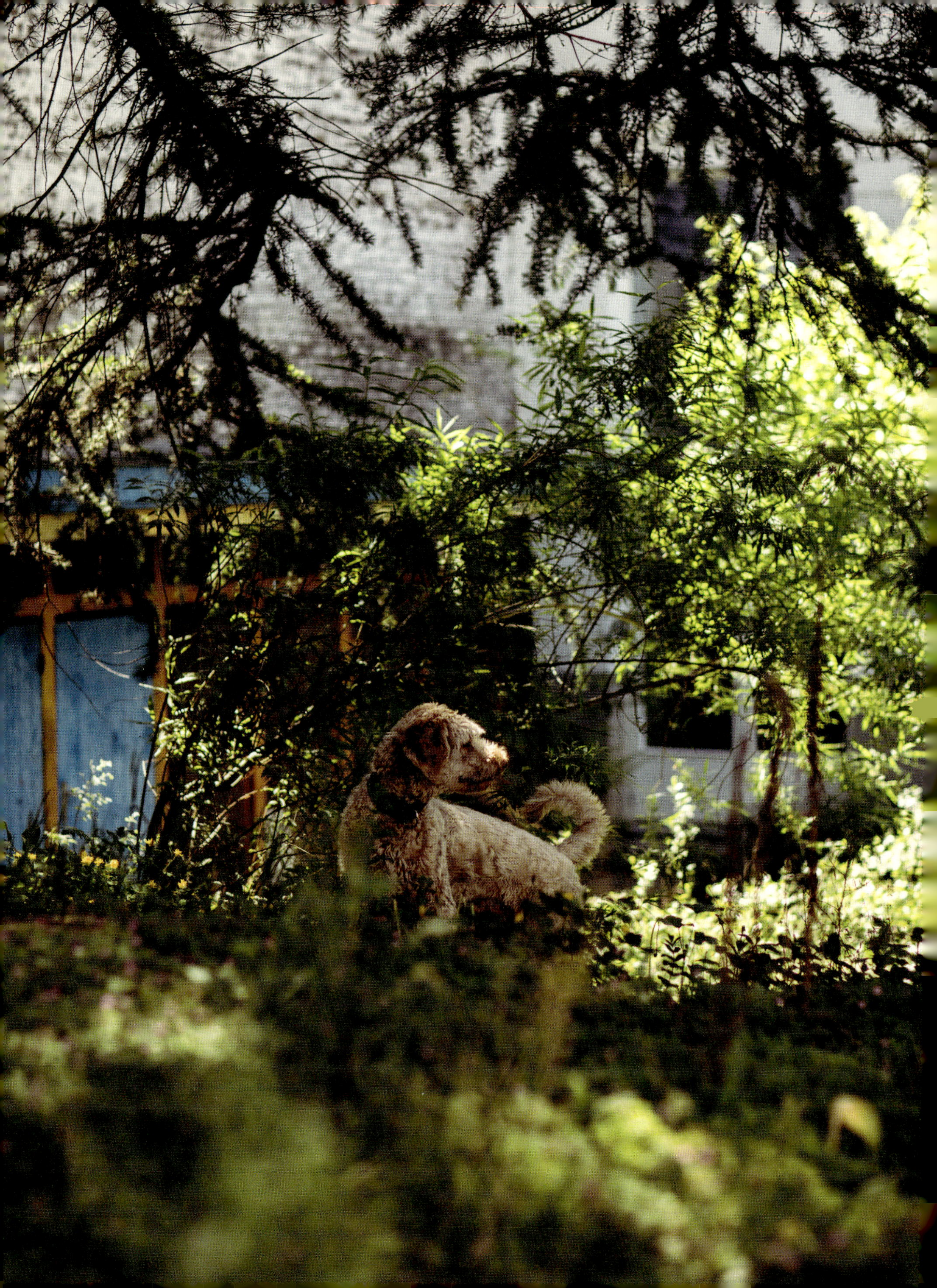

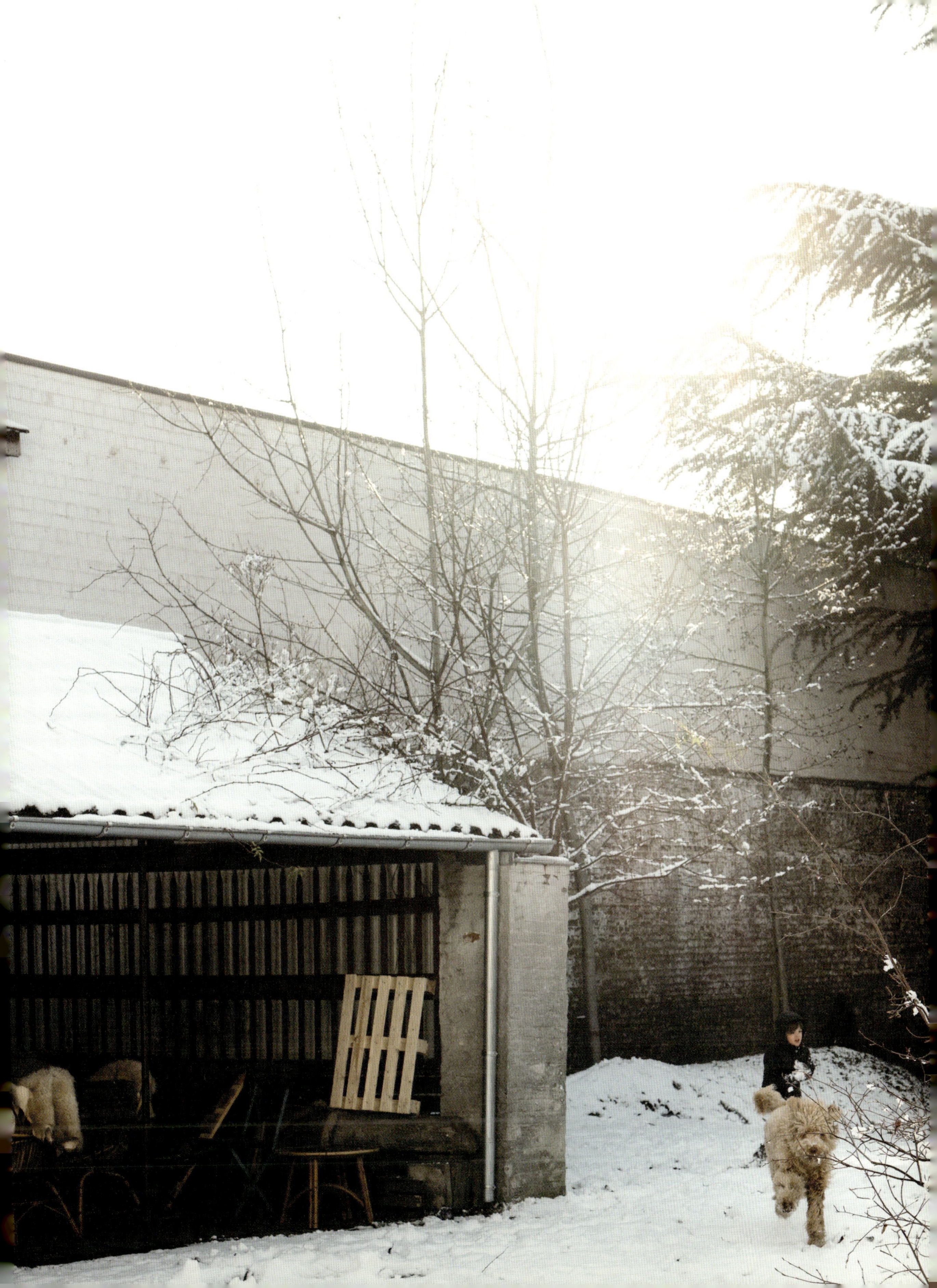

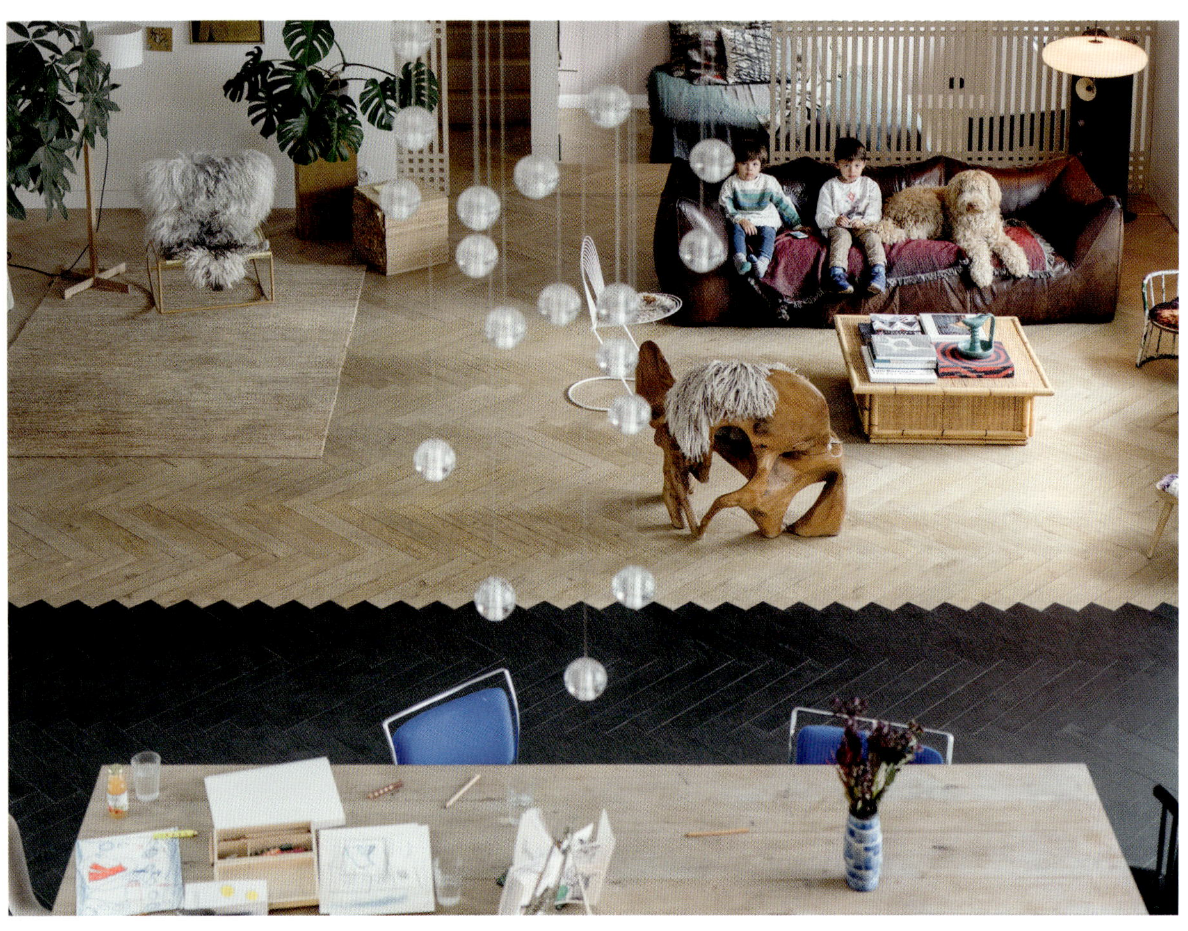

The dog gets a proper brushing once a week to avoid matting
and remove any loose hair from his coat. He undergoes it
gamely and also gets into the bath without a protest.

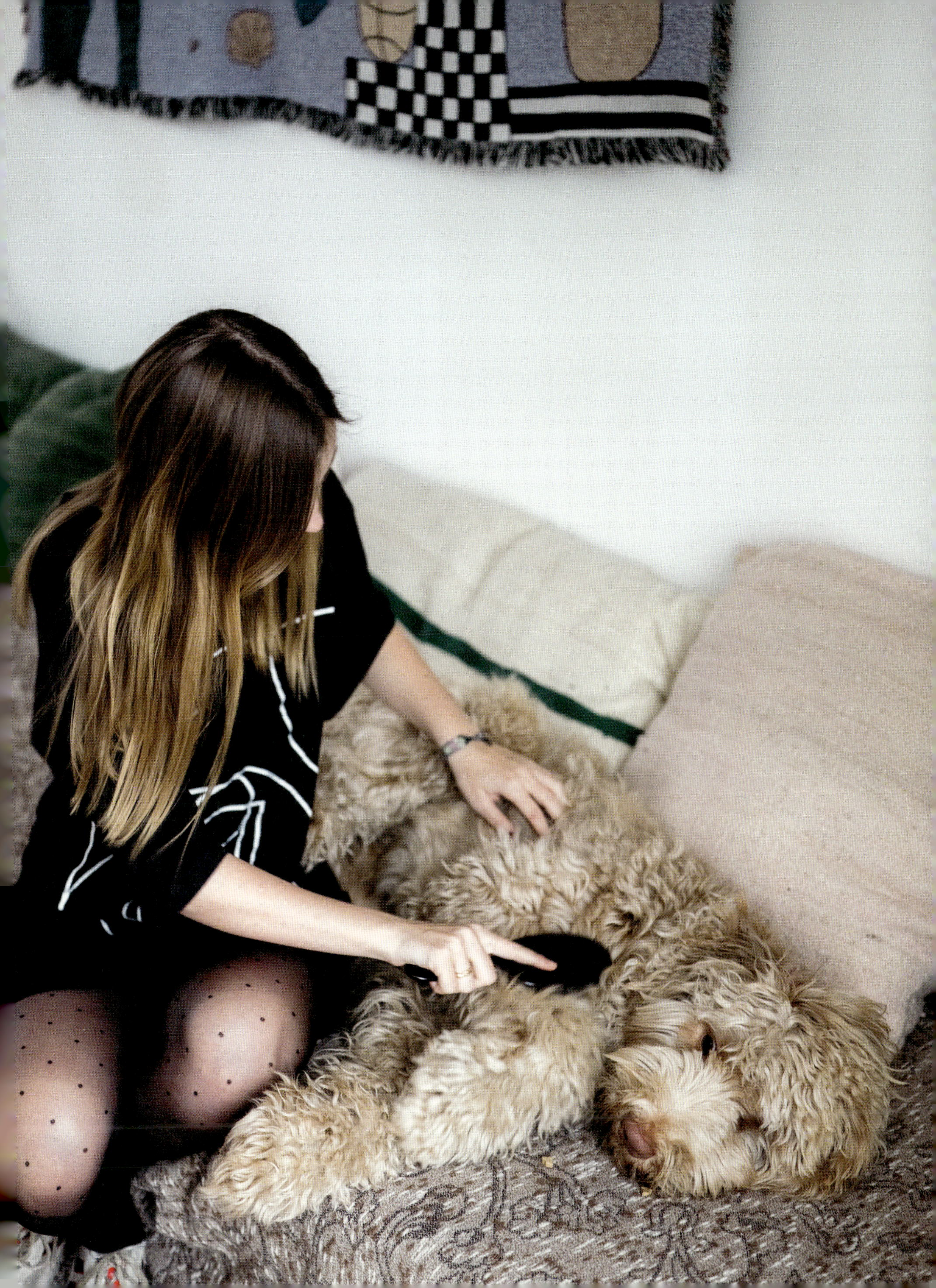

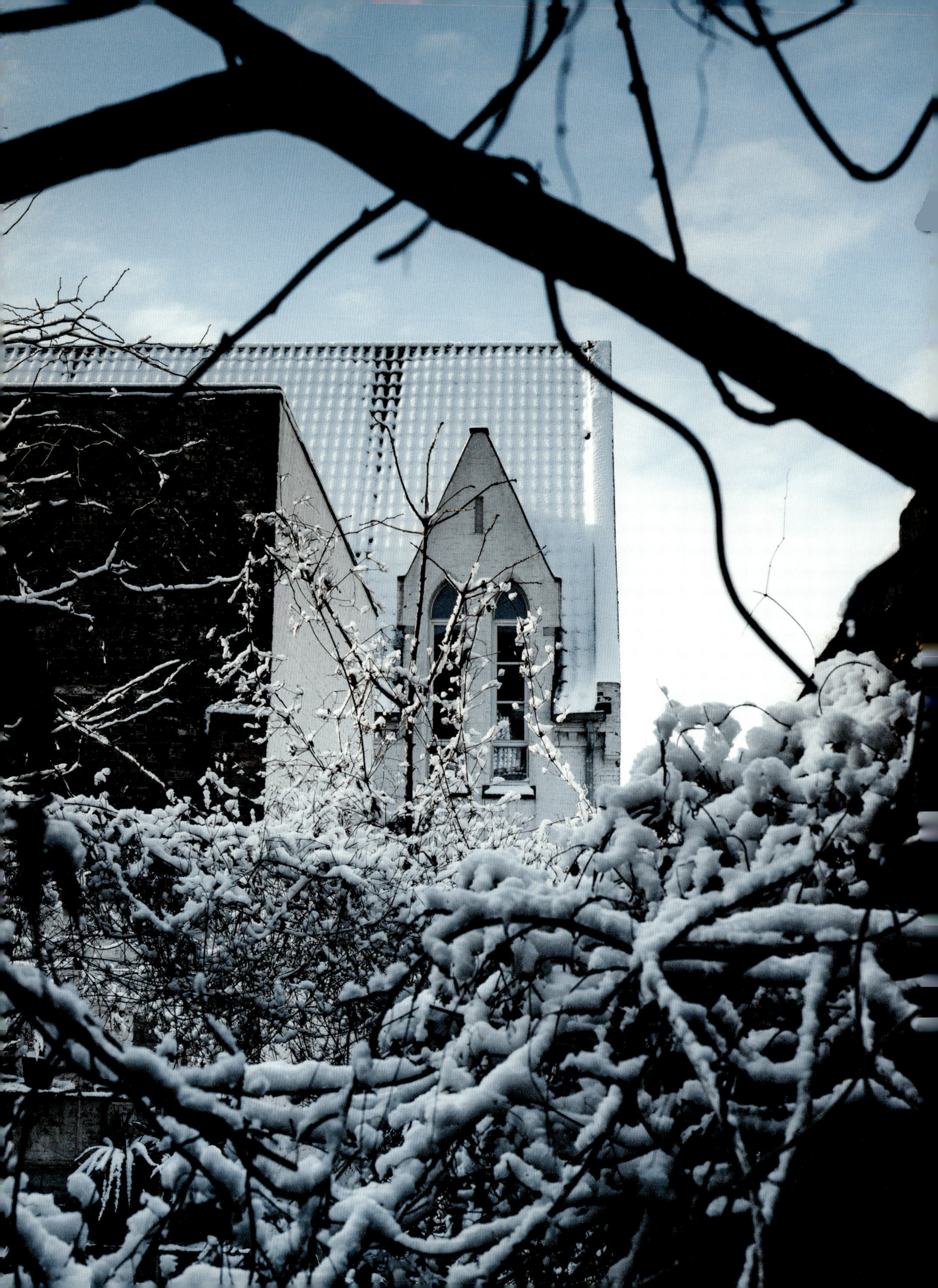

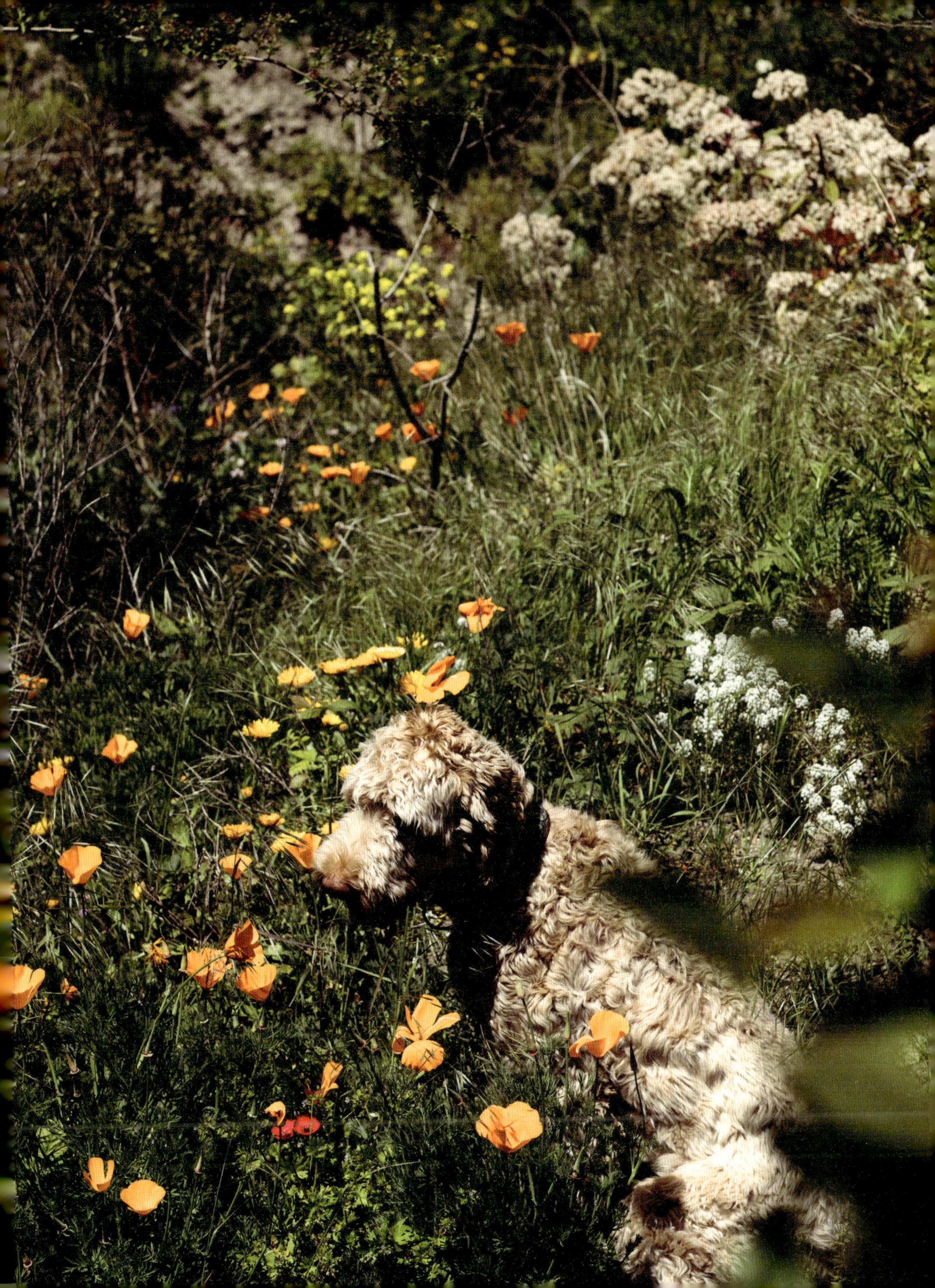

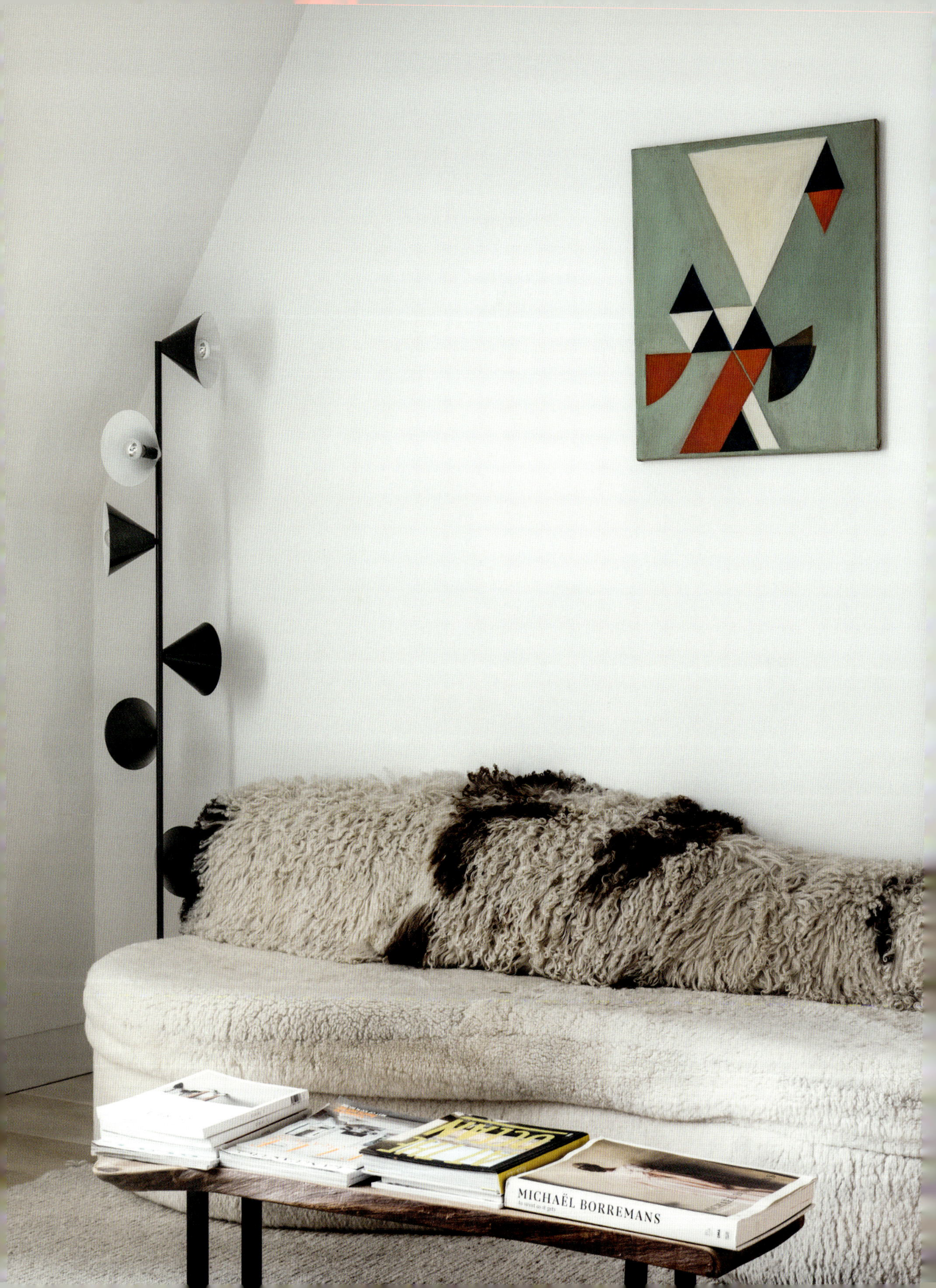

MICHAËL BORREMANS

Veva is able to give her interest in interior decoration free rein
in the building. The spaces are showrooms, which she has
adorned with products from her online shop.

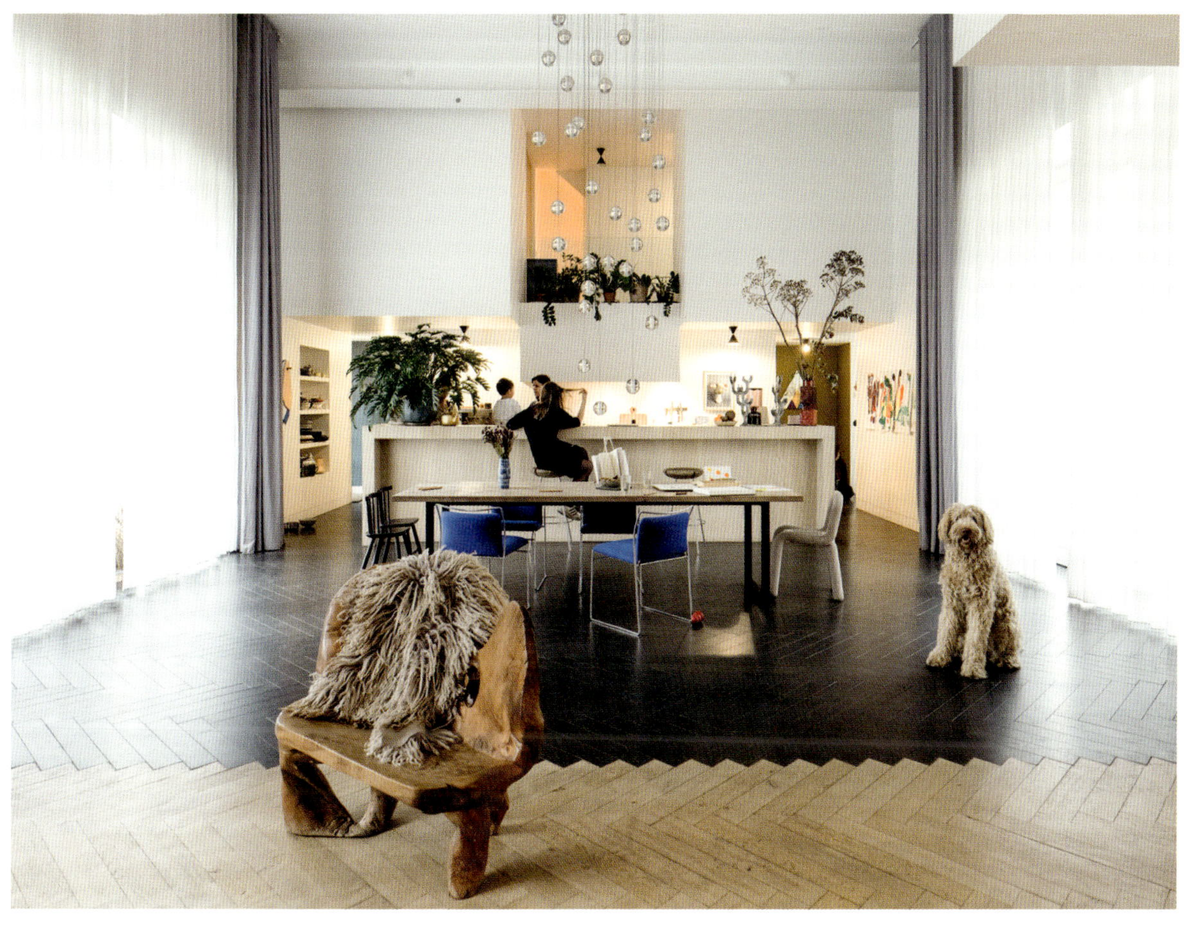

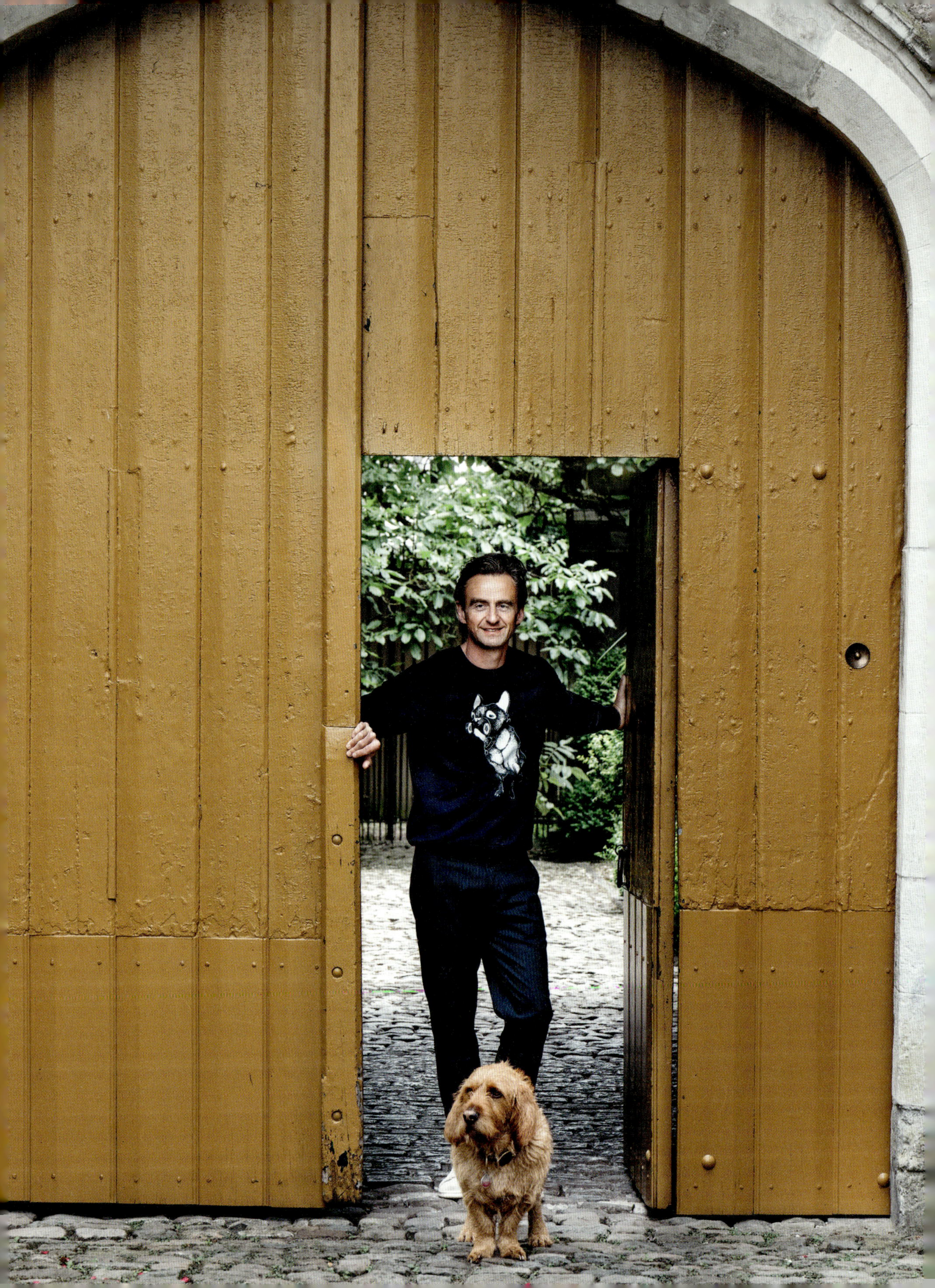

It looks like a fairy tale: a hunting dog guarding a medieval castle. The interior designer and antiques dealer Jean-Philippe Demeyer lives in an impressive 13th-century monument with his pedigree dog. Their home is an example of fearless living. It's a mix of objects in different styles, colours, textures, and materials. Items that do not feel too serious or harmonious. A very quirky and personal interior, where life is good and work is fun, and where a pooch with a Napoleon complex is the king of the realm.

View of the world

Our entrance is immediately noticed. As we arrive at
the castle, we are startled by a small brown guard dog,
which stands on the other side of the moat and barks
at us. As we approach the bridge, the same dog pokes
its head through the gate. The subtle green dog flap
which Jean-Philippe later refers to as 'Ludo's TV screen
or window on the world' is quite a sight. Ludo is the
name of this basset fauve de Bretagne. As an interior
designer, Jean-Philippe has a knack for originality,
and his dog is not an exception to this rule. 'I first
spotted this breed in a French hotel. There was only
one breeder in Belgium, and we were one of the first in
Flanders to get one. Now you see them more often.'

A short-legged hunting dog

A basset fauve de Bretagne is a real hunting dog that
also makes a friendly and gentle pet. Jean-Philippe
is proud of Ludo's physical force, 'in spite of his short
legs and lazy nature.' Given the fact that the castle
has such a magnificent garden (which he designed
himself), you'd think that a dog like Ludo spends his
days exploring it, but this is not the case. When he is not
on the jetty or out walking with his owner, he relaxes in
the office. He also has a favourite spot upstairs, on his
blanket on the sofa. Ludo likes structure and routine.
And he hates socialising. After sniffing out other people
or other dogs, he returns to his basket or hides behind
the curtain, from where he observes you. Jean-Philippe
has never considered getting a second pup. 'We used
to have two labradors, one of which was like a mum to
Ludo. After her death, he became the top dog. Since
then, Ludo feels superior, he clearly suffers from a
Napoleon complex. He doesn't want to please like most
dogs, he wants to be pleased.'

Unconventional loners

The decorator talks about his dog as it were a family
member. And during the conversation, he regularly
likens himself to Ludo. 'He lives in his own world.
He's stubborn, won't back down and won't follow.
And I'm just like him. Together we are loners, and
we each like to do our own thing.' That said, the
pet doesn't like being alone. He even suffers from
separation anxiety. That is why Jean-Philippe takes
him everywhere, or he stays on the estate with the
housekeeper, where he lives in luxury and is treated every
day to healthy snacks: a combination of carrots, chicken
hearts, and rice. Ludo is very well trained. He doesn't
run into anything. It's as if he's keenly aware of his
regal surroundings, which is a good thing because the
castle is not just Jean-Philippe's private home. He also
uses it as a showroom in which the interior is regularly
changed. Twice a year it is opened to the public.

Animal motifs

A dog as a companion is fun, but also inspiring.
'I like dogs because they exude a certain placidness.
When I'm working on several things at once, I always
ask myself why I can't be a little more like Ludo.
He really has taught me to live in the moment.'
The pet's presence also manifests itself in his design
jobs, more specifically in the choice of animal motifs.
You'll find porcelain dogs throughout the house, as
well as vases shaped like animals, or leopard and tiger
prints, which, he says, 'add a playful accent to the
interior.' The designer collects these objects for himself
and loans them now and then for projects. On a fun
side note, Jean-Philippe is wearing a jumper with an
animal pattern during the interview.

A quirky interior

Now and then the decorator is asked to design a
special item of furniture for a pet, such as a luxurious
dog cushion that matches a sofa, or a real house for
a pooch or a cat. Whether he creates, customises,
or collects items, all the objects he uses are always
unique and surprising, sometimes even eccentric.
'Fearless living' is not just the title of his book. It is a
concept, a method. He is not led by a style, but by a
theme. 'My home is not just a place to look at. It's a
lab, where I experiment by combining different items.
The result doesn't have to be perfect or harmonious.
I find quirky interiors much more fascinating.
Decorating is an intuitive process. It's fun, light-hearted
and involves a lot of humour because the world is
much too serious anyway.' That said, we are chased
out by Ludo. High time for a walk.

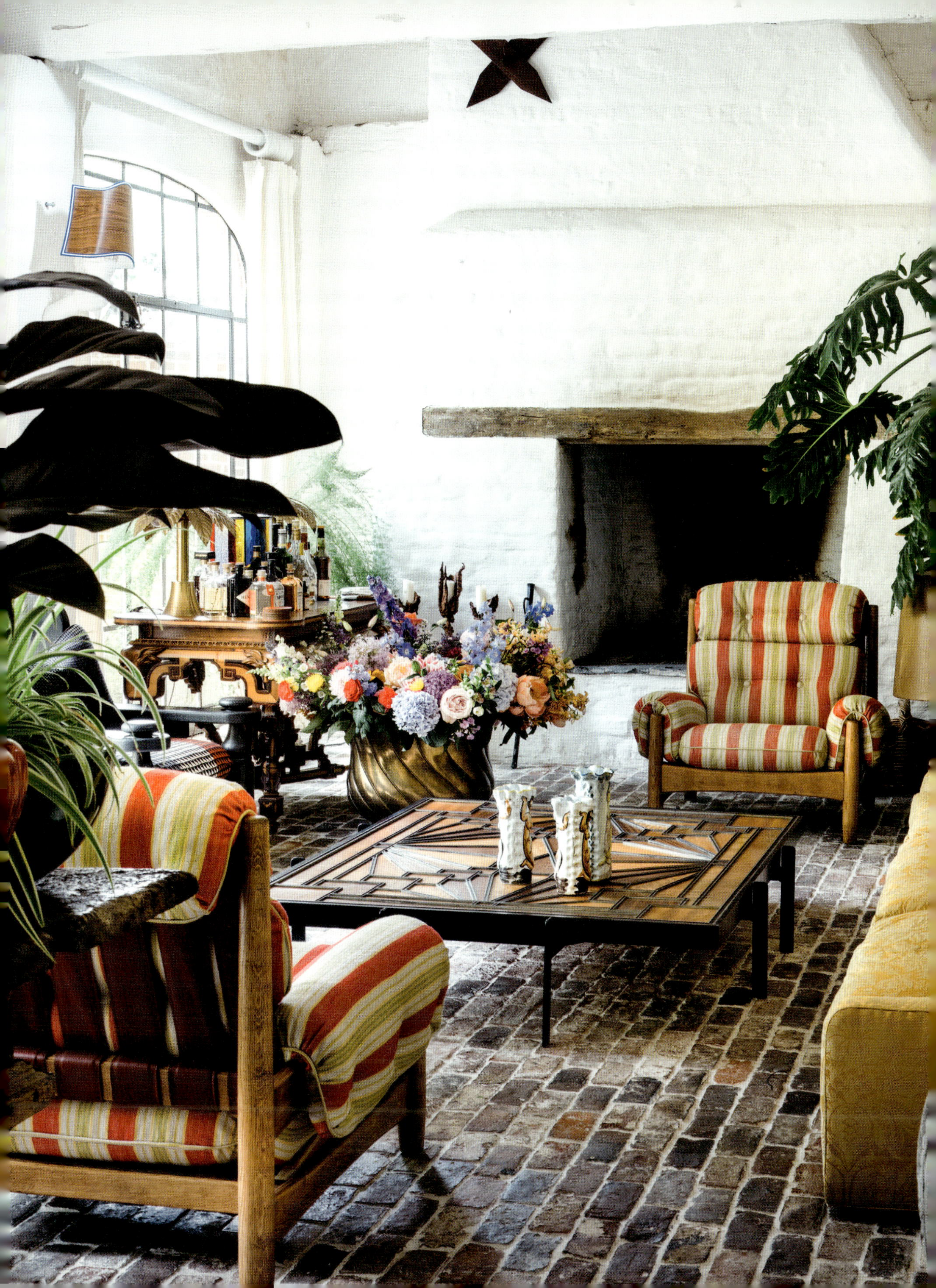

Jean-Philippe lives in a 13th-century castle. The interior is a mix of objects in different styles, colours, textures, and materials.

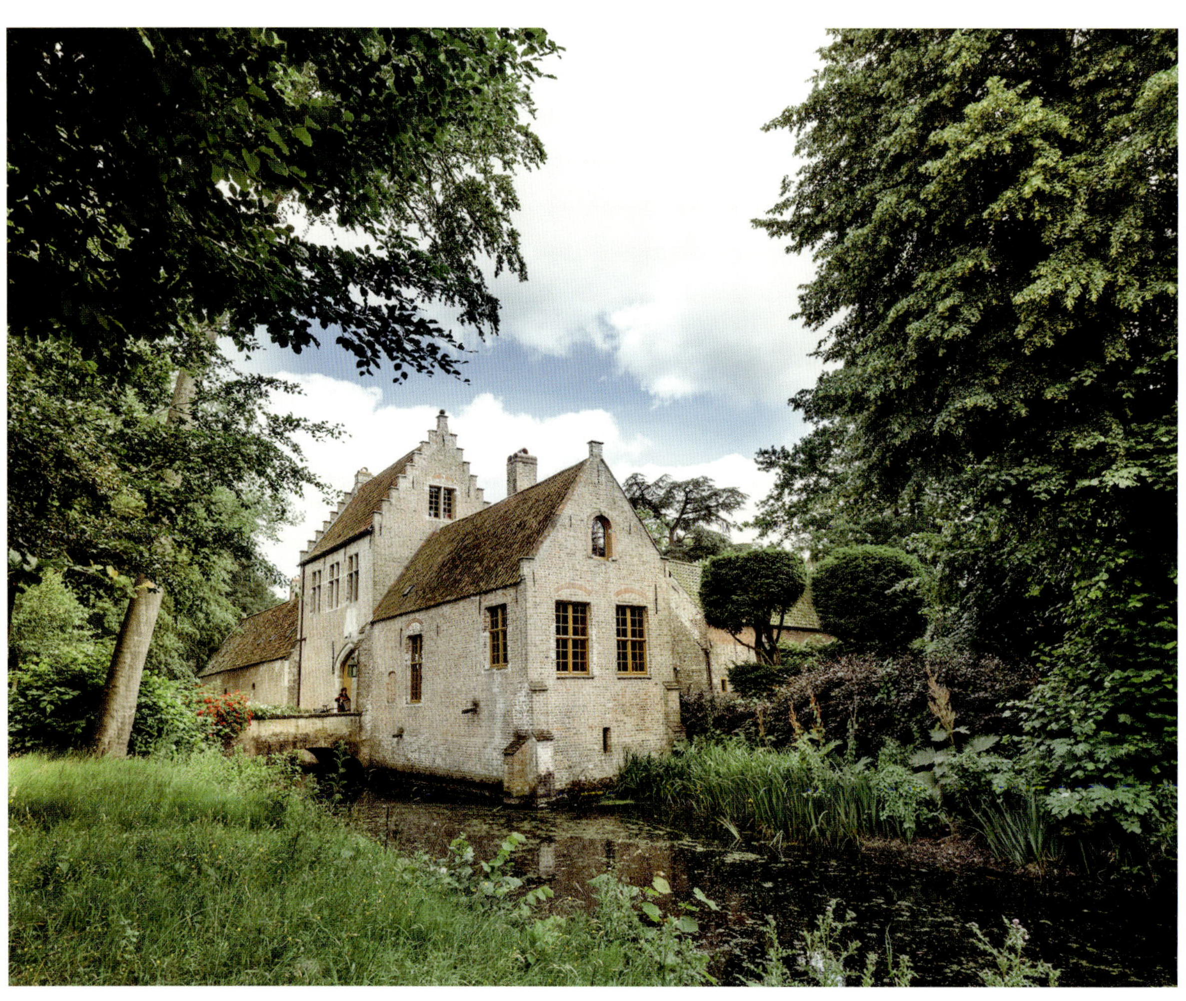

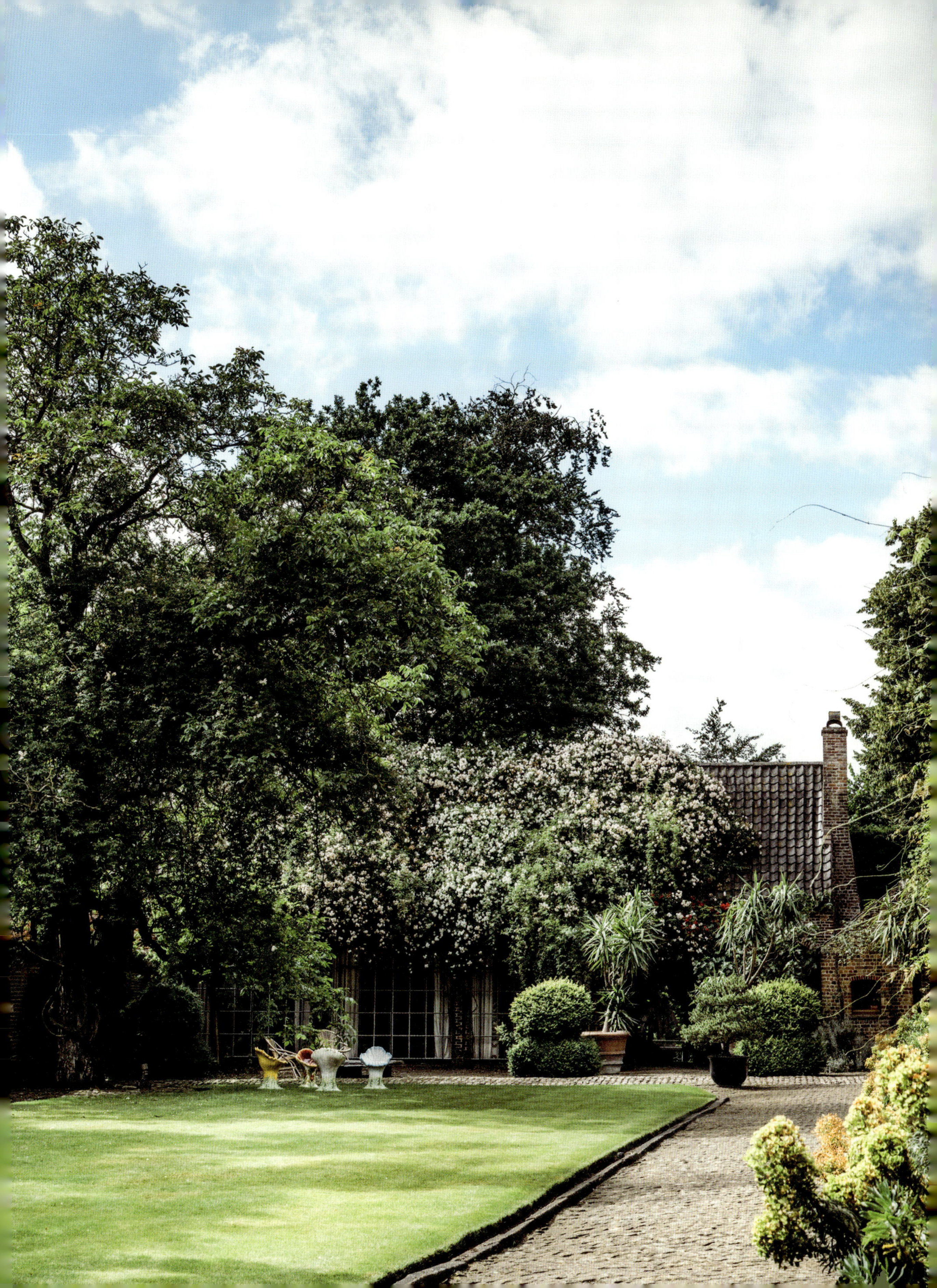

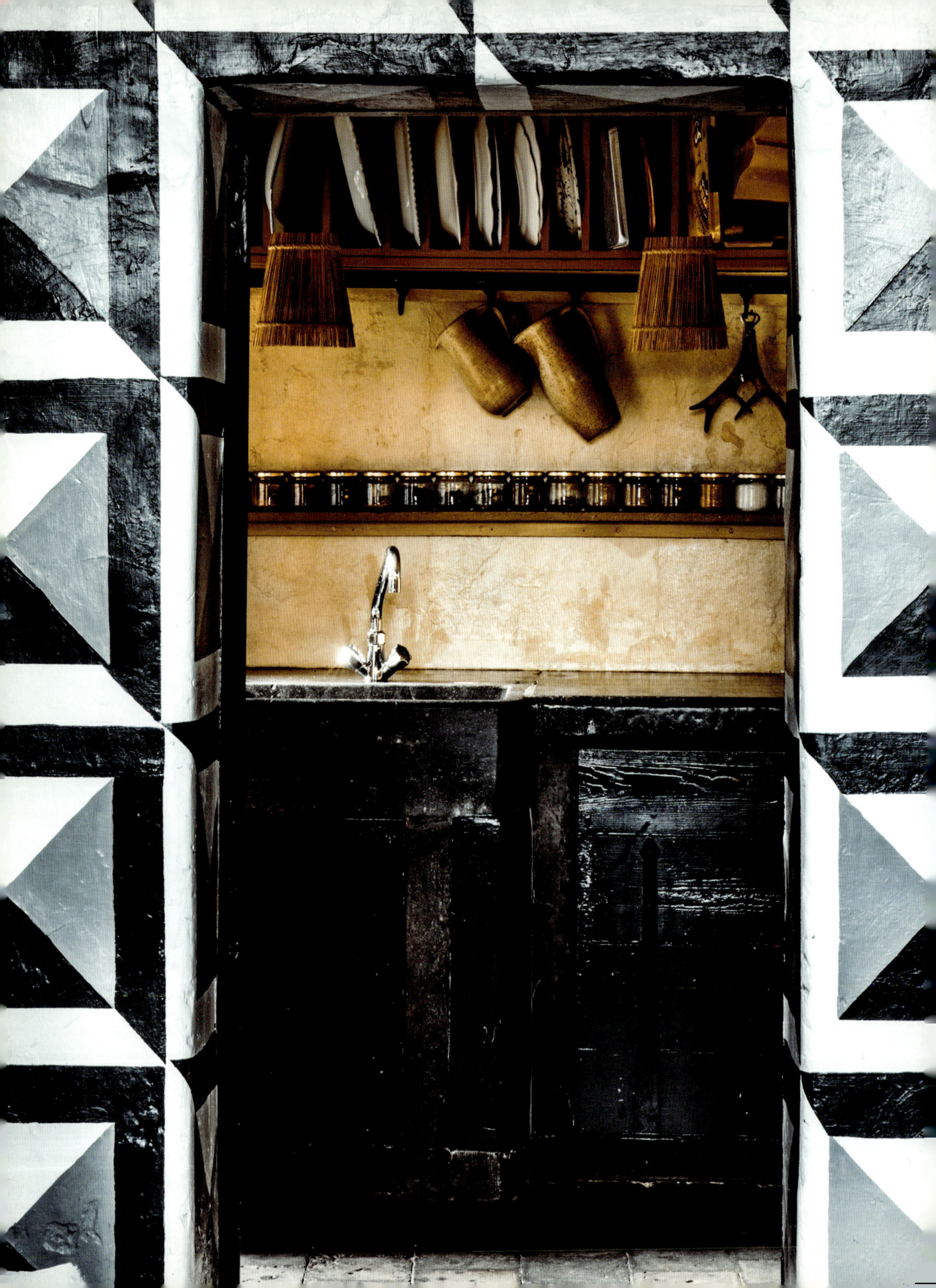

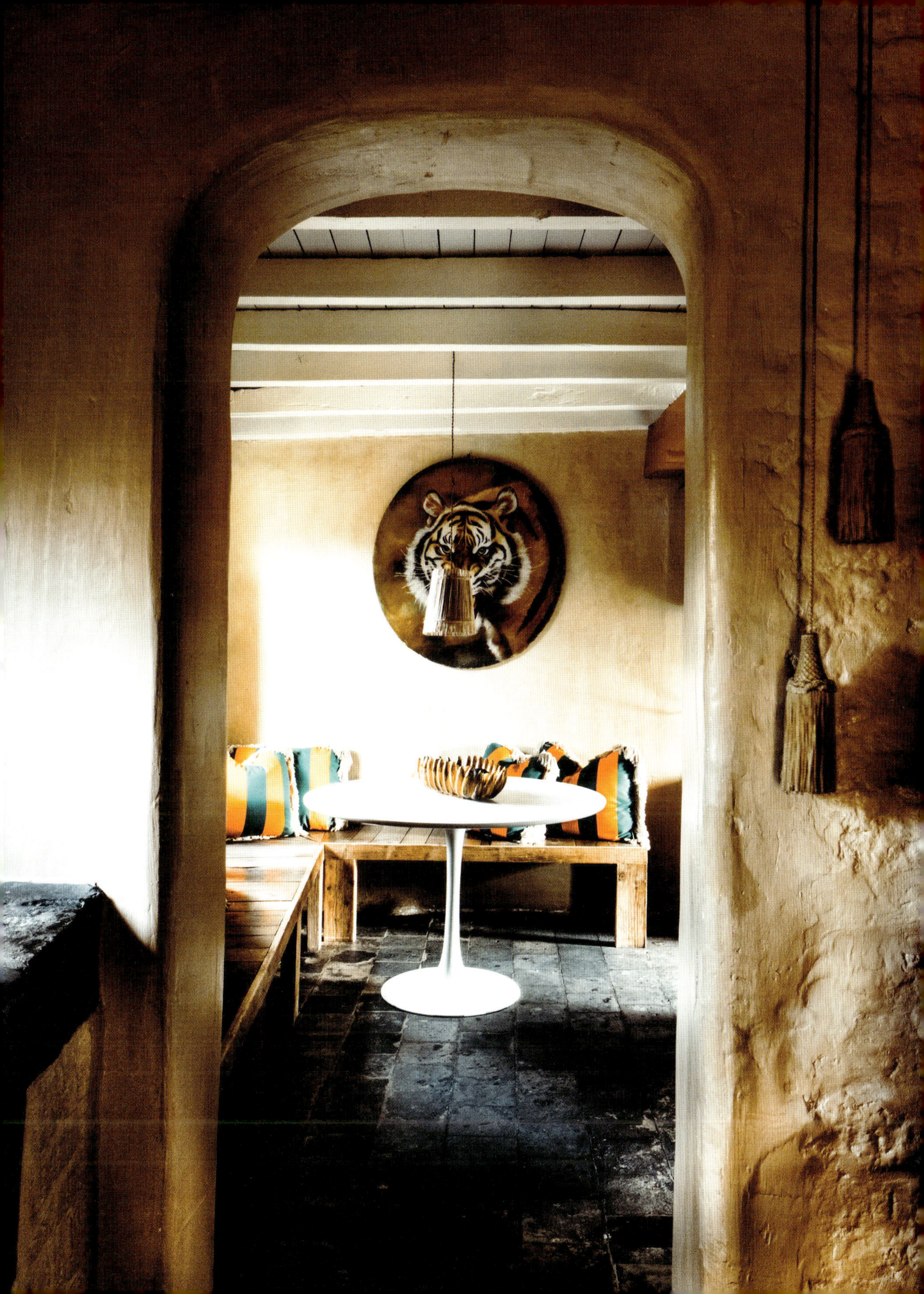

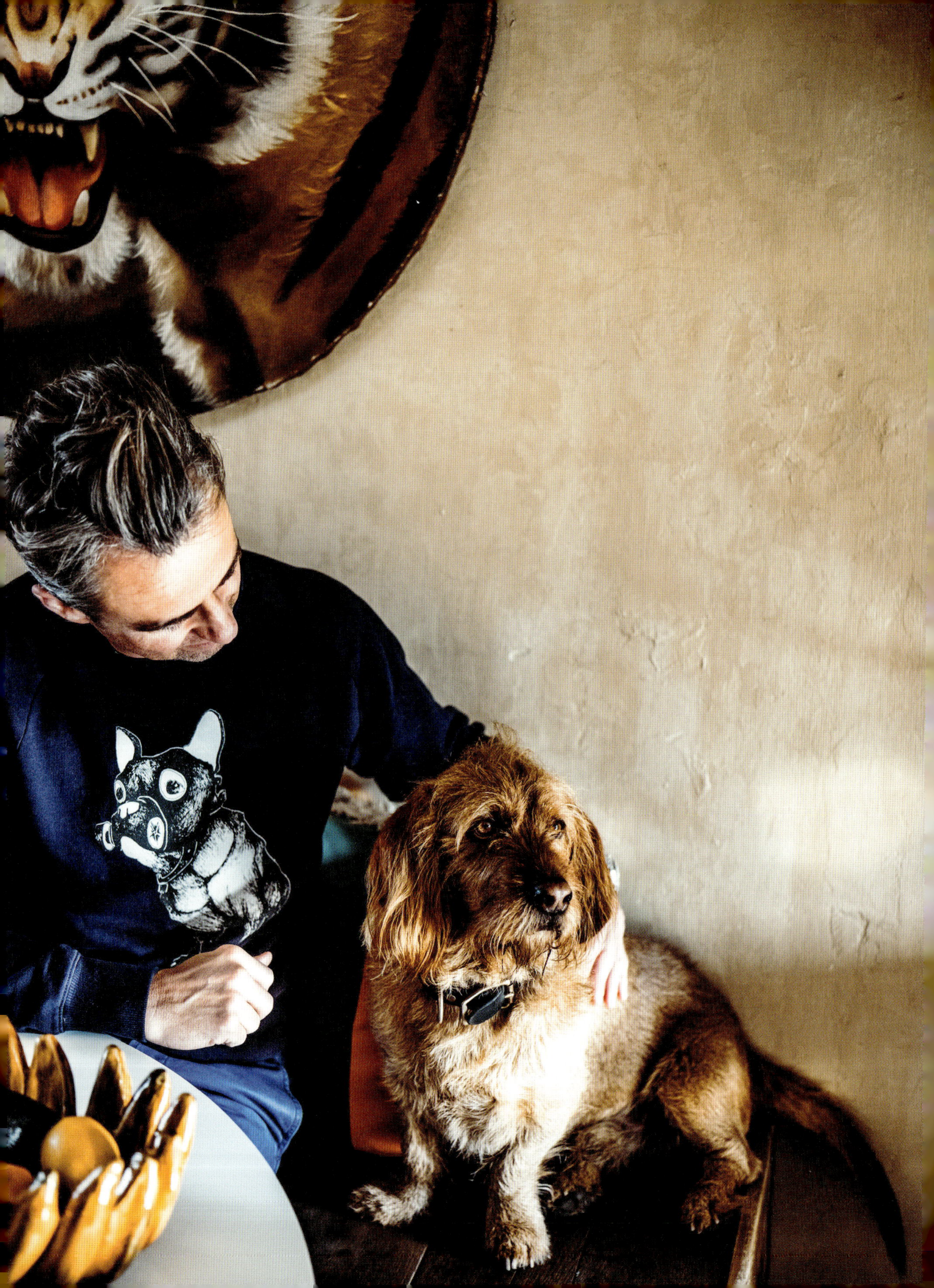

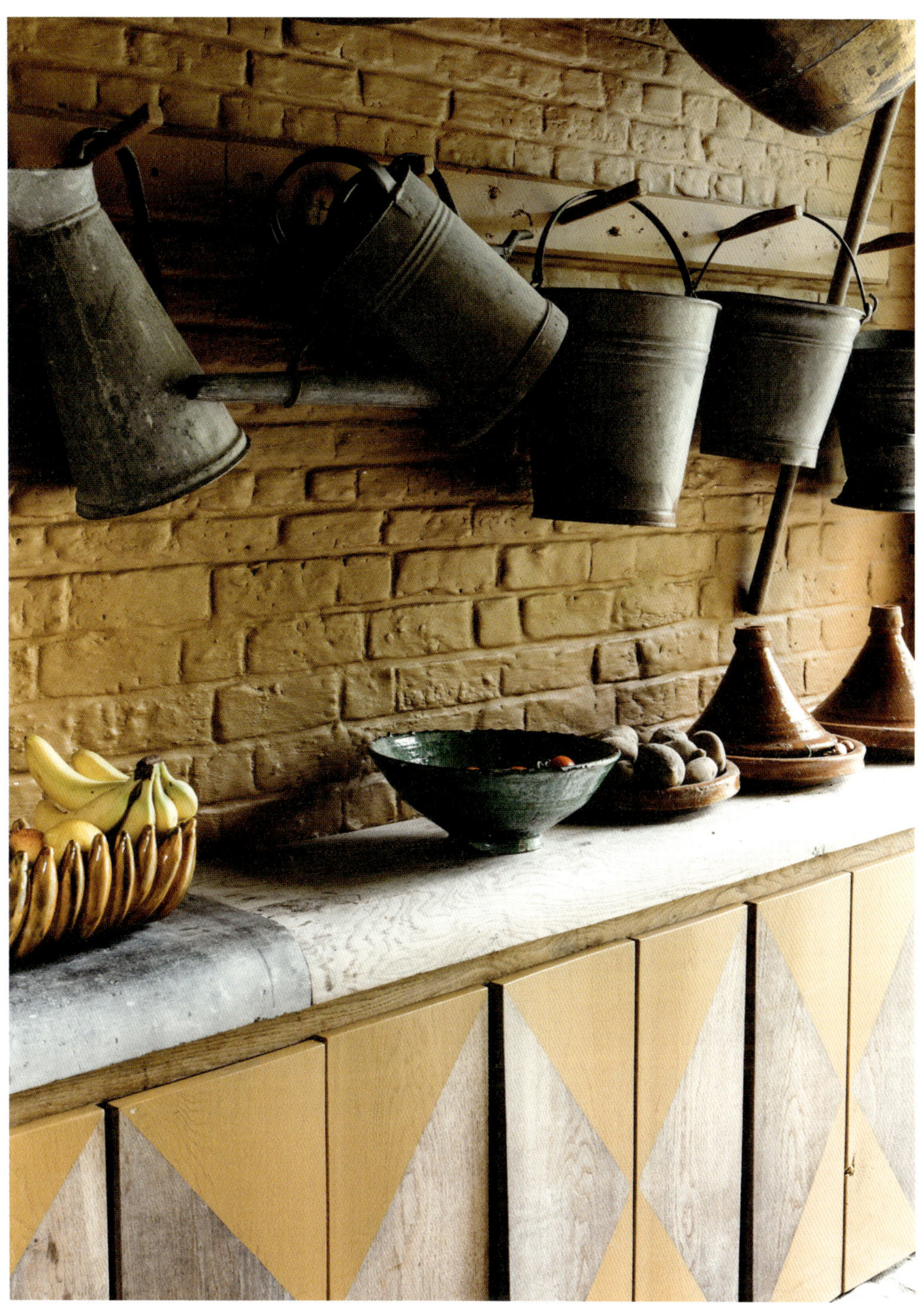

Ludo is a pedigree dog. Like his owner, he's stubborn and lives in
his own world. He feels superior, likes to be pleased, and suffers
from a Napoleon complex.

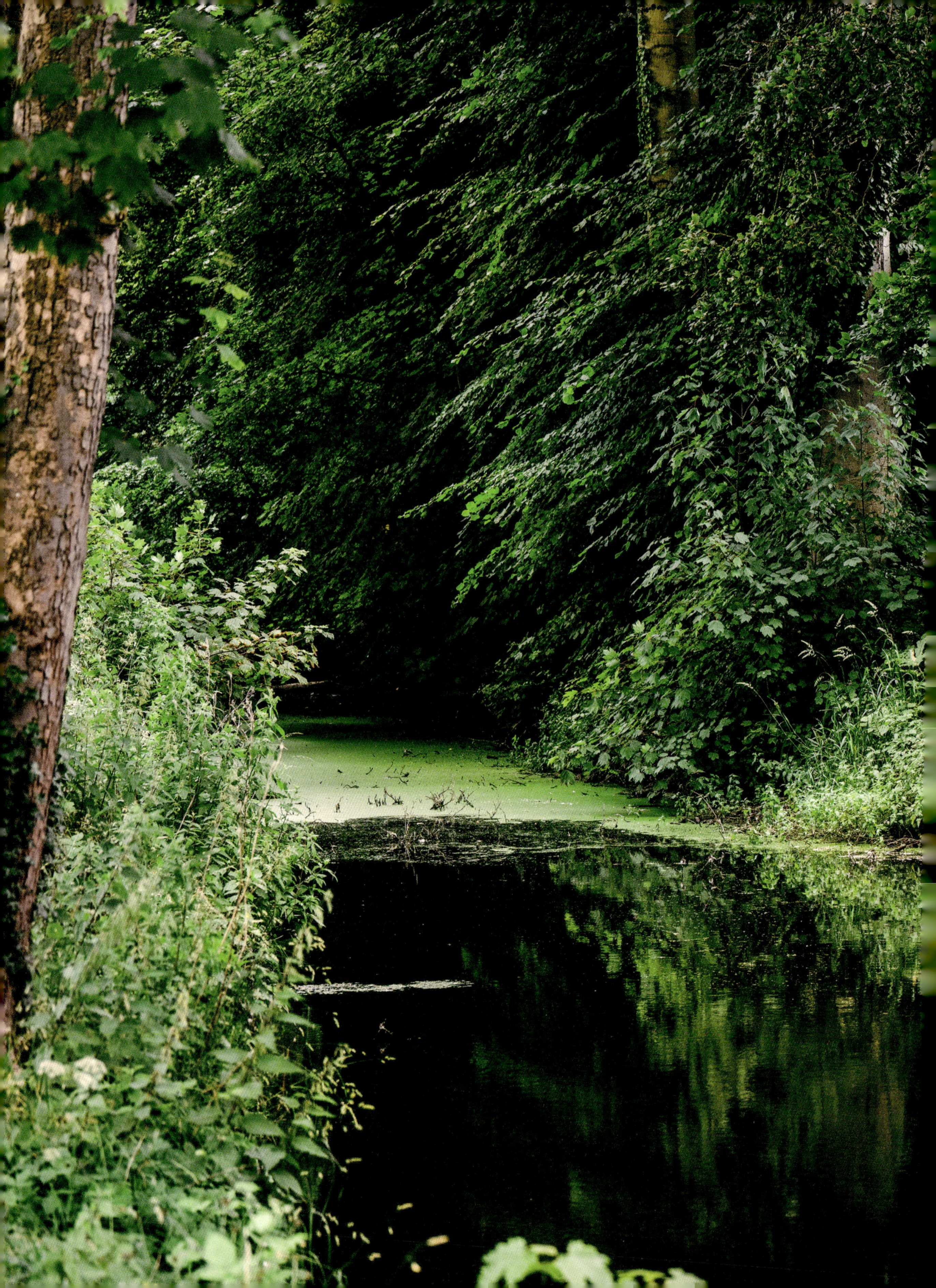

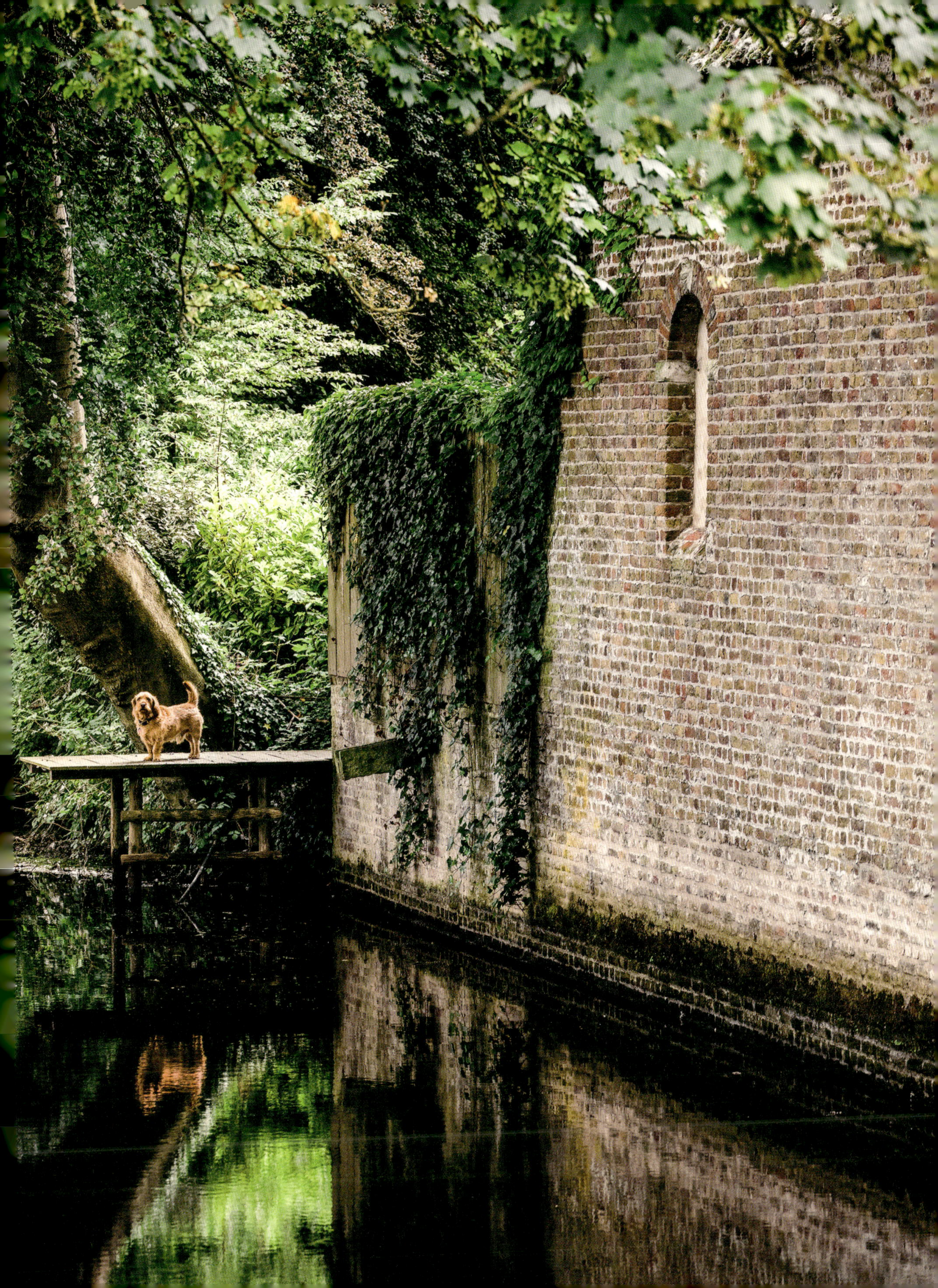

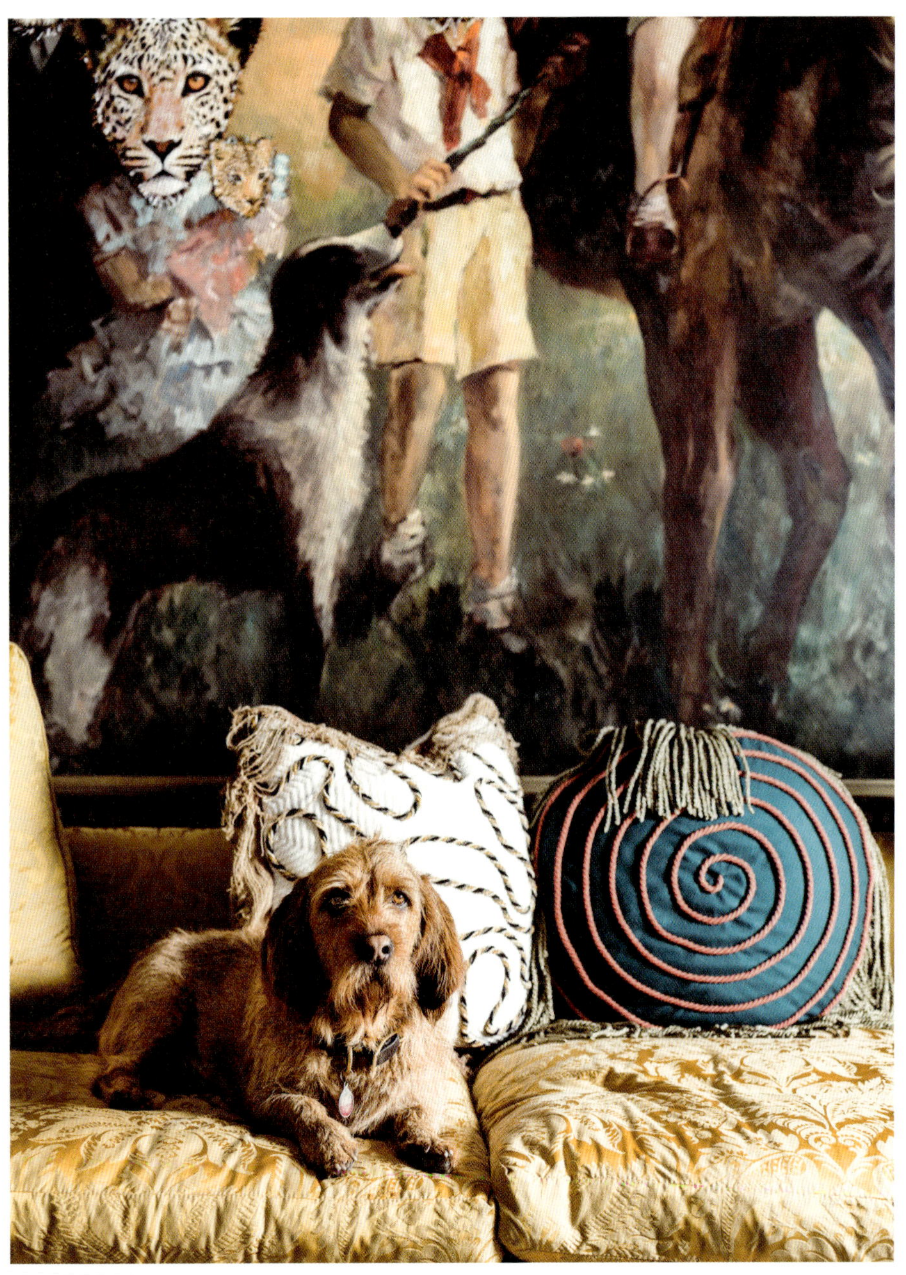

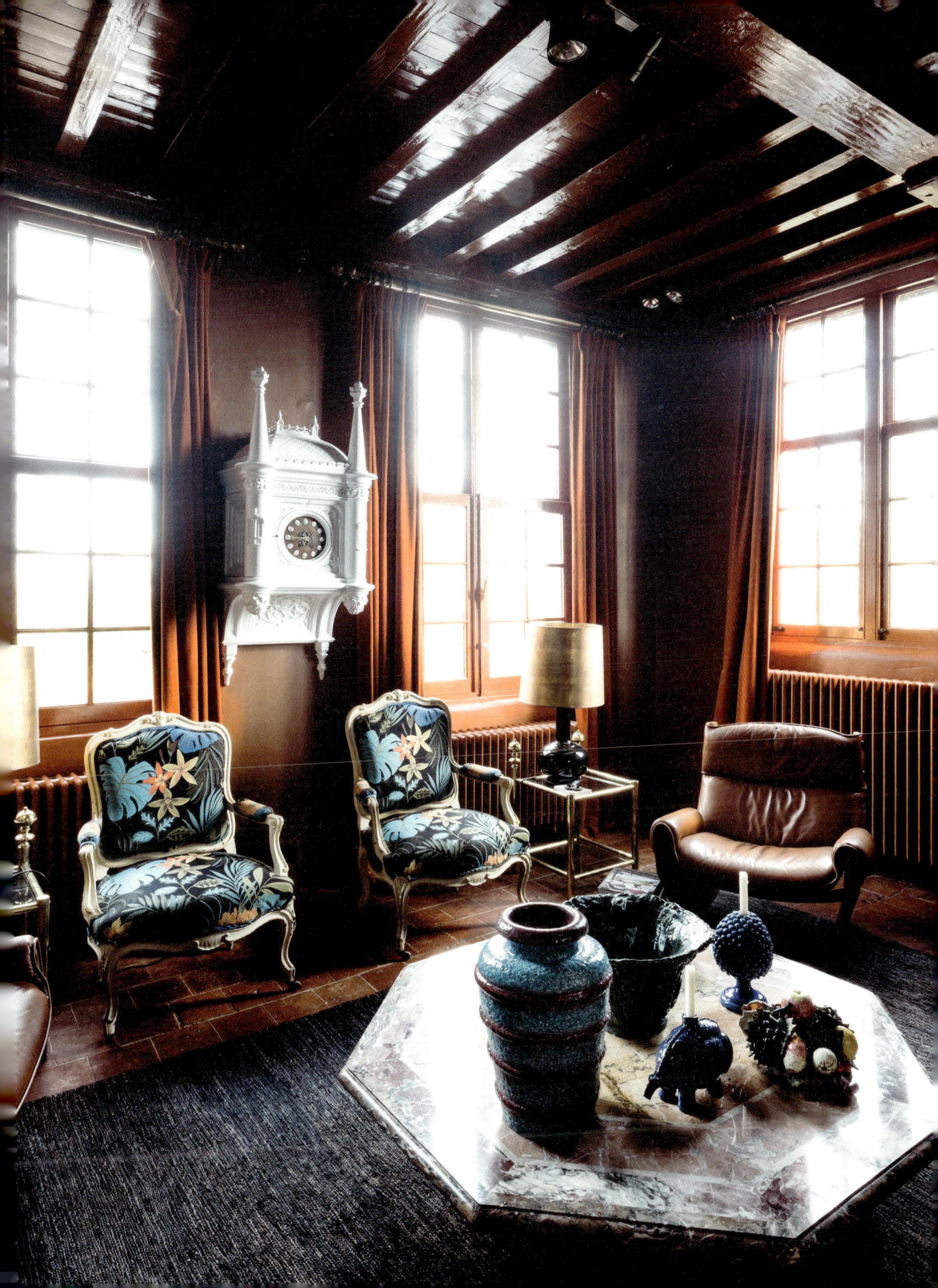

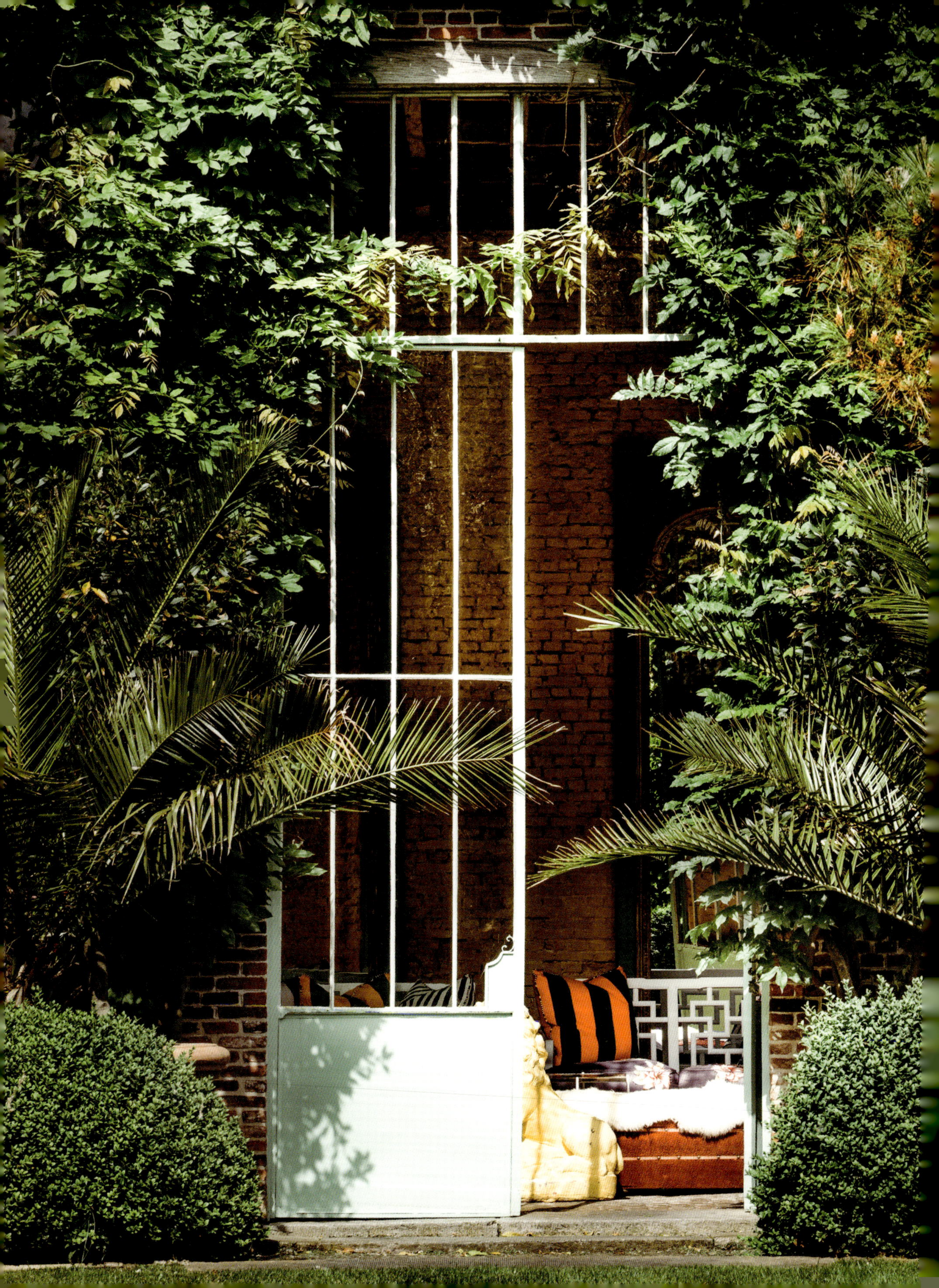

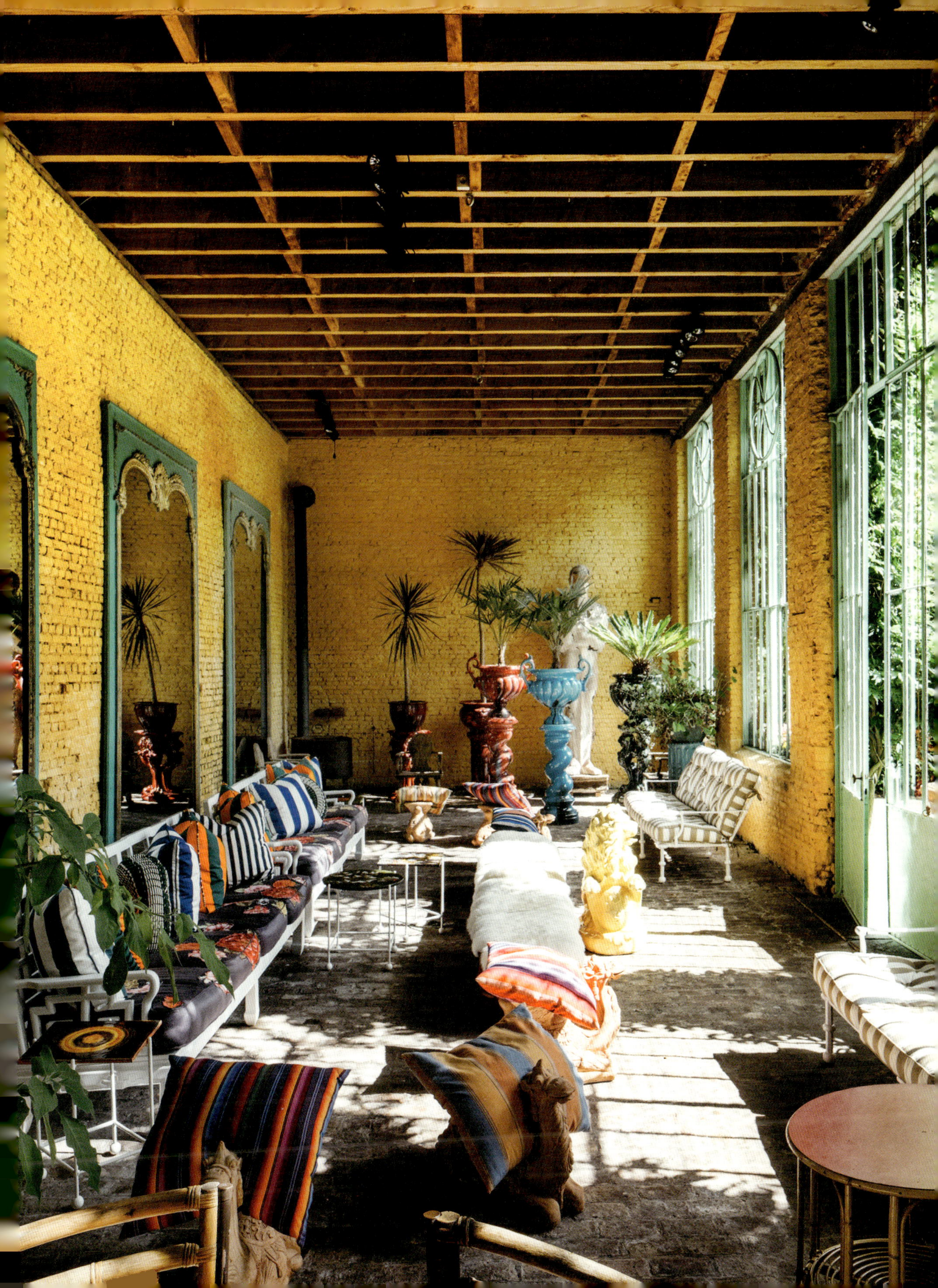

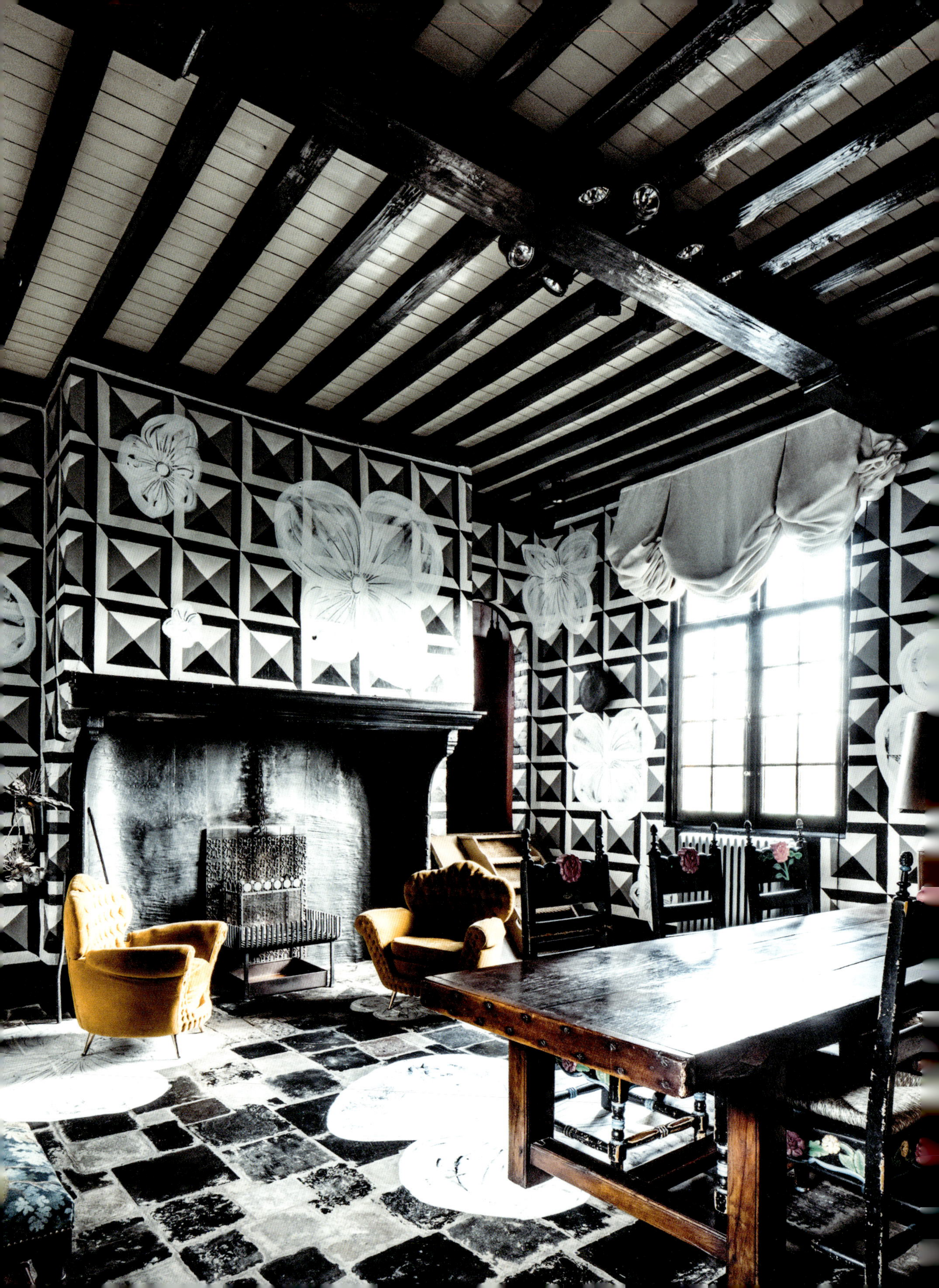

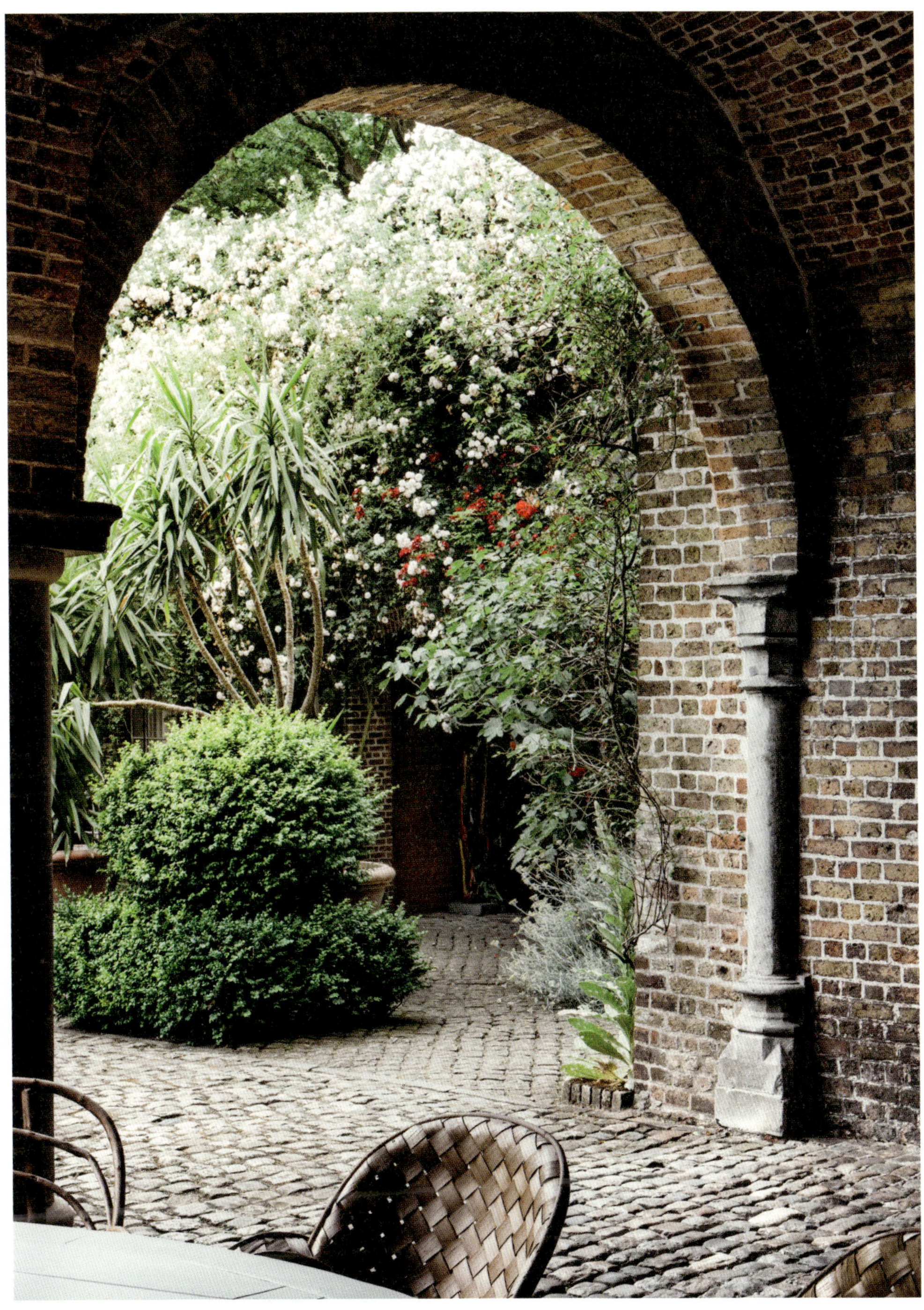

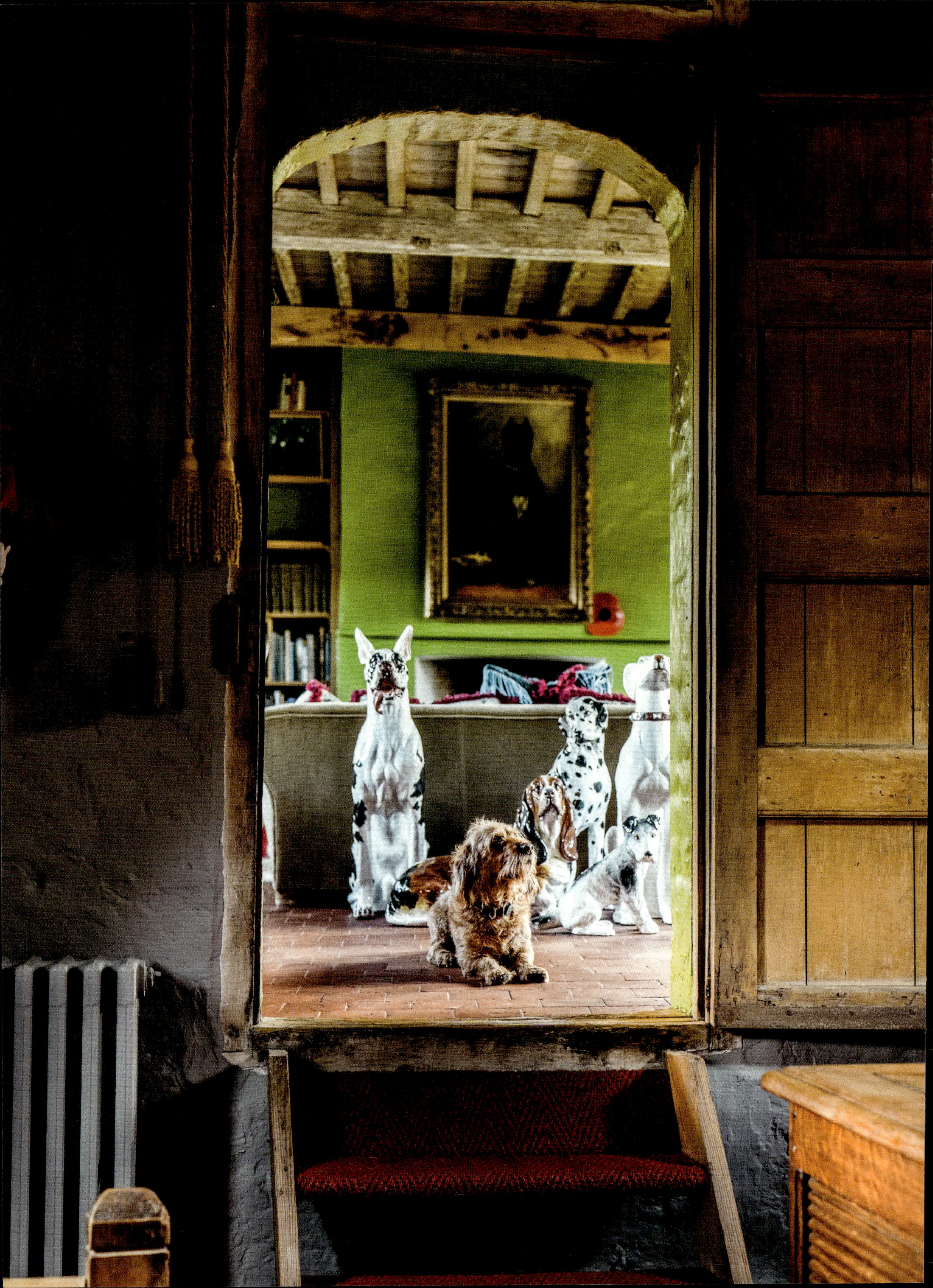

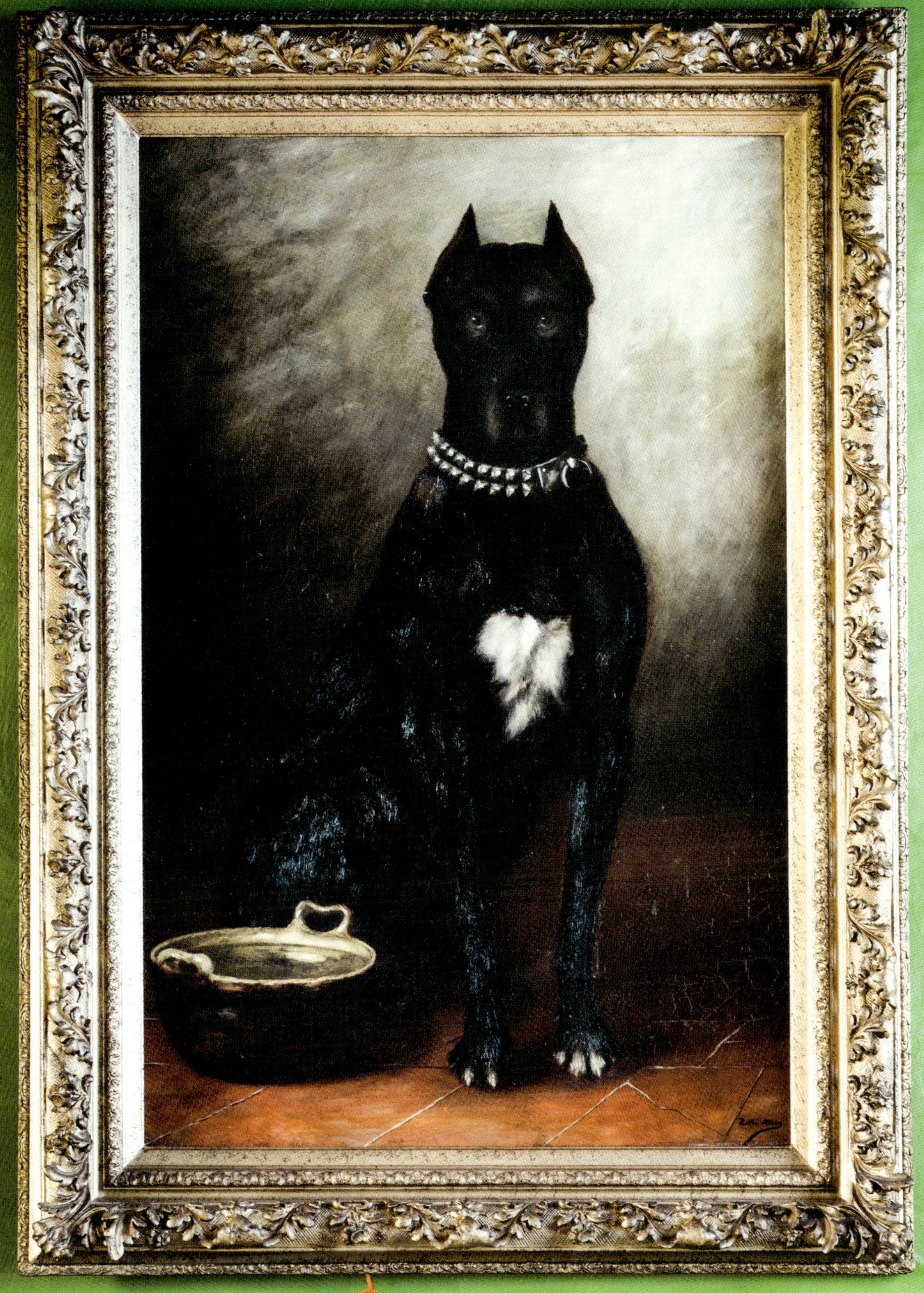

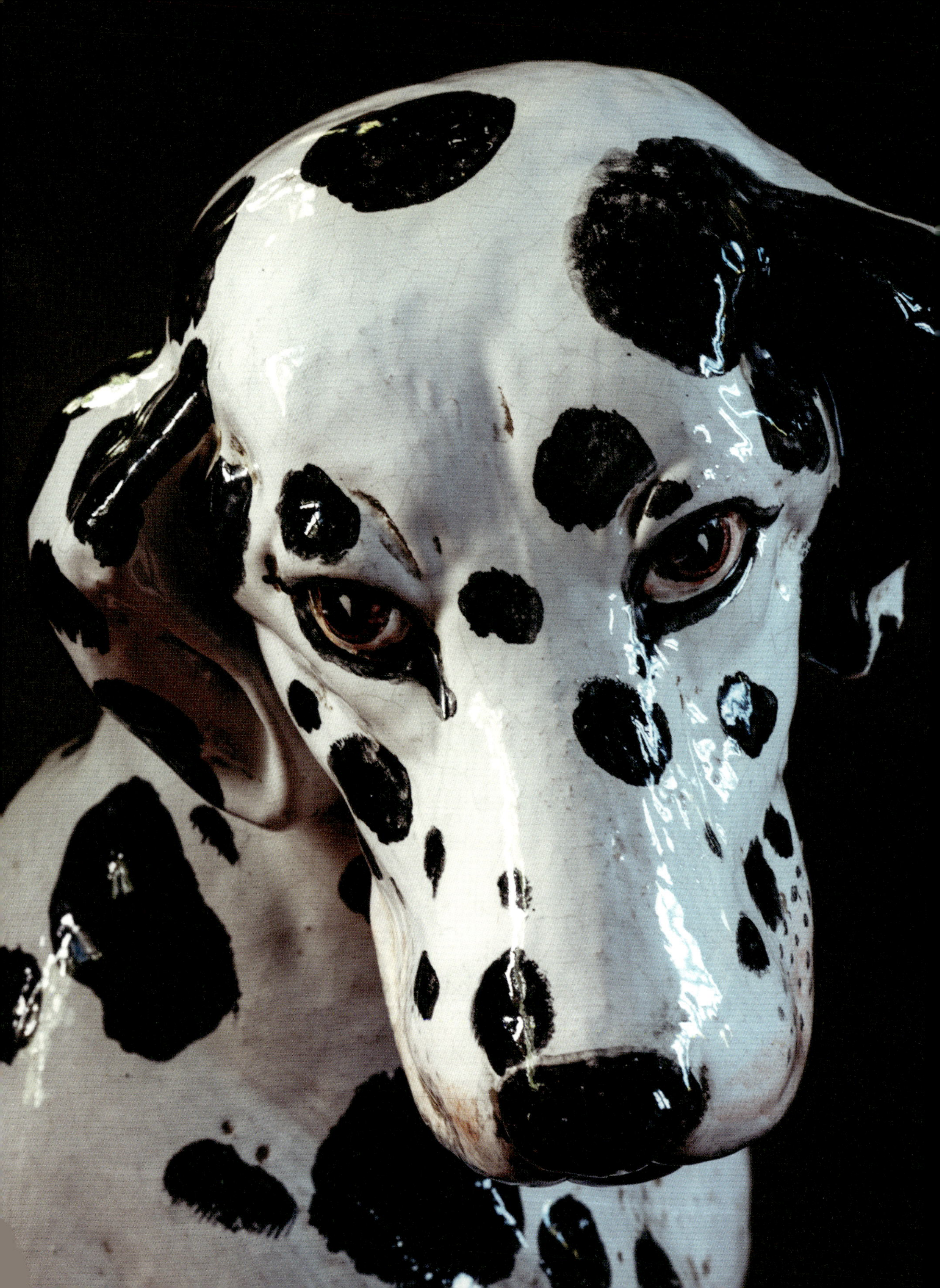

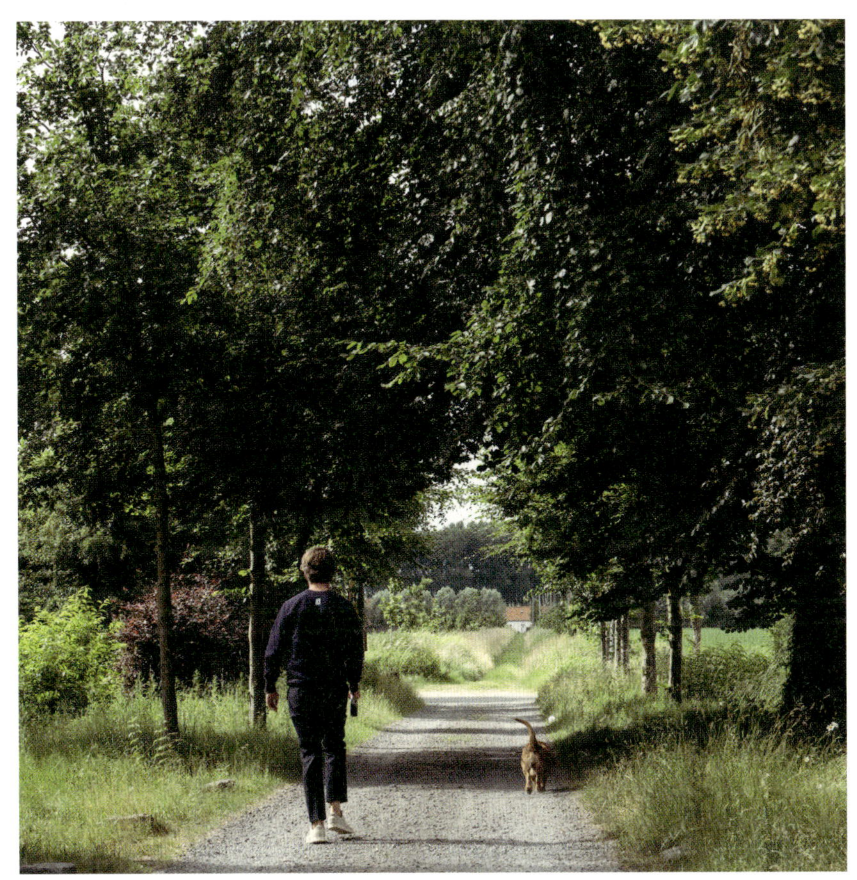

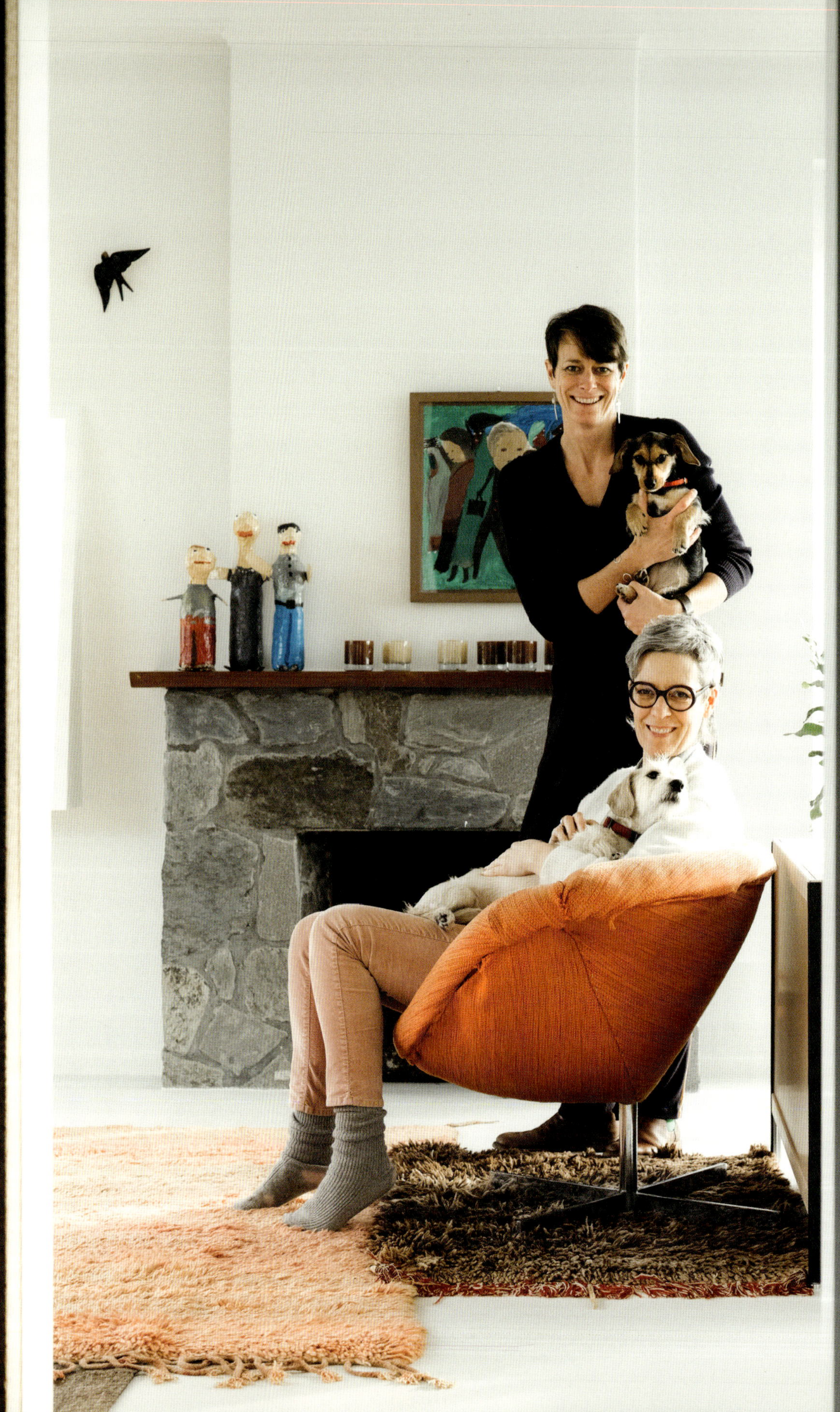

Adopt, don't shop. Kim and Sofie strongly believe in rehoming animals from the rescue centre. In fact, they adopted most of their pets from there. The two dogs, who get on like a house on fire, and the abandoned alley cat perfectly match their welcoming interior and active lifestyle. On weekdays they all share an apartment in the city. The oldest dog accompanies his caretakers to work. On the weekend, they all make the commute to their farm in the countryside, where the couple's dream project is gradually taking shape.

A dream project

Buying, renovating, and selling rundown houses, that
is what interior architect Kim Verbist does best. She is
currently restoring an old farm, with a home and two
sheds, surrounded by fields, in the countryside. Kim
describes it as 'the dream' which she shares with her
partner Sofie Van Waeyenberge. While Kim draws the
plans and makes interior design decisions, Sofie sets to
work. Kim is a dreamer, Sofie is all about action. They
complement each other beautifully. In the meantime,
they have transformed the dilapidated dwelling into
a warm and colourful cocoon. The interior is very
simple, with patinated furniture, ethnic accessories and
anonymous outsider art on the walls. Kim compares
their home to a caravan because it's so compact.
The large windows look out onto the sheds and the
fields. Nature invades the house, just like the sun, which
embraces the interior with its warm glow. It is a magical
place where the animals feel happy too. They run
in and out of the farmstead and play anywhere
they can. There are no valuable objects, and all the
furniture can take a hit.

Office dog

The adopted pets are part and parcel of the family.
And because they have separation anxiety, they make
the commute from the city to the countryside and back.
Seraphine, the oldest dog, even goes into the office.
'I left her home alone once. She howled so loudly that
the neighbours thought there was a baby in the house,'
Kim laughs. Taking your dog into work is the new
cool thing to do apparently because Seraphine now
shares the building with seven other animals. 'For now,
everything is going smoothly. They never fight, but
when they play, it's like a race course.' Seraphine is a
mix of a dachshund and a West Highland terrier. It's a
small hunting dog that is smart but stubborn. Terriers
are very independent, although this does definitely
not apply to the rescue dog that Kim decided on six
years ago, after having gone through 14,000 pics
online. 'She was already quite old when I adopted her.
Seraphine was stuck in the rehoming centre with her
puppy and her little brother. Unfortunately, they had
already been reserved. Otherwise, I would have taken in
all three of them,' Kim confesses, who strongly believes
in adoption. 'Many owners kick out their dog when their
family situation changes. Often, the problem is not the
animal. You just need to take the time to choose a pet
whose personality matches yours.'

A puppy with a cat bell

Odile, the four-month-old puppy, a mix of a dachshund
and a jack russel terrier, is also a rescue. You don't often
see puppies in the pound, but I unexpectedly had the
opportunity to adopt one,' says Kim about the pooch
that Sofie also loves with a passion. 'I didn't grow up
with pets, and I definitely am not a dog person. But I
love Odile because she is quite a character. Like most
dachshunds, she is very stubborn,' Sofie explains. 'And
she gets into so much trouble. We always know where
she is because of the bell around her neck.' She likes
to cuddle up close to Seraphine to sleep. Kim and Sofie
worry about how Odile will cope when her buddy is no
longer there. Seraphine's cancer has come back and is
incurable. Kim has already lost many rescue dogs, and
yet she always saves another one. She just can't help
herself, she loves animals too much.

Cat with an arched back

A few years ago they found a cat, called Poes in a
box on the street. 'We think her owner threw her out
of the car window.' After she recovered, she stayed
on. She also commutes, with the dogs. She likes
Seraphine but hates Odile with a vengeance. When
the pup approaches her, she hisses and arches her
back. The dogs want to spend most of their time in
the living room, which is why Poes has claimed the
bedrooms as her own. She goes out now and then, into
the fields, to chase mice. During our visit, she accepts
to be petted. Kim likes the tranquillity that emanates
from the pets. 'They teach me to relax,' she says, with
Odile on her arm. But the peace and quiet ends abruptly
when the puppy spots a partridge. She manages to free
herself and runs off, chasing the bird.

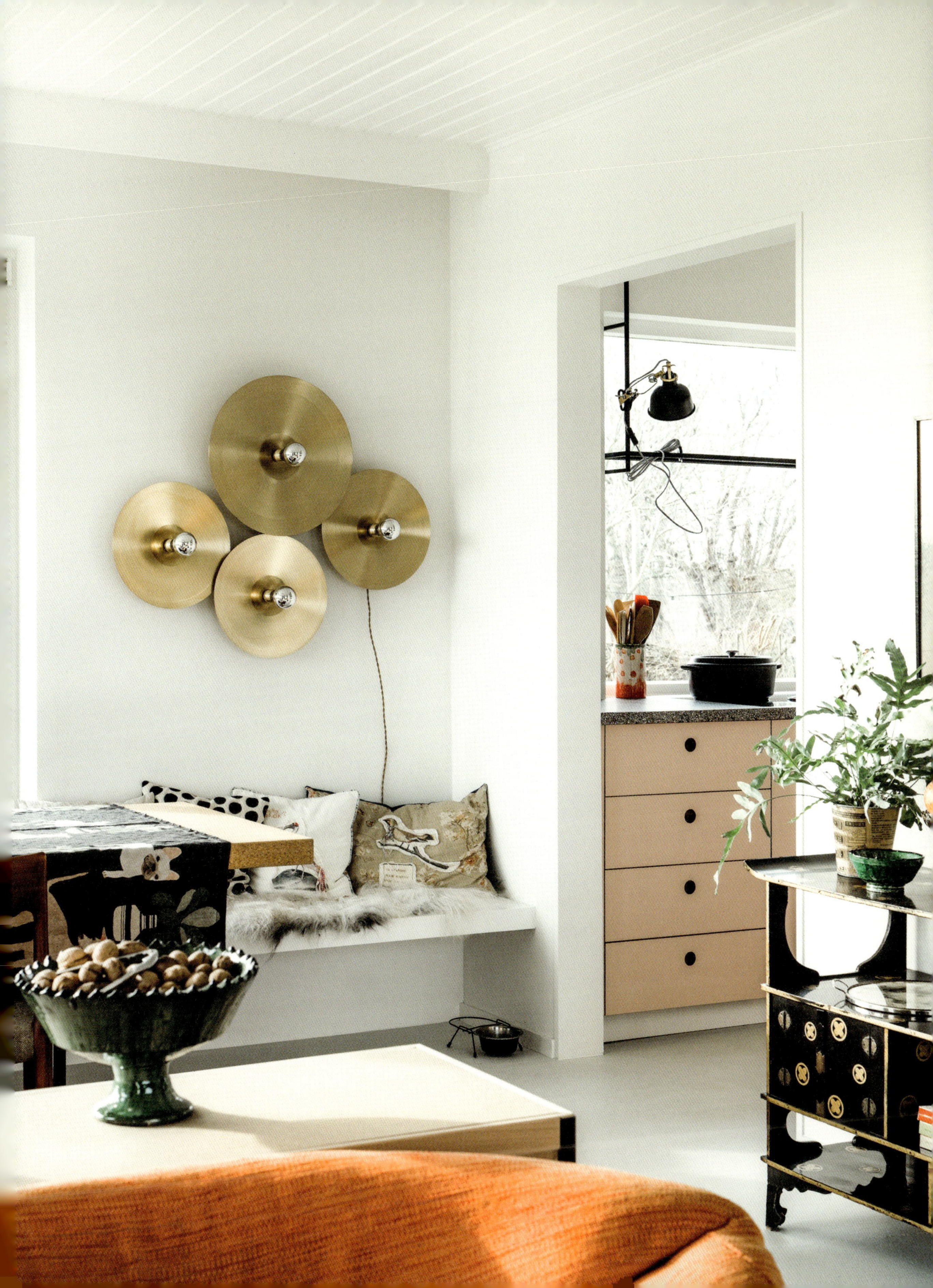

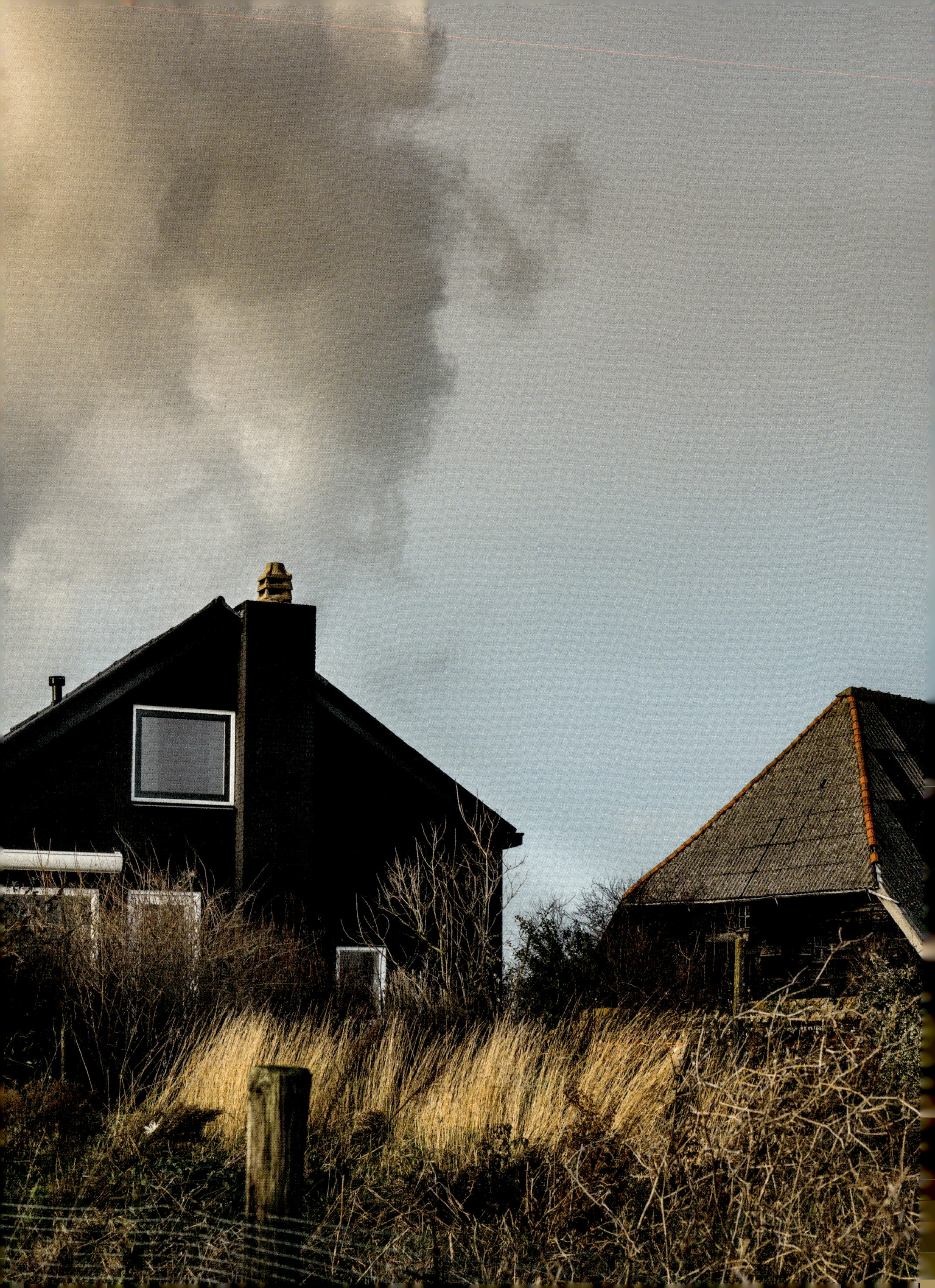

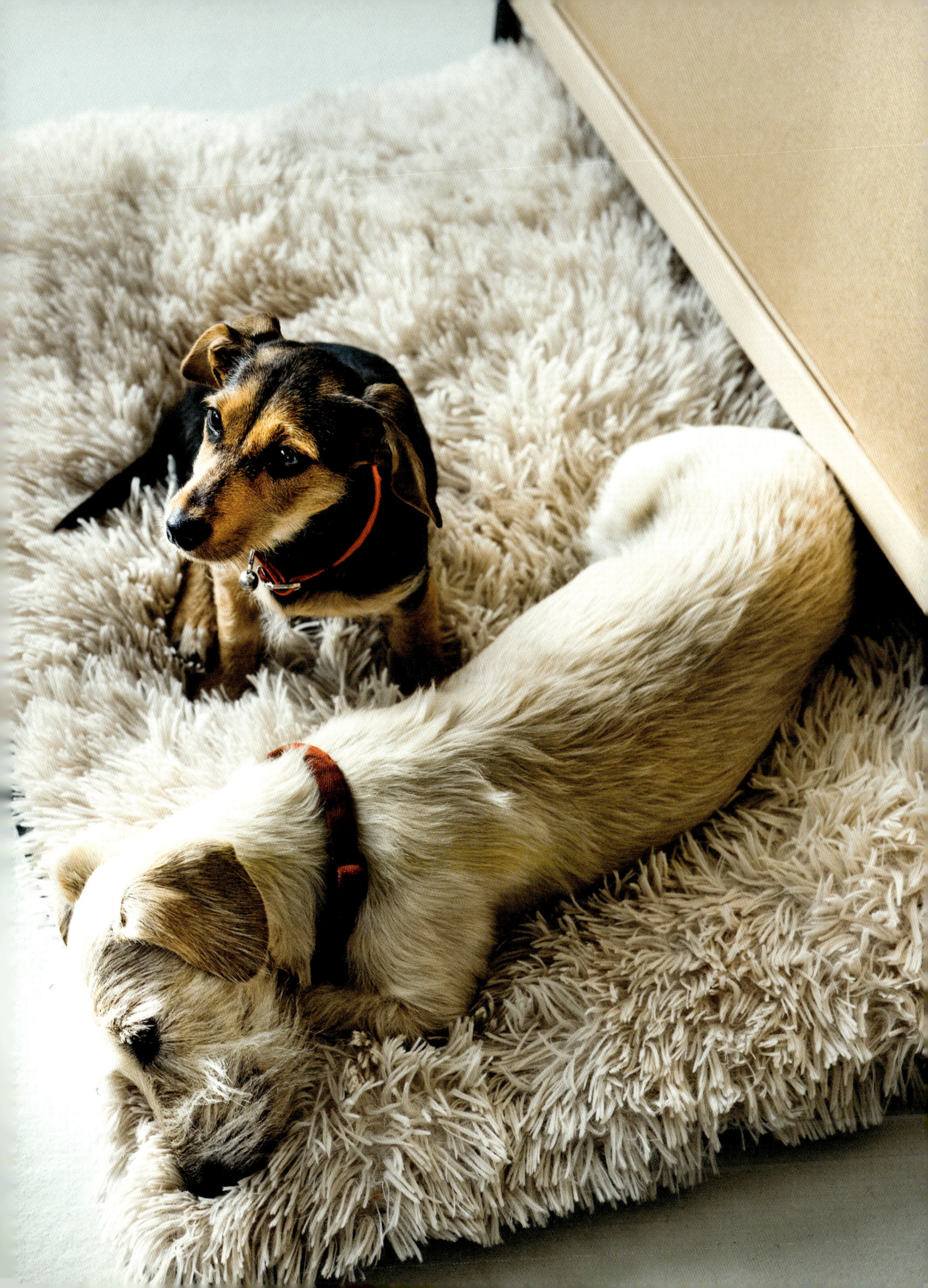

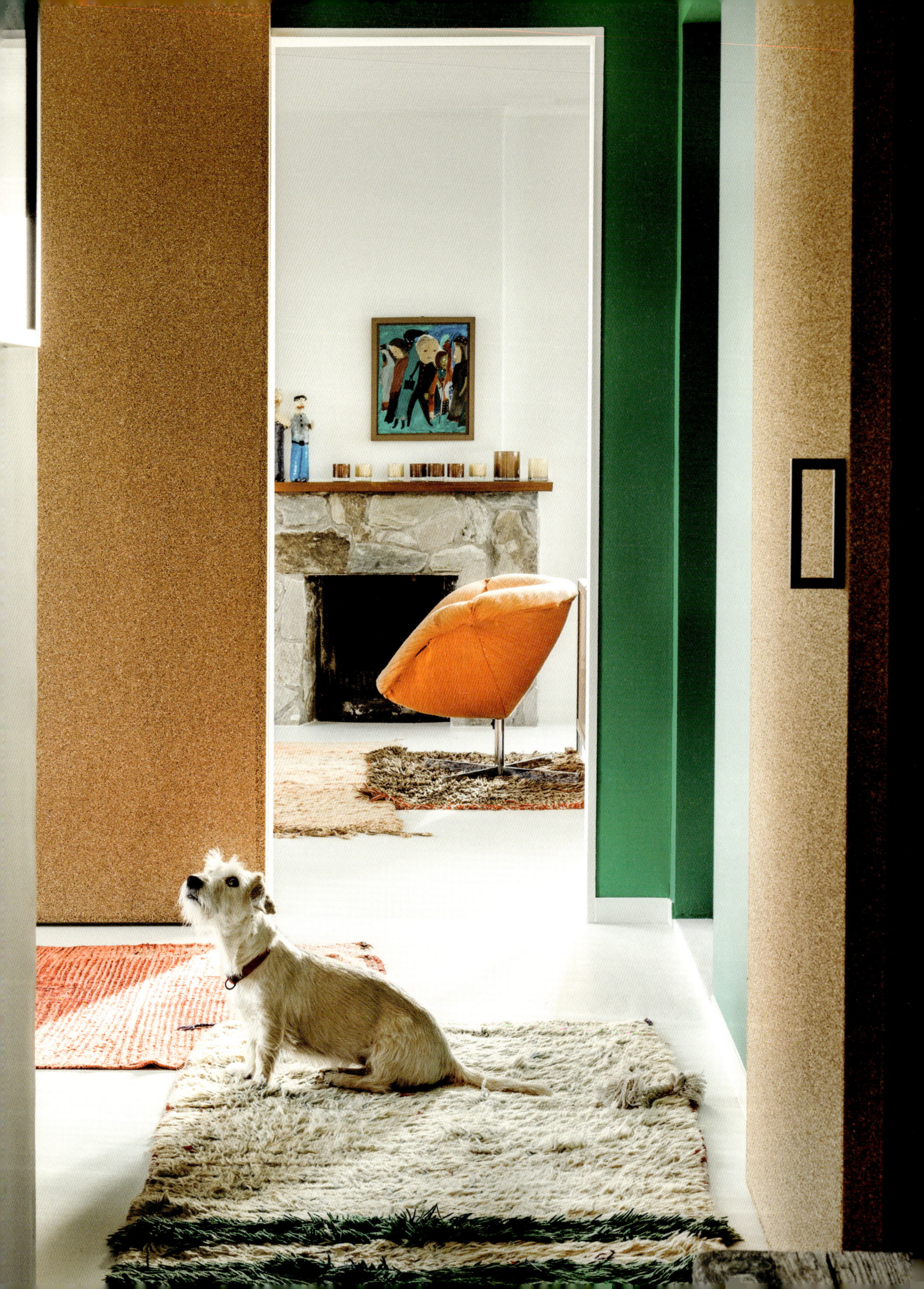

The farmstead has been renovated and decorated with simple,
secondhand furniture and outsider art on the walls.

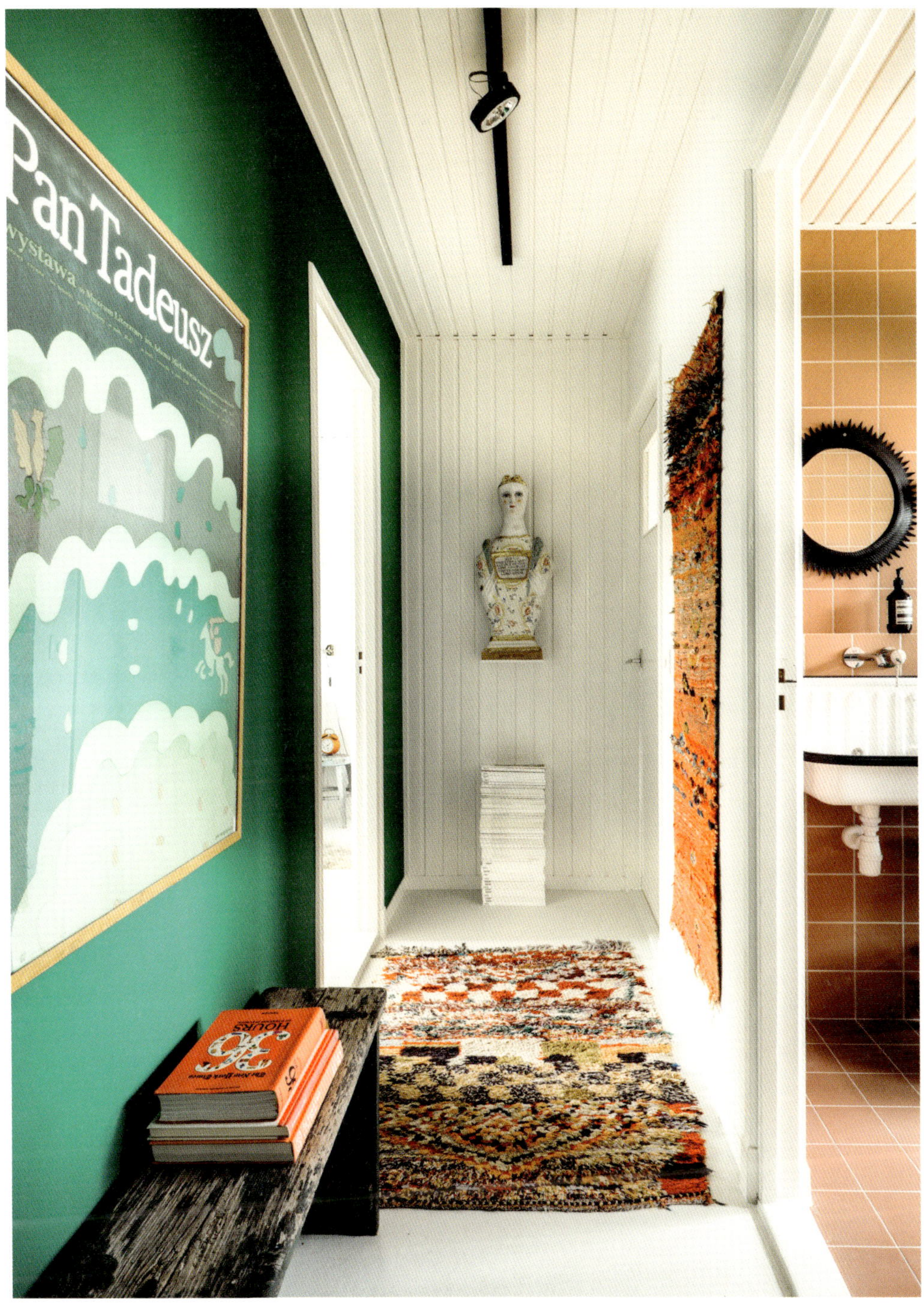

Kim and Sofie strongly believe in rehoming pets from the
rescue centre, like their two dogs. They found their cat in a
box on the street.

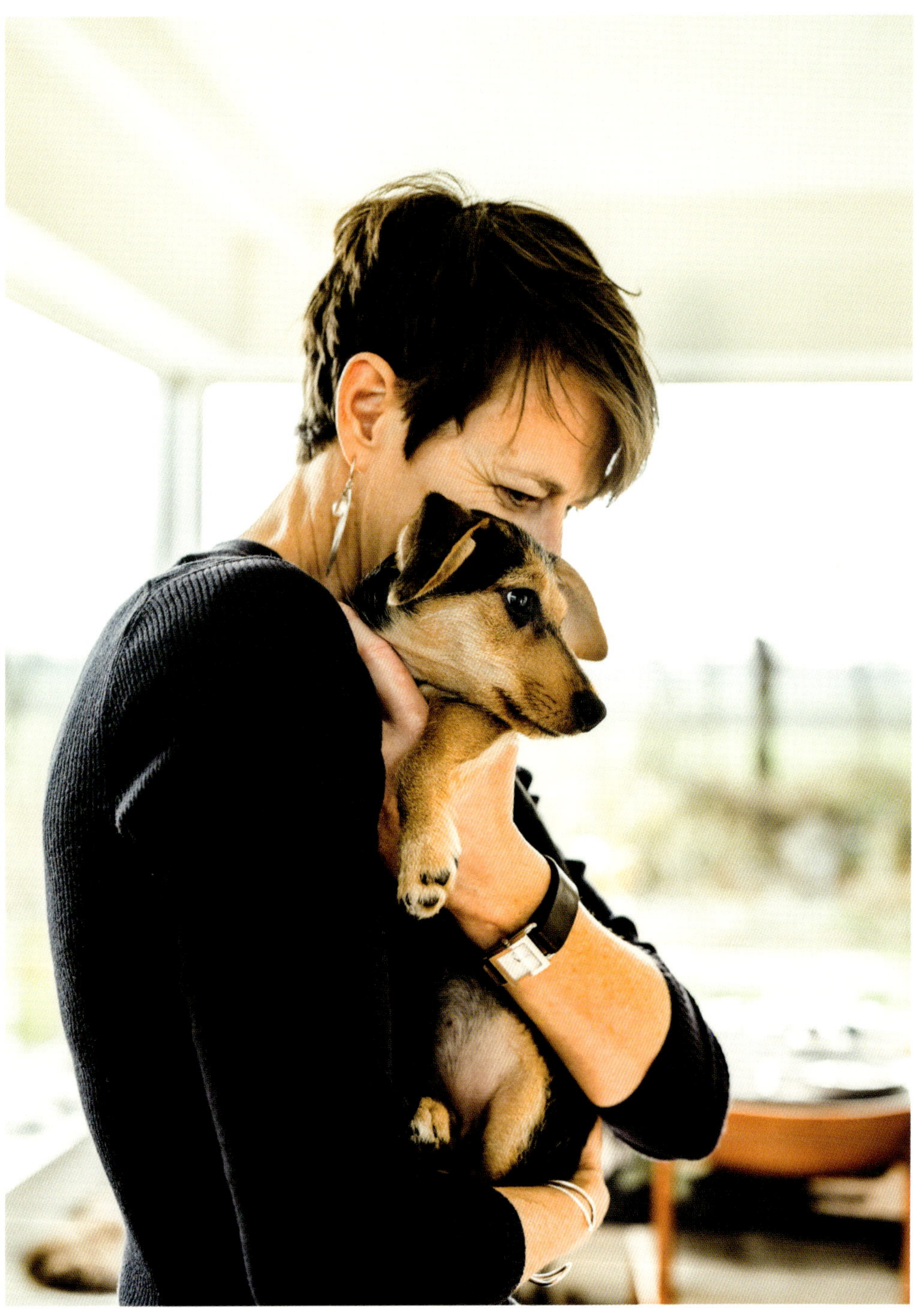

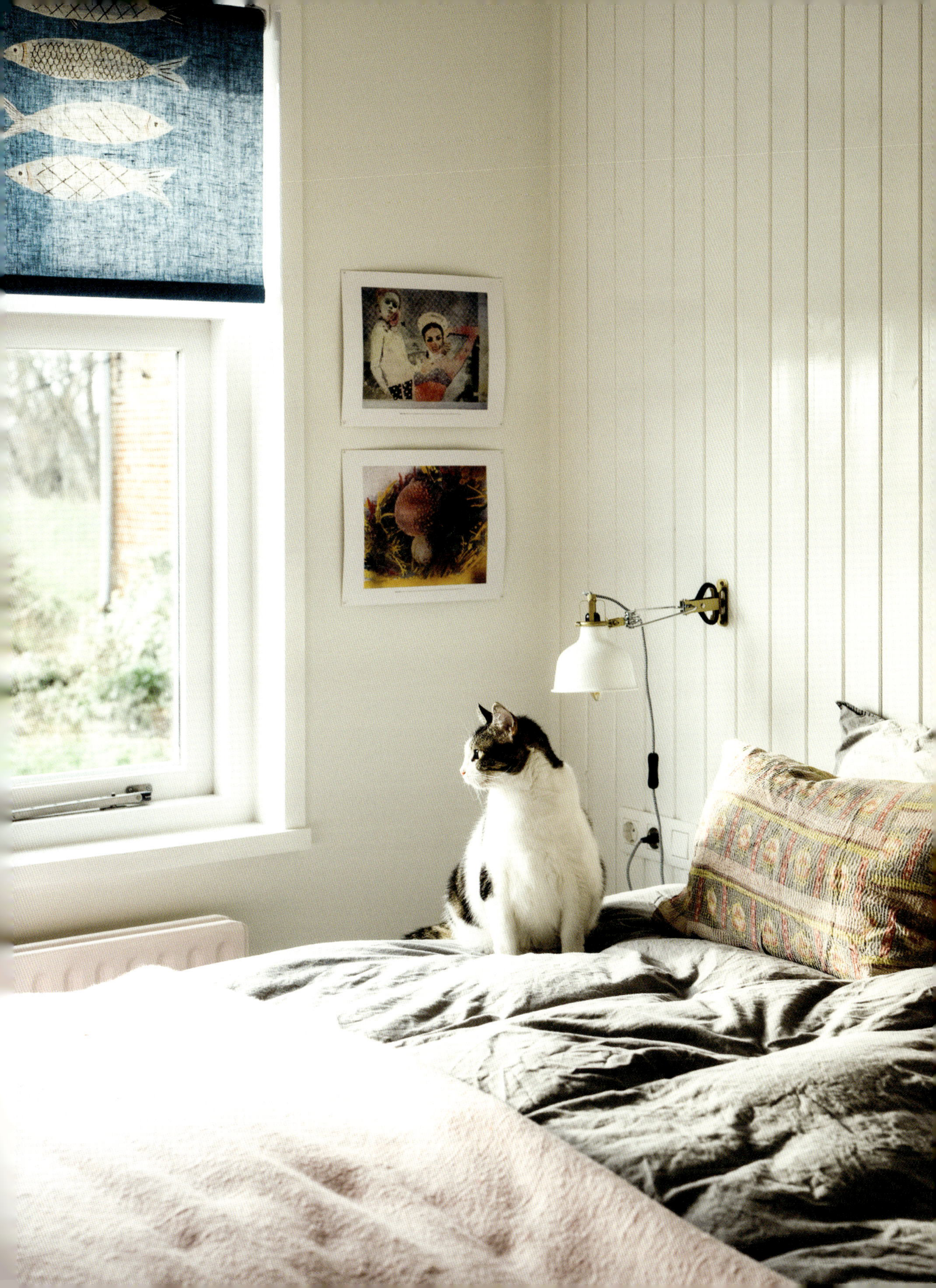

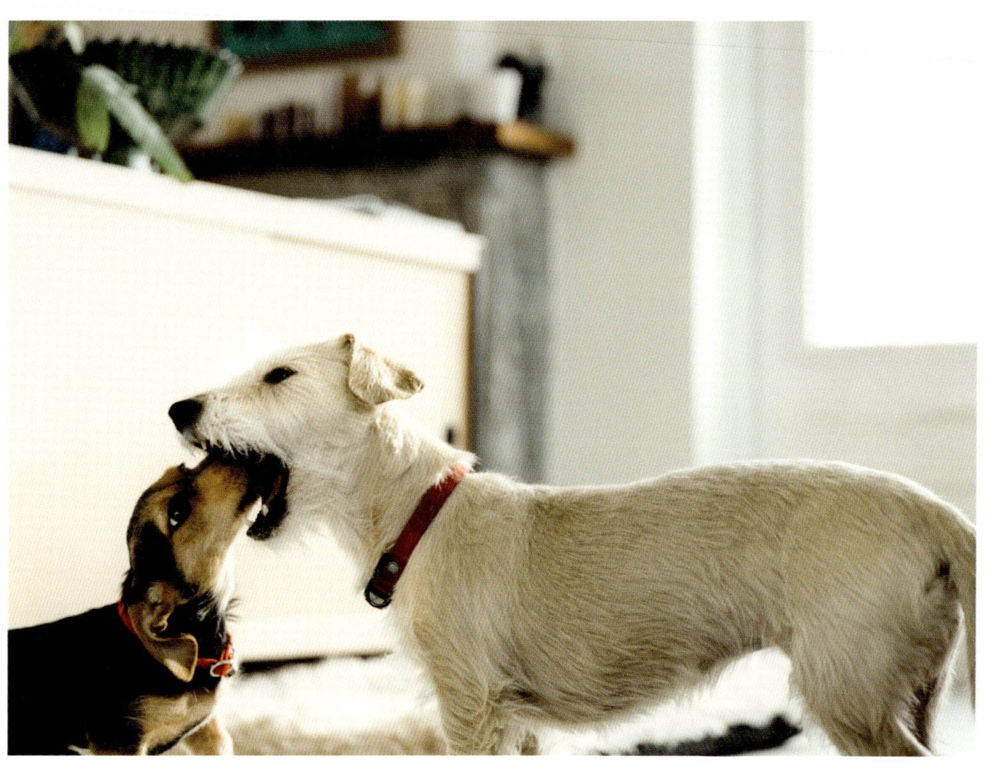

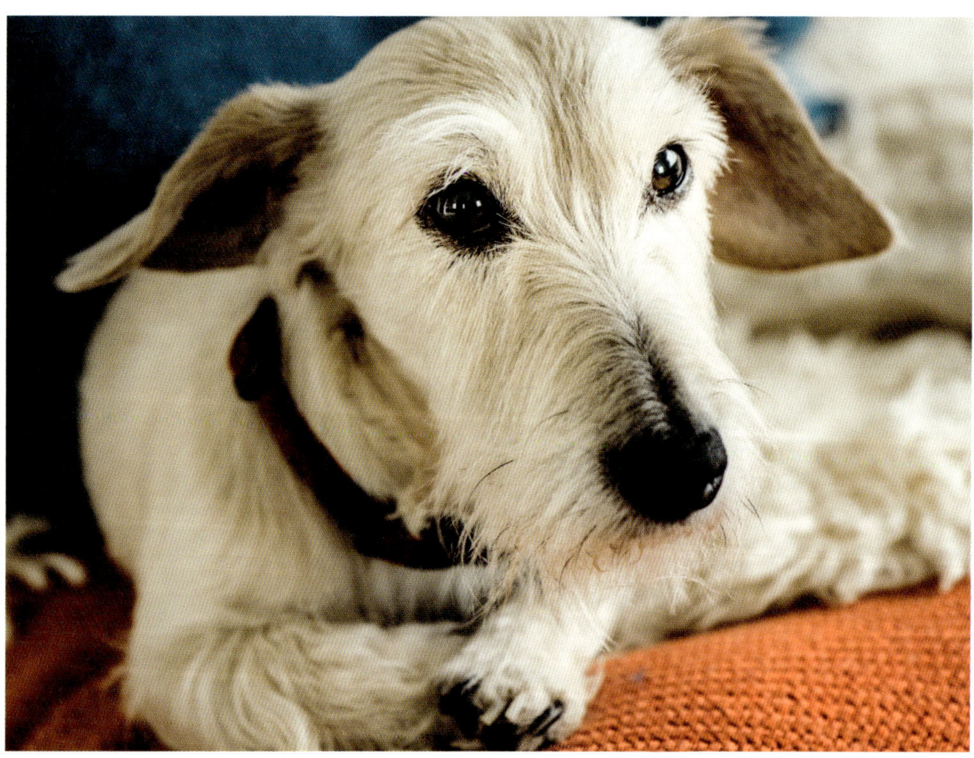

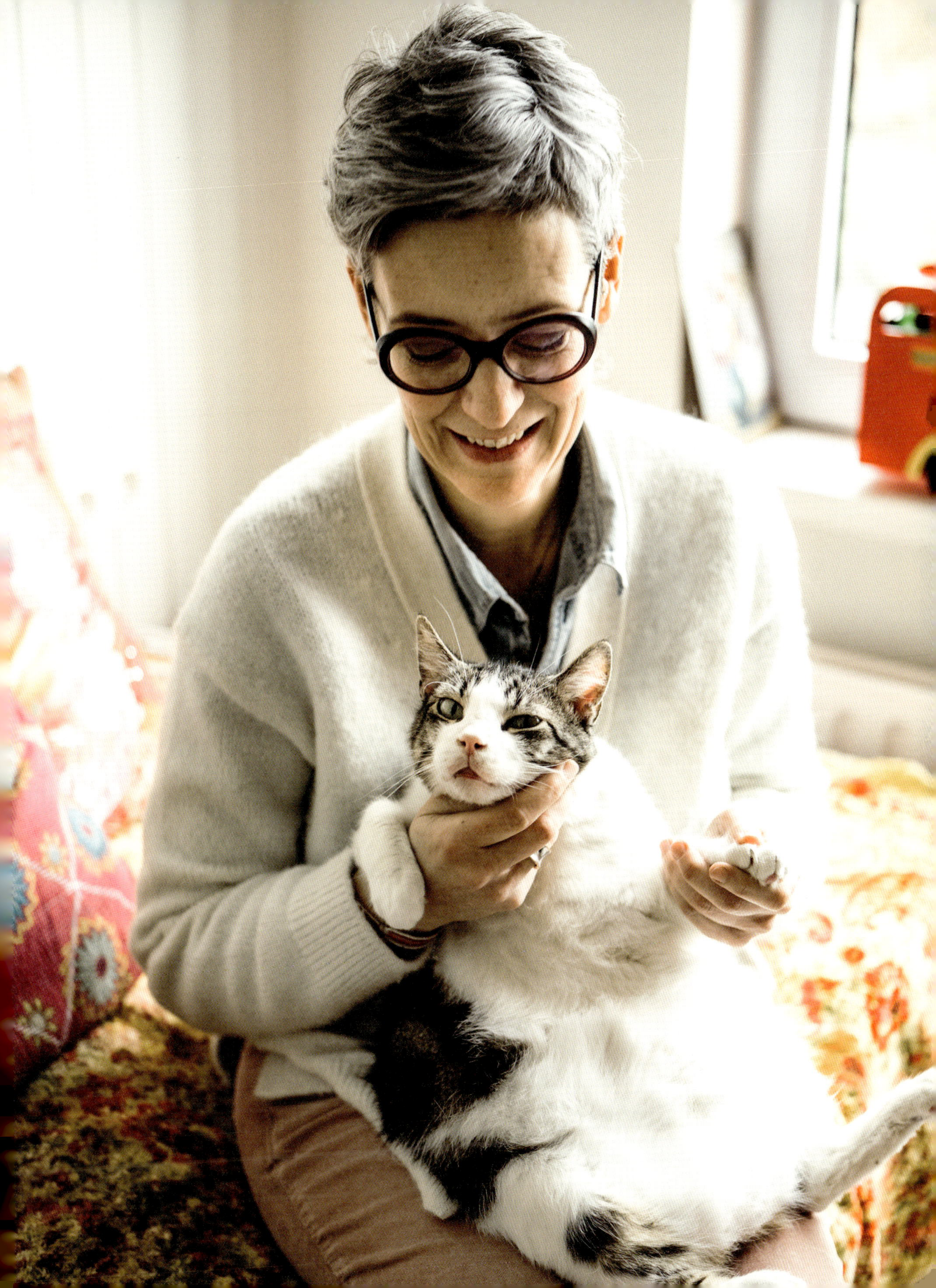

The large windows look out onto the barns and the surrounding fields. Nature finds its way into the house, just like the sunlight.

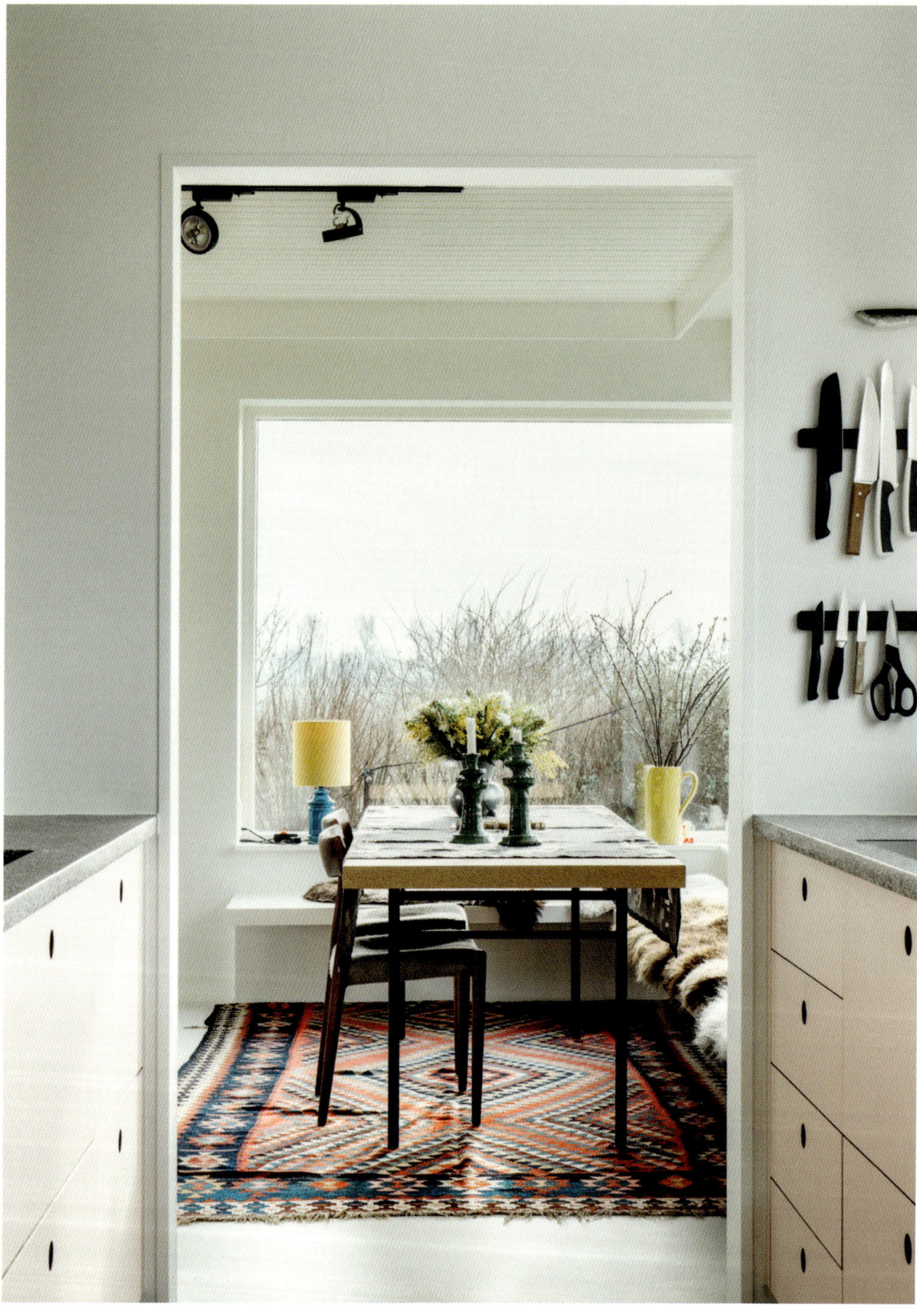

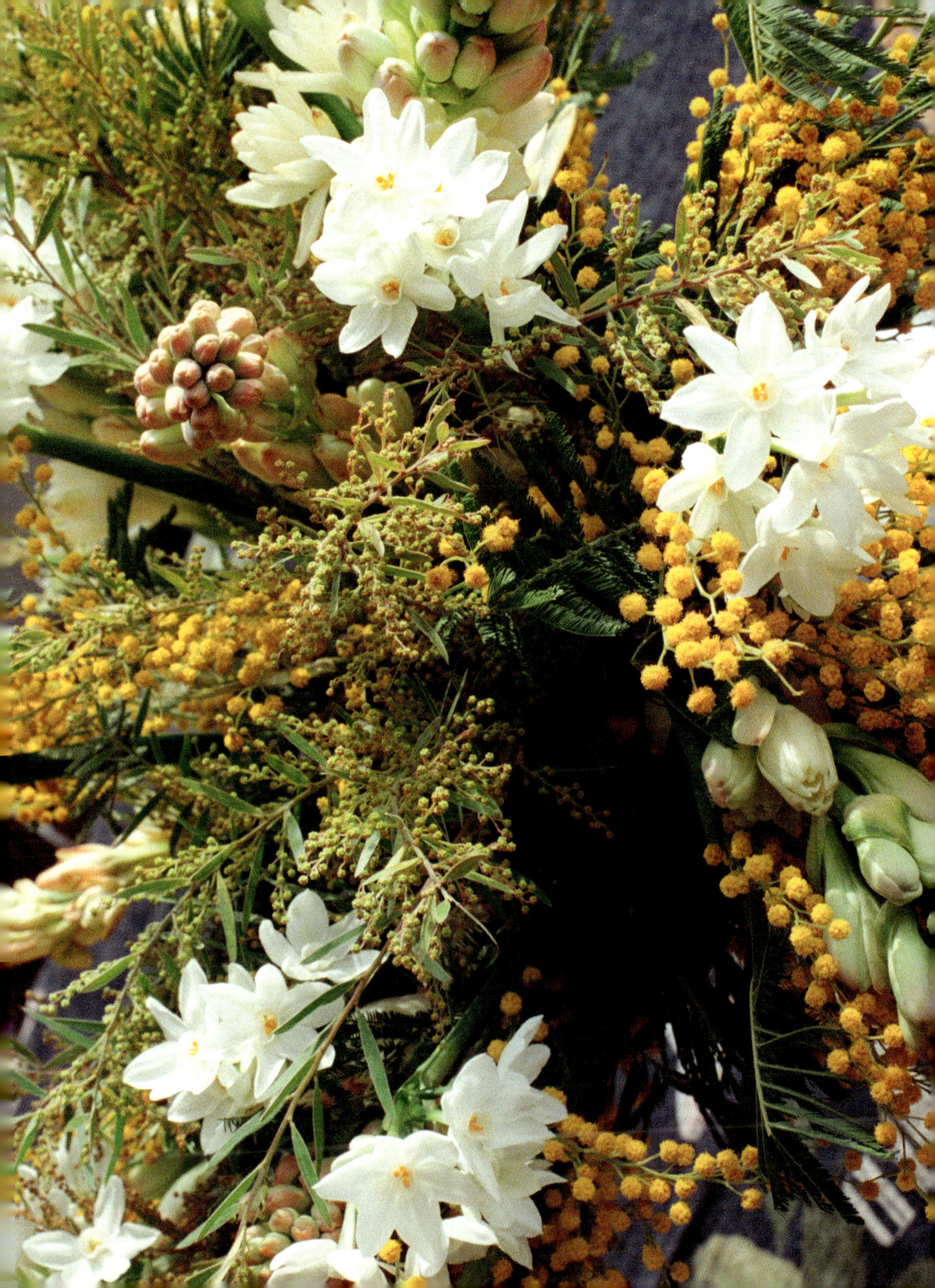

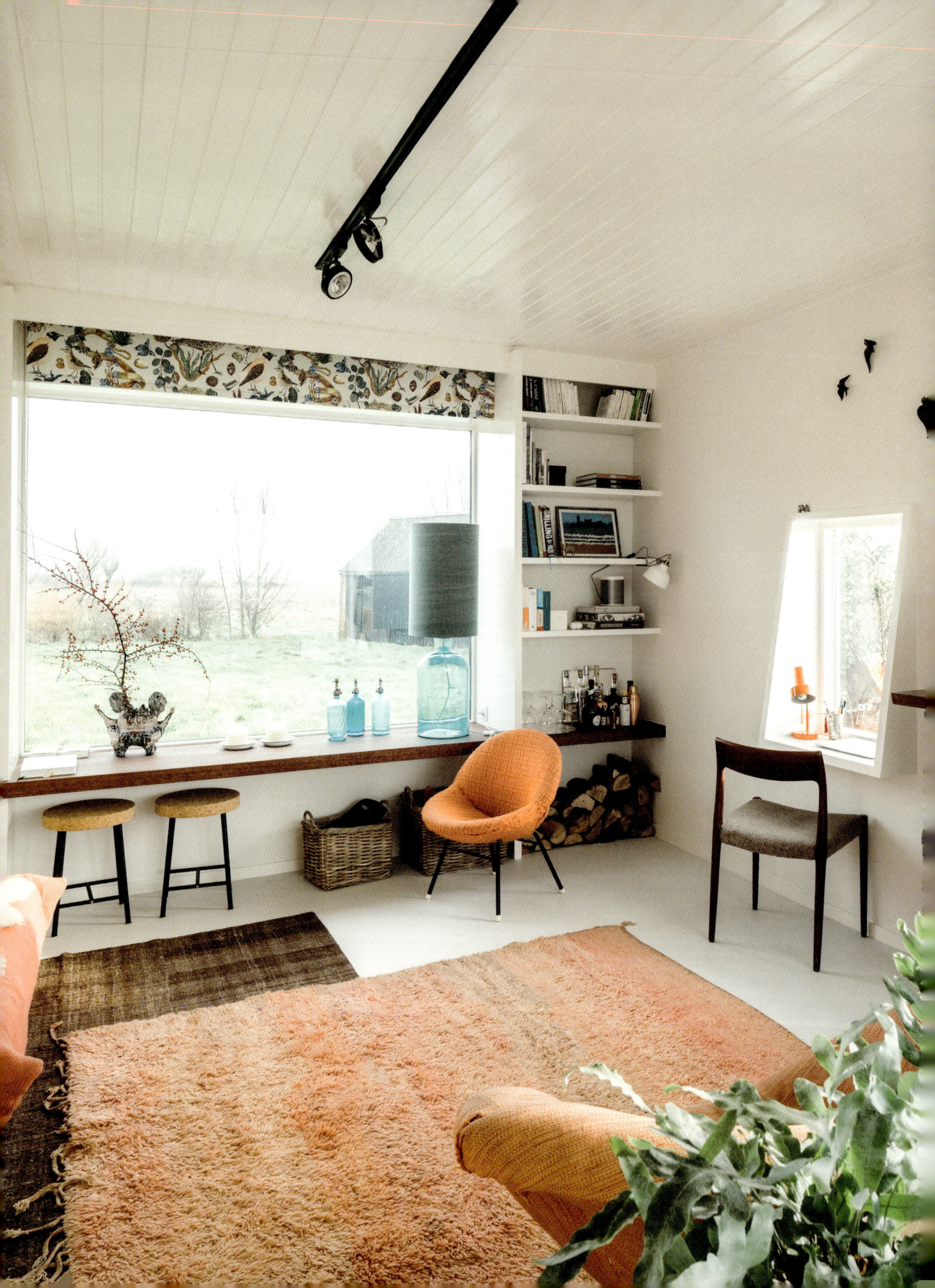

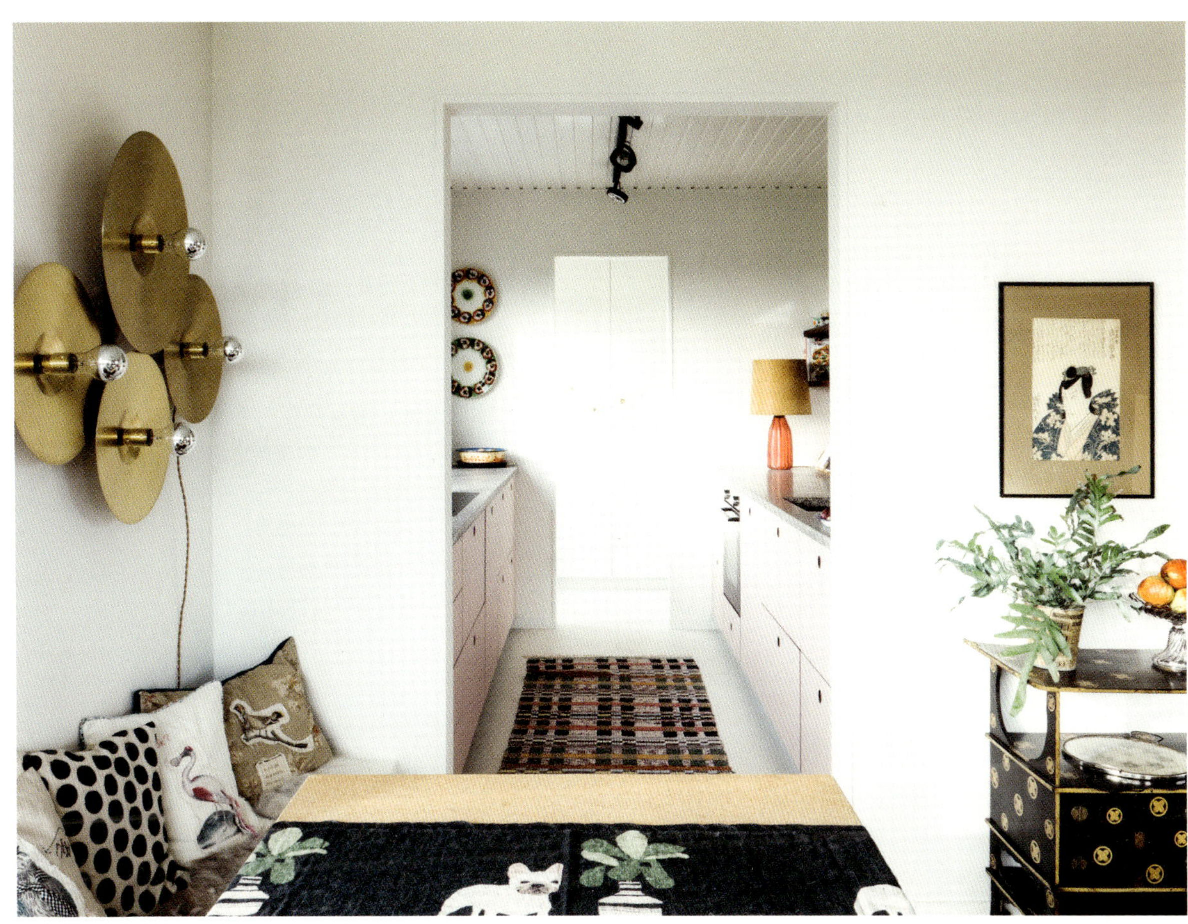

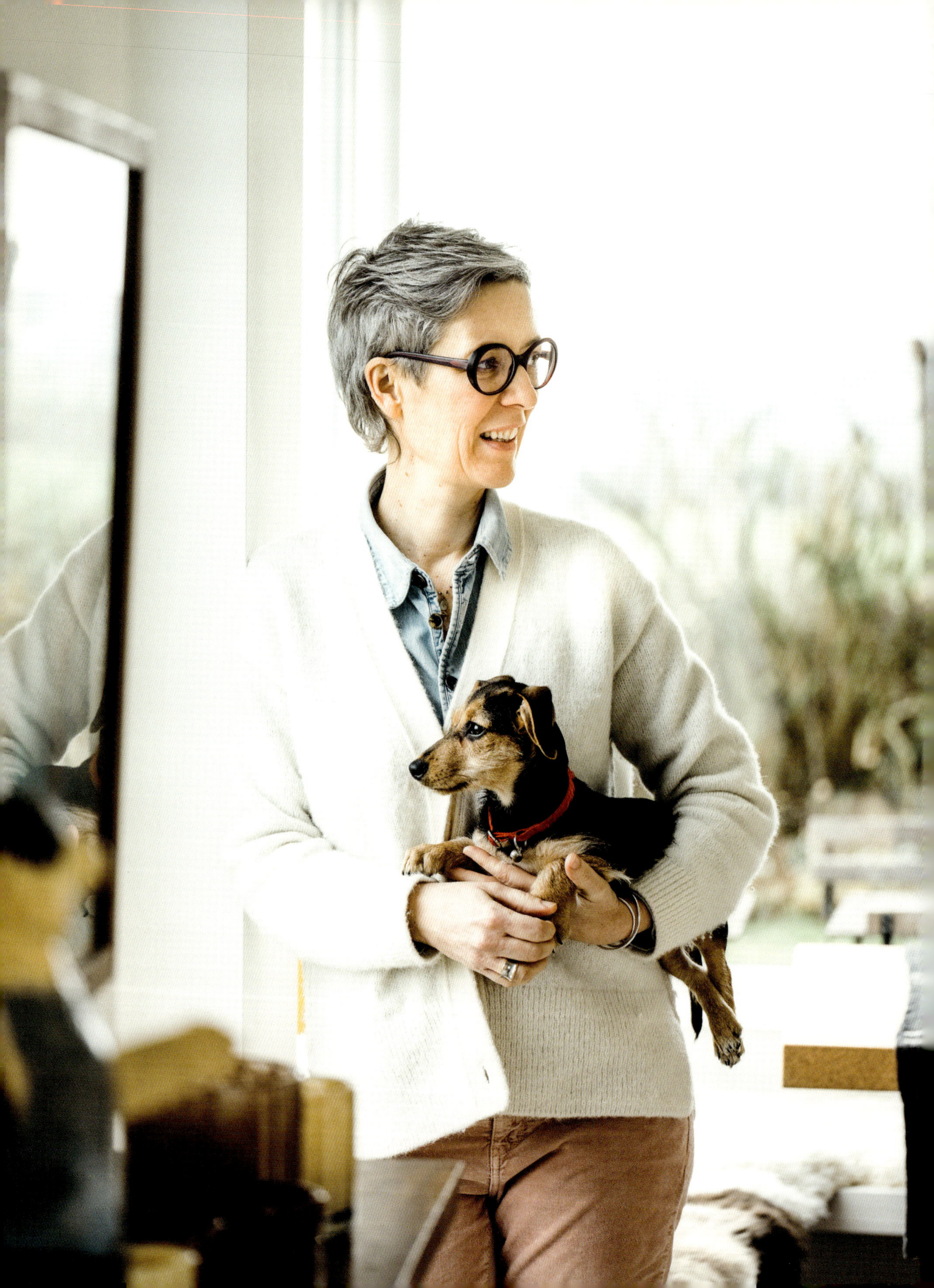

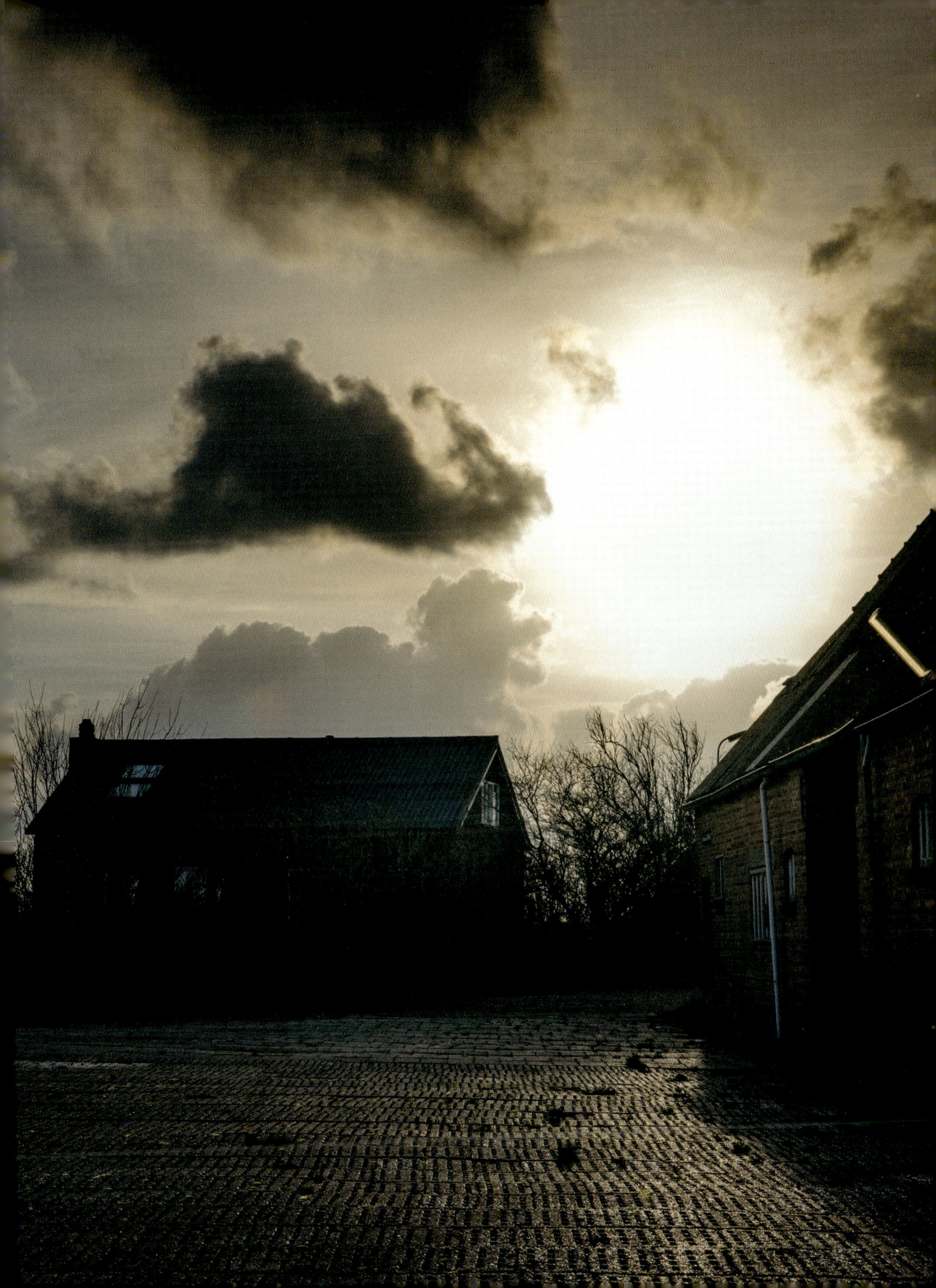

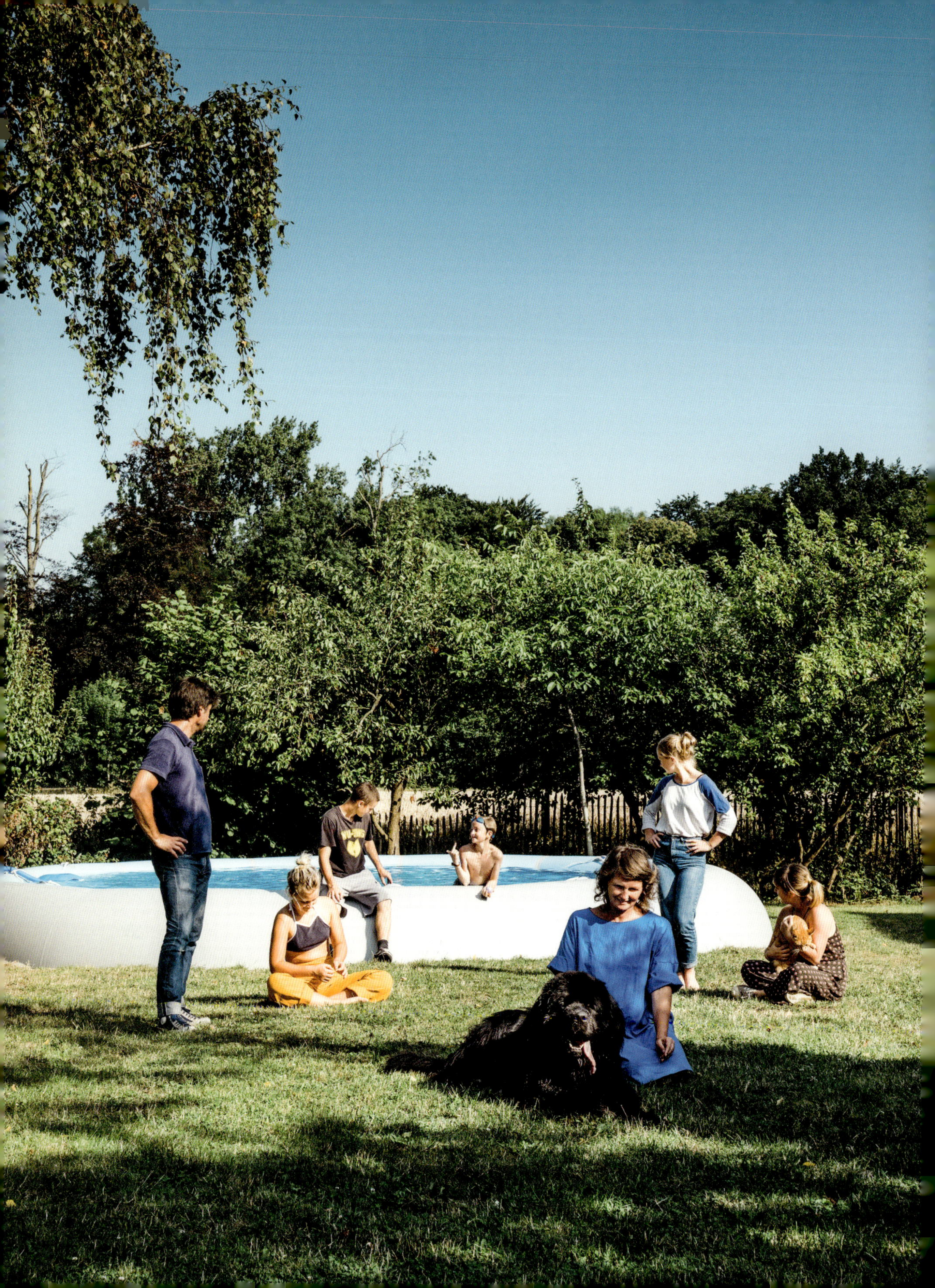

In many ways, this old farm, with its pink roof, in a golden cornfield resembles Pippi Longstocking's home, Villa Villekulla. This romantic setting is the perfect home for Annick and Frank, their six children, and their pets. The family left the city ten years ago, moving to the country, in search of some peace and quiet, more space and healthy outdoor air. Annick likes macramé, Frank is a helicopter pilot, and in his free time, he likes to work in their home, which is continually evolving.

A warm welcome

If we learnt one thing while compiling this book, it's that you should always be prepared for wild greetings and never wear your Sunday best. As we unload the car outside the house of Annick Geers and Frank Oosterlynck, a large, black dog jumps up against us. 'Mojo, down,' Frank yells, slightly embarrassed. 'What a welcome,' Annick laughs. 'Mojo loves it when we have visitors.' And that is how our interview begins. The home of Annick and Frank is cosy and ever so slightly chaotic.

A lifesaver

Mojo looks on with interest, as the six children Babette (21 years), Zsa-Zsa (19 years), Feigy (17 years), Lolita (15 years), Mowgli (12 years) and Senne (3 years) play in and around the pool. 'He'll never jump in although you would expect him to,' says Frank. Mojo is a Newfoundlander or Newfie as he is sometimes called. His breed comes from the island of Newfoundland in Canada, where it helps fishermen drag the nets out of the water and saves people from drowning. These dogs are eager to learn and loyal, and their webbed feet help them immensely. Annick thought he would make the perfect friend for Frank, who works as a helicopter pilot. Mojo is very gentle and a real family pet.

A large home, a large dog

The couple has always had dogs. Before Mojo, they had a border collie named Nifty. The small Scottish brown and white shepherd was better suited to their previous, smaller home in the city. Border collies are very energetic, and as he was unable to expend all his energy there, the family decided to move to the country. When Nifty became old and blind, he was joined by Mojo. 'Our rule is, the larger the home, the larger the dog,' Annick says. And the scale of their house does truly match that of the dog. The renovated farm they live in was designed by architects De Vylder Vinck Taillieu. The studio always strives to create homes that feel 'unfinished', which is in tune with the rough aesthetic that Annick and Frank love so much. They describe their home as a work in progress because Frank is still working on it. They preserved the façade and as many of the original elements as is, to retain the soul of the property. The ornament on the roof was painted a striking pink. They added new joinery, and the roof was opened up to emphasise the connection with nature. The couple loves living in the country, which is why they aim to integrate their farm as much as possible in the surroundings.

Visiting animals

During our visit, the children run in and out of the home, with the dog and the cat hot on their heels. Senne, their youngest son, loves to chase their ginger cat Ouistiti out of the house, who prefers to spend his time purring on the bed. He turned up one day, as a kitten, and never left. 'That's what happens,' Annick says. 'When people no longer want their pets, they just dump them in nature. It's really bizarre, and I actually find it's shameful. Our pond is full of abandoned frogs.' In addition to the cat and the frogs, they also have plenty of other curious visitors, like a fox, who ate all their chickens. Frank had built a fifties-style coop for them, after a design from a book called 'Reinventing The Chicken Coop' by the American architects Matthew Wolpe and Kevin McElroy. The remaining chickens and cockerel were soon driven out by a bunch of pigeons which now occupy the coop. The chickens sought refuge on the lawn and in the hedge, where they lay their eggs. Once Annick even found eggs in a T-shirt drawer, after they managed to invade their bedroom covertly.

Macramé all the way

Annick stresses that the birds do not enter the house or her atelier, which is located in an old barn next to the house. She creates plant hangers, lampshades, hammocks, beach chairs, curtains and handbags in macramé under her own label, Triconick. This type of thread work was also hugely popular in the seventies, the prevalent style throughout the dwelling. Annick regularly scours antiques markets, vintage shops and jumble sales in search of vintage design treasures, which she sometimes repaints or covers with a new fabric. The annex looks spectacular as it is bisected by a vertical window and mirror. The architects named it 'Matta' after the American artist Gordon Matta-Clark, who sawed houses in two. The workshop looks just as unfinished as the abode. Although the family loves the country, Annick does not exclude that they will move back to the city one day. Their oldest daughter recently went back, taking her cat Poupinette with her. Who knows, perhaps this is the beginning of a new family adventure?

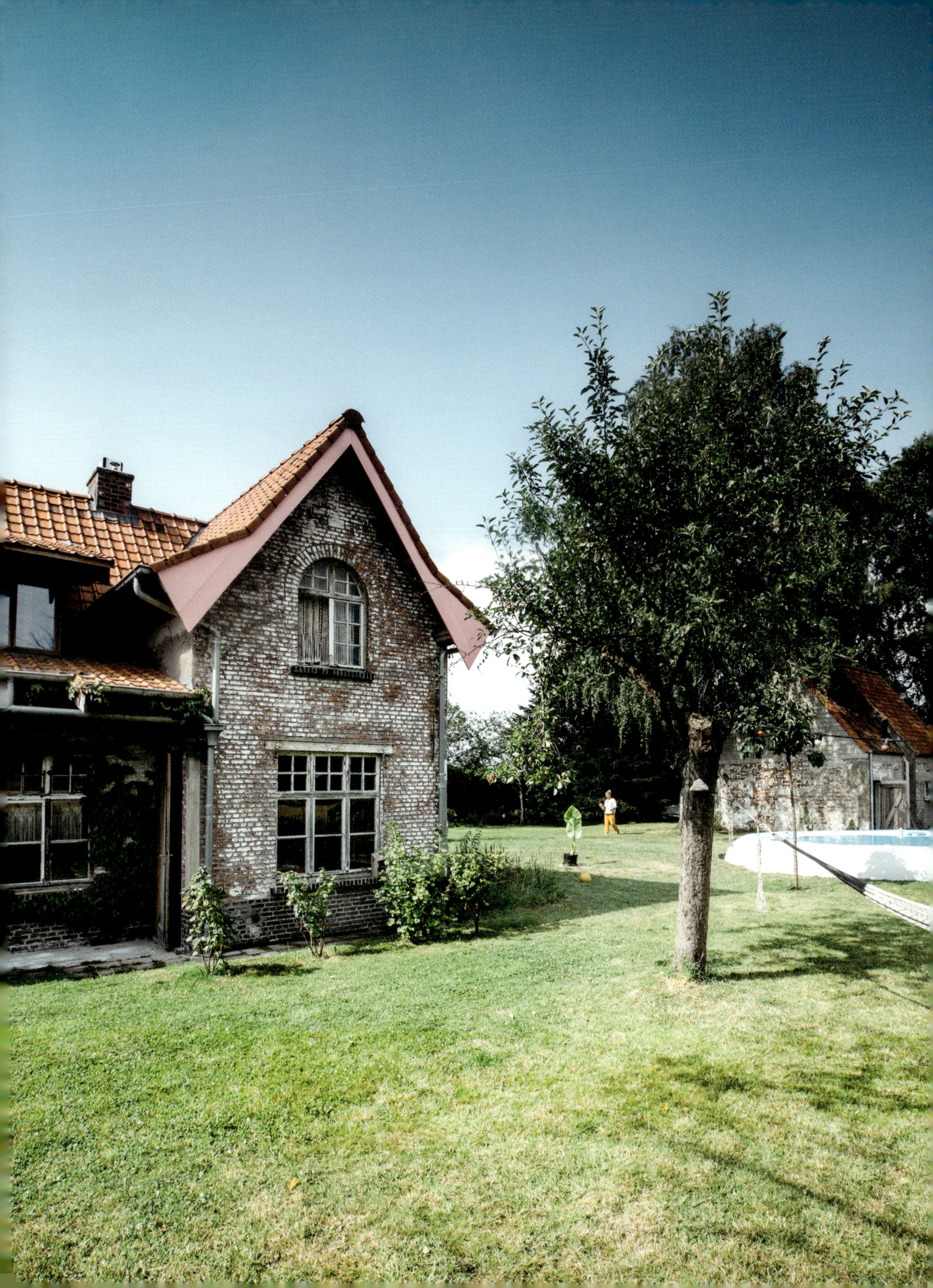

The country house of Annick and Frank looks quite idyllic in the
middle of the cornfield. It is renovated by architects De Vylder
Vinck Taillieu.

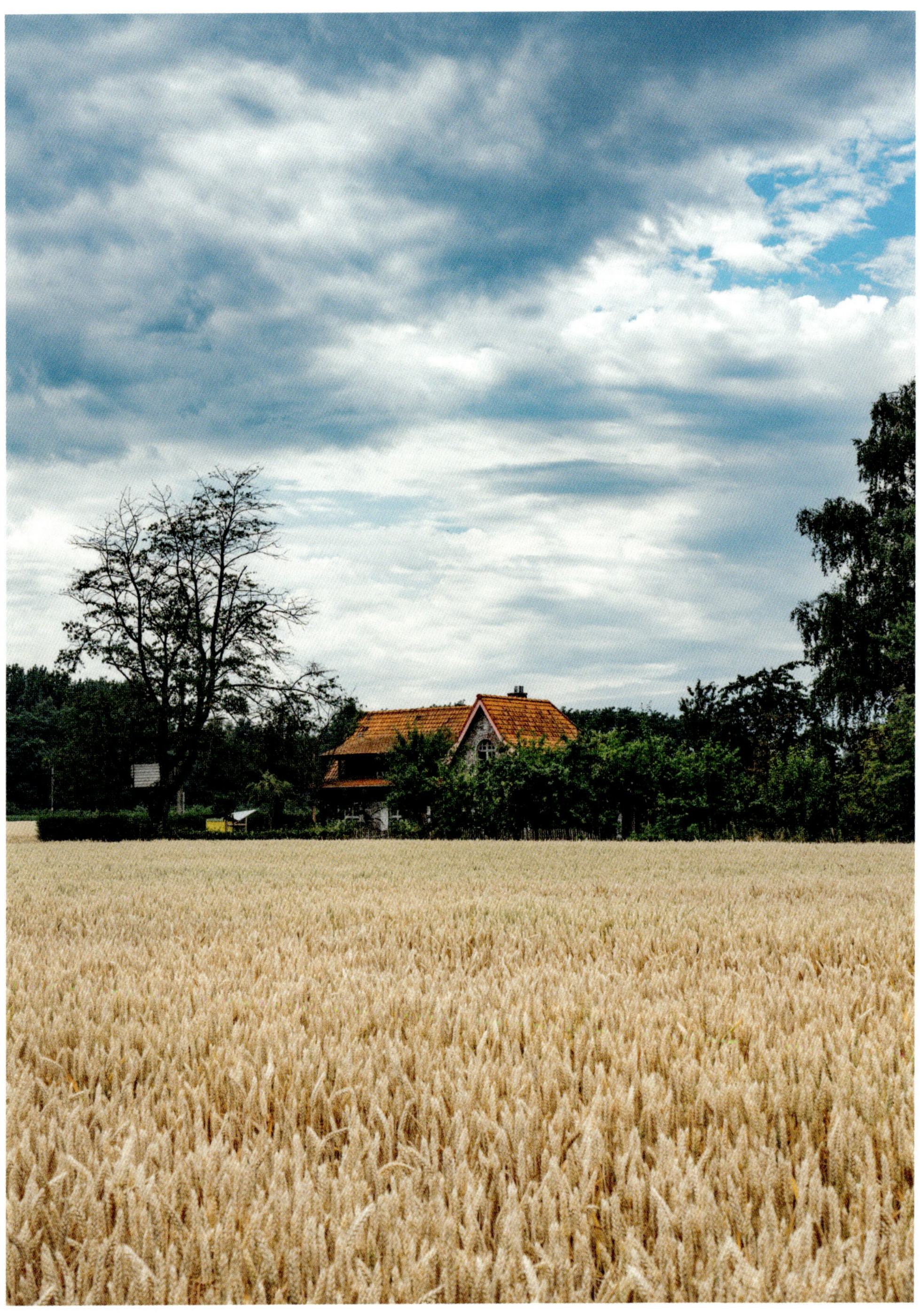

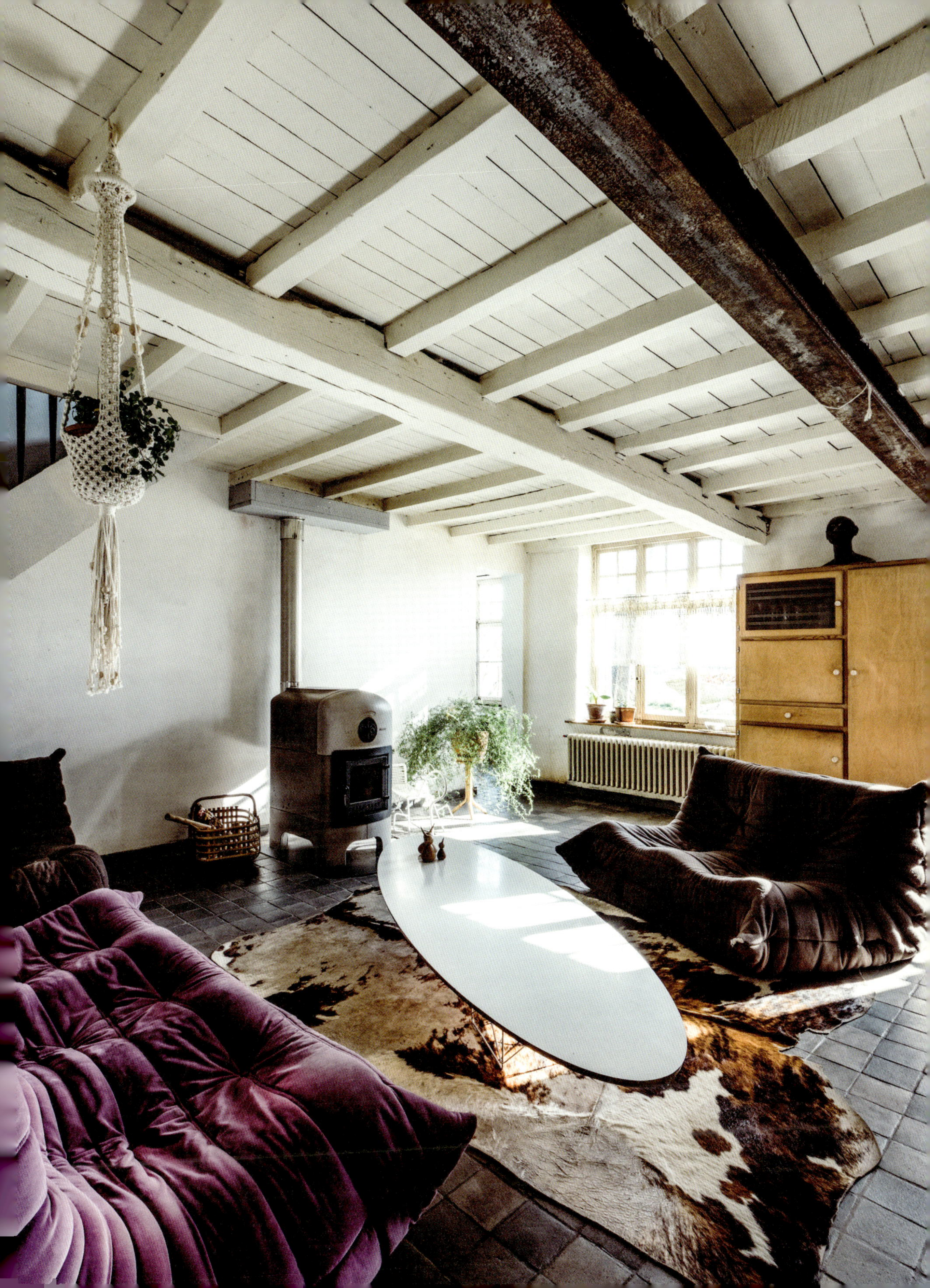

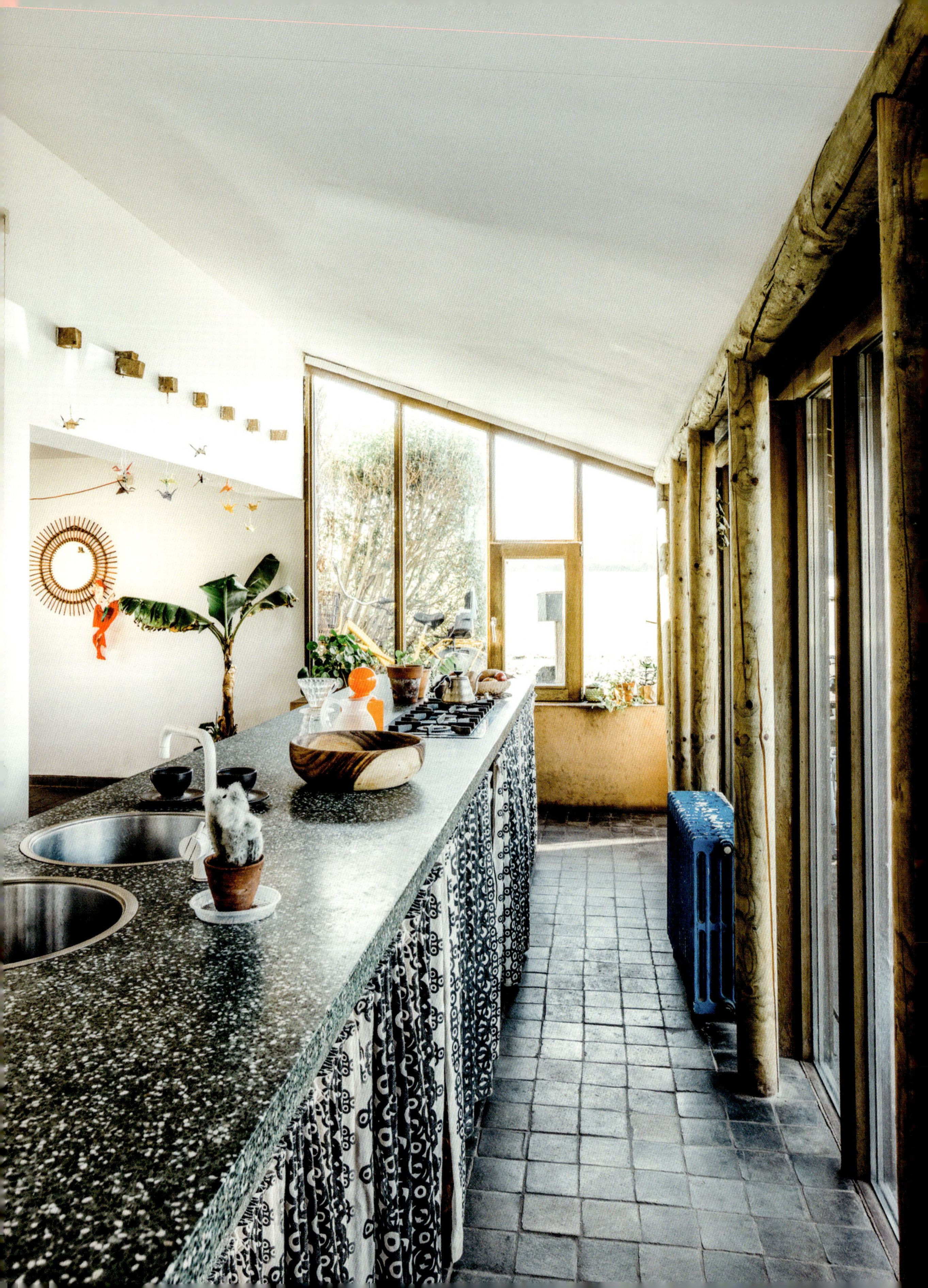

The interior is colourful and a mix of design classics and second-hand objects. The house continues to evolve and change because of all the work that Frank does in it.

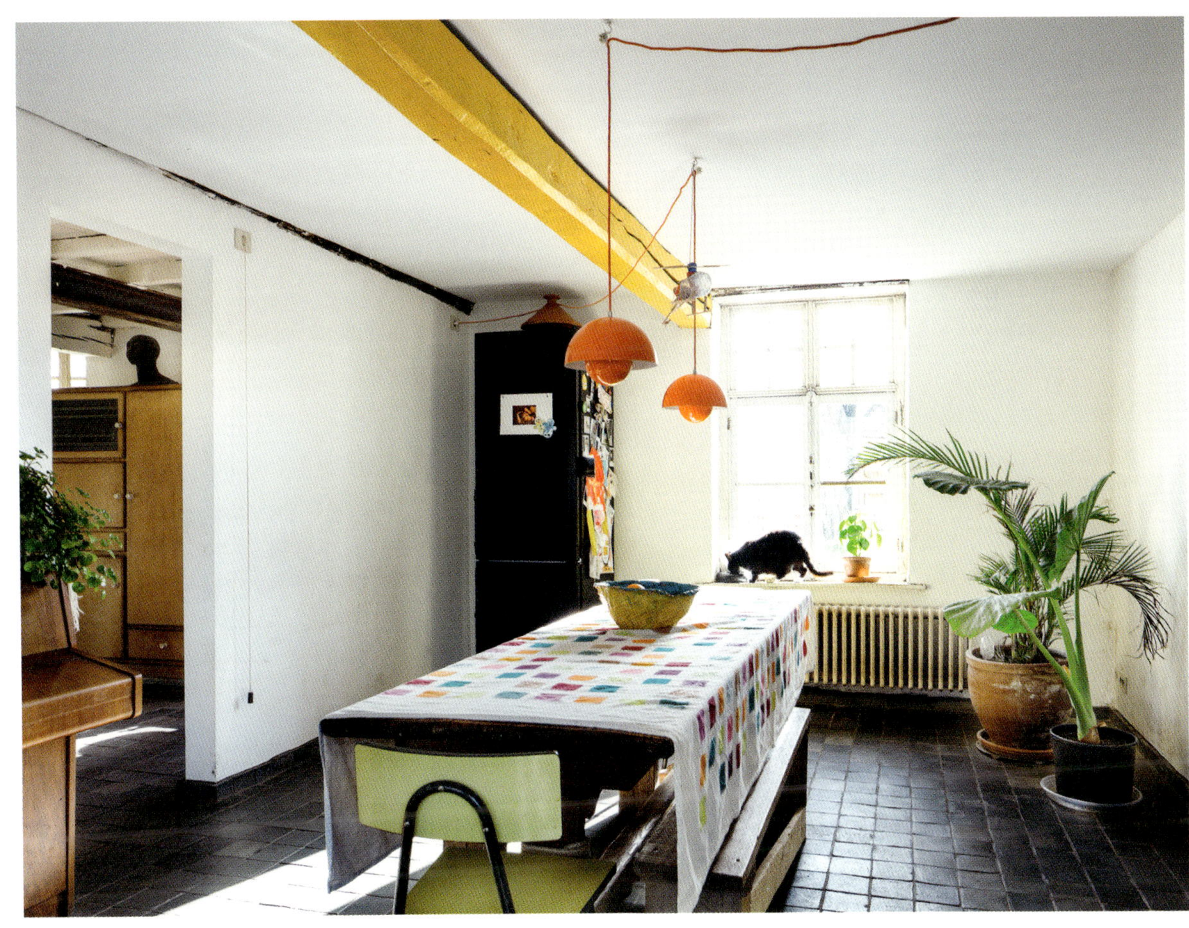

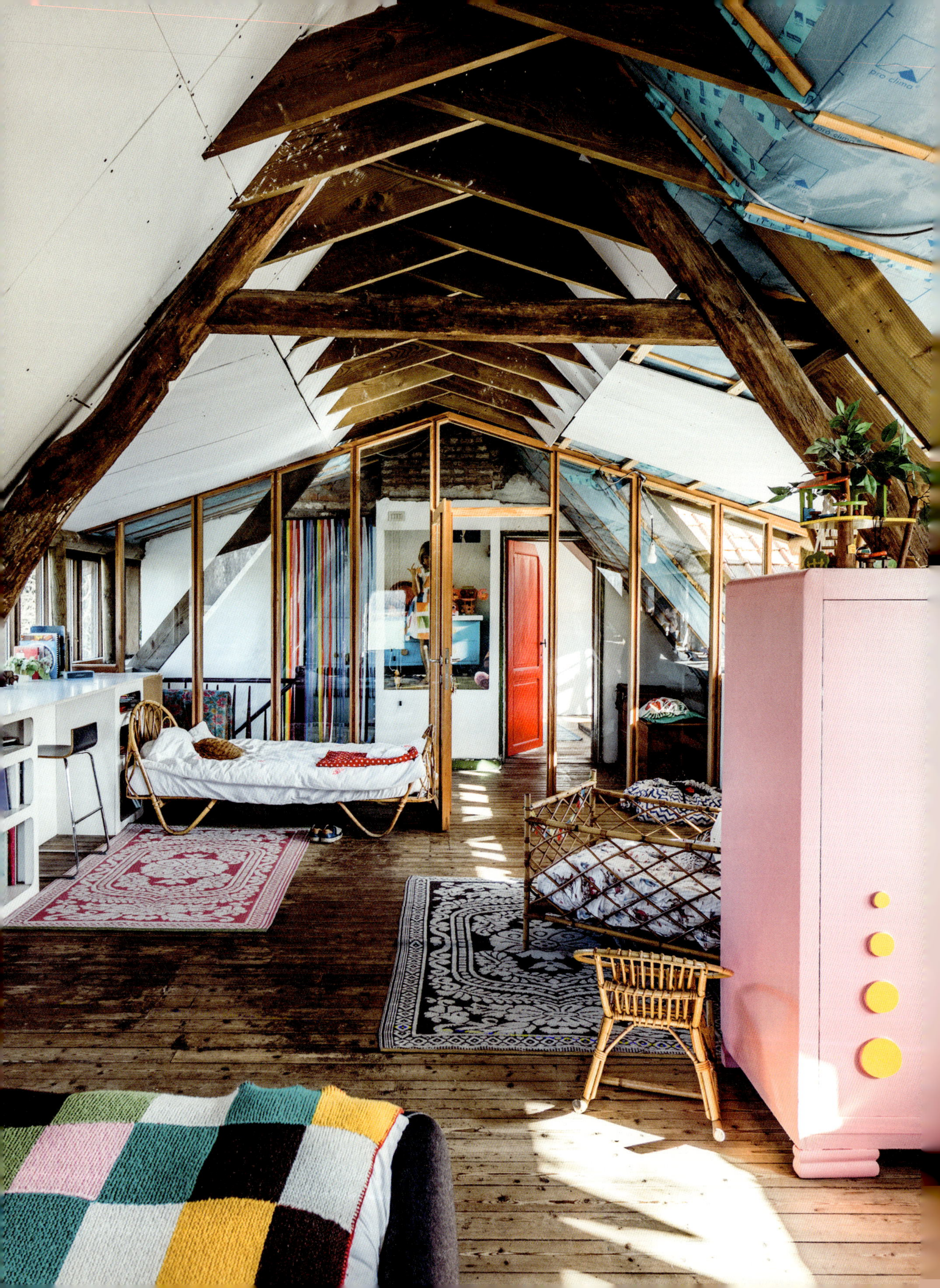

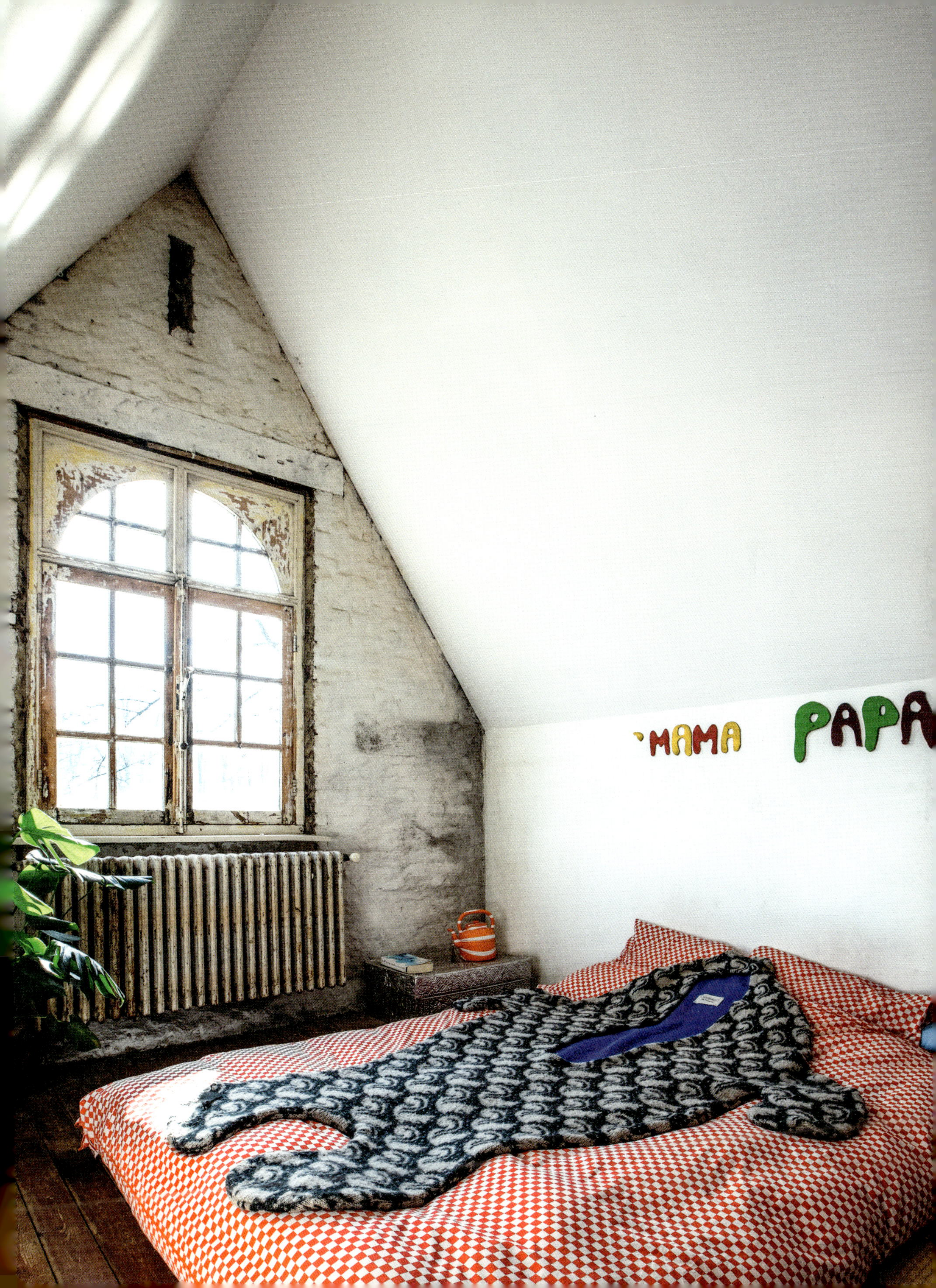
MAMA PAPA

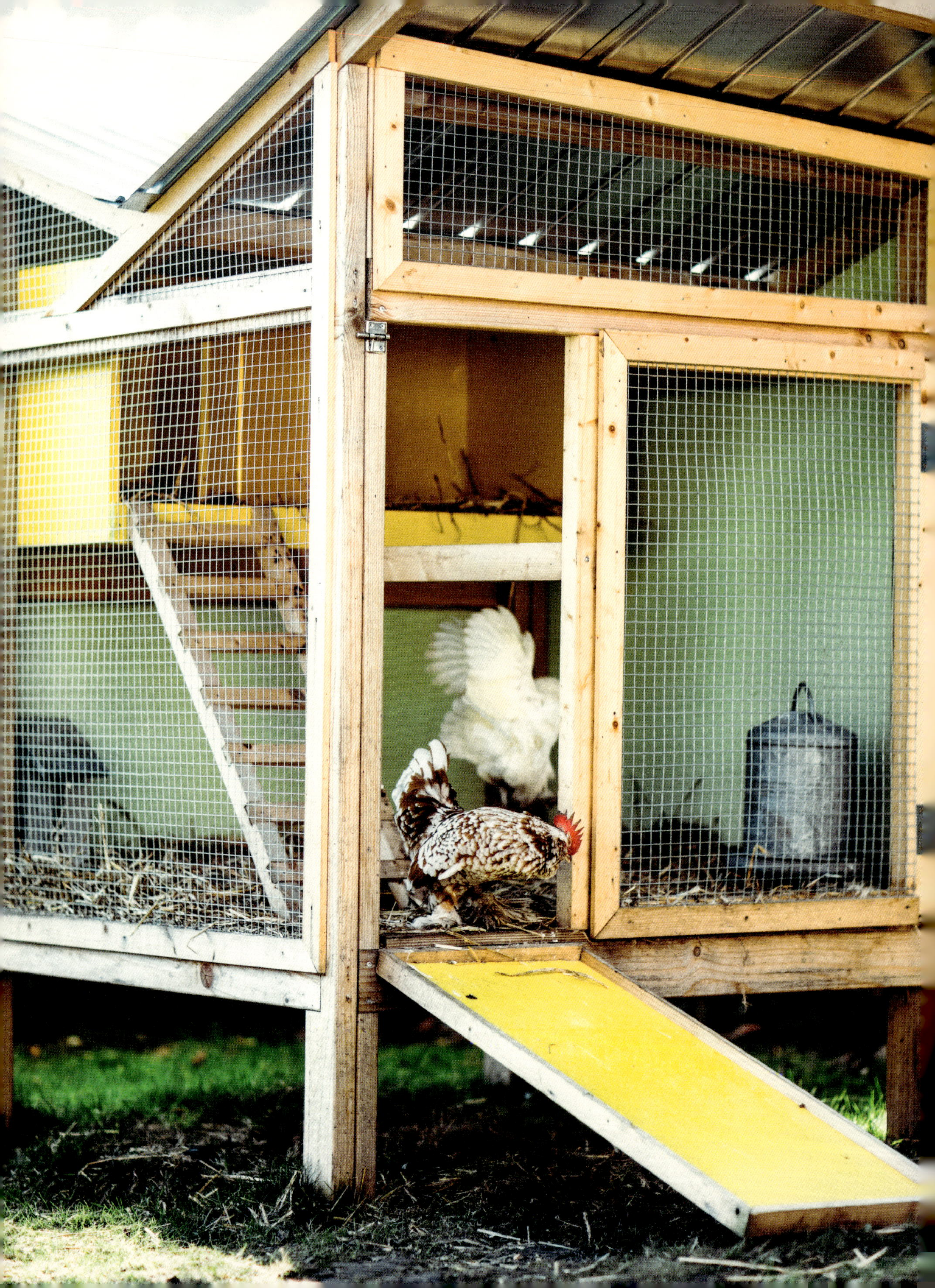

Mojo is a real family pet and gets on well with the other animals.
He cuddles the cat and sniffs at the chickens who were driven from
their chicken coop by a bunch of pigeons.

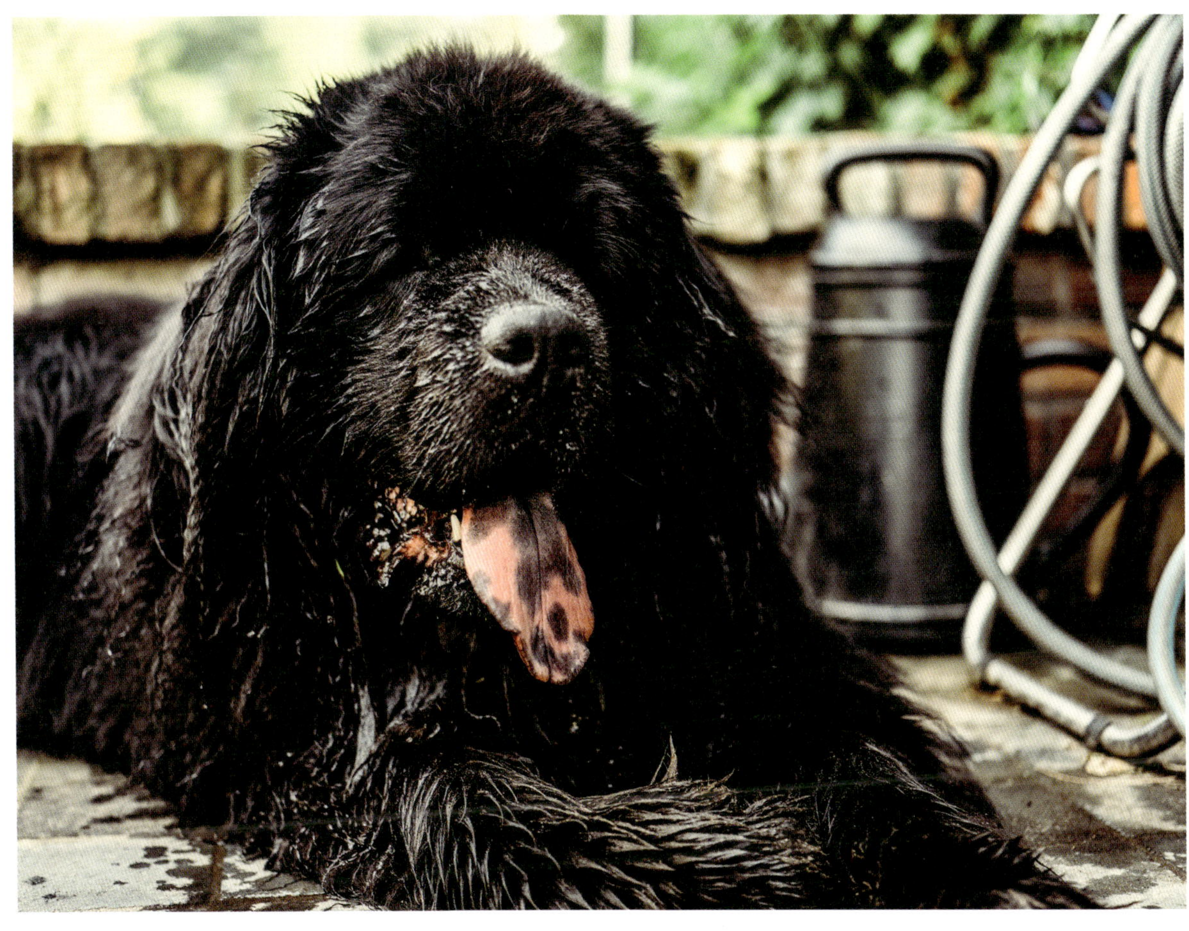

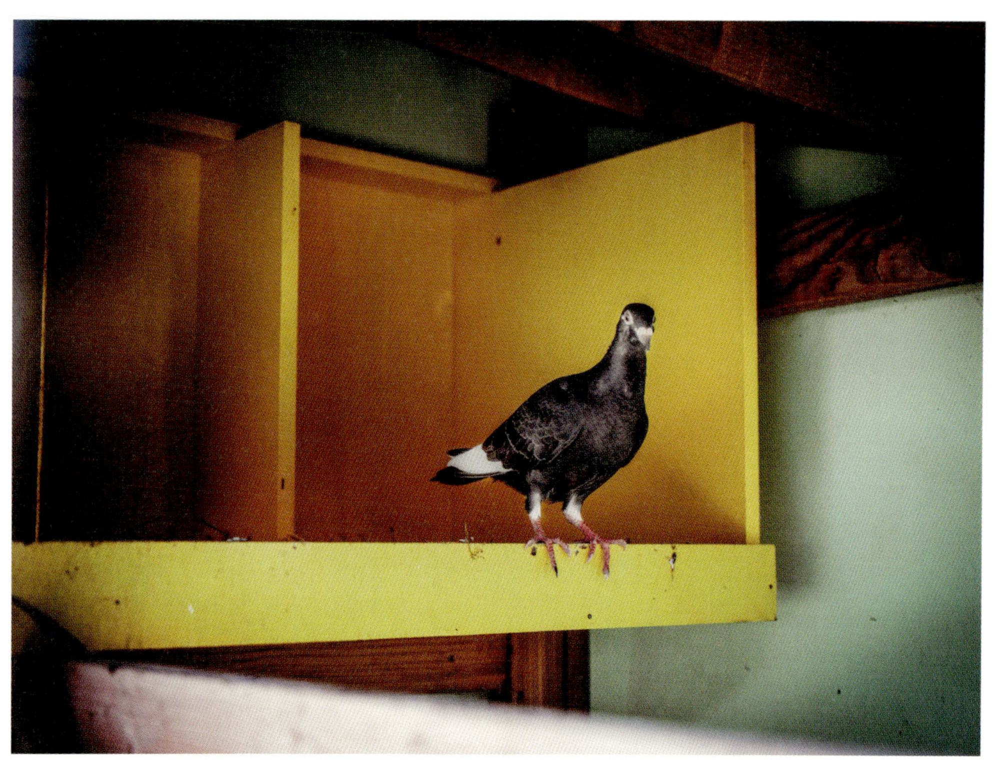

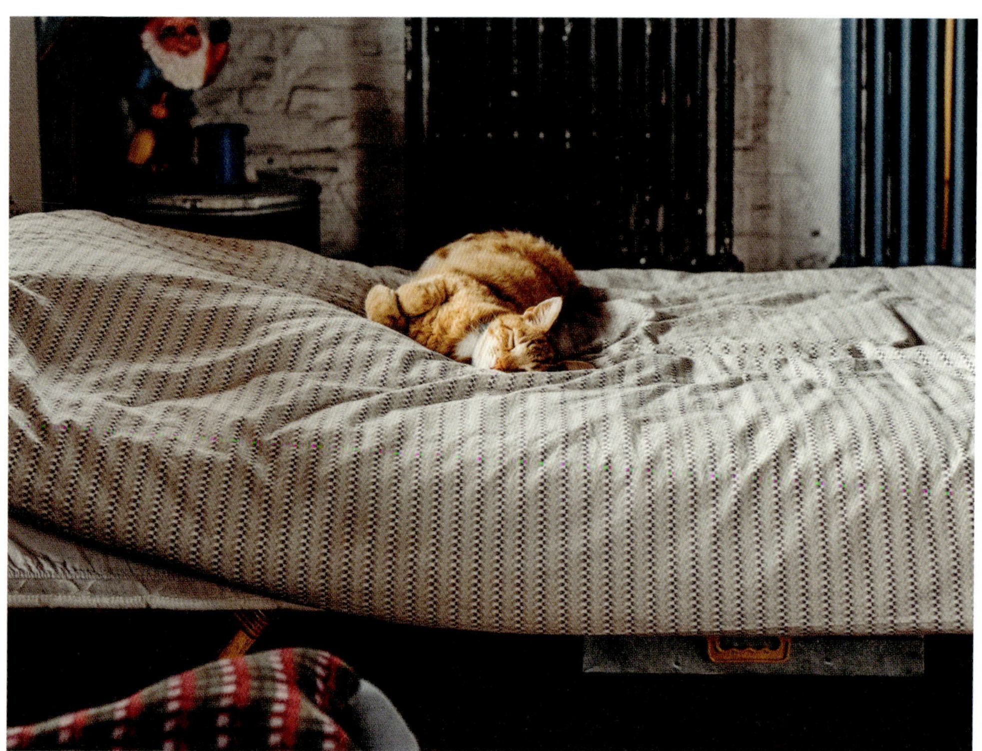

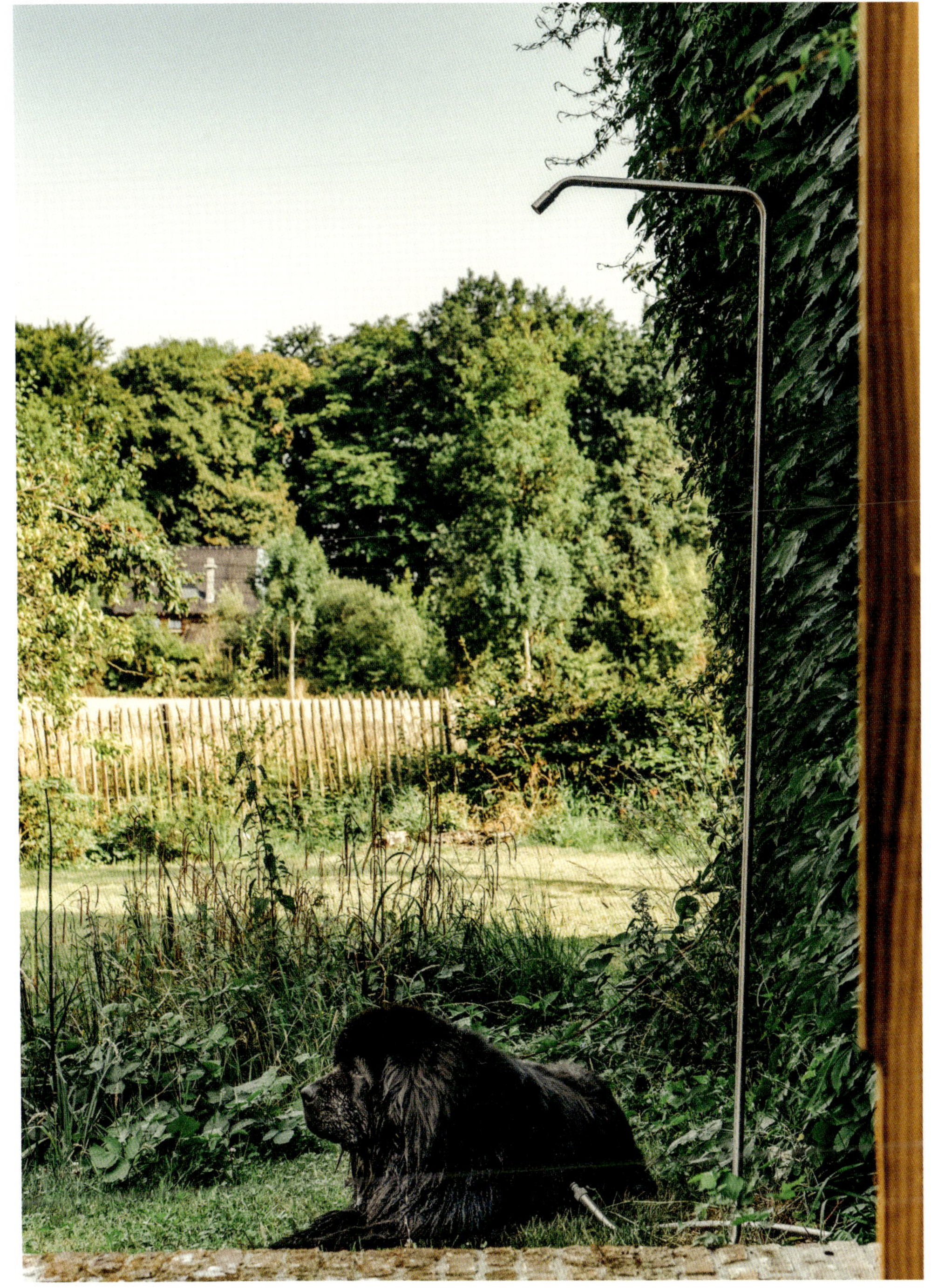

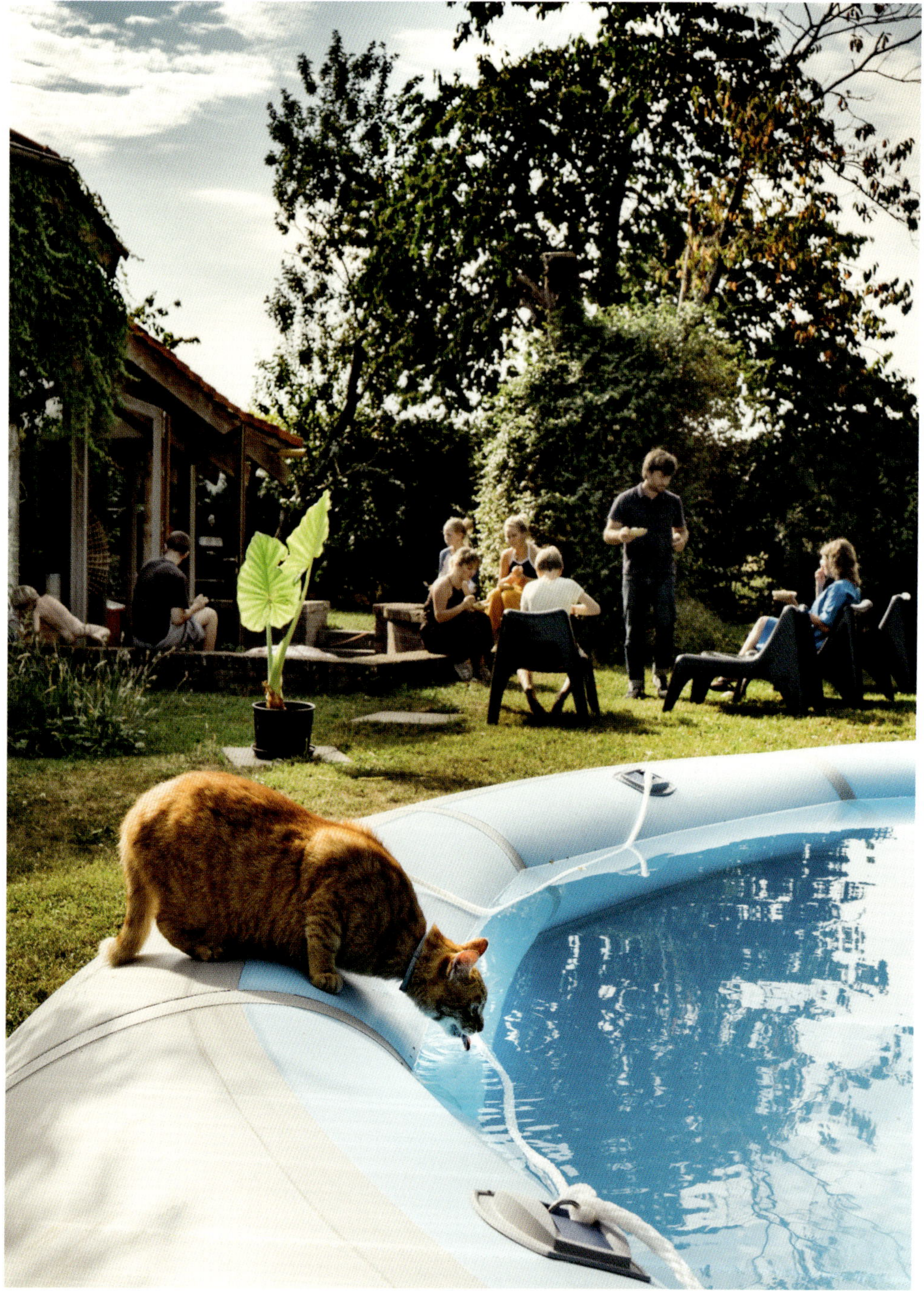

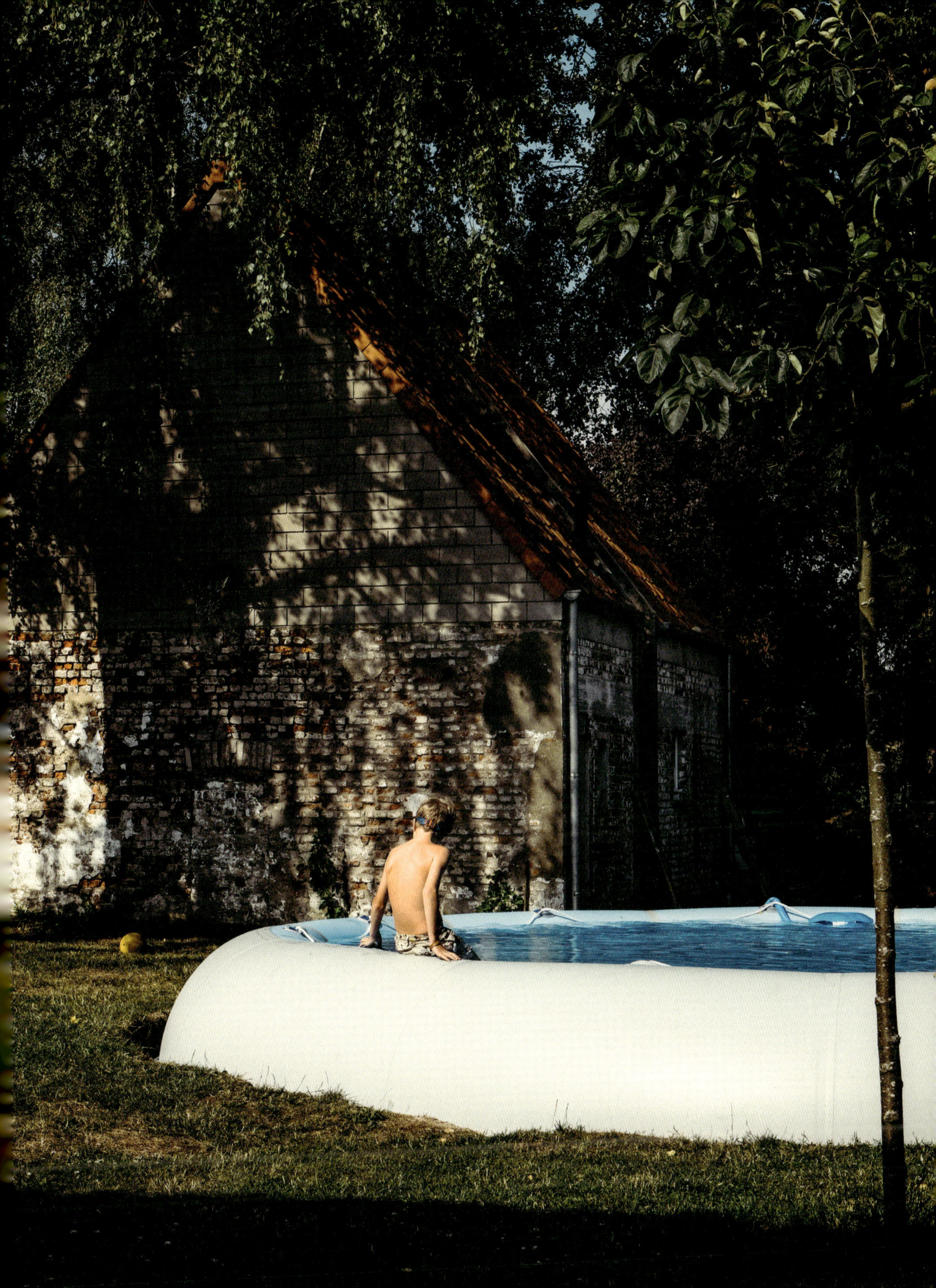

Life here is generally chaotic with six children. They all gather in
the kitchen and the living room. And they run in and out, usually
with the pets right behind them.

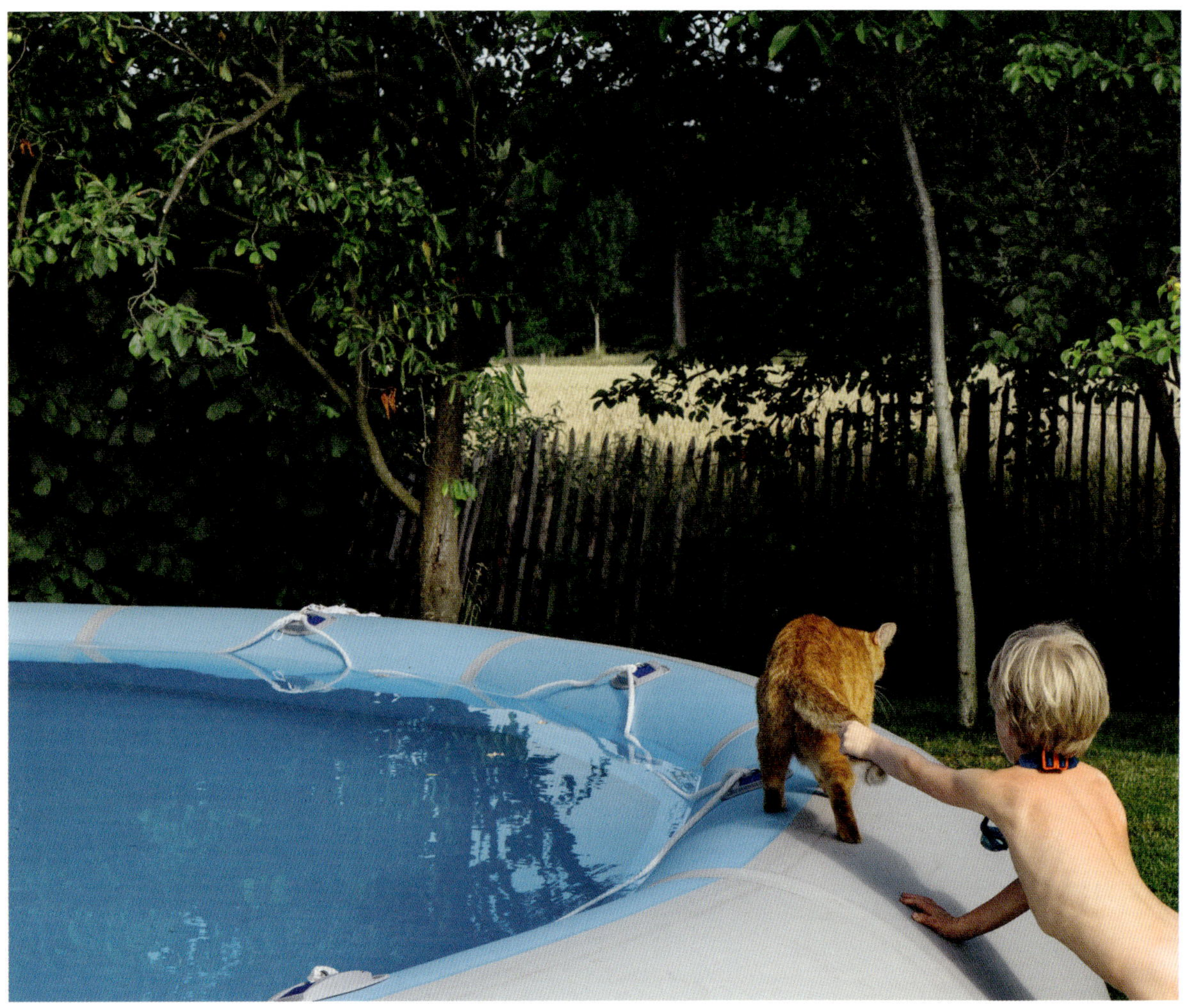

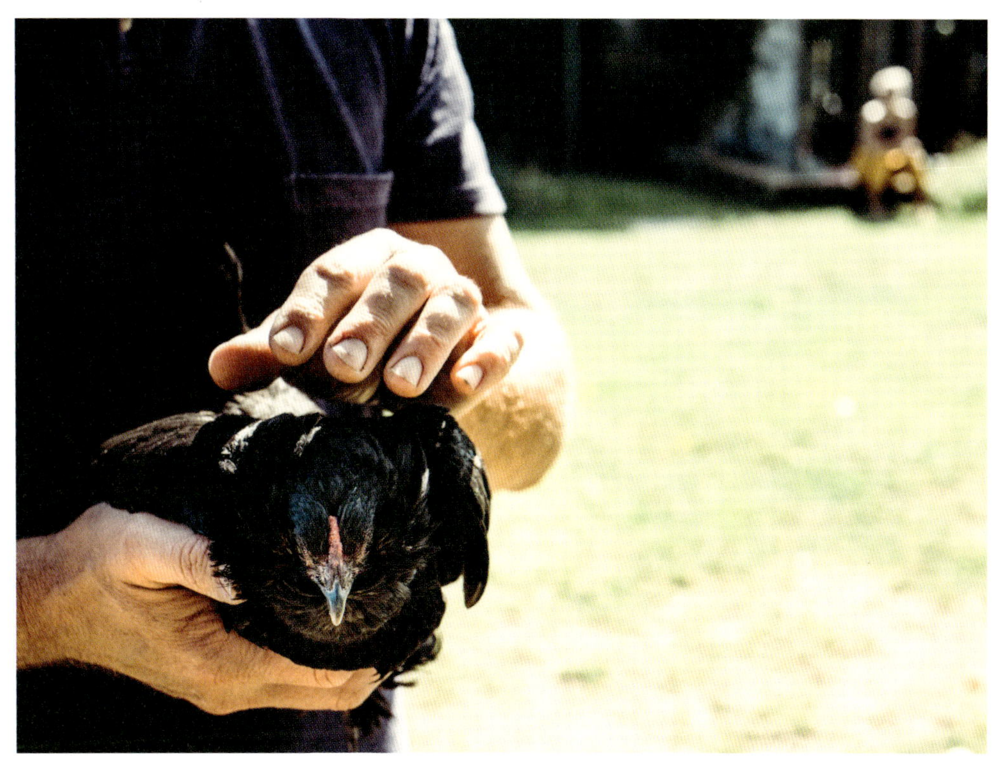

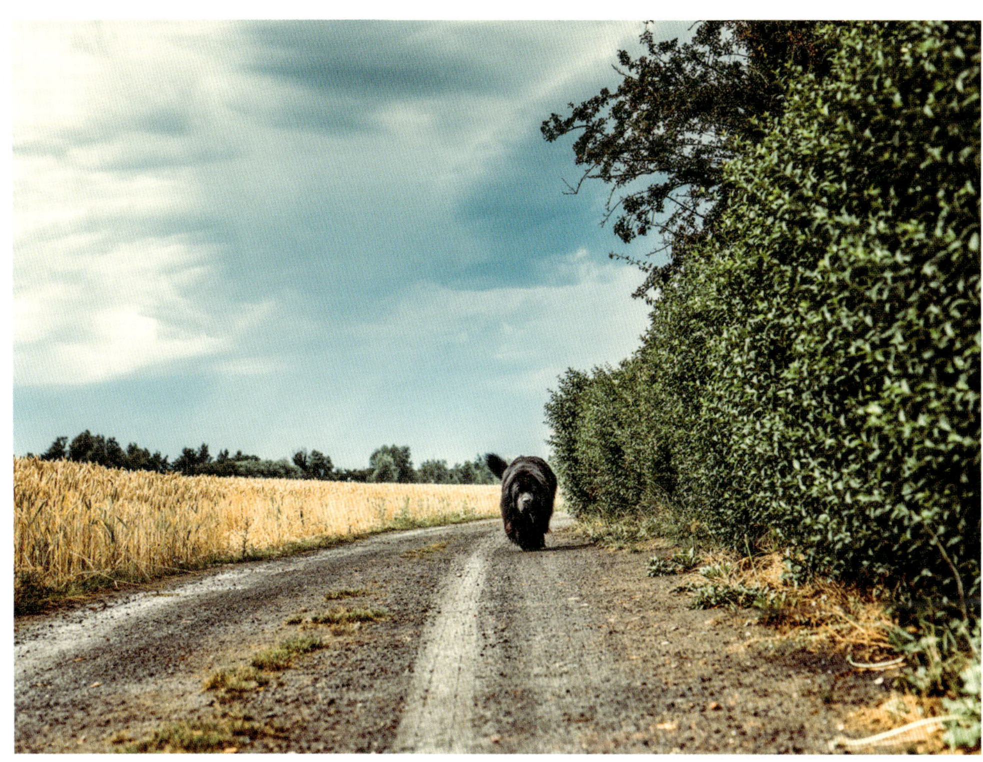

Annick has her own textile label, Triconick, specialising in
macramé. In her studio she creates bags, plant hangers,
curtains, and so on.

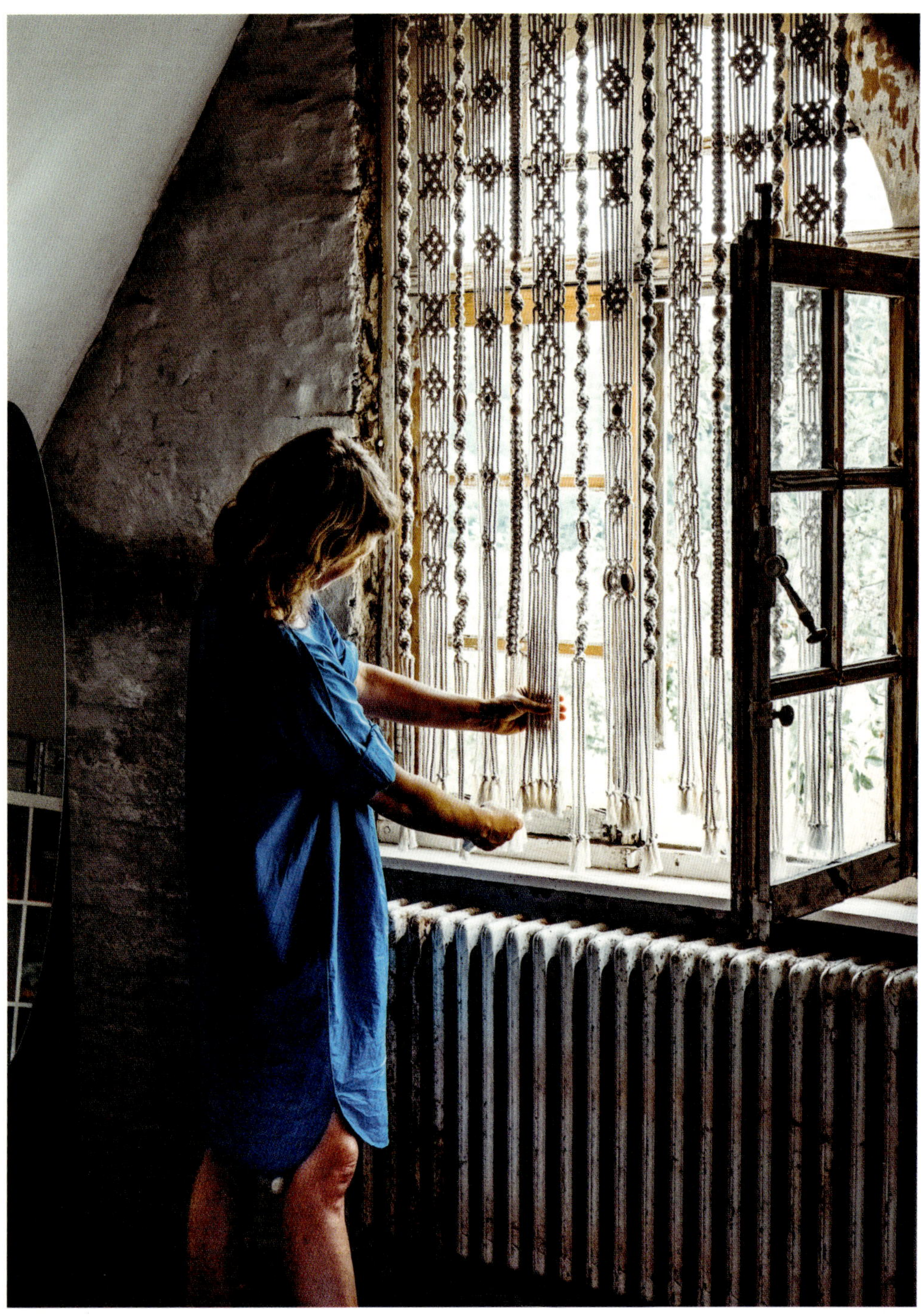

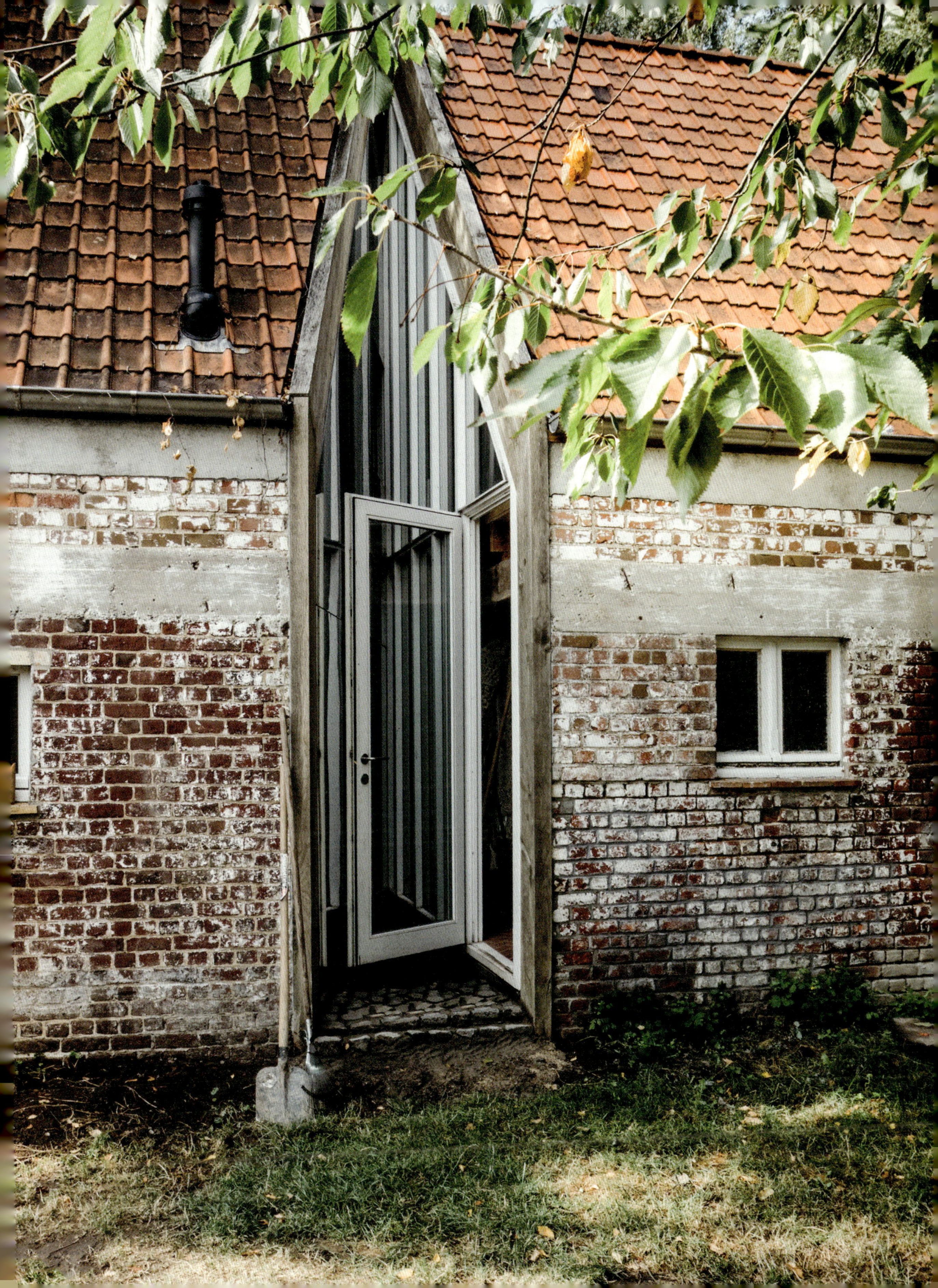

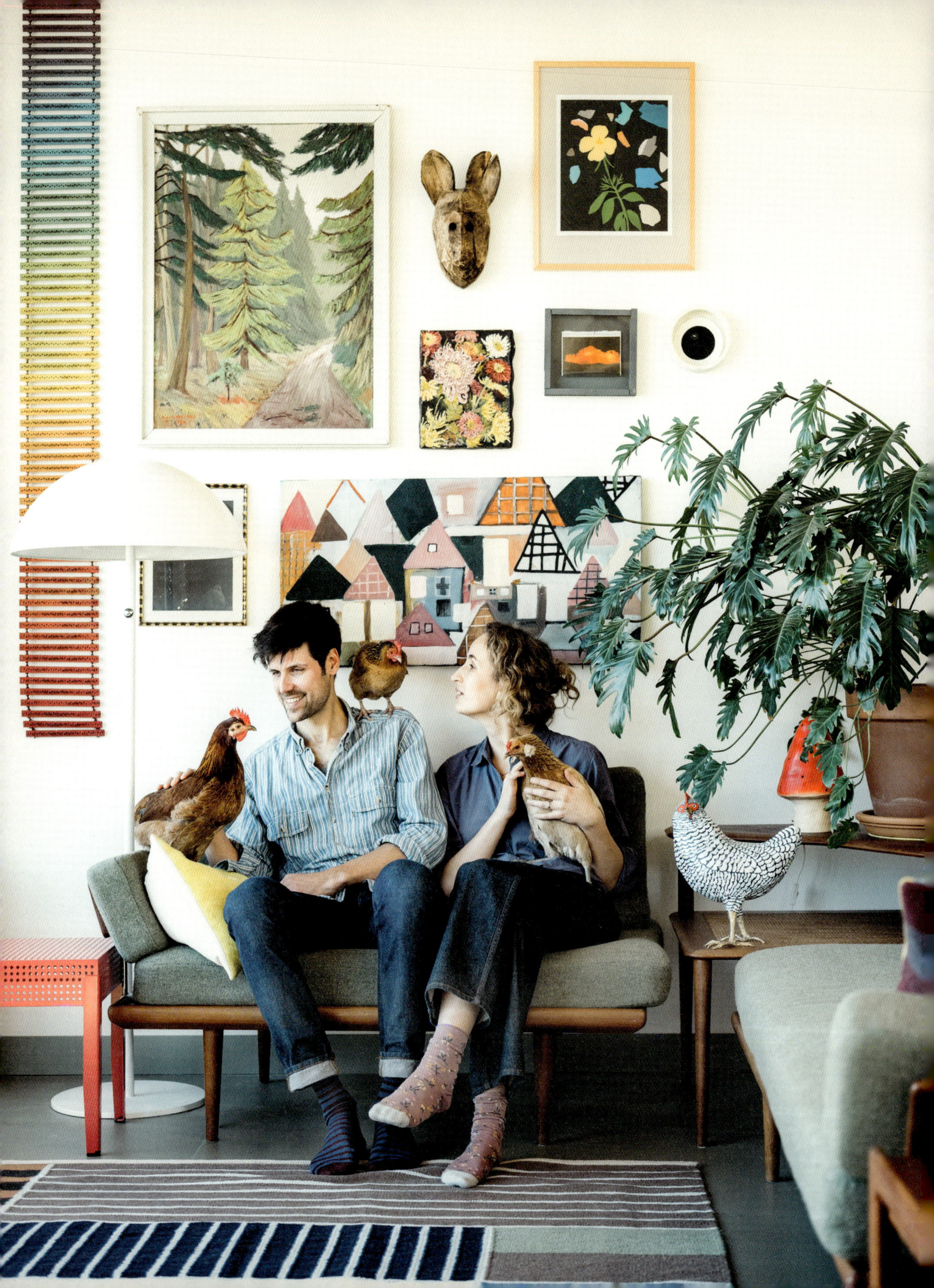

It's a daily ritual for Foekje and Marcel. They release their domesticated chickens from their favela hutch in the garden. Then they take them upstairs, into the living area and the kitchen, where they are washed, receive a blow-dry and plenty of cuddles. They share a new, ecological and colourful home, which they largely built themselves, with their birds. She is a product designer, he makes documentaries. They both love their pets and believe in gentle activism as the way forward to a more sustainable world.

Light, spacious and sustainable

We've been following Foekje Fleur, Marcel IJzerman and their chickens for quite some time. When we first met them, they were living in a tiny apartment, and the birds walked in and out freely. One creature was actually so tame that it would hop on Foekje's shoulder and rub up to her. This wonderful image made quite an impression on us. Those animals have since died. The couple now lives in a new home, an ecohouse, which they built themselves. The land they wanted was so popular that they spent three days camping in front of the realtor's offices. 'The house was delivered to us as a building shell. We did the rest ourselves,' Marcel says proudly. Besides being sustainable, the house is also very spacious and light. The couple lives on the upper floor, in a spacious living room and kitchen with large windows. The bedroom, bathroom, Foekje's workspace, and Marcel's editing studio are downstairs. There is a small parcel of land around the house, which they use to grow vegetables and which is the home of their three chickens.

A luxury chicken residence

In the beginning, the birds used to roam freely around the neighbourhood. Some of the residents complained, which is why they now live in an enclosure in the garden. The hutch, which resembles a favela, will soon be replaced with a large shed, in which Foekje and Marcel can stand up. They have already drawn the plans for the new chicken coop. Now they are just waiting for a contractor, to pour the concrete plate for the hutch. You can tell that they really love their pets. 'The chickens don't require much care, and you get so much back in return,' says Marcel while he points at a filled basket. Two of the three birds are Araucanas, which are famous for their shiny green eggs. The origin of the third animal is unknown. 'Her name's Bea,' says Foekje. 'She is the boss and always wants to be in control. Pippi is deaf, she was born without ears. She's very gentle and easy to get on with. Patricia is very curious. She's the only real escape artist.' They all have their own character but get on well with each other.

Washing and blow-drying

During the day, the chickens live outside in their hutch and enclosure. At night, they are taken inside, where they can roam in the living area and kitchen. They hop onto the windowsill and walk over the carpet. Foekje and Marcel eye them closely, always with kitchen paper on hand. 'The big disadvantage of chickens is that they poo everywhere, except when you hold them on your lap,' Foekje laughs. 'Unlike other pets, they don't shed, and they don't make much noise.' We mainly notice how tame they are. They like to be petted and will eat from your hand. The secret is repetition. 'The more you take them inside, the tamer they become,' Foekje says. What is even more remarkable is that they don't mind being bathed in the sink. We look in the kitchen. 'They also love a blow-dry,' Marcel adds. We are lost for words.

Gentle activism

When they decided to go vegan, the couple got chickens – and eggs. We wonder whether vegans can eat animal products. Marcel doesn't like strict labels and explains: 'We want to be more conscious consumers and help improve animal welfare as much as possible. So we don't eat living beings, but we enjoy an egg now and then. If you take good care of your chickens in your own garden, it's ethically justified to eat their eggs.' It would be sad not to eat them if you bear in mind how much energy a bird expends when it lays an egg. Something you have no idea of when you buy twelve eggs in the supermarket. The couple is very much opposed against the industrial chicken industry and consumption. But instead of expressing their dissatisfaction on the streets, they prefer a gentler style of activism. They want to make people aware of the impact of their consumer behaviour on the environment and inspire them also to get chickens. That is why they share their love for these creatures on social media.

Ceramics can save the world

Activism also inspires Foekje's pastel-coloured creations. She is addressing the growing problem of the plastic soup with her ceramic Bottle Vases, which look like sustainable replicas of plastic bottles. But she goes one step further: her designs are made from recycled materials, like the Bubble Buddy, a vegetable-based soap with a matching soap dish. She wants to raise awareness and make the world more sustainable for everyone, including for her chickens. In anticipation of their new home, the pets flap around and pose proudly for the camera. Life in the lap of luxury.

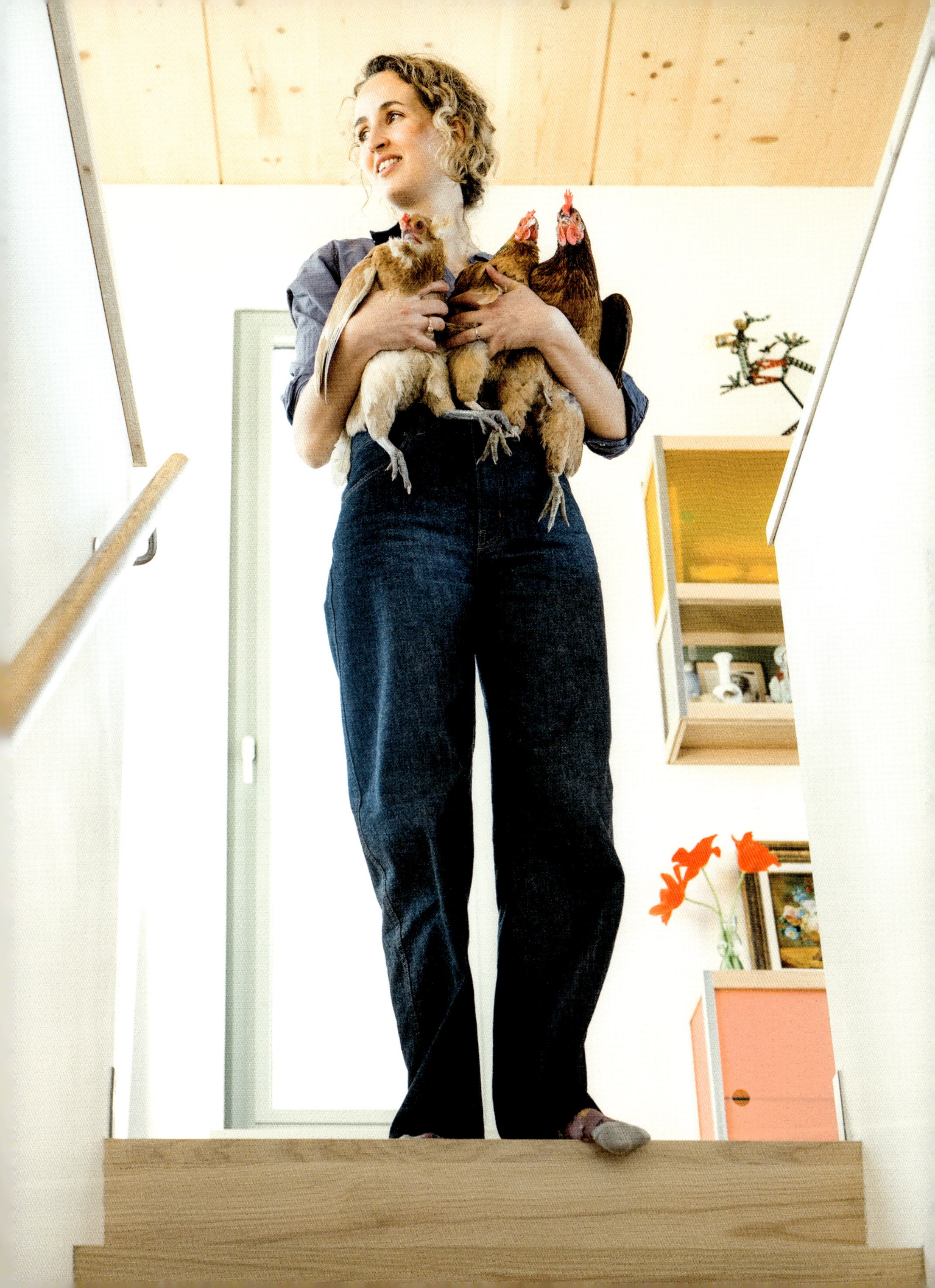

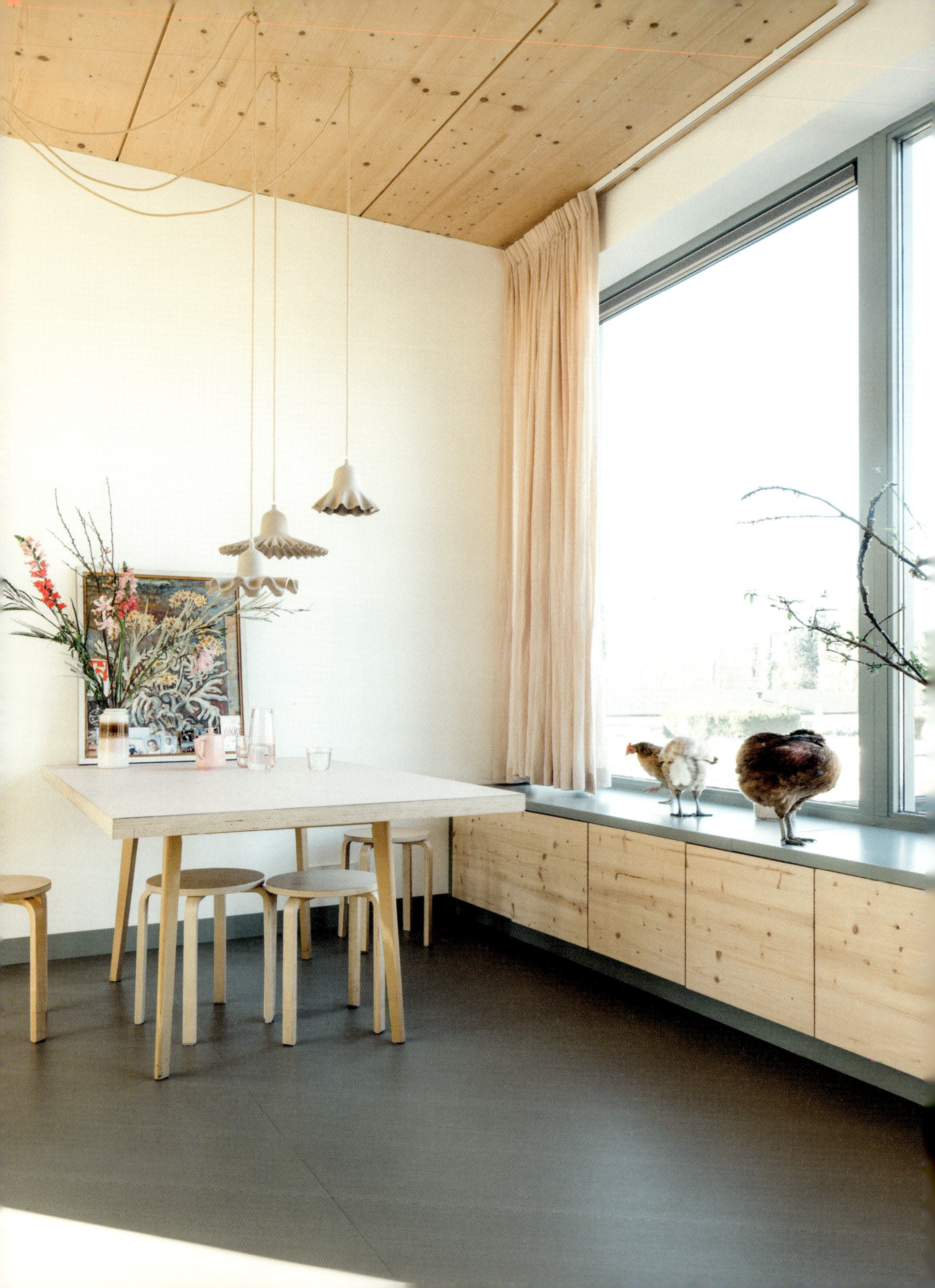

Besides being sustainable, the new ecohouse of Foekje
and Marcel is also very light and spacious. The couple lives
upstairs and works downstairs.

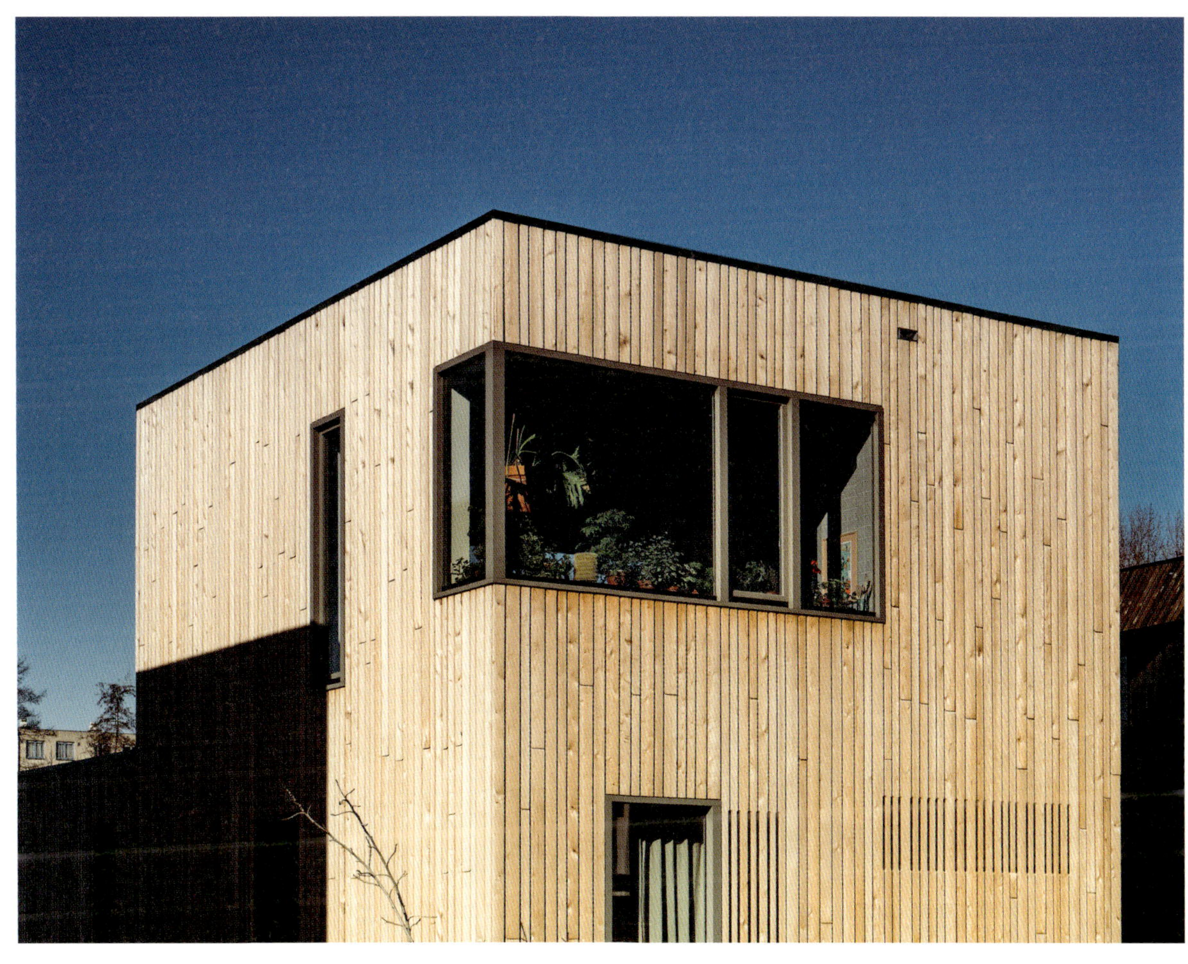

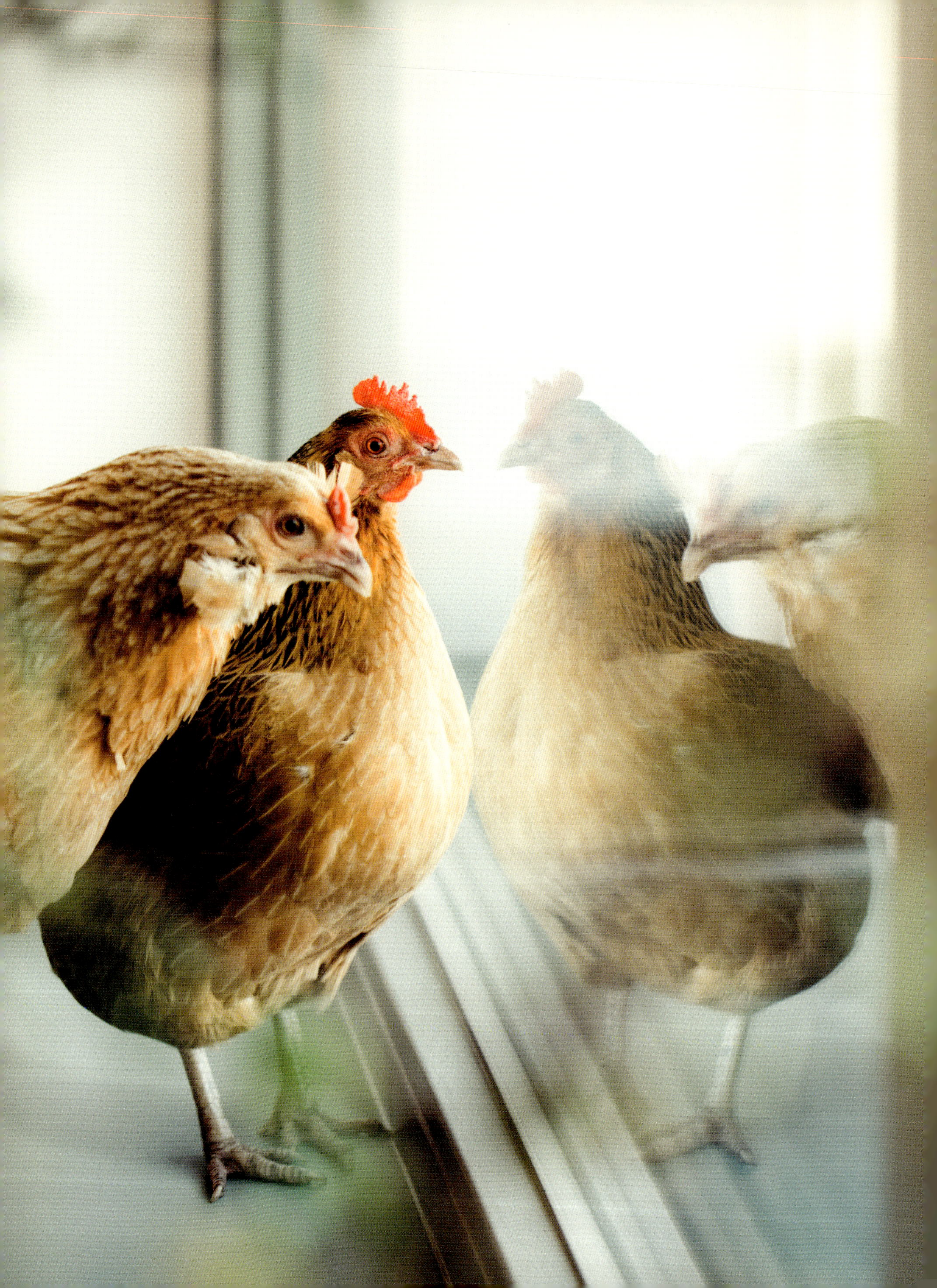

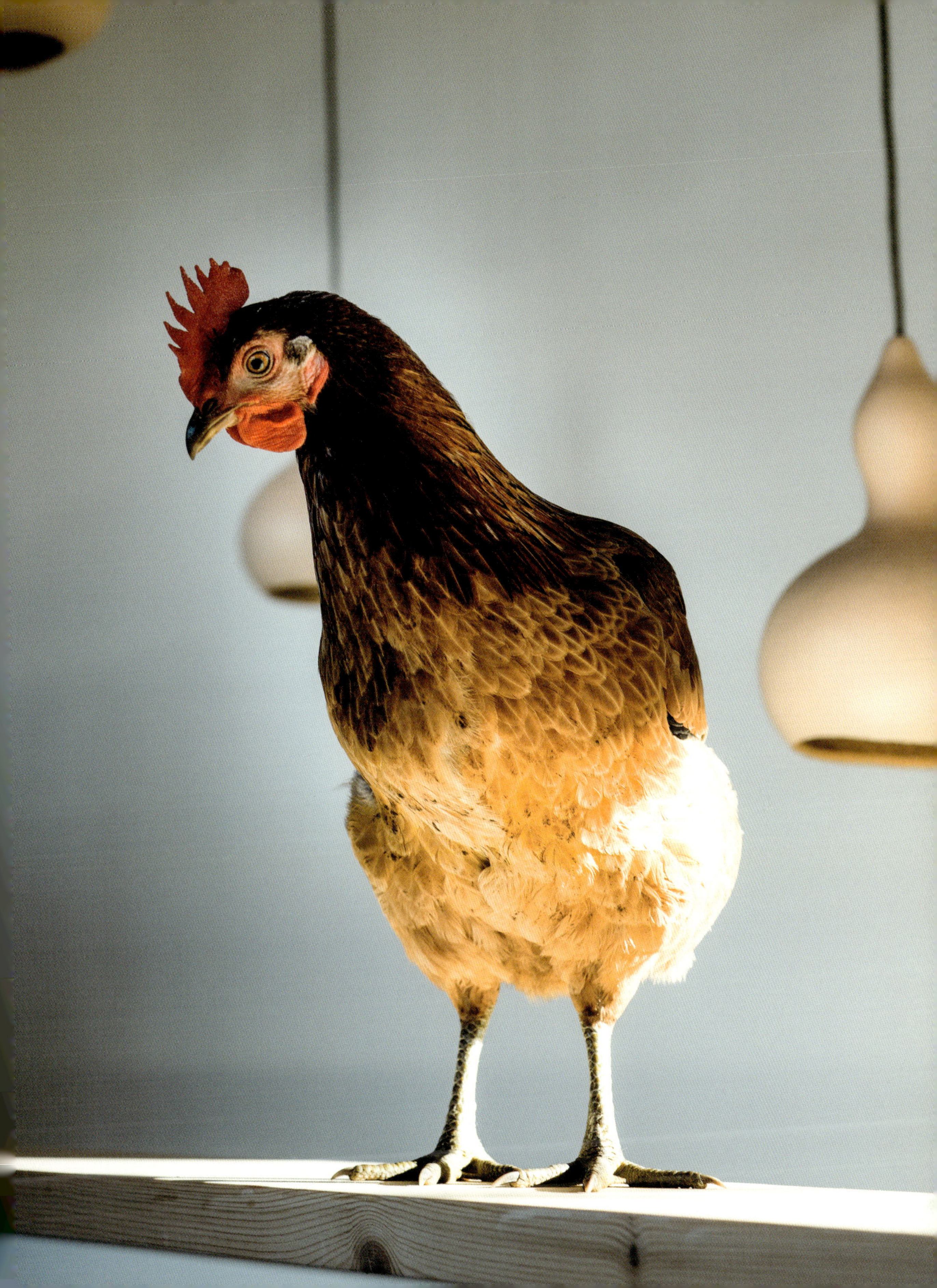

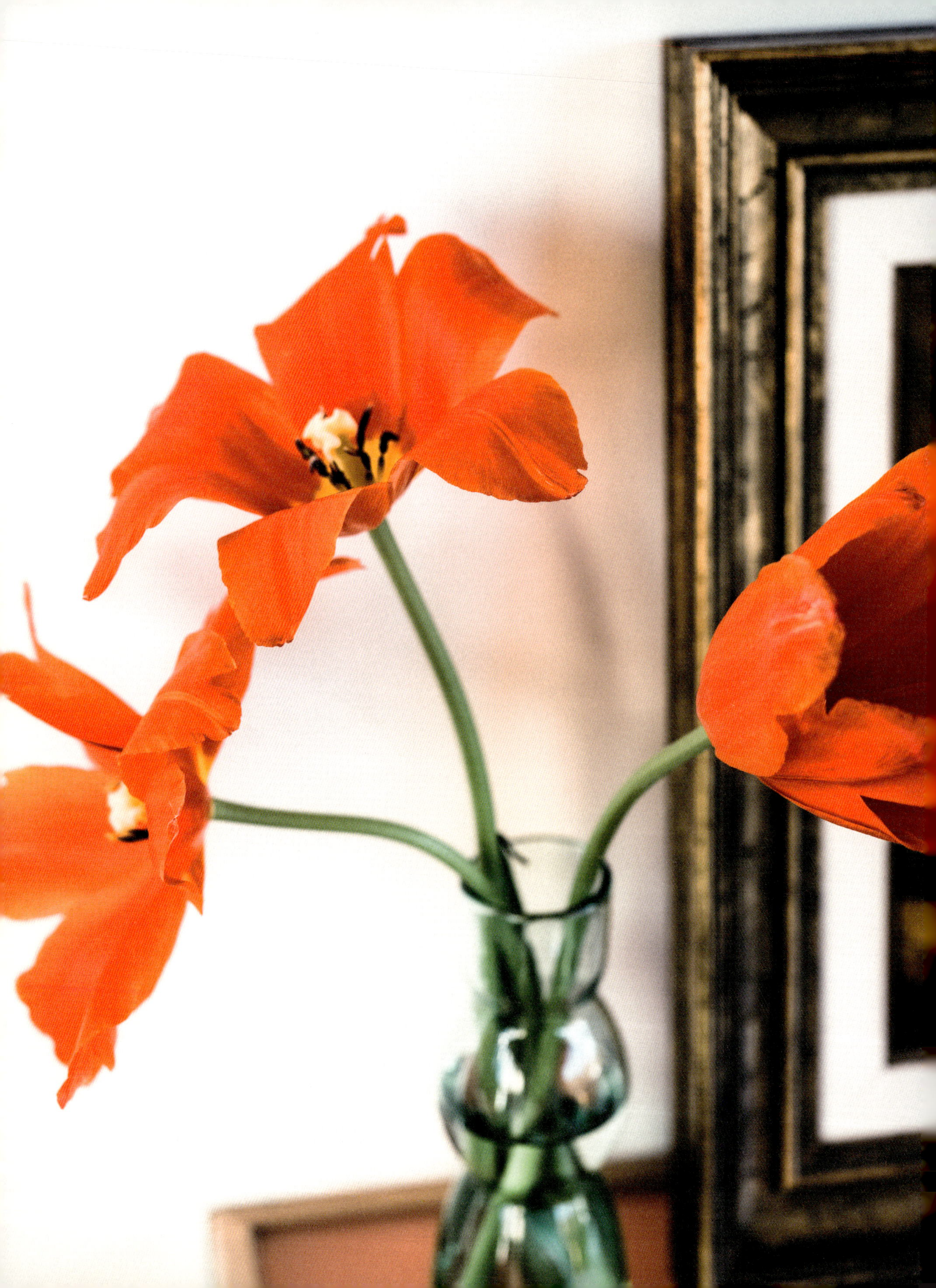

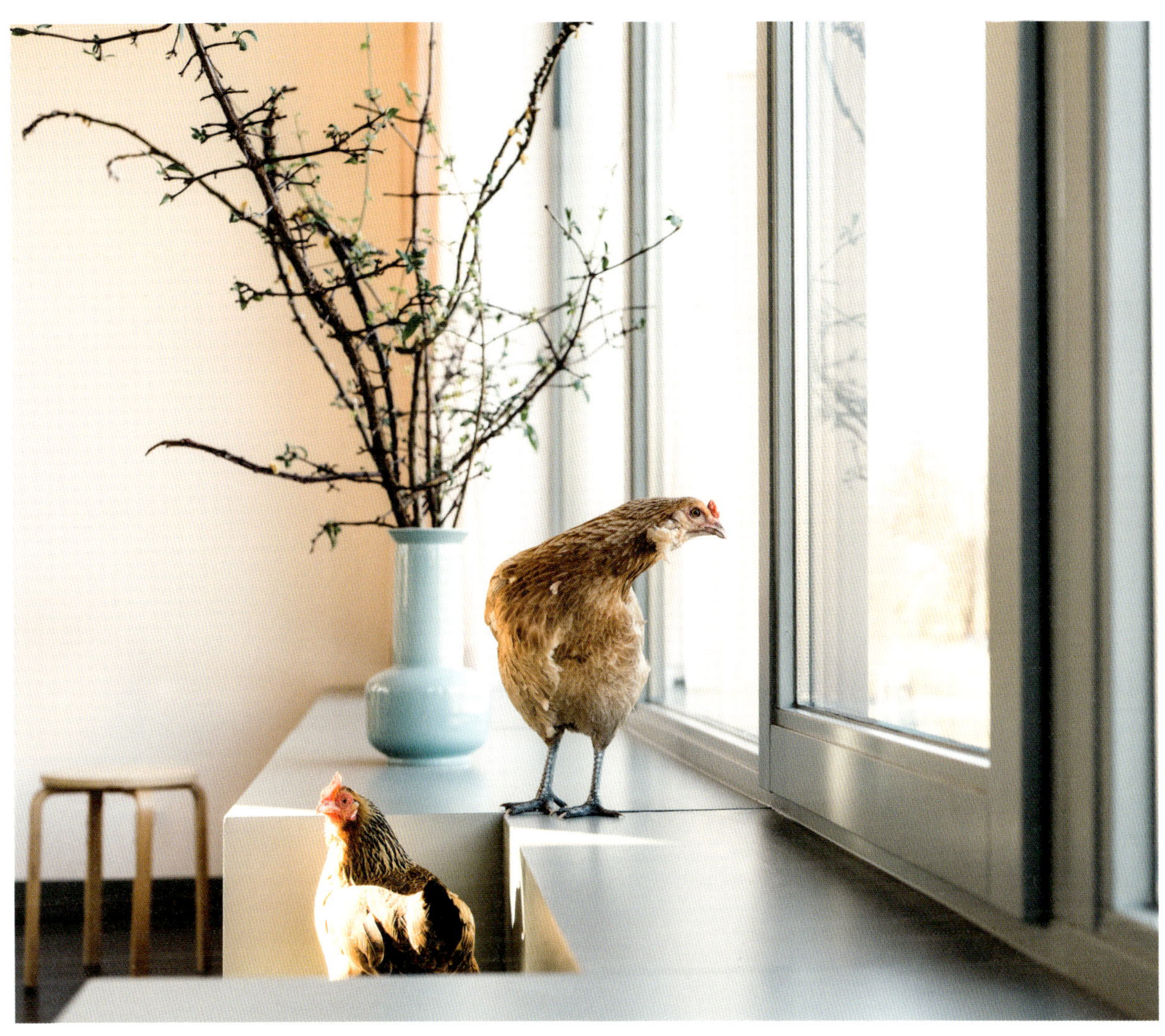

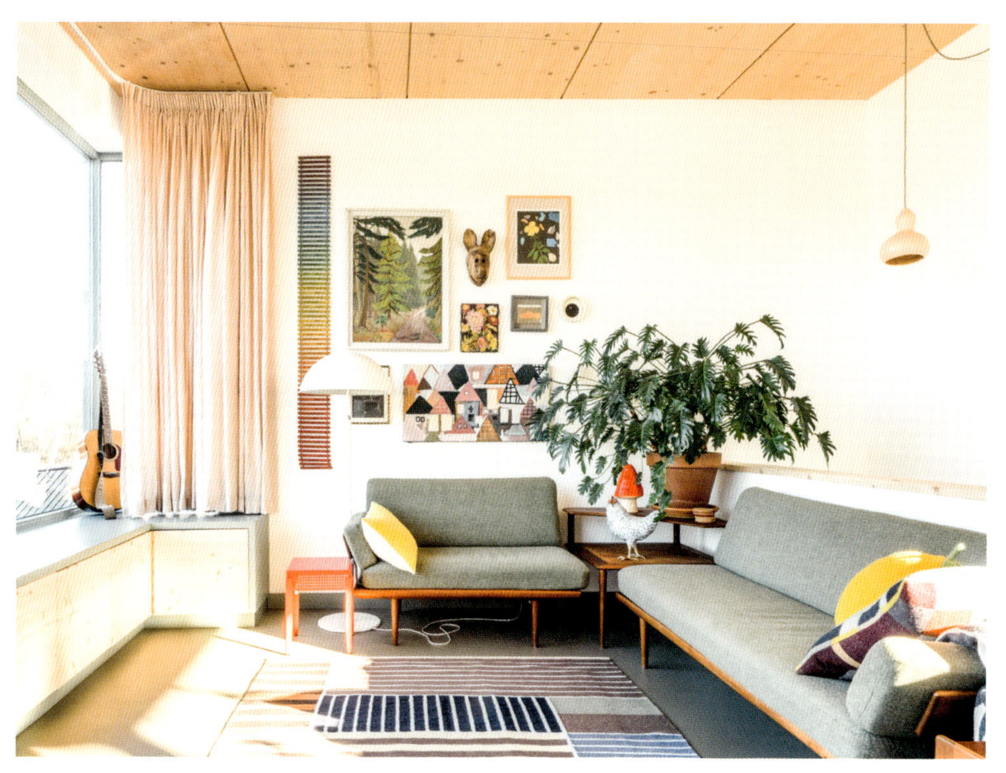

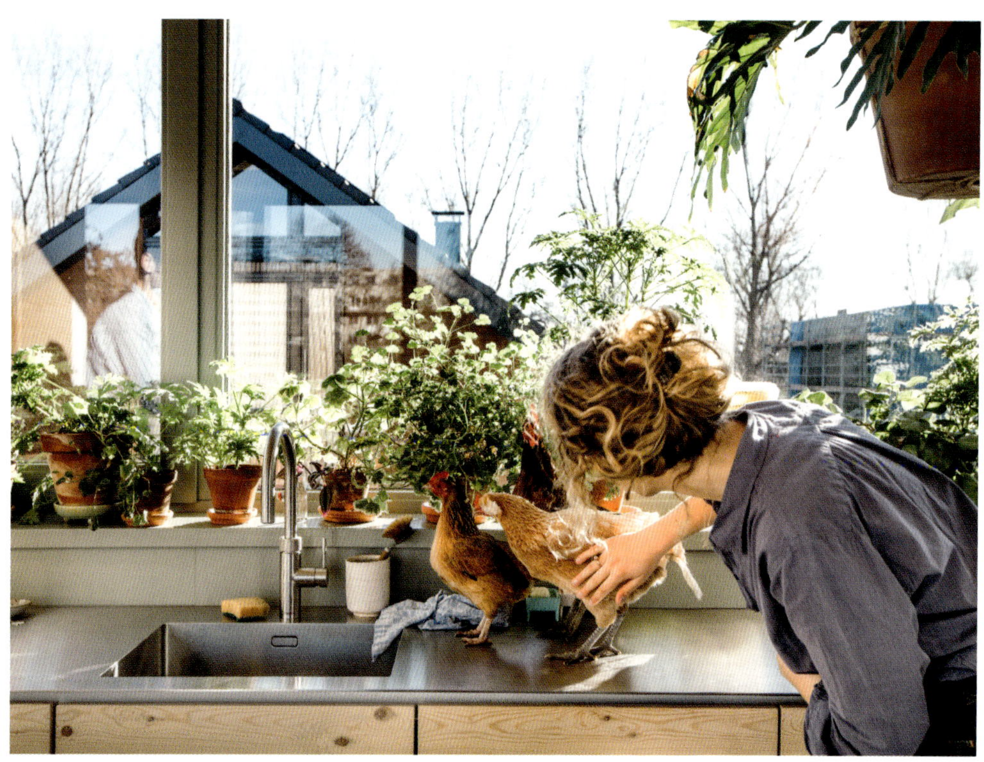

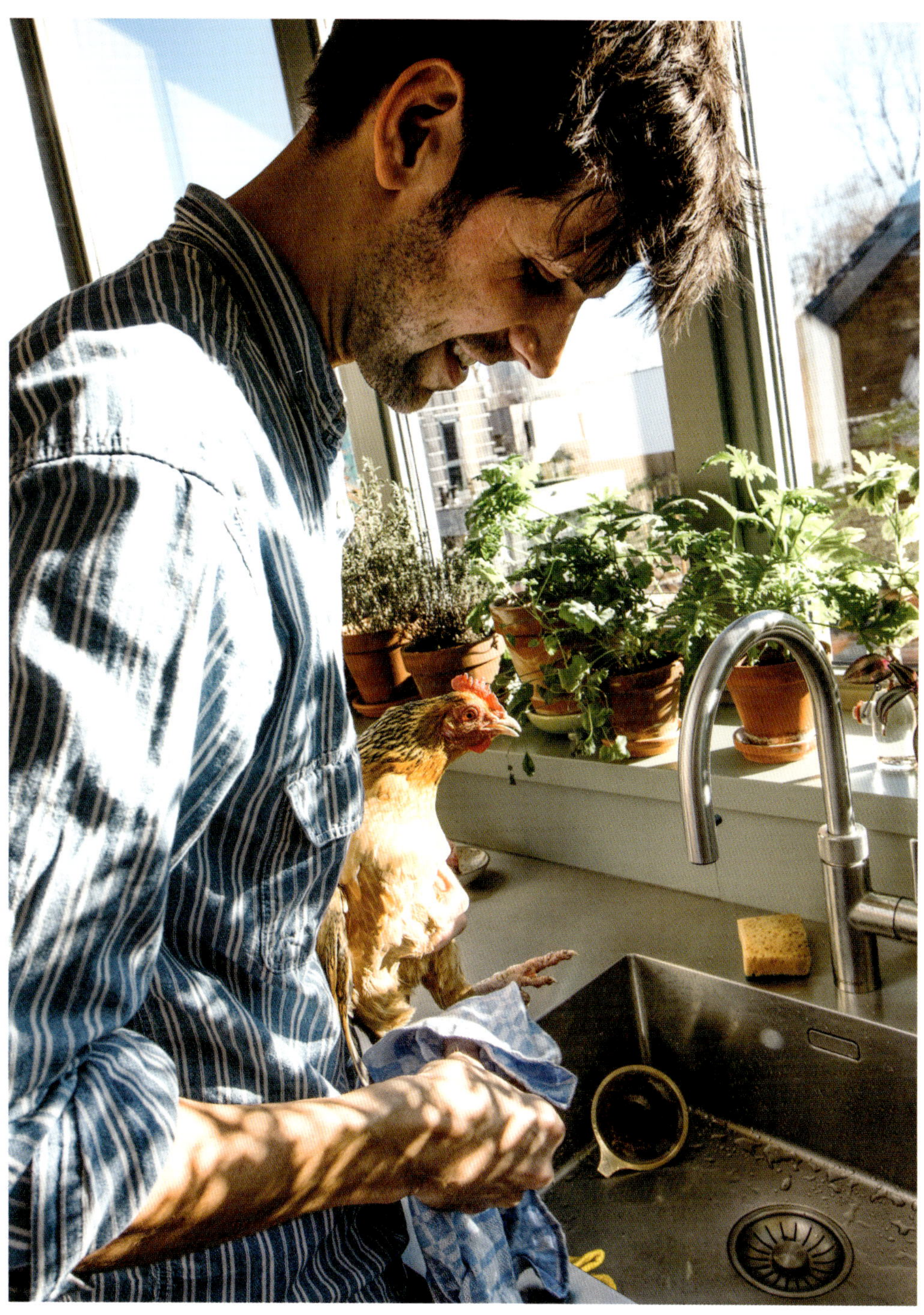

The chickens are domesticated. They eat from your hand and like
to be petted and washed in the sink. The secret? It's all about
repetition. The more you take them inside, the tamer they become.

The pastel colours that Foekje uses in her work are combined throughout the house with brighter hues and natural materials.

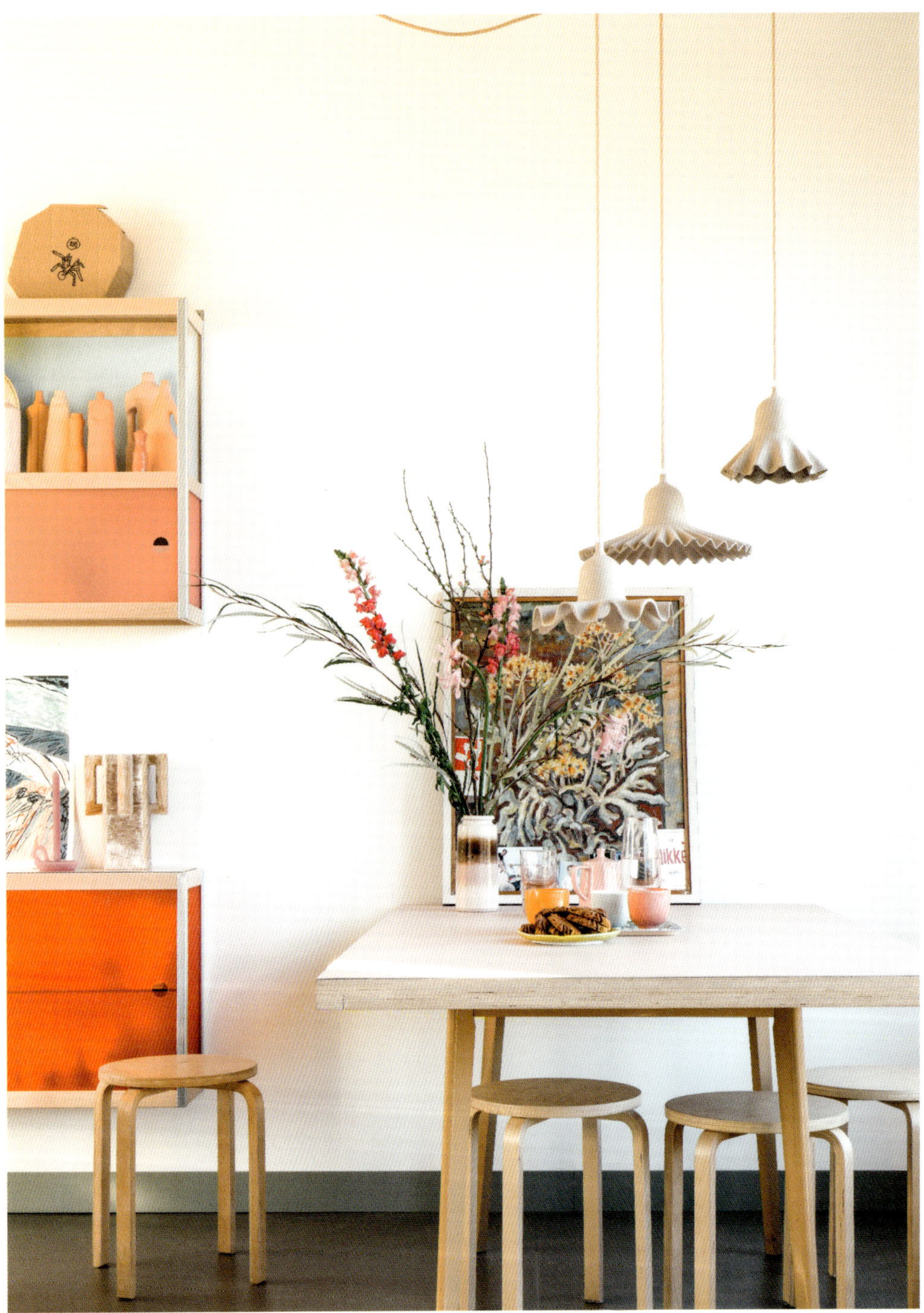

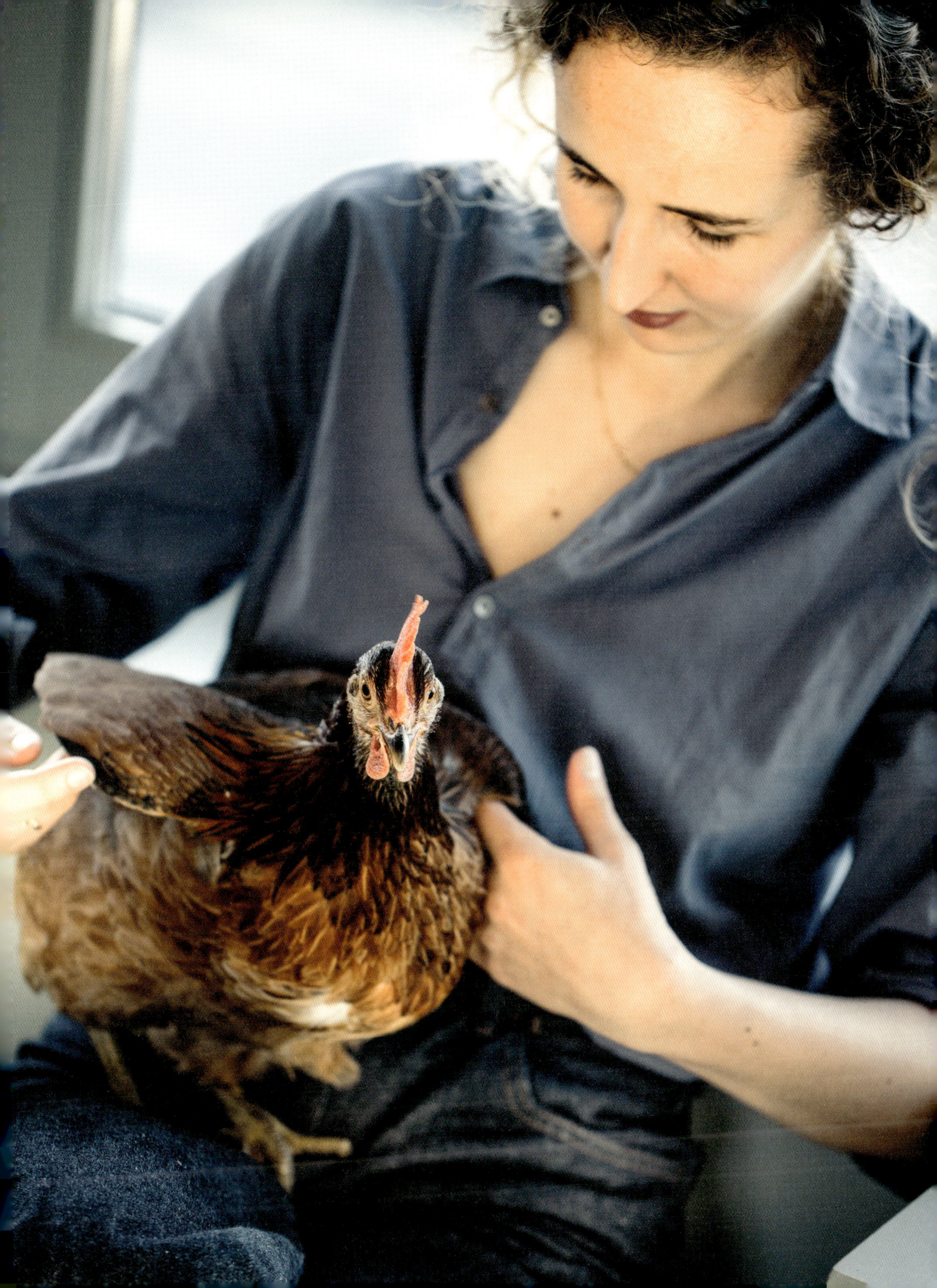

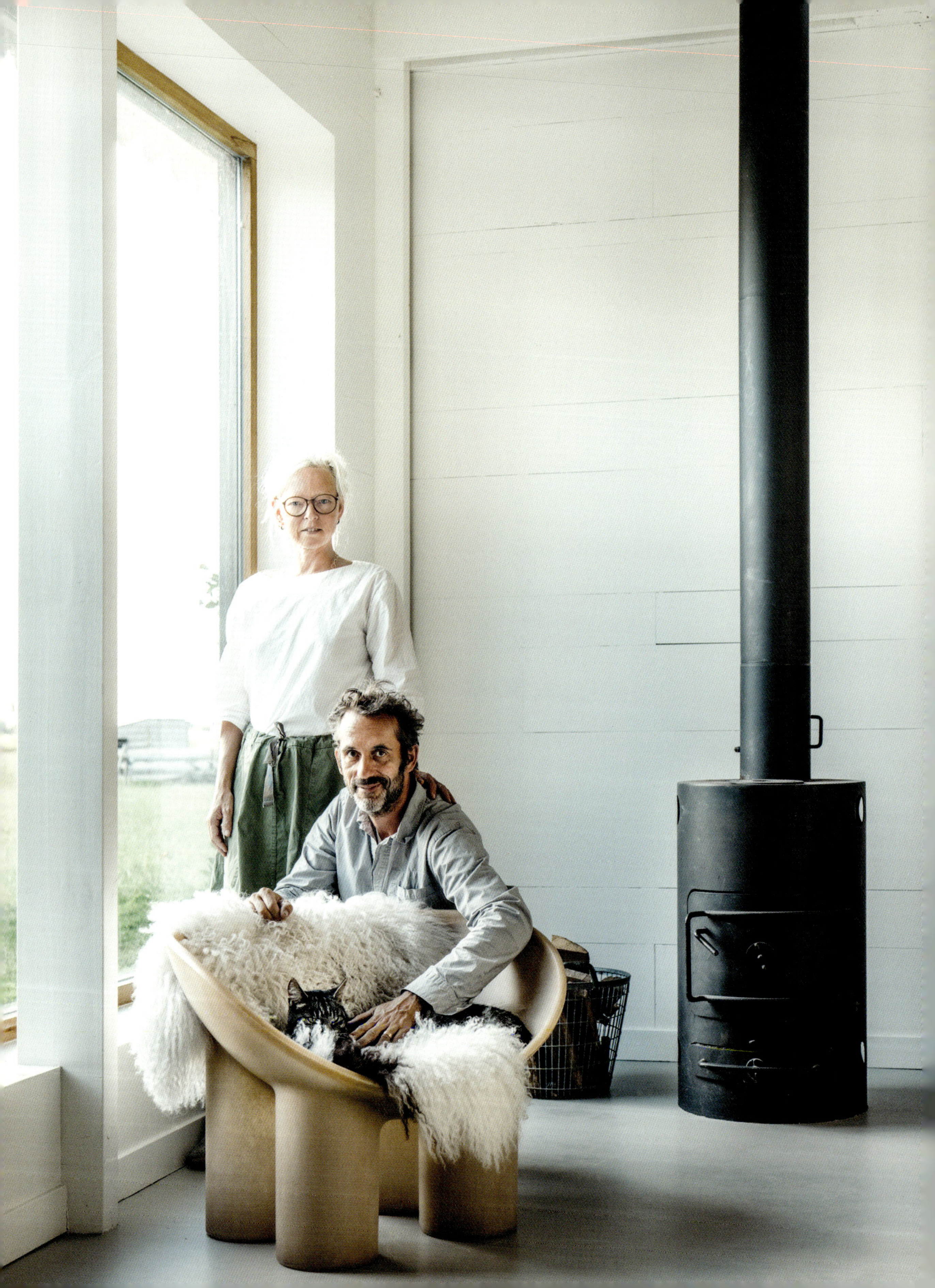

Ina and Matthijs of studio Inamatt ended up in the country by chance. They used to live in the city and were not really looking for a new home. Until such time that they stumbled upon two empty barns, which they converted into an inspiring place to live and work. The animals, whose presence can also be felt in the interior, are part and parcel of the experience. Their home is filled with drawings and visuals of creatures, which they bought or received because everyone knows the occupants of this house love pets.

A bit of a zoo

Fate and two old stables led us here,' says Ina Meijer. 'When we renovated the farm of one of our friends, we ended up falling in love with this empty stable and carriage shed on the opposite side of the road.' The renovation was quite radical. One of the most striking interventions in the larger of the two sheds was the lowering of the floor, making the space look taller and wider. The doors and windows, which open out, were incorporated in the design to bring in more light. The windows vary in size and were arranged at different heights. Some are at 'hare level,' just above the field. The animals walk past, as we sit on the sofa during our visit, looking us straight in the eye. As a result, the boundary between the exterior and the interior becomes almost entirely obsolete. Matthijs van Cruijssen explains that pets are an essential part of these residential barns, adding to the ambience: 'If your home is surrounded by fields, the aspect of sharing becomes crucial. We keep animals because this is where they belong.'

Donkeys can't be alone

The most fascinating creatures in the pasture are two donkeys, called Olga and Abel, and Toos, the sheep. 'The neighbours wanted to use them as part of a nativity scene, but they refused to budge, and we were unable to move them out of the field,' Ina says with a laugh. 'Toos hates being shorn, but when we do get around to it, the donkeys protect her. And vice versa, when their hooves need care. They are such good friends,' says Ina, while petting Olga's head. Donkeys love to be cuddled, but they can also be very stubborn. 'They do what they want, rather than what you want. When we work in the garden, they seek us out. They like contact, but they decide where and when. They hate being alone, it kills them,' Matthijs explains. Donkeys are very social animals, and they need at least one friend. Preferably another donkey, a pony, a goat or a sheep. Without company, they become depressed and can suffer from all kinds of physical ailments. They need a well-drained field and a dry barn. And if you take good care of them, they can live until the age of thirty. Ina loves their woeful eyes and their upbeat nature. 'They make great friends, like cats,' she adds.

Inspired by animals

With Olga and Abel in the farmyard, you can see why Ina and Matthijs's friends think they like pets, which is why they often receive donkey-related gifts and souvenirs. When we point out the sizeable collection of animal figurines, they look surprised. They absolutely refuse to be called animal freaks.

And yet... everywhere you look in the house, you see stuffed creatures, drawings, paintings, and ceramic objects that represent farm pets. And on the sofa, you can find cuddly toys made by Ina's mother, Meintje. She uses wool to create all kinds of imaginary creatures, which have clearly become a source of inspiration in the home and work of the designer duo. A good example is Miniverse, their platform for children between the ages of 0 to 8 years. The main character is Nilo, a futuristic figure, whose shape is reminiscent of an animal. Matthijs explains the link: 'We developed a fascination for pets, because their shape fuels our fantasy, creating associations. They are accessible and approachable. There is something tactile about them. You want to touch them and hold them, like babies, and you instantly feel affection for them.'

Pizza cats

Matthijs and Ina feel a lot of love for their felines, the two 'pizza cats'. They got them from a nearby pizzeria, for which they designed the visual identity. The couple initially wanted one kitten but ended up coming home with two almost identical cats. 'We couldn't choose, and because they resemble each other so much, we wanted to call them both Broer (Ed: Dutch for brother),' Ina recalls. During the interview, they join us at the table. And when Ina steps inside, they follow her. The house has no cat flaps. The felines indicate when they want to go out or come in. The pizza cats also regularly visit the design studio, sitting on your lap, or on steel textile, to test their 'cuddle factor'.

Chickens under the table

The chickens were not an immediate success. They had unexpected visitors, like a fox or a stone marten. Of the eight original chickens, only one survived. She soon was joined by a cockerel that arrived on the farm one day and a set of new birds, bantam Barnevelders and a Sussex chicken from the UK. During our lunch, they peck around under the table, and the cat sits on Ina's lap. This scene shows how comfortable the animals feel in their surroundings. They are more than just good company, they are family.

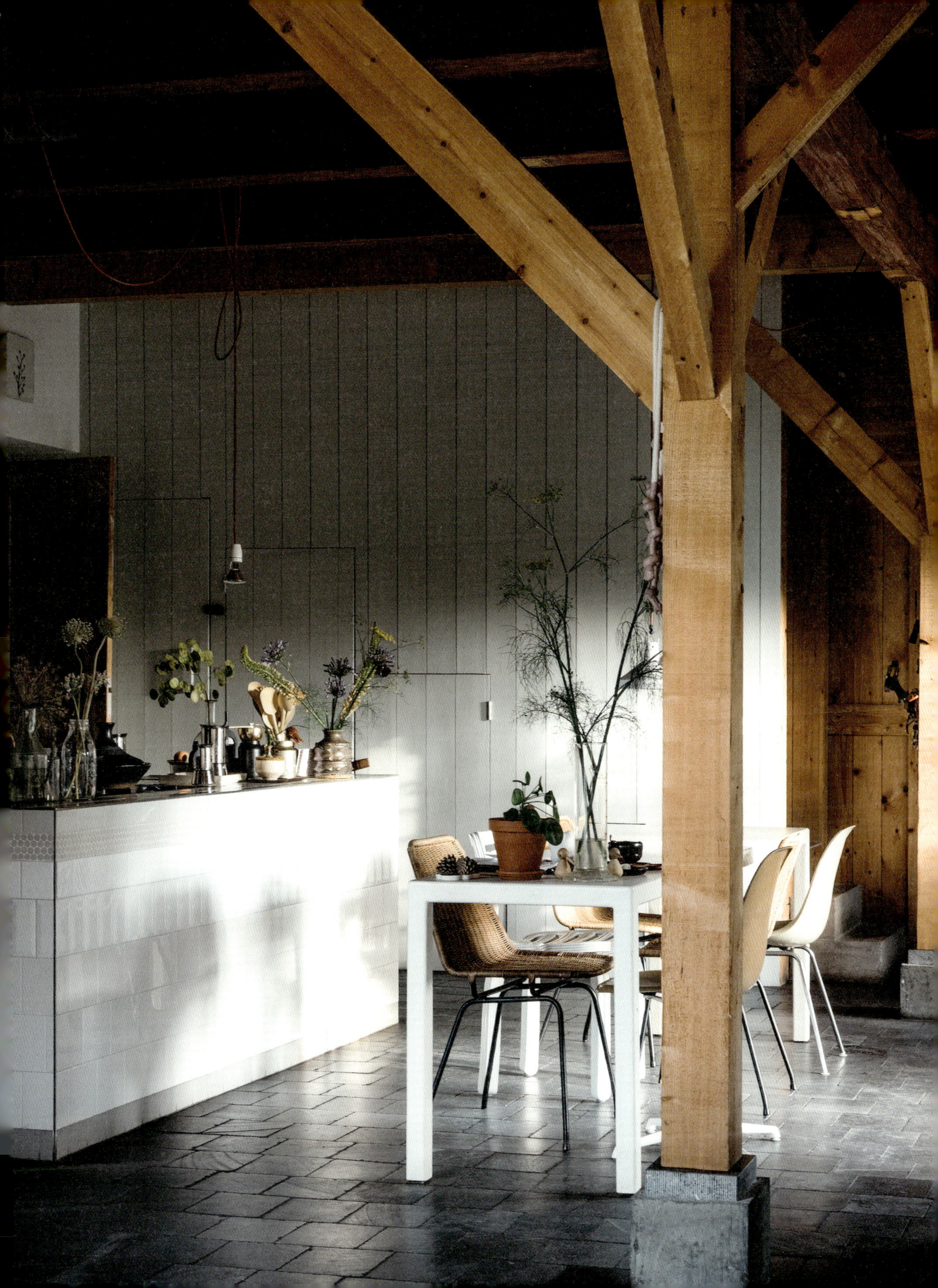

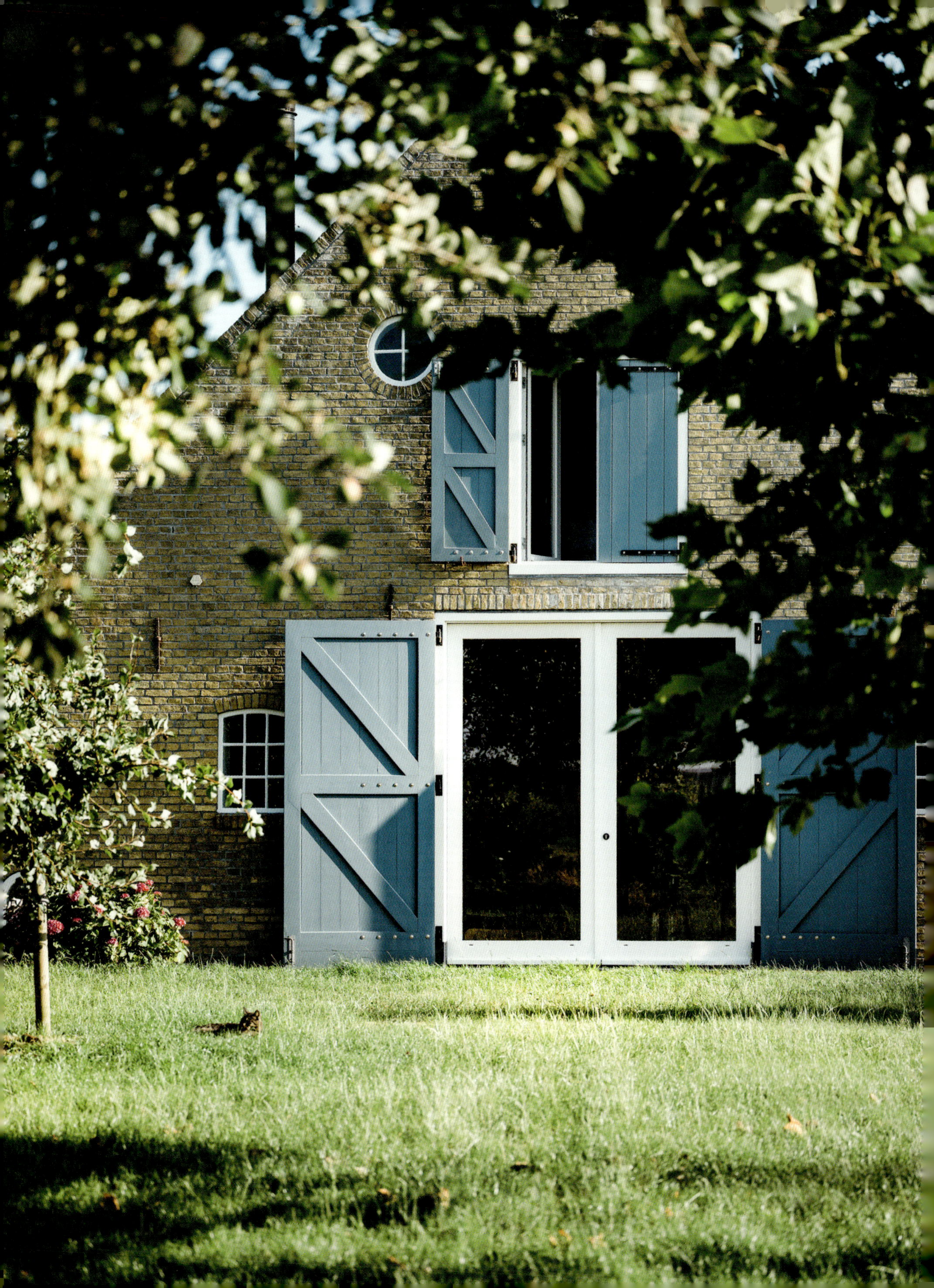

Ina and Matthijs live and work in the country, where they
converted two former barns into a studio, home, and workshop.

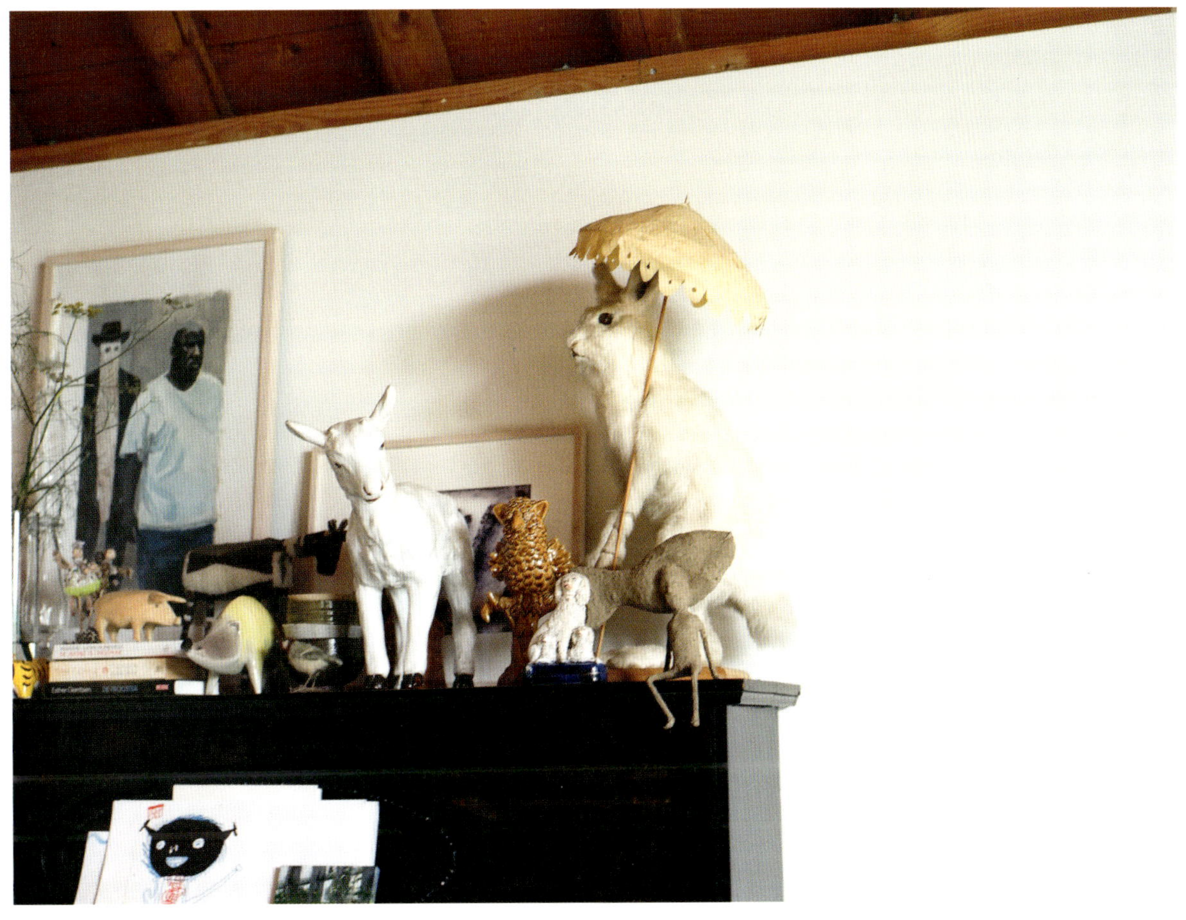

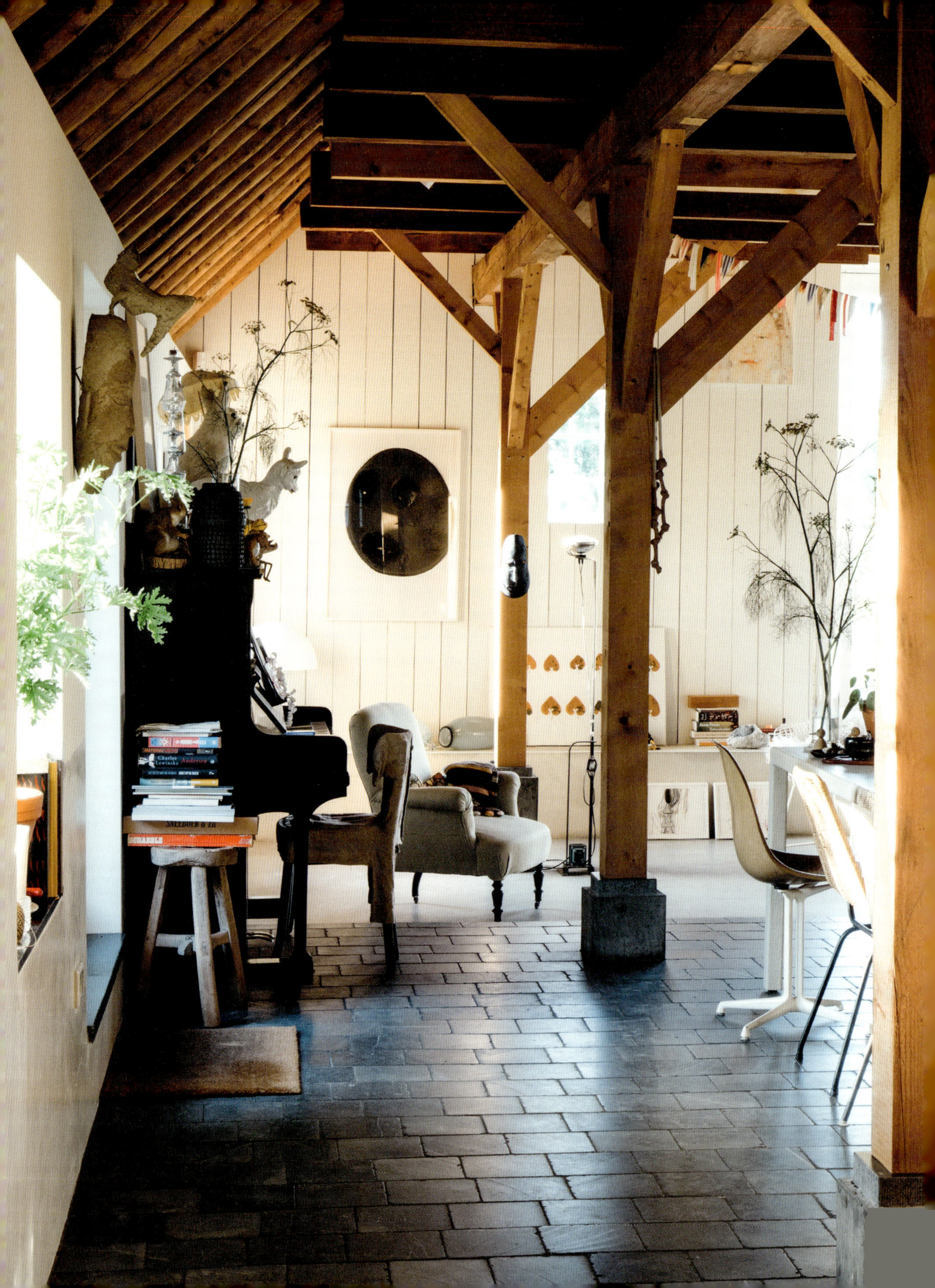

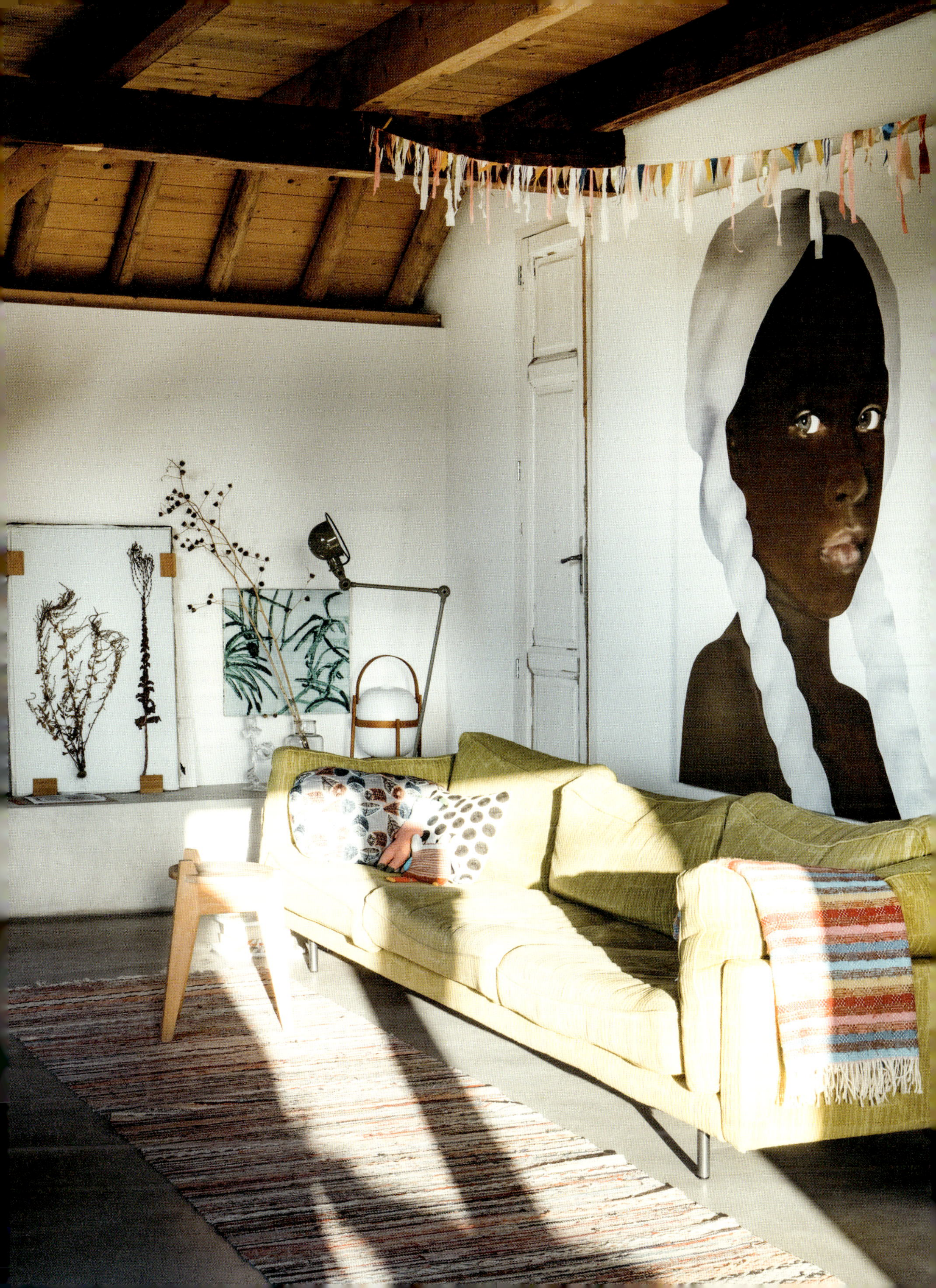

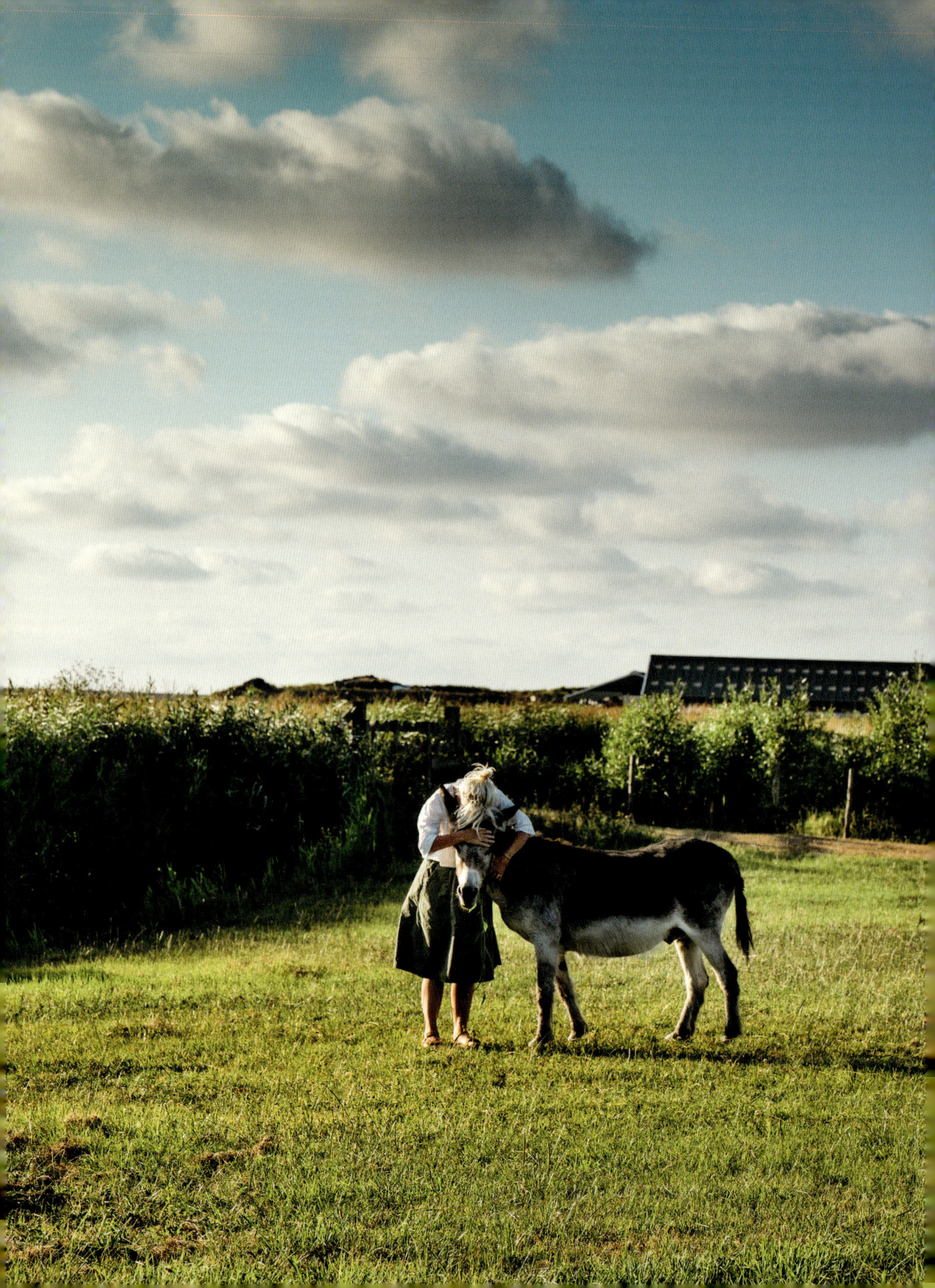

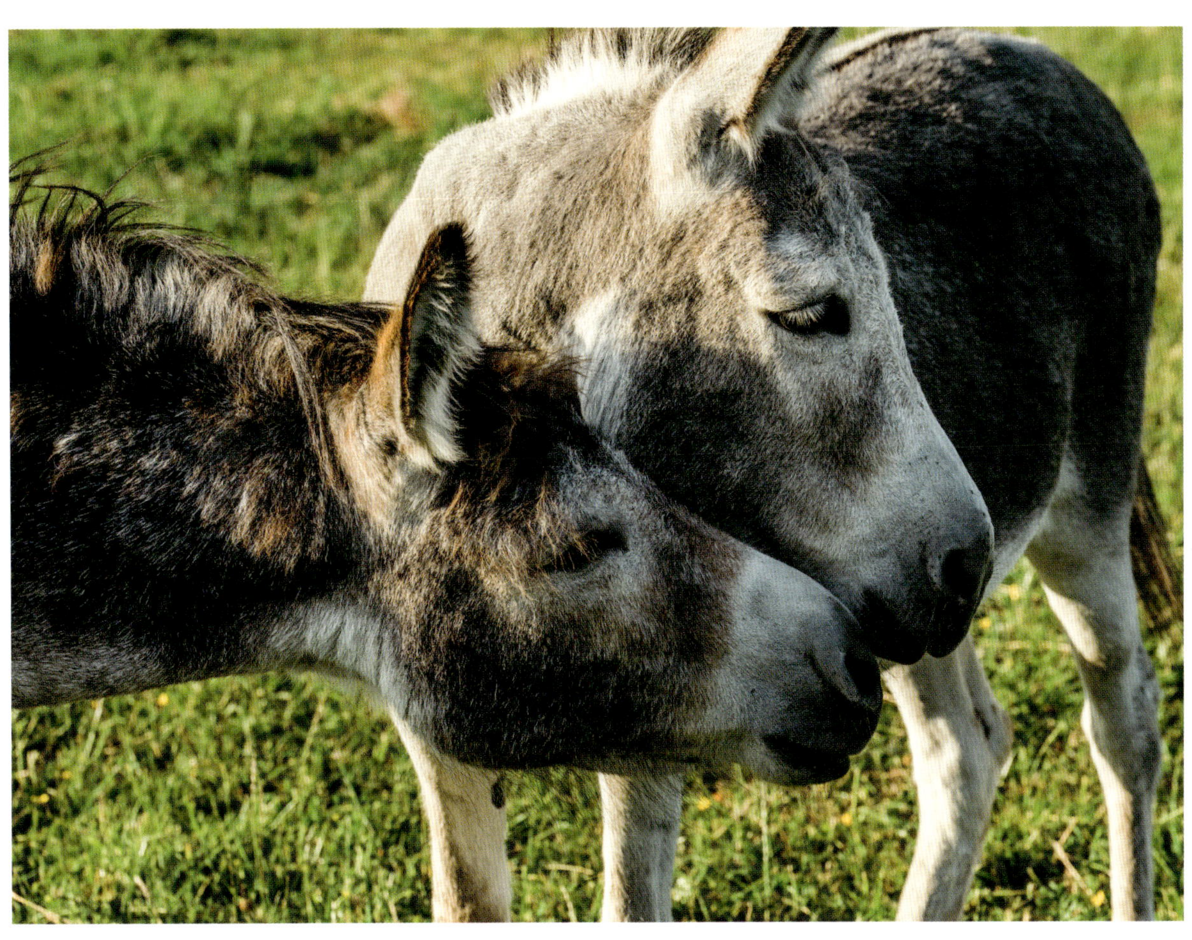

You can't help but notice the two donkeys and a sheep in the
pasture. Olga, Abel and Toos are inseparable. They also have
two cats, and chickens that like to roam around the farmyard.

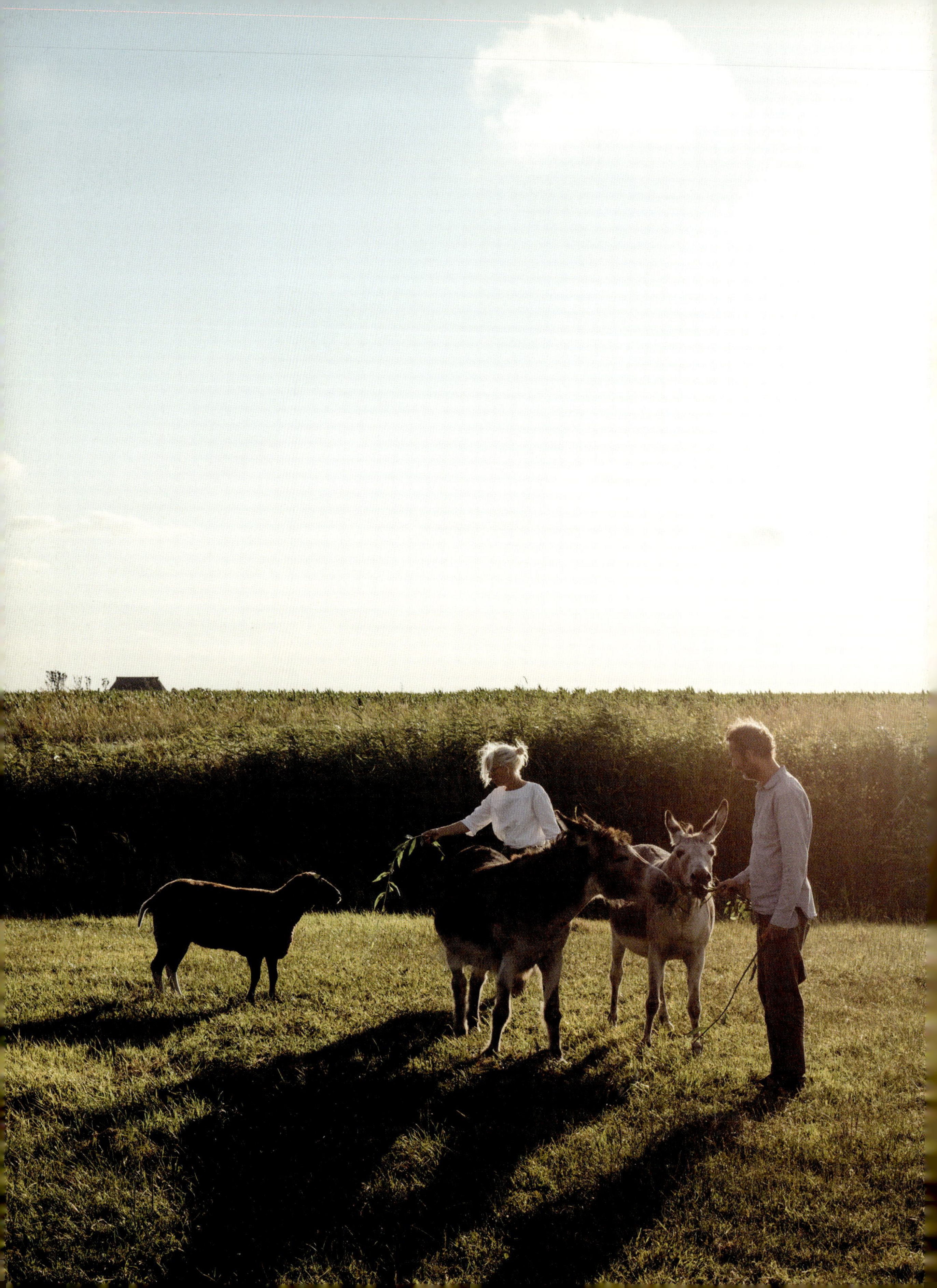

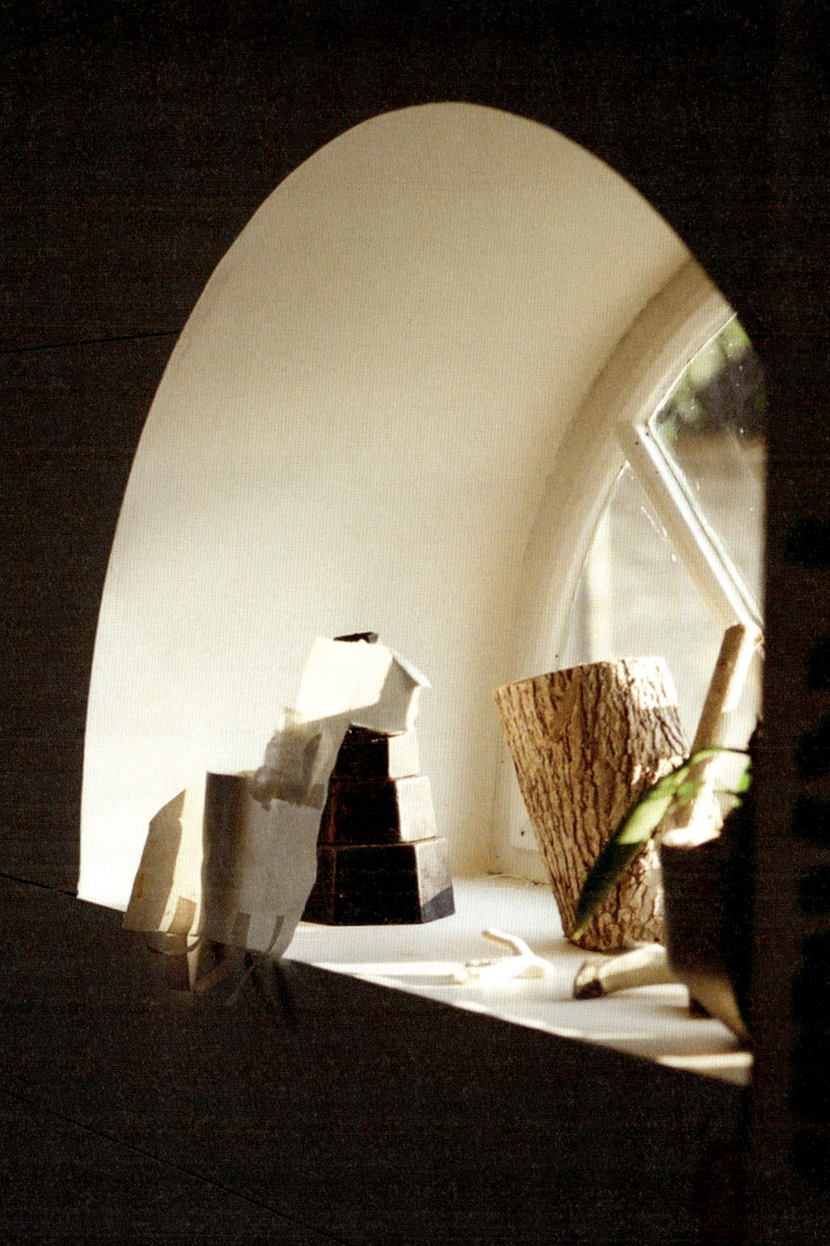

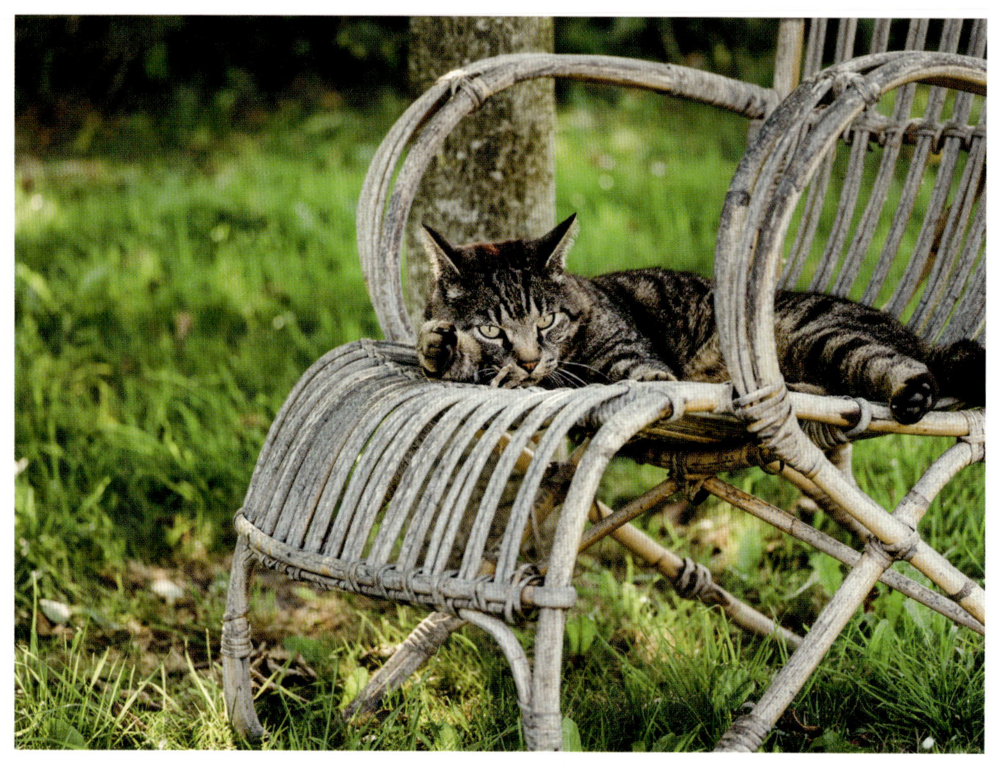

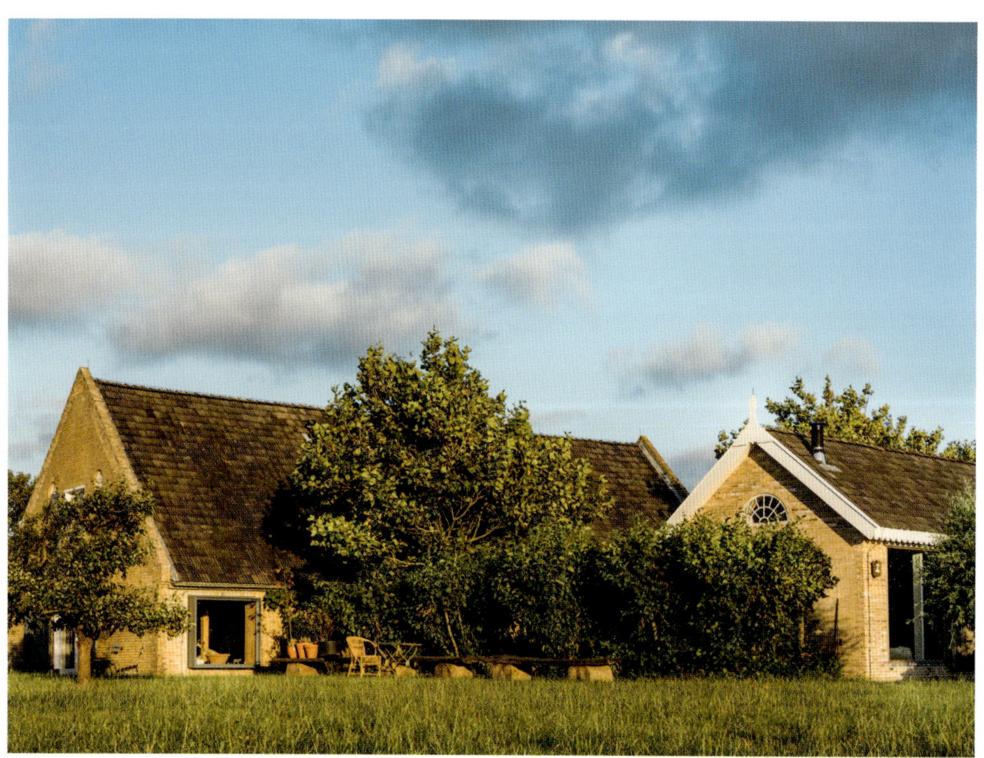

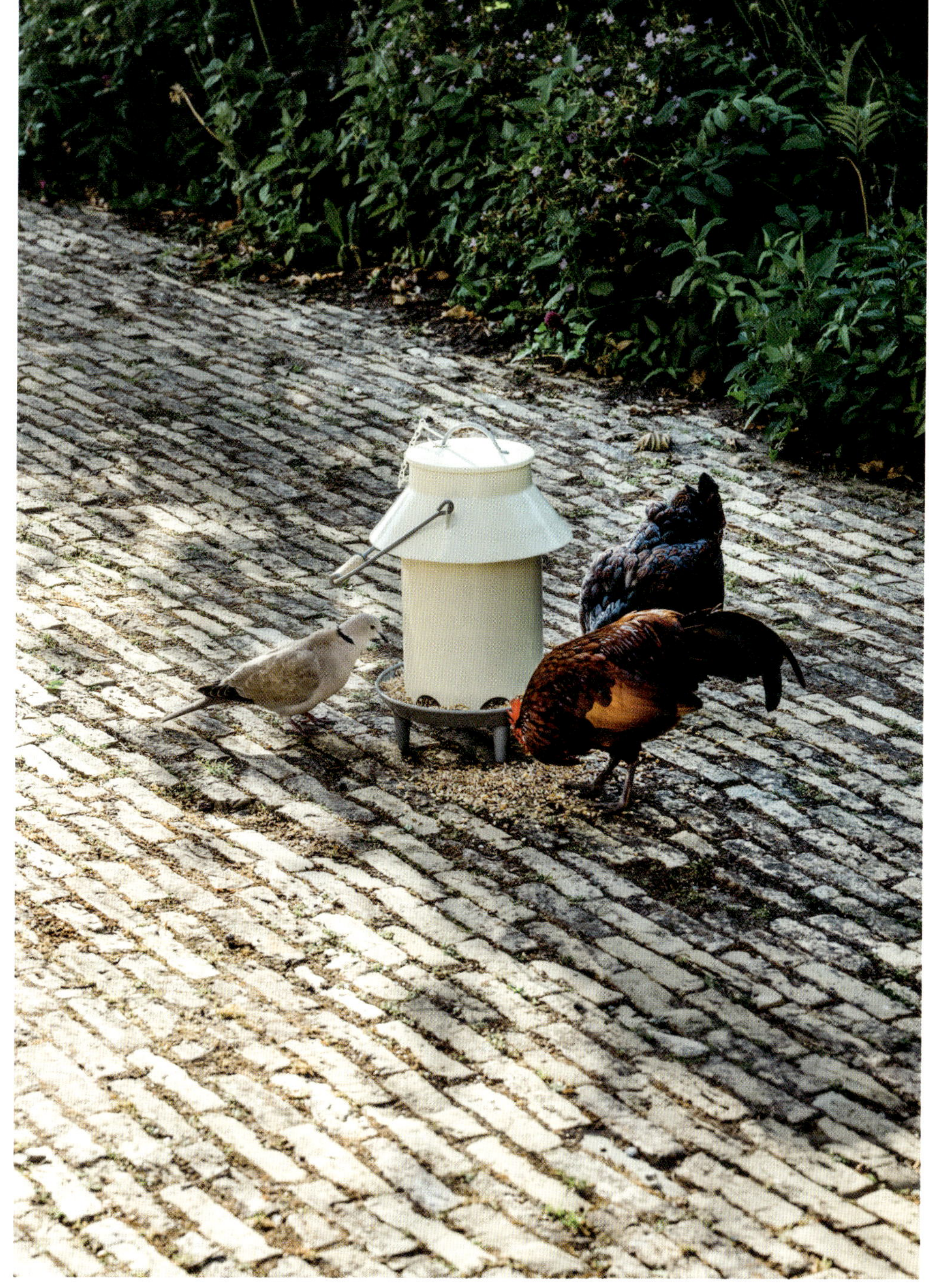

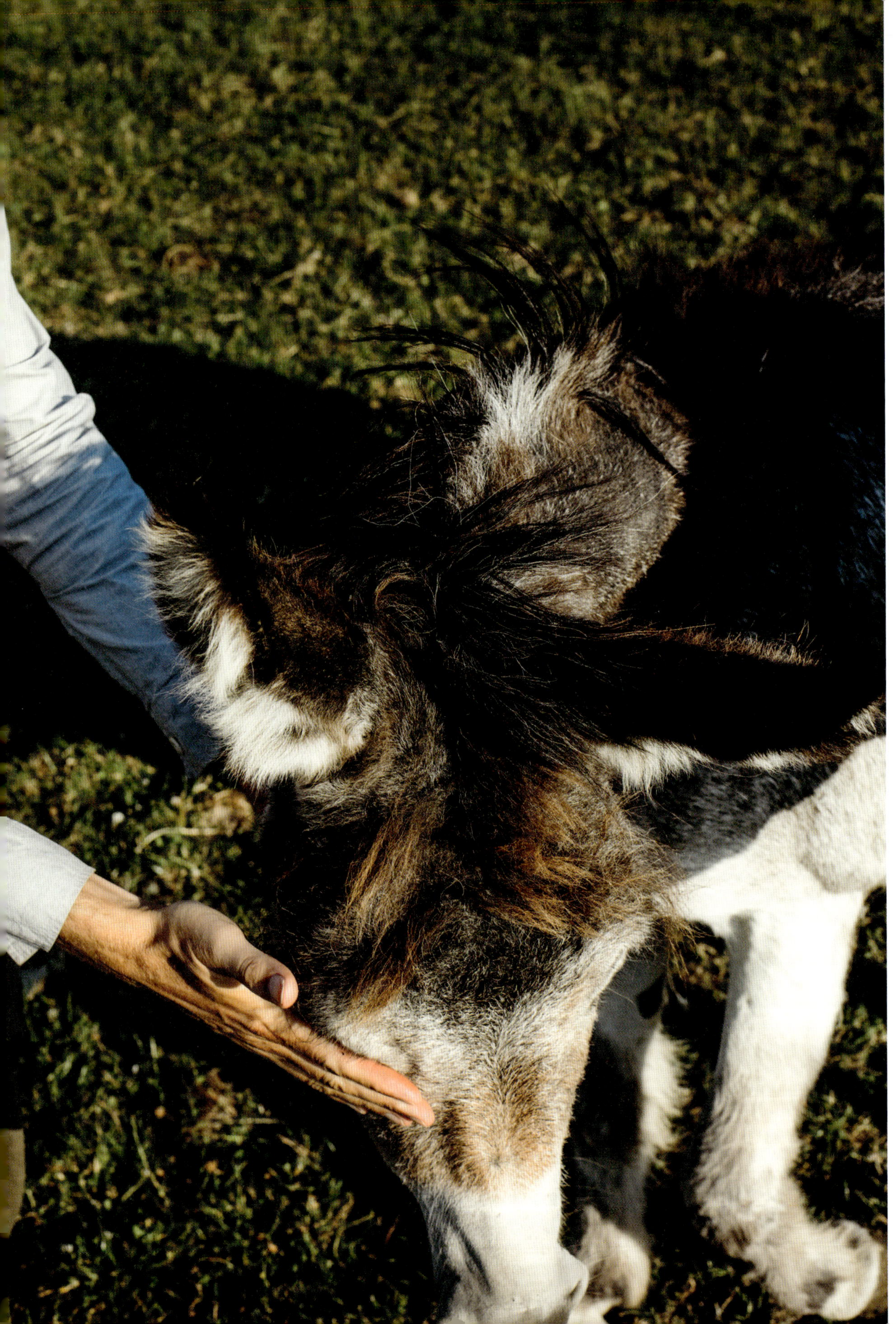

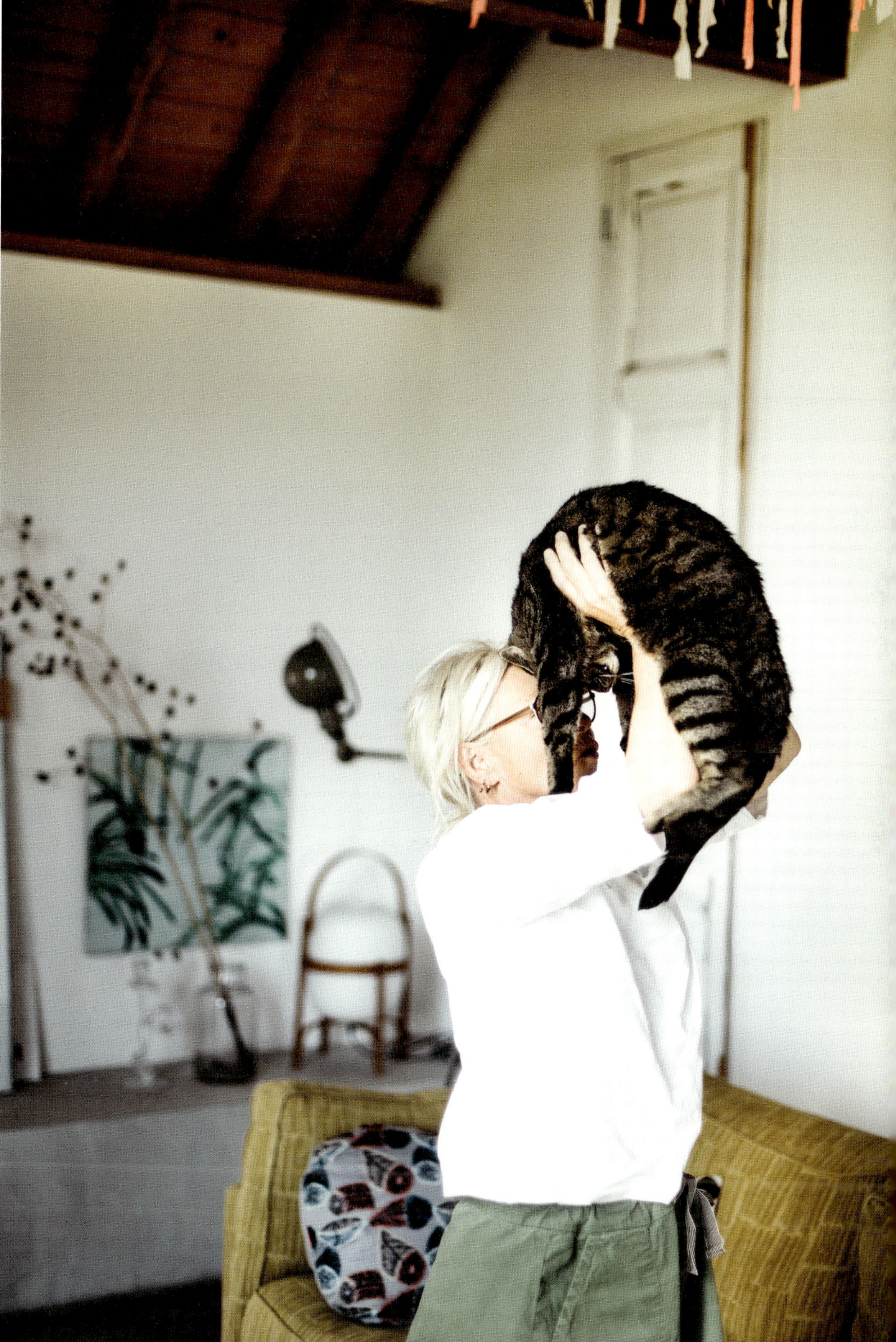

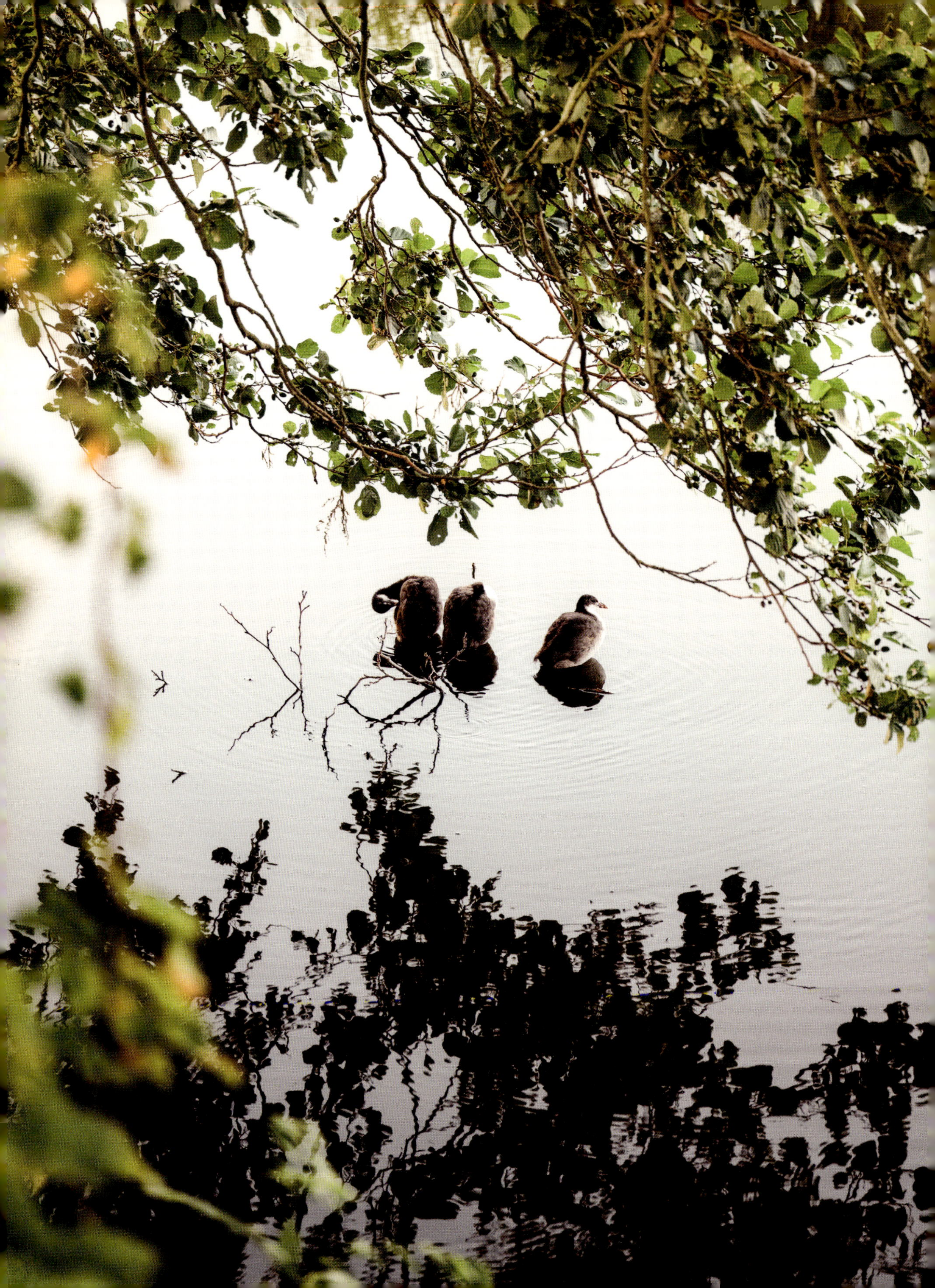

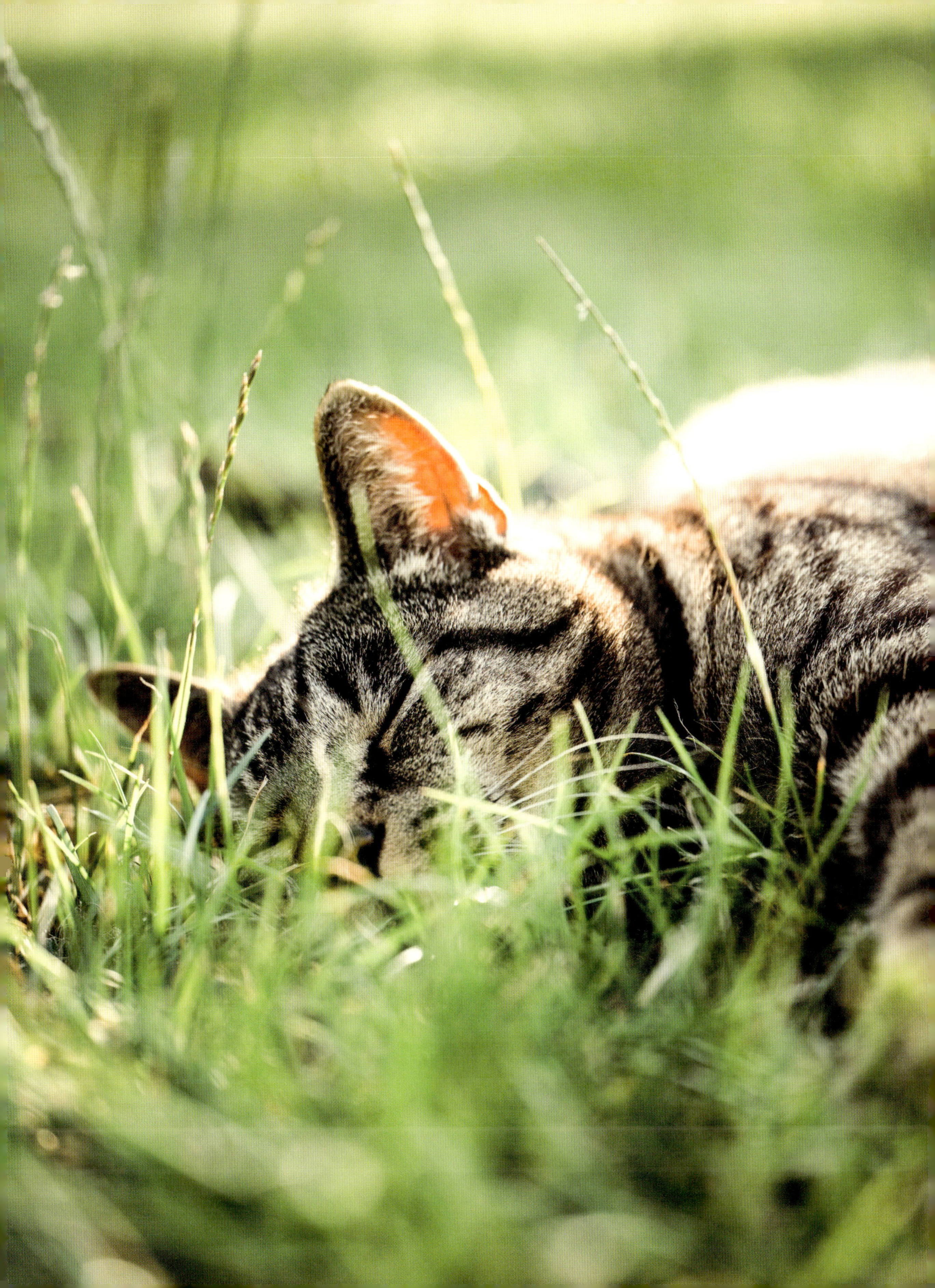

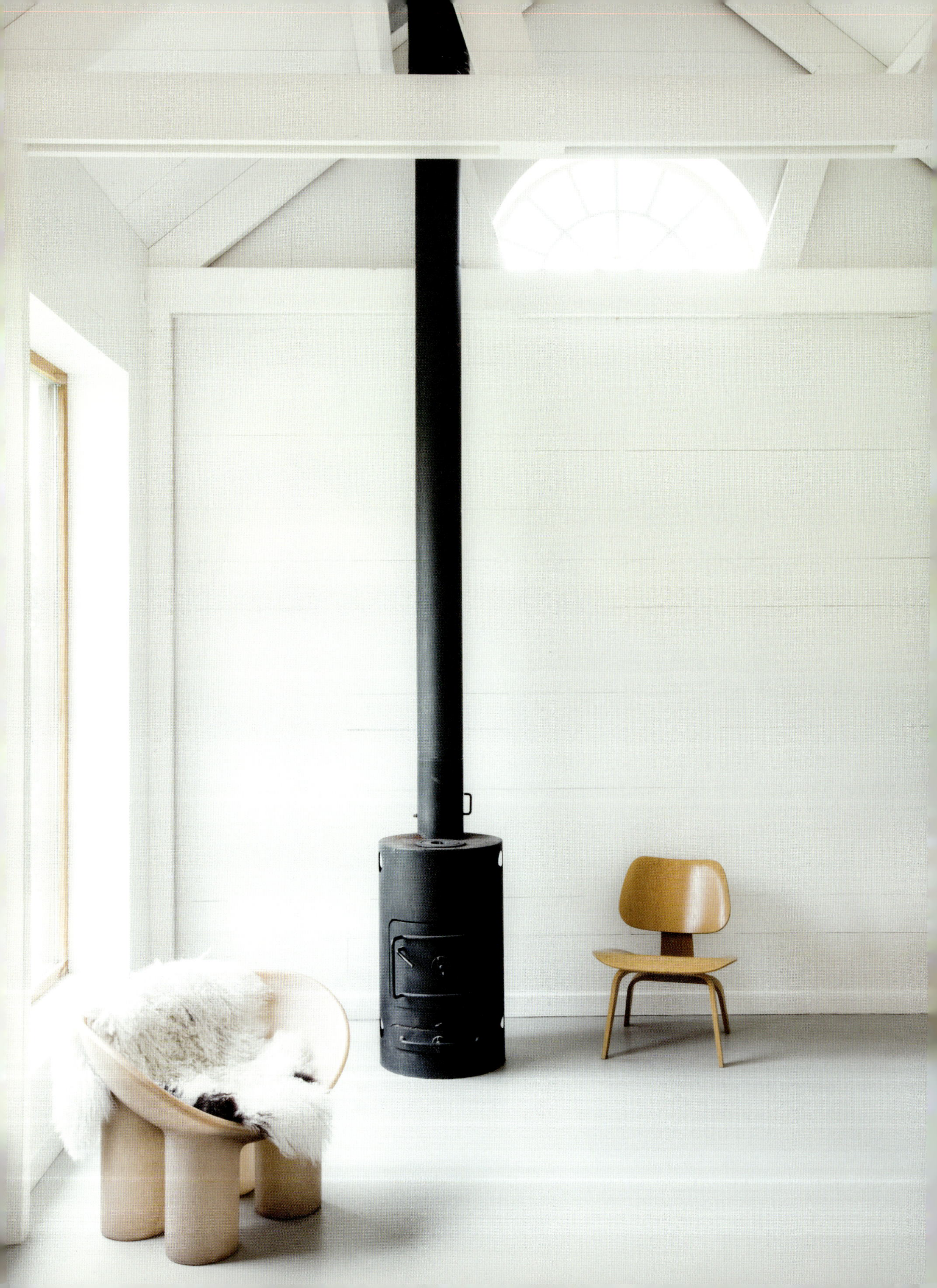

The atmosphere in the studio is very tranquil, with
white-washed walls, light furniture, and large windows,
which give out onto the surrounding countryside.

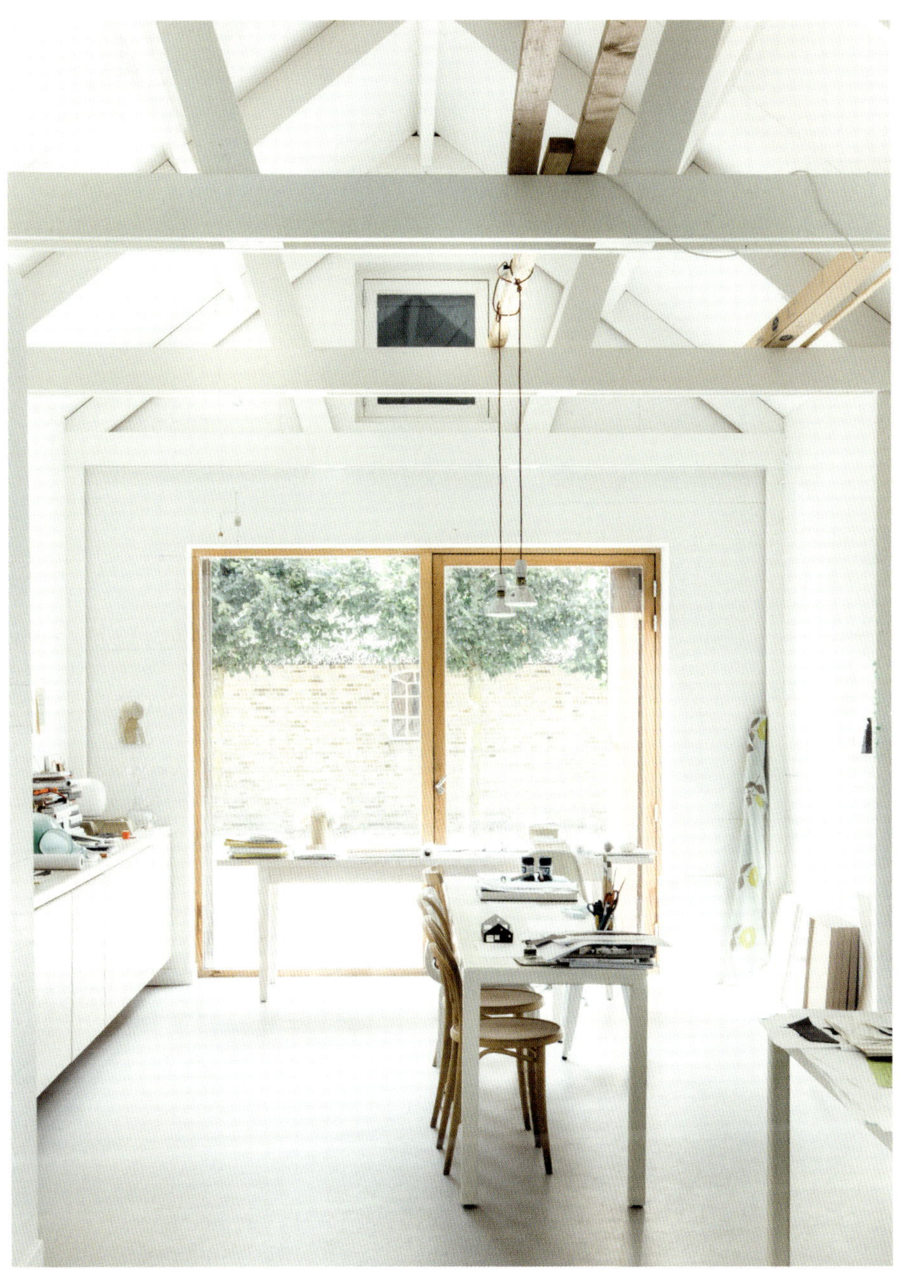

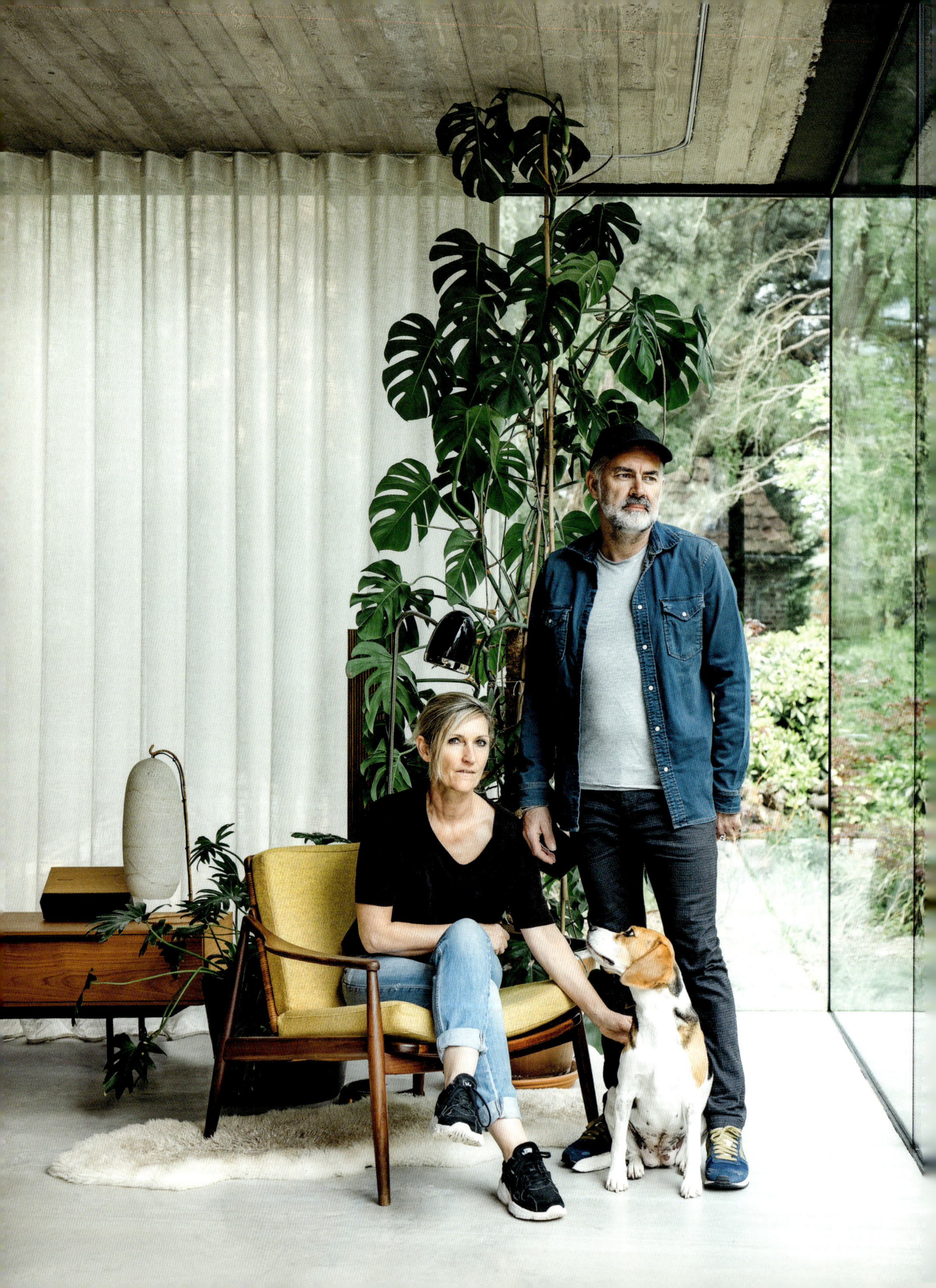

The red-brown brick sculptural volume behind a steel gate in green surroundings, looks downright impressive. It is the home of ceramic artist Alex, advertising exec Philippe and their three sons. A beagle stands guard, rushing down to welcome us. The dog blends in completely with the warm tones of the interior. We have to look twice to spot the cats, and the tone-on-tone effect is also reflected in the ceramics, which seem to be an extension of the house. Or perhaps it's the other way around?

A curious beagle

When Billie spots us from the first floor, she goes bonkers. 'It's completely normal,' says Philippe De Ceuster. 'She gives other dogs that walk by the same treatment.' Billie is a beagle, an active and curious hunting dog. The breed, which has been around for hundreds of years, is famously energetic and known for its deep bark. Usually, they limit themselves to barking and wagging their tail because beagles are fun dogs that love people and get on like a house on fire with other pets. That said, it took Billie some time to get used to the cats, that already lived in the house when she joined the family. Alex Gabriels and Philippe have always been cat people. Wherever they lived, they had a cat. And then there was that one time that a bird fell through the chimney and they decided to raise it. But that was an exception. Their sons Luka (23 years), Nino (20 years) and Noah (18 years) had wanted a dog for quite some time. So imagine the surprise when they returned from their scout camp.

Dog training: not everyone's cup of tea

Alex and Philippe imposed two conditions when they agreed to get a dog: the new house had to be finished entirely, and someone had to take care of the beagle. Before her arrival, the couple worked full-time in advertising until Alex decided to follow her heart and dedicate herself full-time to her passion, ceramics. Their new home has a workshop and a showroom for her collection. They made a deal that the boys would take care of the dog, but it is mainly Alex's job. Billie is very attached to her and follows her to the atelier. During the day, she sleeps in her basket while Alex turns her pottery. In the evening, Billie and her basket move to the bedroom. Philippe also loves the pup a lot and regularly takes her on long walks in the fields around the house. 'Billie is a top dog, she's so sweet.' Because she is so stubborn, like most beagles, they only went to dog training a few times. 'After two years, she knows exactly what she can and cannot do. It doesn't mean she always listens. She can be quite headstrong. But that makes it even more fun,' says Philippe with conviction. Billie is a female dog and gets on well with male dogs. Every Thursday, one of her furry friends visits.

Dividing the attention

We agree with Philippe: Billie's mild-mannered demeanour is an extension of her character. During our visit, she lies down happily next to our 9-month old son. She gently licks him and doesn't mind it when he tugs at her fur. The two cats are much less forthcoming. Spook is a black and white cat and is fifteen years old. He is very independent and is already used to his new home. On winter days, he leaves the house through the cat flap. In the summer, he walks in and out through the sliding windows in the kitchen. The couple has no scratching posts or litter trays, Alex thinks they're dirty. The cats poo in the garden, and they sharpen their nails on the trees. Now and then Spook brings home a prize, which Billie proceeds to gobble up. 'Fortunately, he catches mice for the most part. Once he hid a dead hare behind the freezer,' Philippe recalls. Krapuul is Spook's mother. She has a recently-diagnosed thyroid problem, which is incurable. 'We have no idea how long she will live,' says Alex, visibly moved. 'We want to have her put down, but the boys objected.' They give the cat medicine a few times a day. Philippe cuddles her. She enjoys it and purrs. Alex confesses that she feels guilty because the cats received a lot less attention recently as Billie tends to demand a lot of it. During the renovation, the felines spent some time in a cat hotel, which they hated.

Concrete, ceramics and wood

While they were renovating the house, the family lived in a tiny studio flat opposite the construction site. What a contrast, compared with the considerable space they now have in the new-build. We feel an instant glow inside when we enter the house. The Indian and Moroccan influences in the architecture of Bart Lens and Thijs Prinsen definitely contribute to this. But the interior also has a nice ambience with a combination of rough concrete, warm wood, and house plants. Alex's ceramic objects and Philippe's paintings only add to the overall atmosphere. The house only feels cosier because of the presence of the pets. While we enjoy the view, Billie draws our attention again, licking the walls this time. The walls were treated with salt and minerals, and the dog loves to lick them. After she has finished, she flops down in front of the fireplace and nods off. Enough action for today.

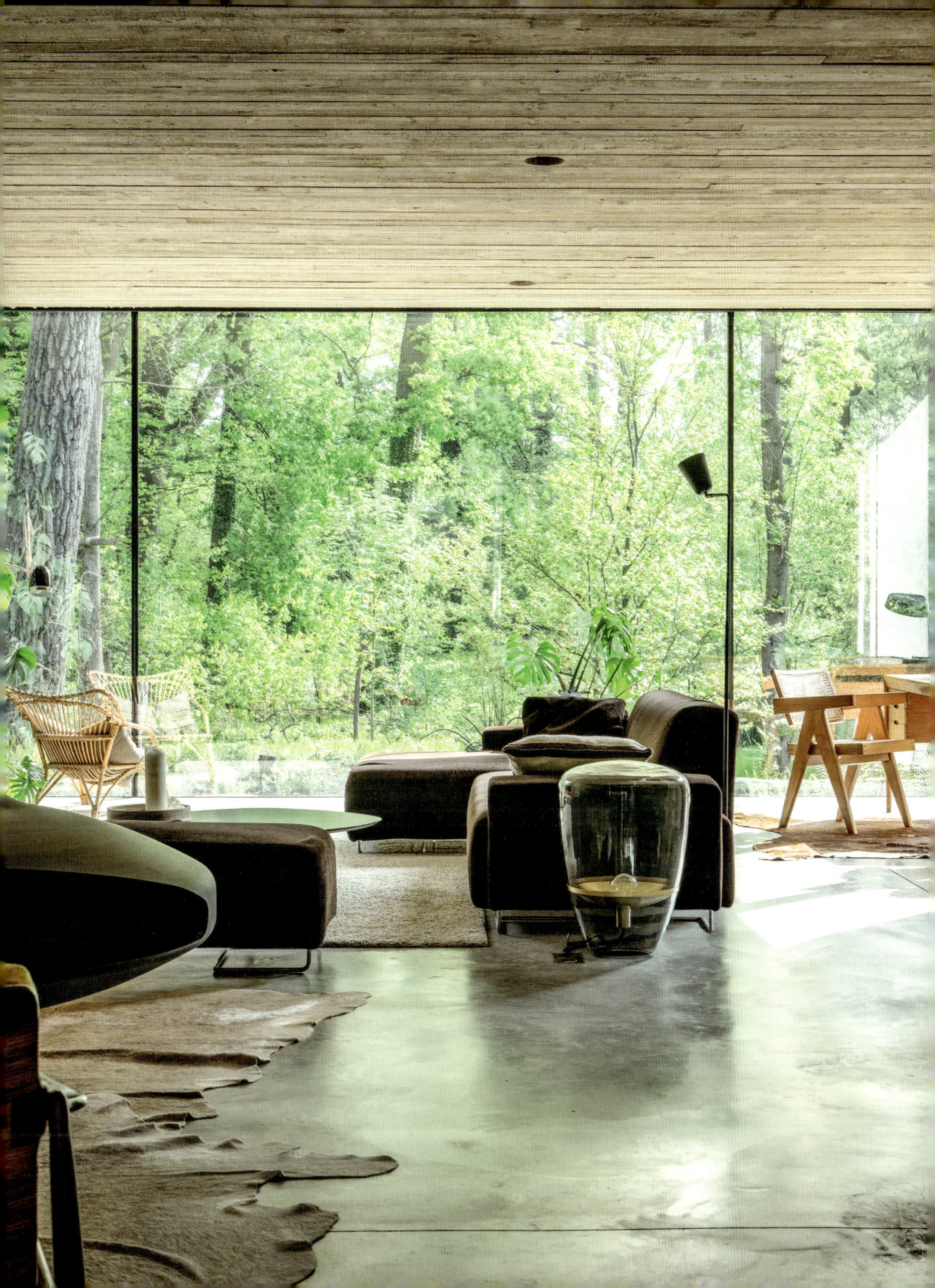

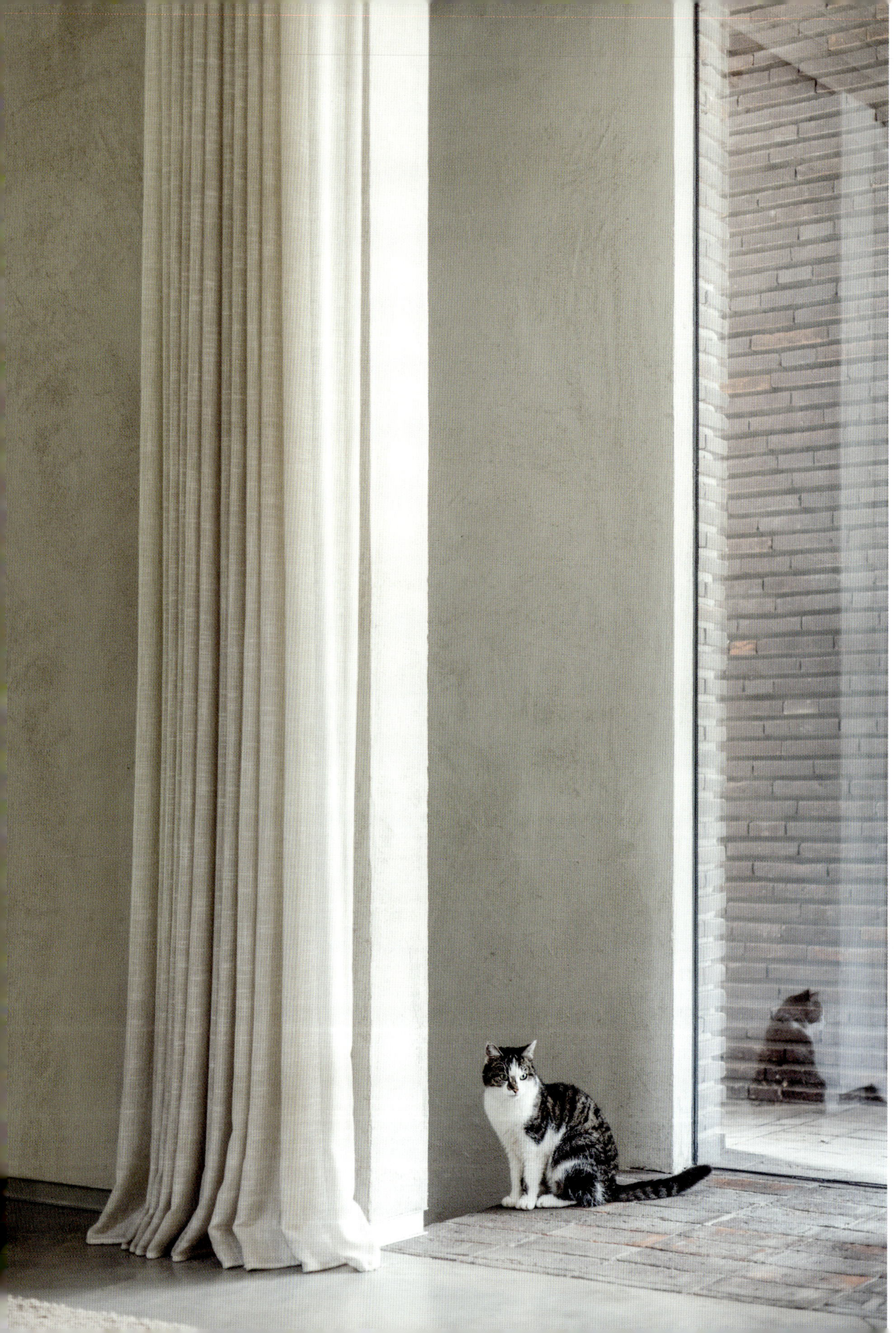

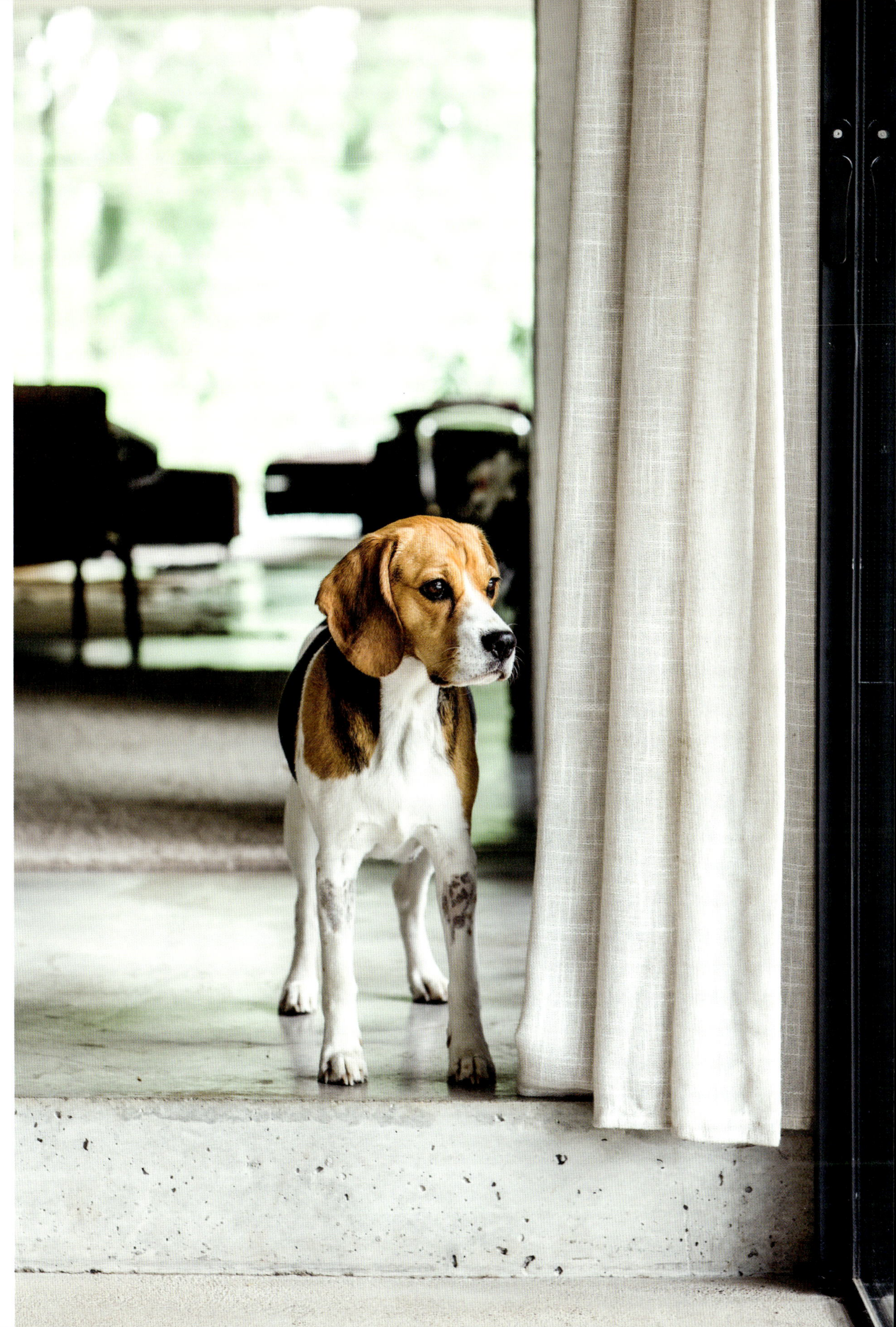

Architects Bart Lens and Thijs Prinsen designed a brutalist house, with influences from India and Morocco. For the interior, Alex and Philippe combined concrete, wood, ceramics and house plants.

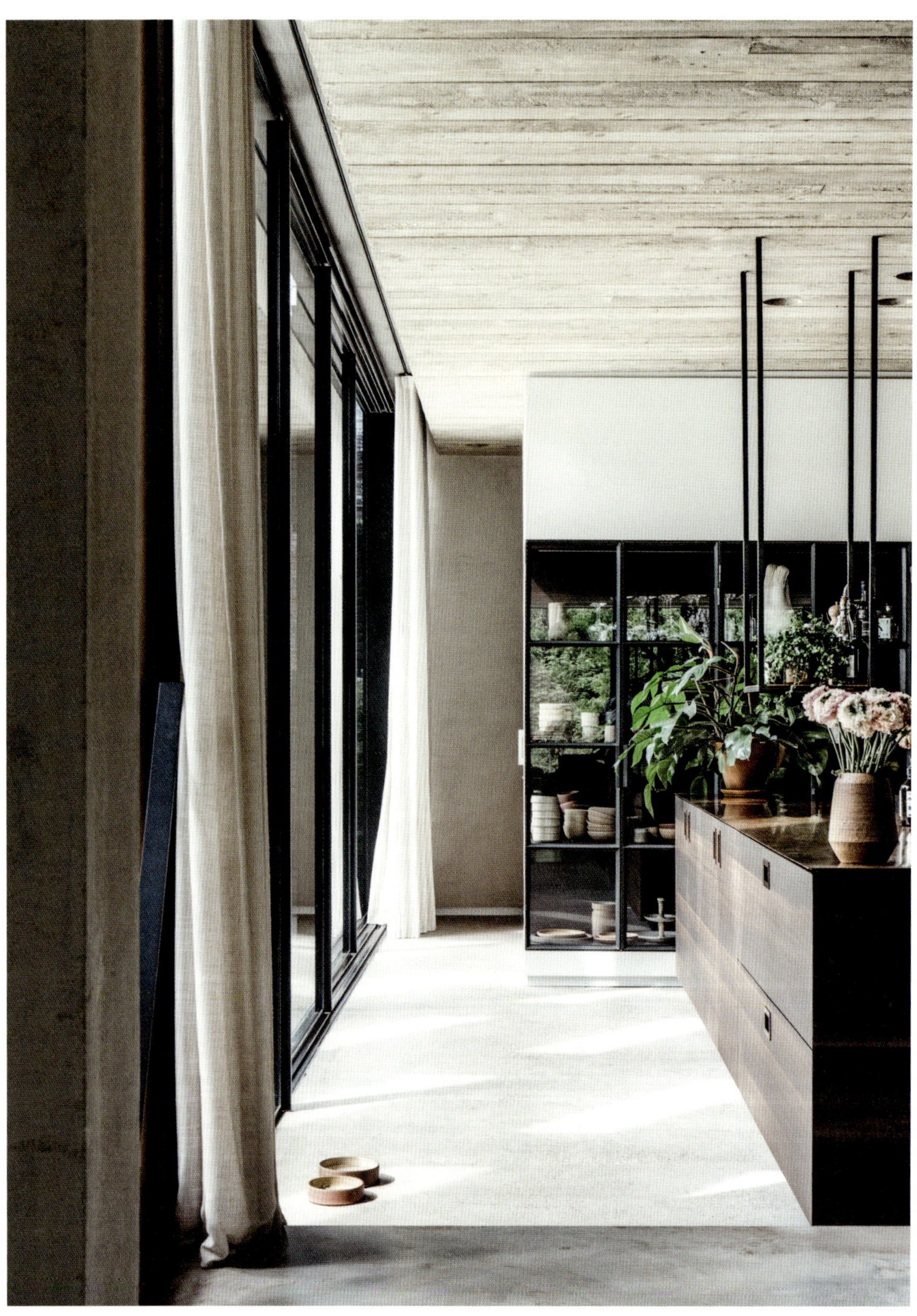

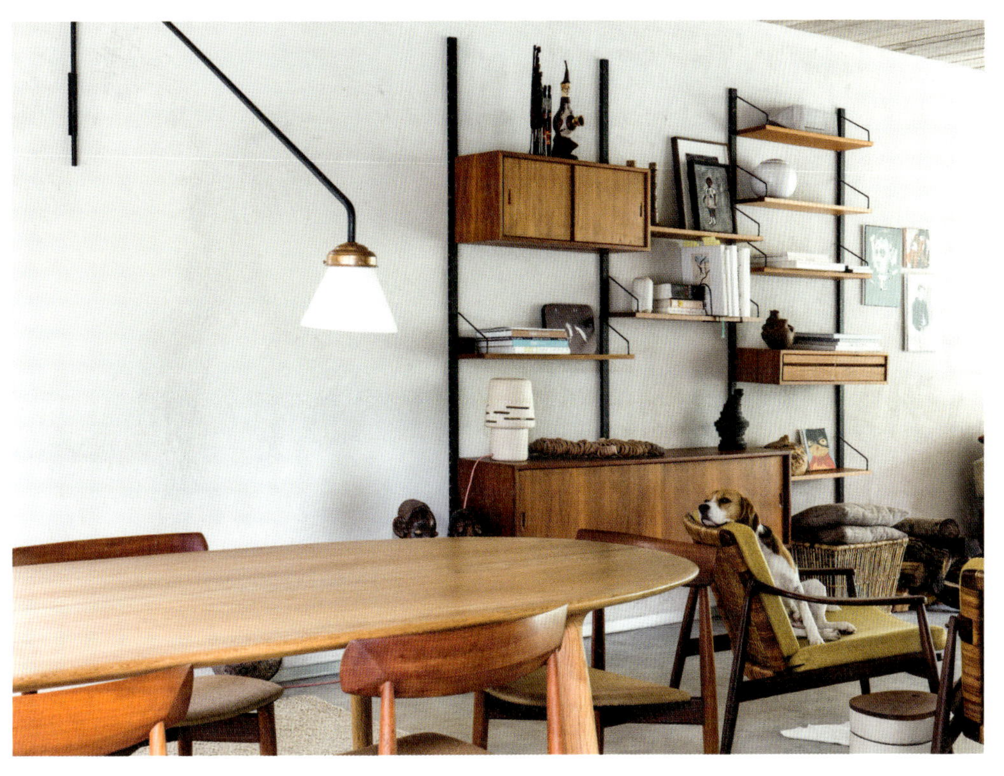

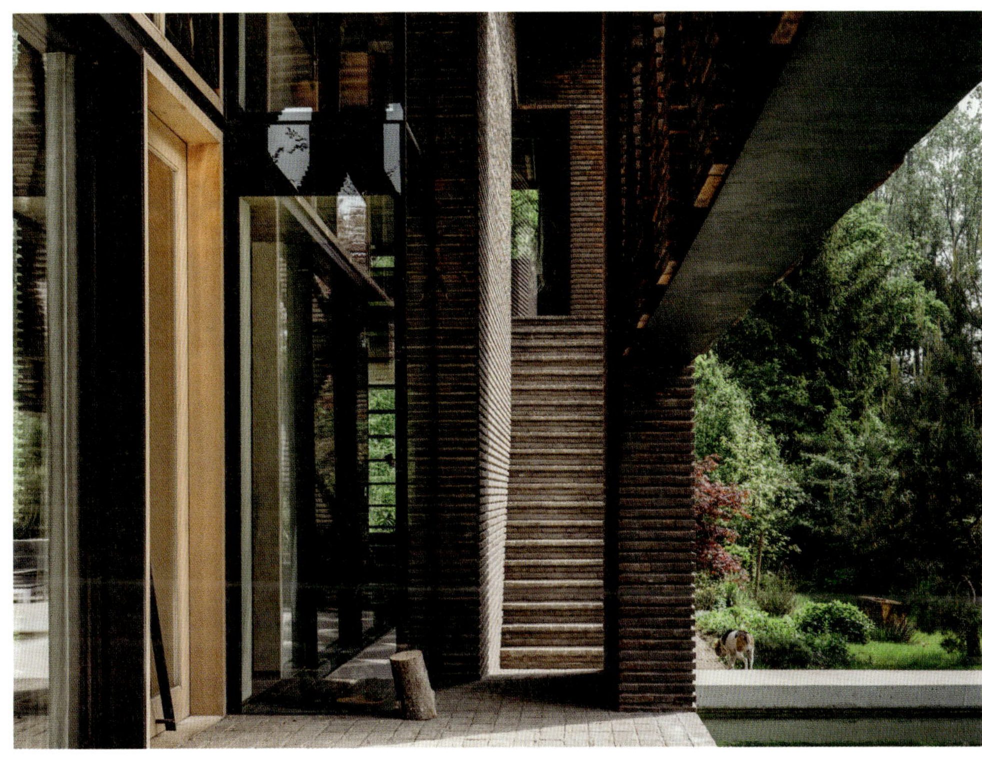

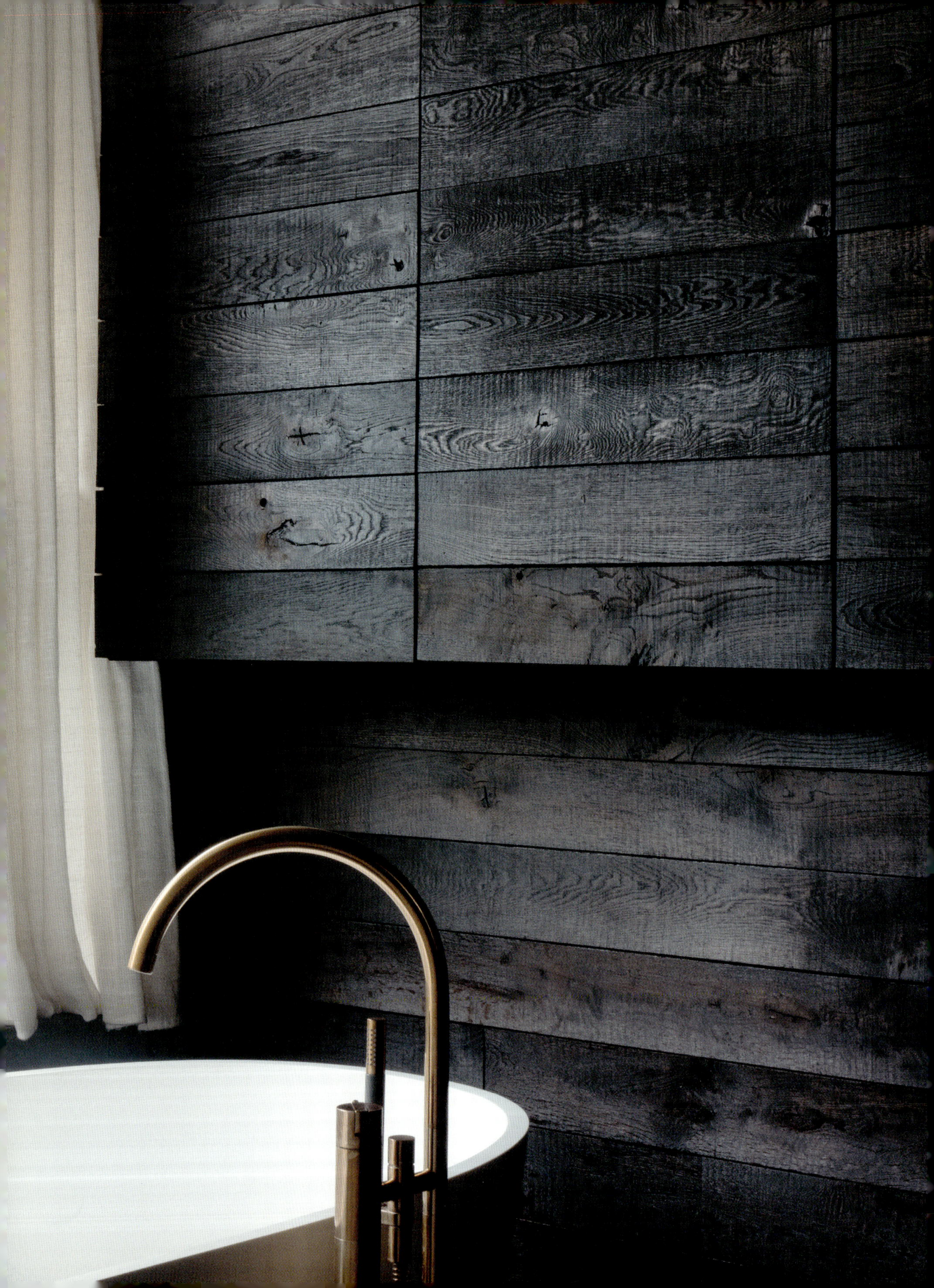

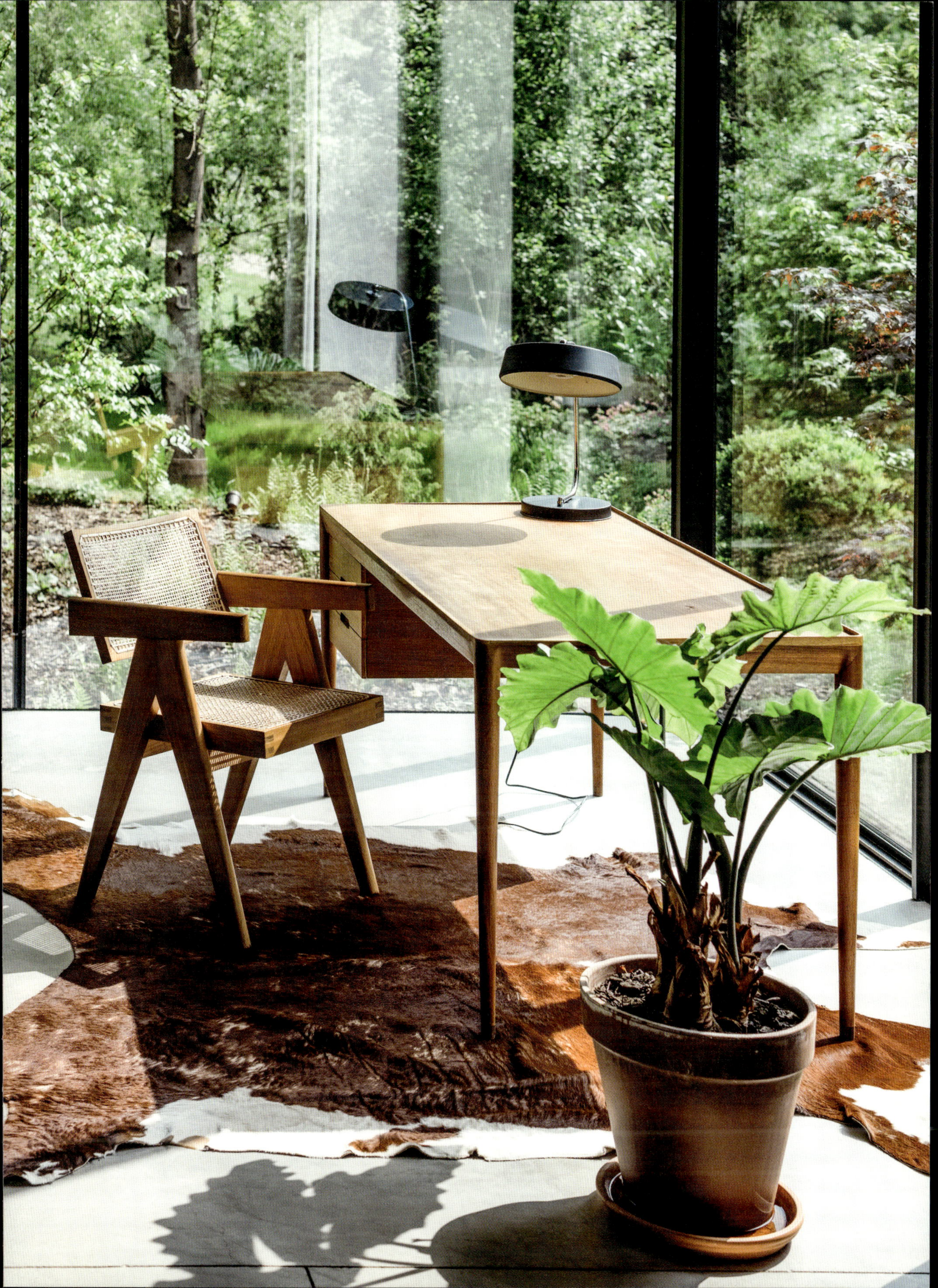

The couple caved in to their children's demands for a dog.
Billie, the beagle, is very active and gets on well with their cats,
Spook and Krapuul.

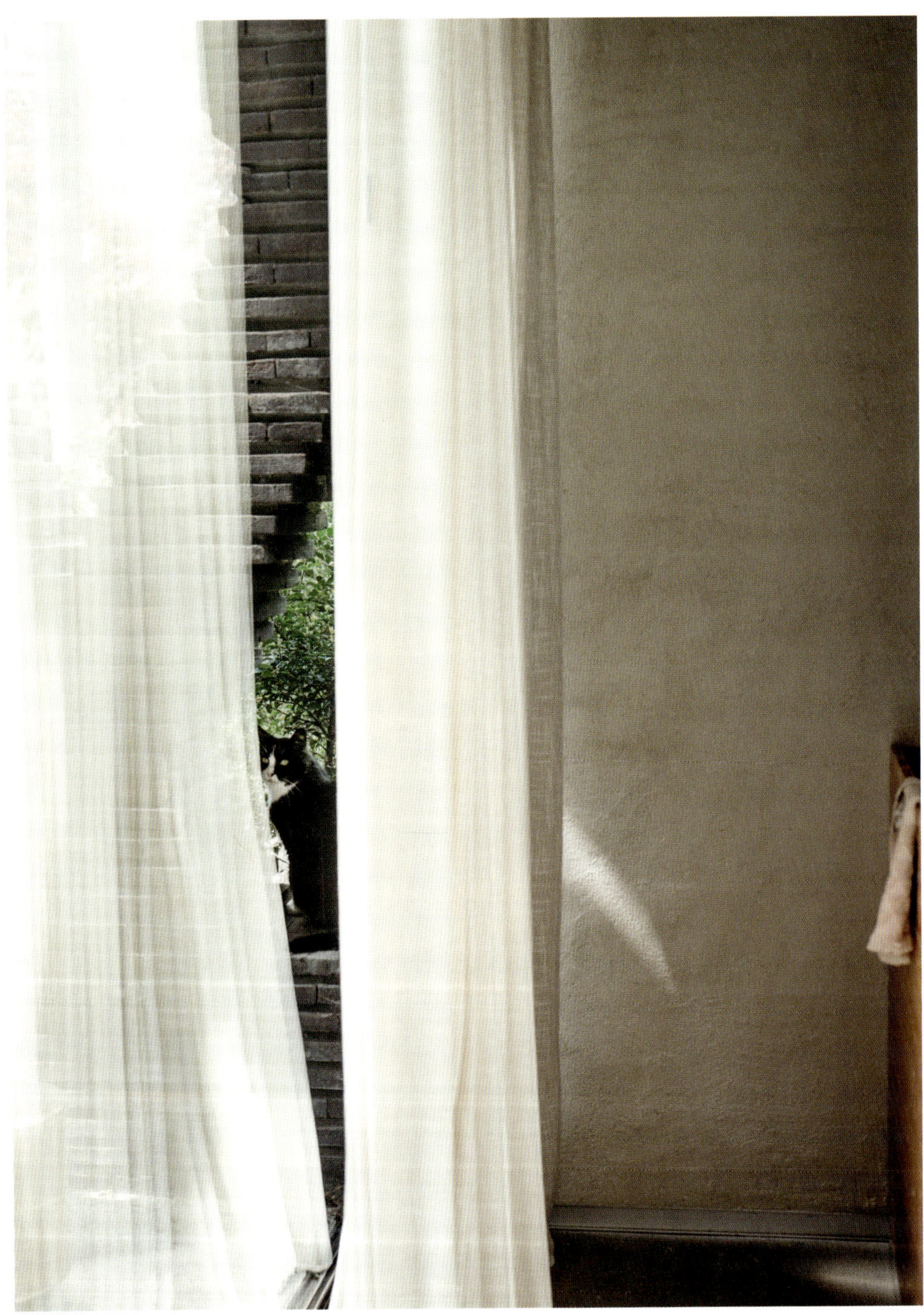

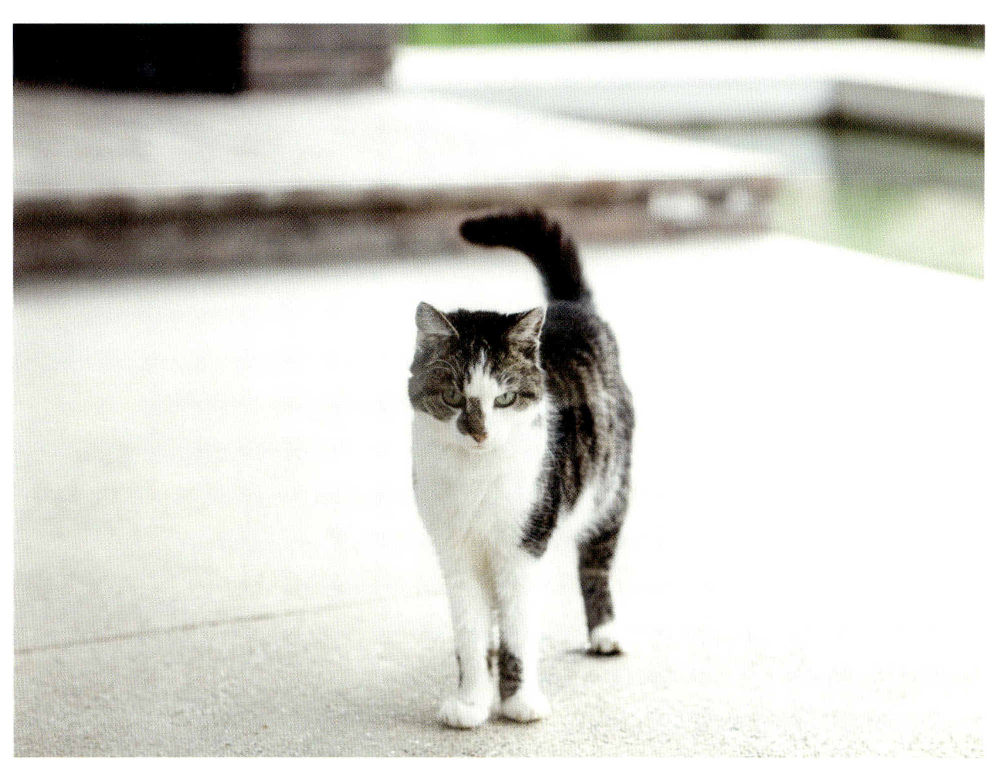

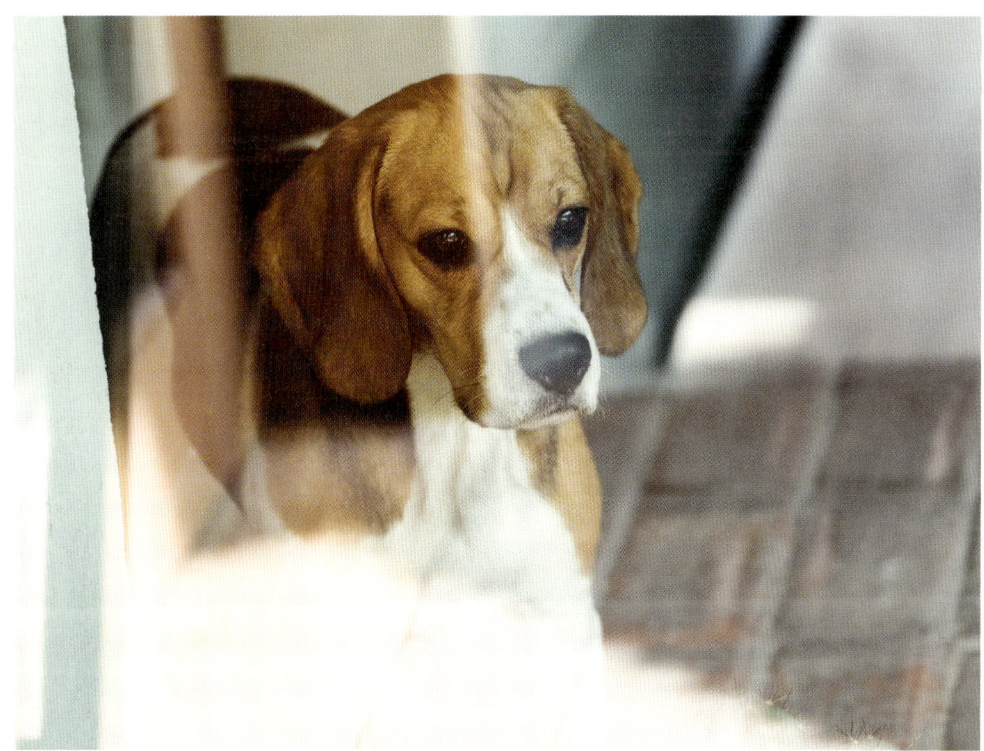

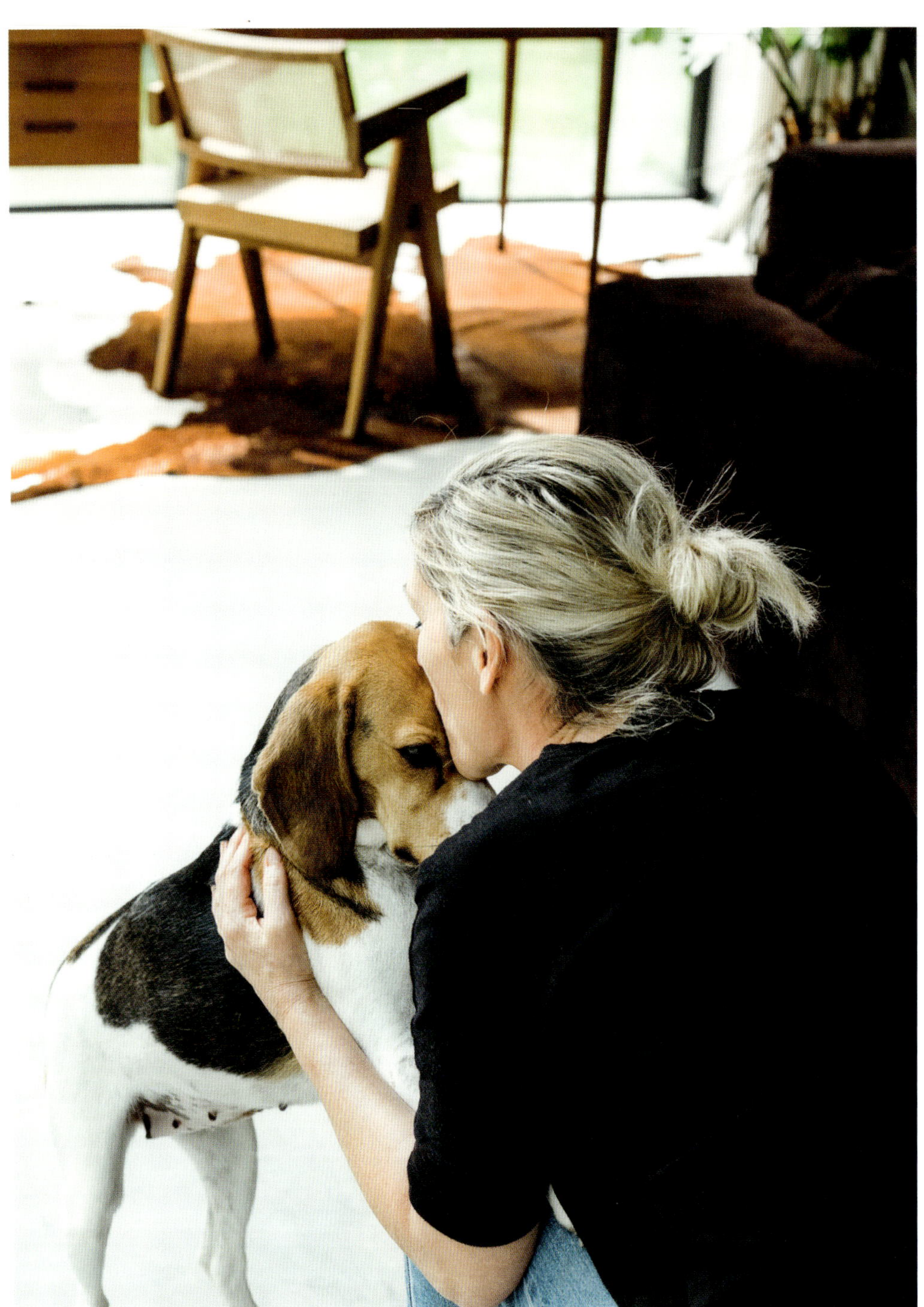

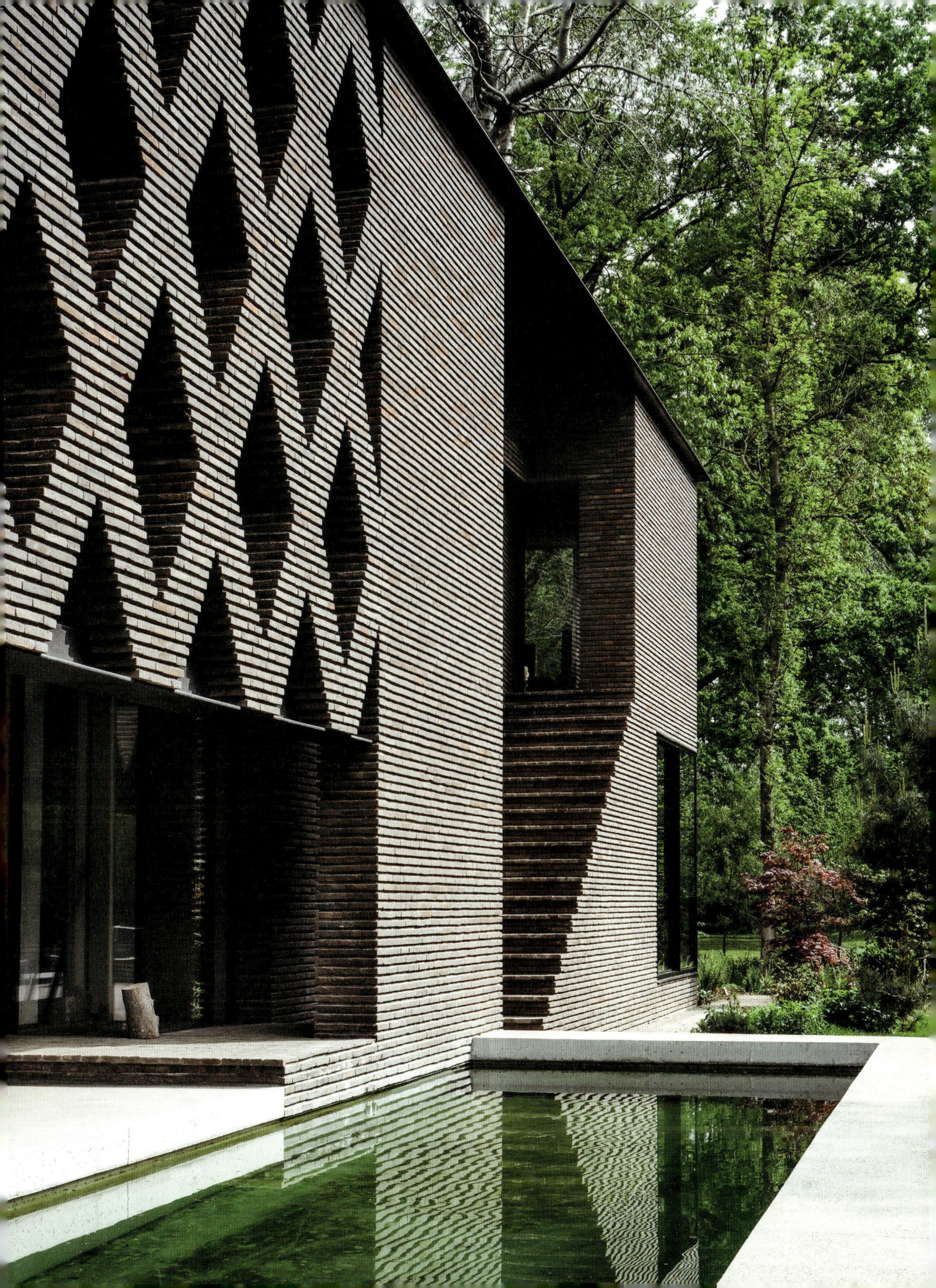

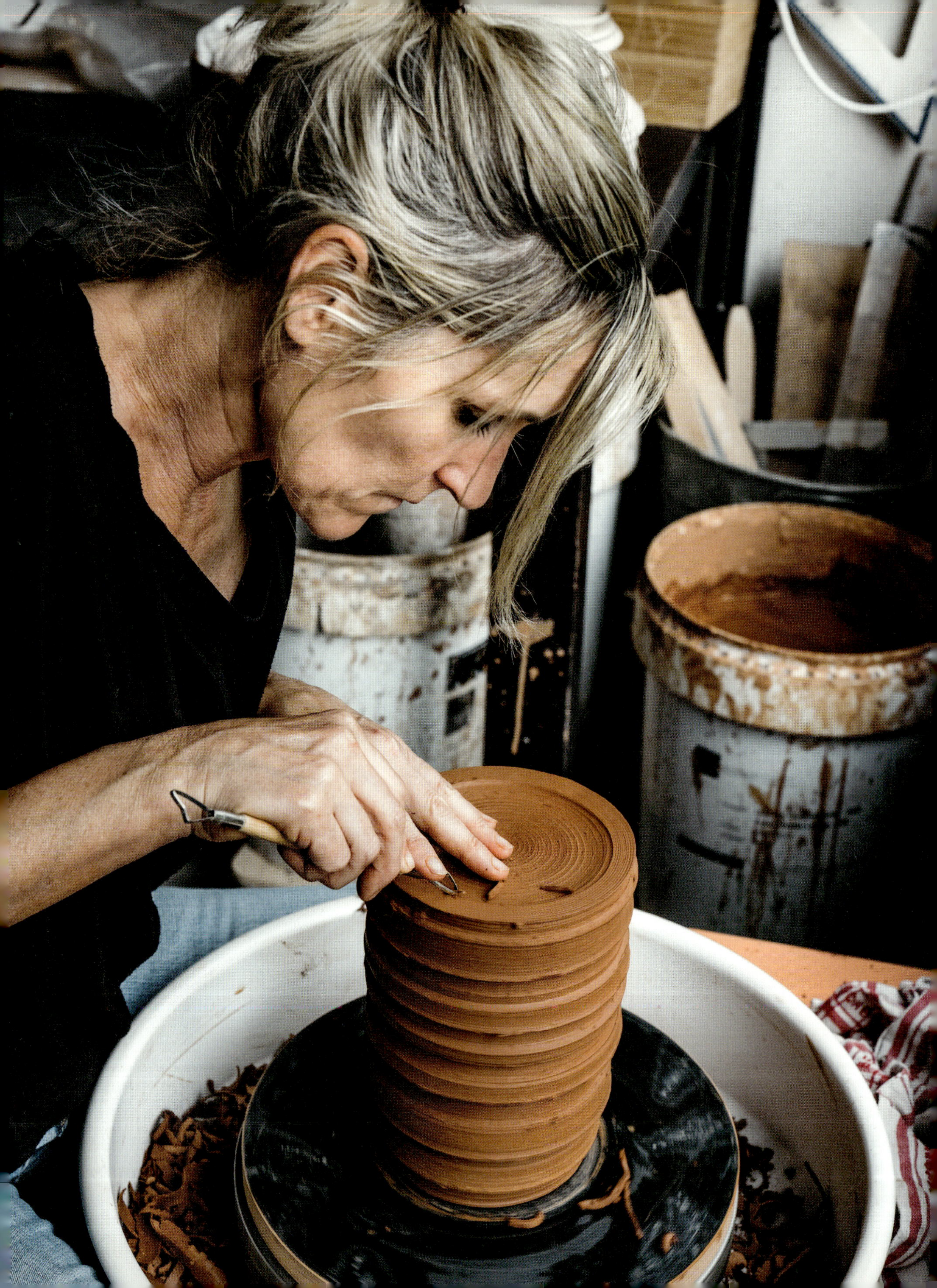

Alex is a ceramic artist and has a workshop and showroom near the
house, where she works with the beagle by her side. The earthy hues
of her works blend in nicely with the style of the interior.

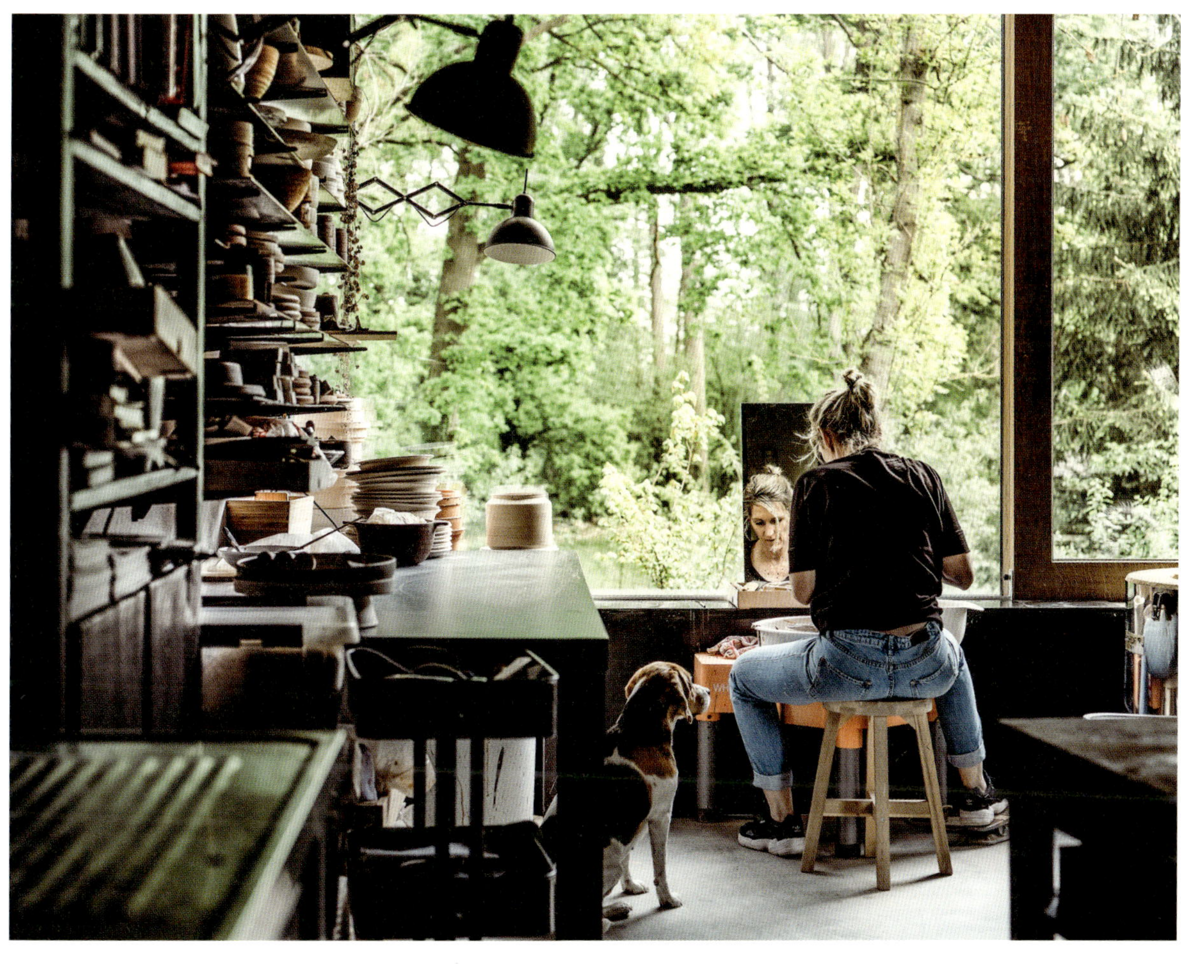

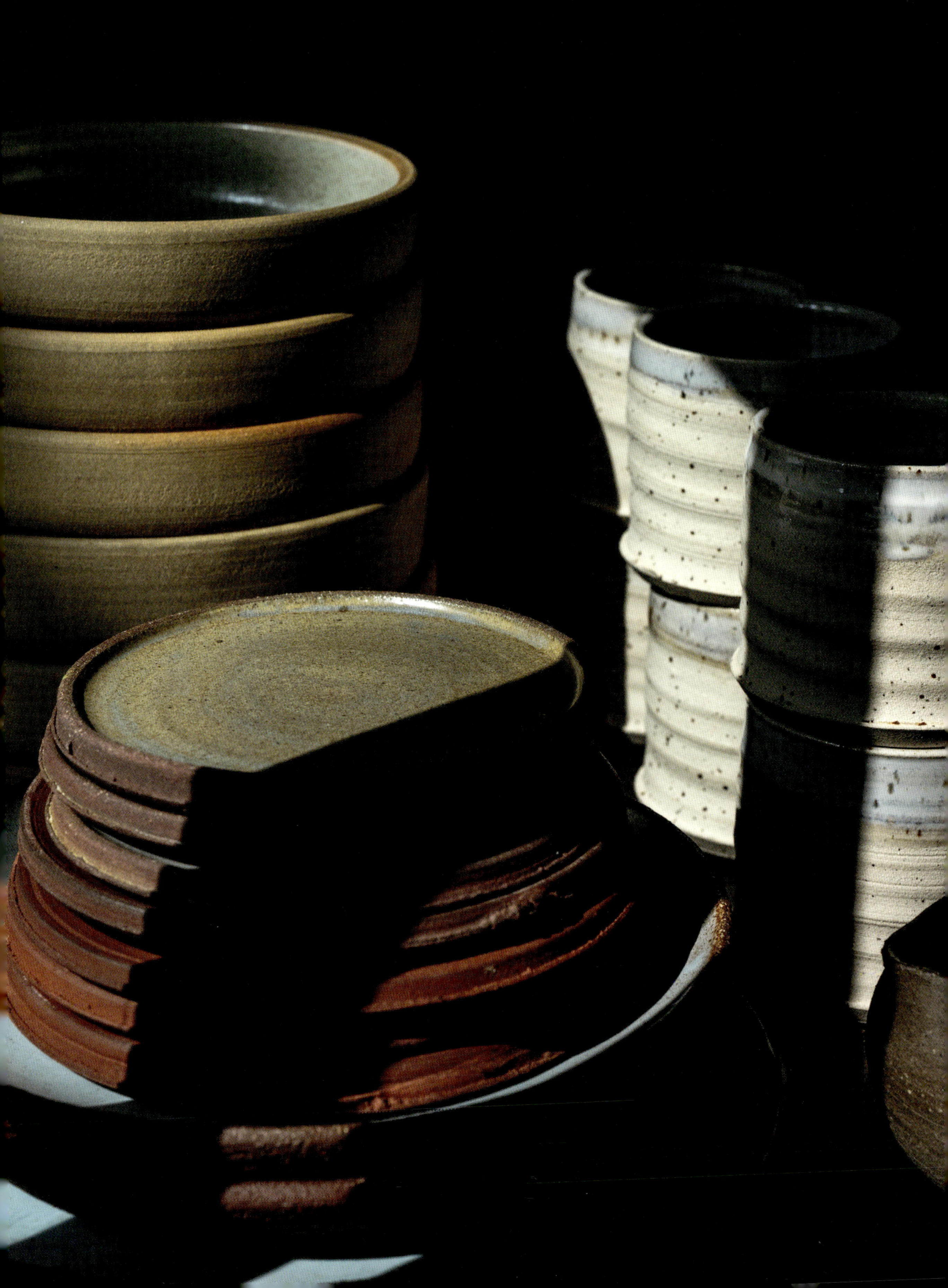

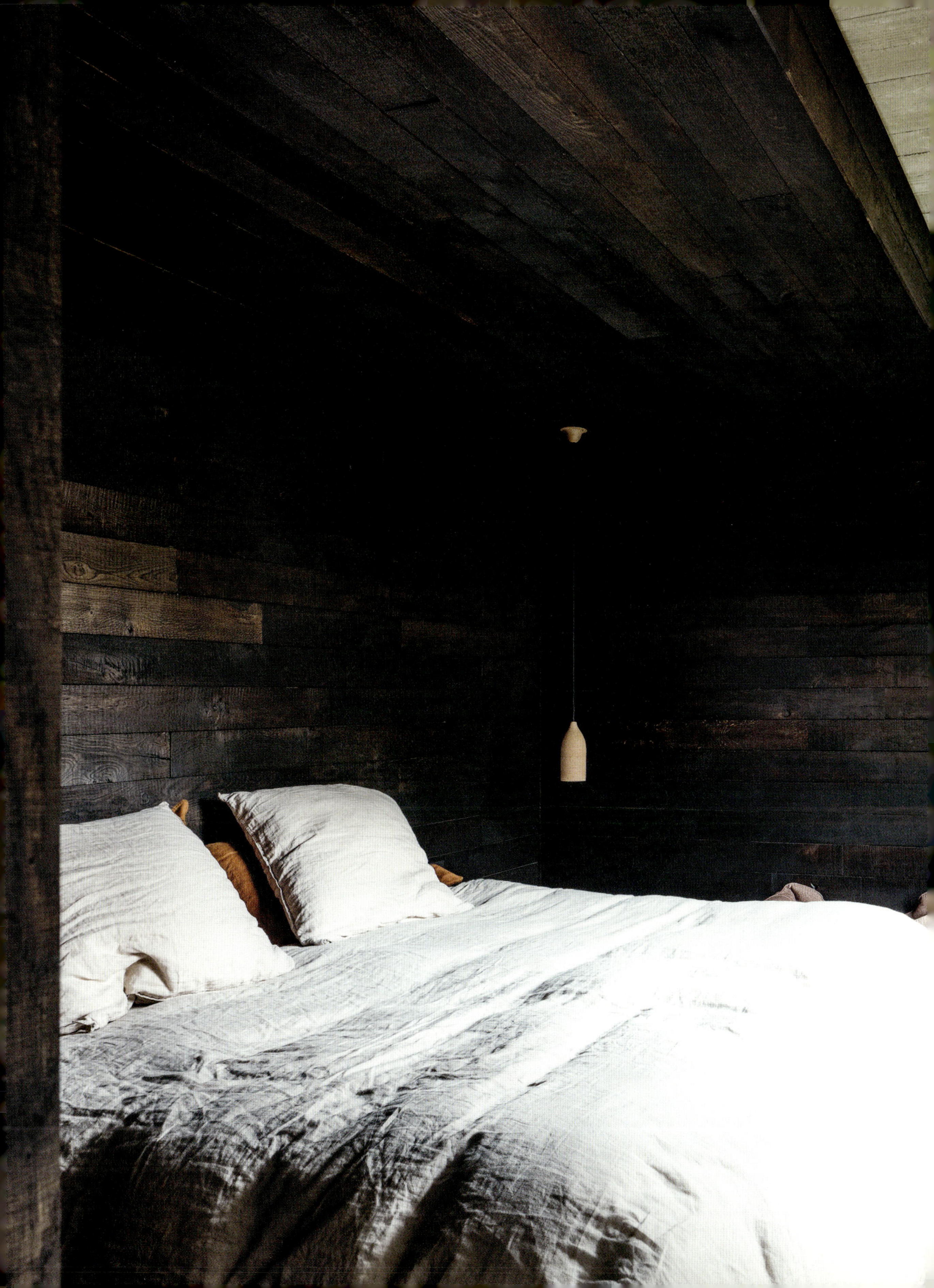

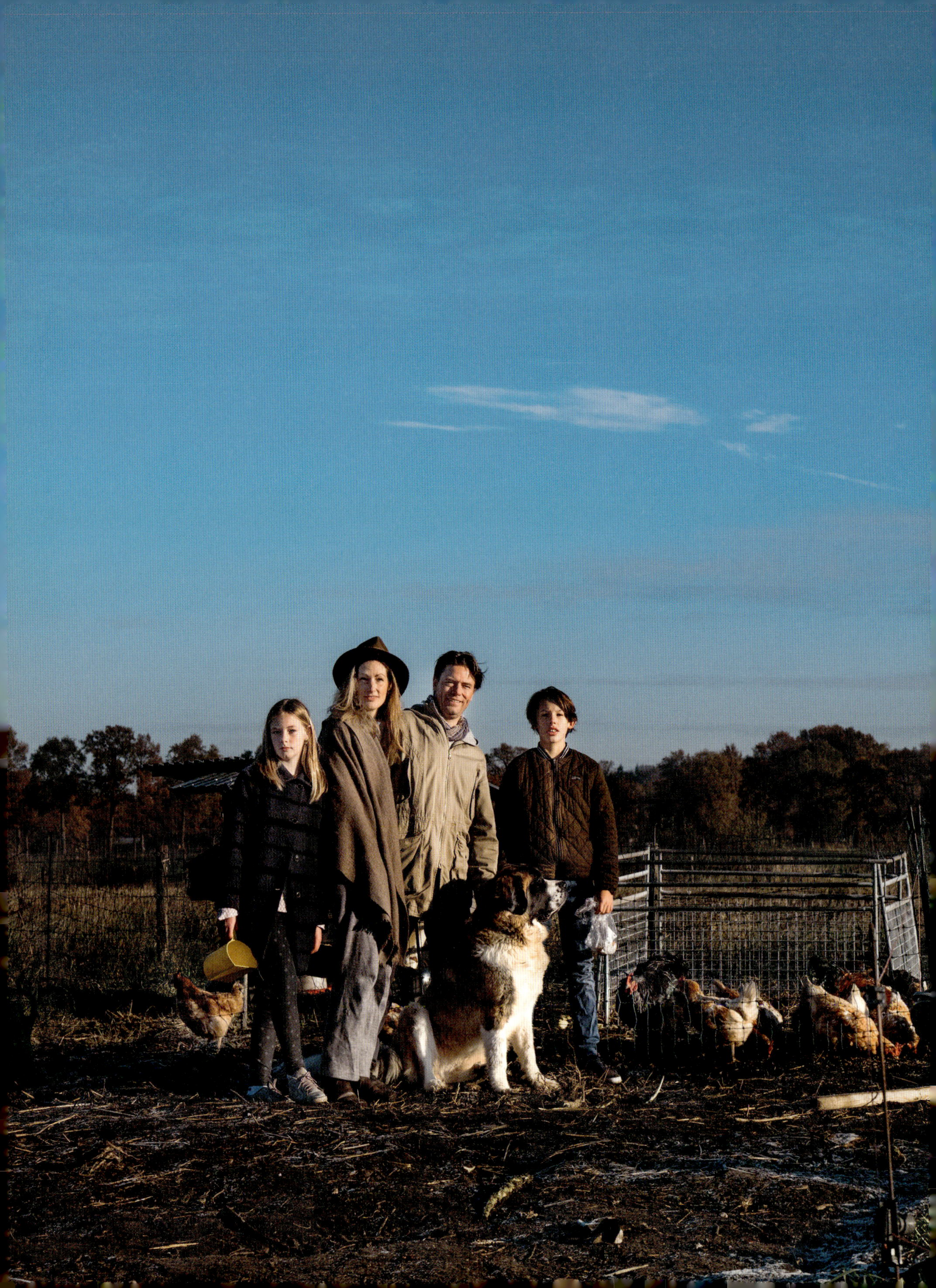

Silence. That is what Mera and Niek were looking for, and that is exactly what they found on an old farm. The children gladly agreed to the move when they were told that they would have more pets. The couple transformed a dilapidated fifties-style house into a cosy, imperfect but beautiful home. The farmyard animals have become part of the family. Everything that happens on their country estate is new for the former city dwellers. But having many pets also means a lot of work, which they don't mind.

Cosy imperfection

There are several advantages to rural living. 'That said, it's not that easy for teenagers to leave the city,' Mera Martinot confesses. 'Moving means starting over and making new friends.' They promised their son Ives (12 years) and their daughter Lana (11 years) that they would have more pets and that their dad would spend more time with them. That was all the convincing they needed. The old fifties-style farm was transformed into a warm, contemporary family dwelling in no time at all. 'While the house may be imperfect, the basic structure is good. There's always something to do, but we don't mind,' says Mera. The combination of natural materials and earthy hues creates a secure and serene ambience. Interior design is Mera's thing. In addition to her work as a stylist, she runs the interior shop Stilleven and rents out Tiny House, the nature cabin on their country estate, together with her husband, Niek Peters.

The excitement of rural life

Tiny House is a home on wheels in a pasture. It is usually booked by people who want to enjoy the peace and quiet. It has become a very popular rental. From the house, you have a stunning view of the fields and the large chicken coop. The four chickens which the previous occupants left behind soon had new companions. Mera calls them real pets. 'You build a rapport with chickens by feeding them every day. I feel as if they know who we are. And they also eat your residual waste of course,' she laughs. To city dwellers, everything that happens on a farm like theirs is exciting and new. But everything does not always go according to plan. In their enthusiasm, they decided to get a few goats in the early days. 'Ives had built a fenced-in cottage garden, but one of the bucks leaped over the fences and proceeded to eat all the vegetables and flowers. It was fun, but it was also very frustrating,' Mera remembers. They rehomed the animals on another farm. 'A bit of a beginner's mistake, really.'

From house pet to farm dog

All their city pets moved with them to the country. While it took some time to get used to their new surroundings, Moes, the oldest cat, now also feels at home here. In the spring and summer, he likes to roam, while he prefers to curl up on their lap during the winter months. In the city, he spent a lot of time with their dog, Tashi, a Lhasa apso, that really adapted well to farm life. This long-haired breed from Tibet is a jaunty little guard dog with a long body, a curly tail, and a sassy demeanour. His eyes are often concealed under his long, luscious fur, and he has a long beard. It's amusing to see. 'In the city, we used to take Tashi shopping in a bag. Now you have to look twice to spot him in the hay. He loves spending time outdoors, even when we call him back inside,' says Mera. Unfortunately, Tashi and Moes are no longer friends. And this is mostly the fault of Ellis, their saint bernard.

Jumping dog and angora rabbits

Originally, saint bernards were bred in the Alps, where they were used as working and rescue dogs. Although Ellis looks enormous, she is easy to train and walk. The pup is very social and likes to be involved in all family activities. Because she needs a lot of space, she feels entirely at ease on the farm. Niek spends a lot of time teaching her. 'Saint bernards are cute, but they are also huge. People are usually shocked when they realise how big Ellis is. And I can see why, because saint bernards tends to jump up to greet you out of enthusiasm.' When we unload the car, Niek keeps her at a distance so she can get used to us. While Ellis does indeed look colossal, she is also a real family pet. She loves Ives, and they often tussle on the floor. In addition to the dogs and the cat, the estate also has two angora rabbits. Pluisje Saar was given to daughter Lana. He loves cuddles unlike Bram, a very timid, adopted animal.

Cats and wabi-sabi

The most recent addition to the family is Tuintje, a young kitten from a nearby farm. He follows us closely during our visit and doesn't mind posing for the camera. She hops up on the table, likes to sit on your lap or sleep on one of the furs and other warm fabrics throughout the house. According to Mera, the cats influenced the interior design. 'Felines provide warmth and a homely atmosphere. I like to use soft textiles because I know they love them. A house without animals feels bare.' The welcoming ambience Mera created fully ties in with the wabi-sabi philosophy she applies in her work. According to these Japanese aesthetic,all the elements in the dwelling have sentimental value. Everything doesn't have to be perfect. Beauty is in the here and now and this includes pets.

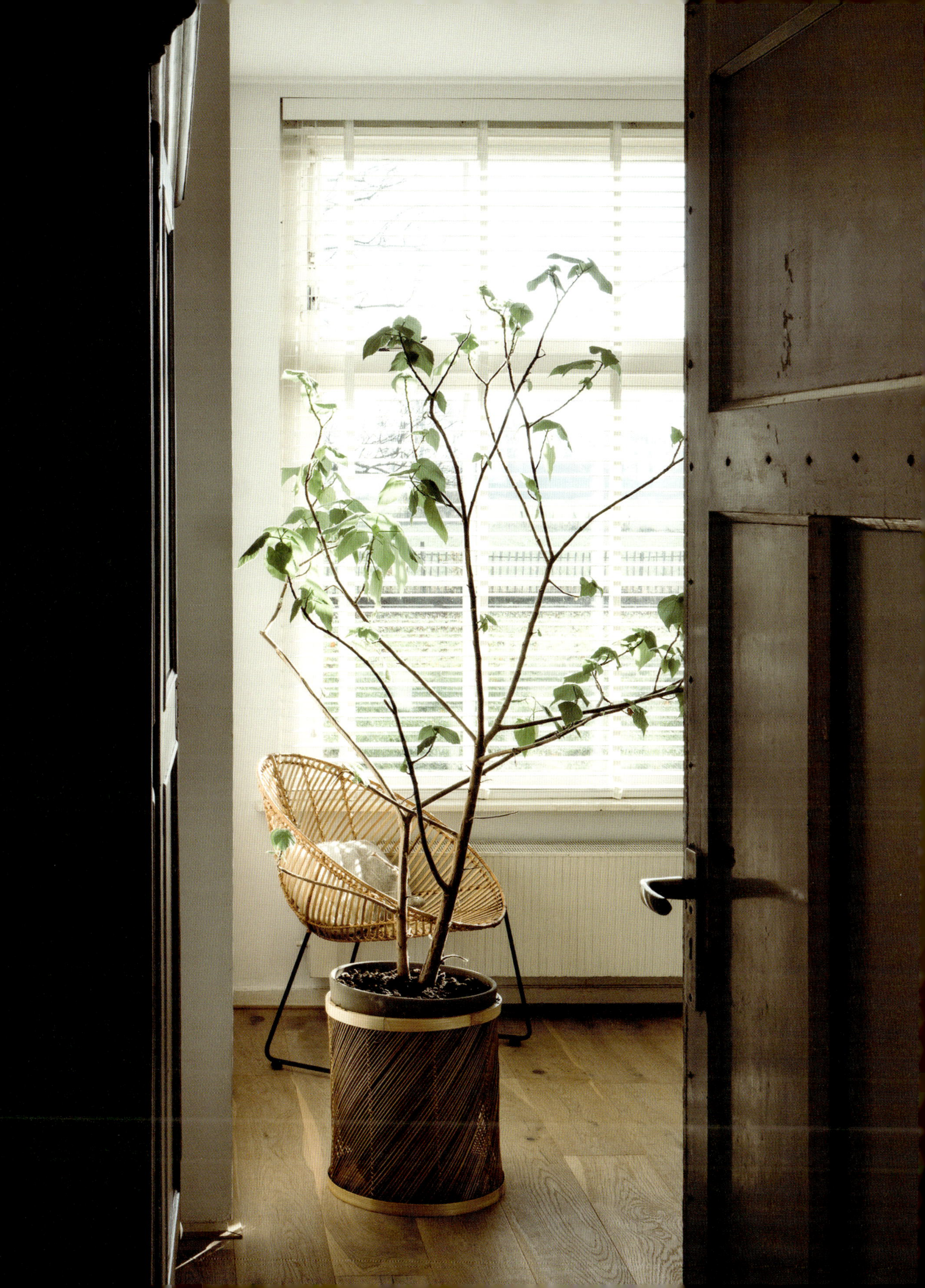

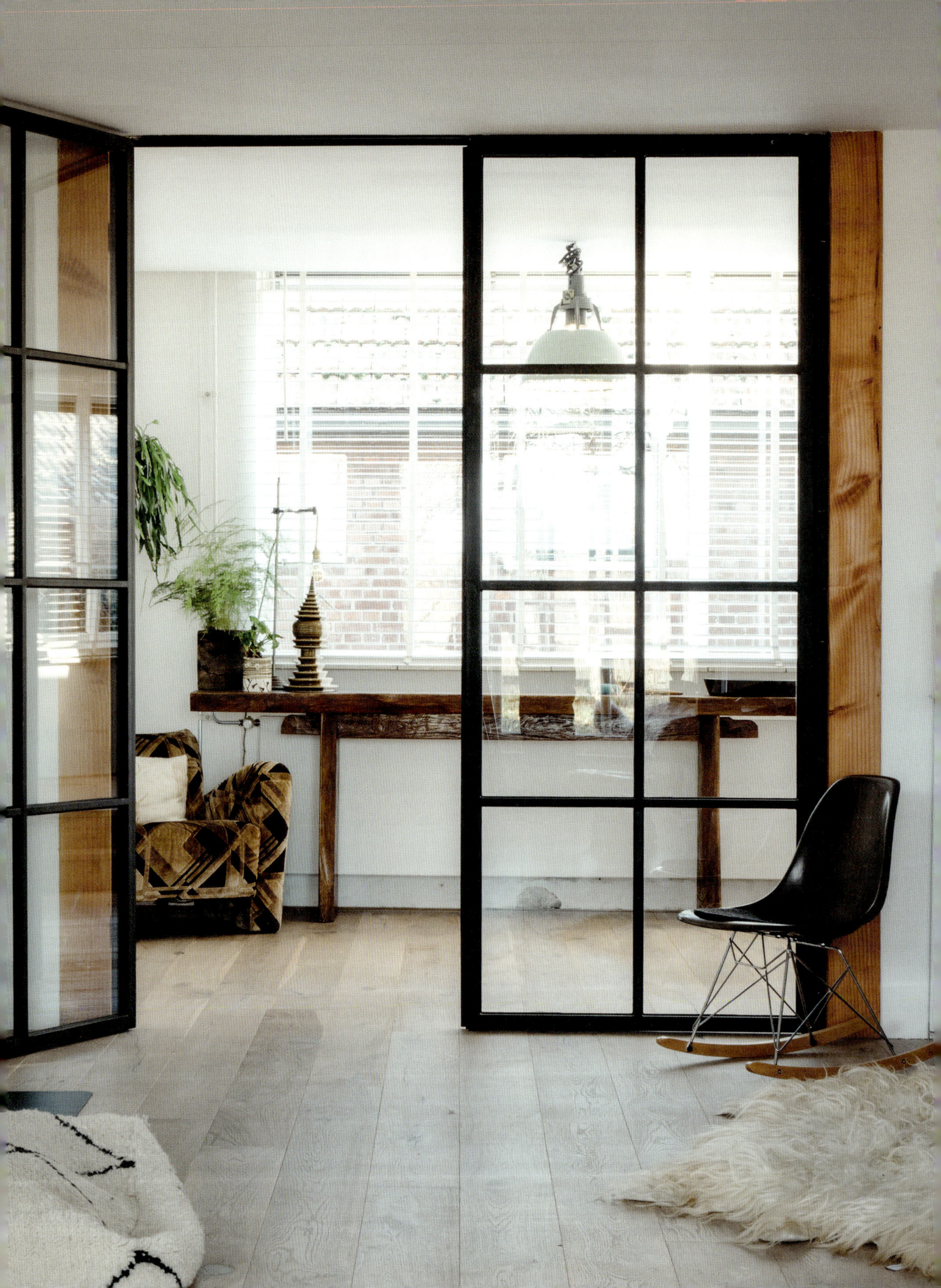

The interior was inspired by the wabi-sabi philosophy.
All the elements in the house have a sentimental meaning,
and everything doesn't have to be picture-perfect.

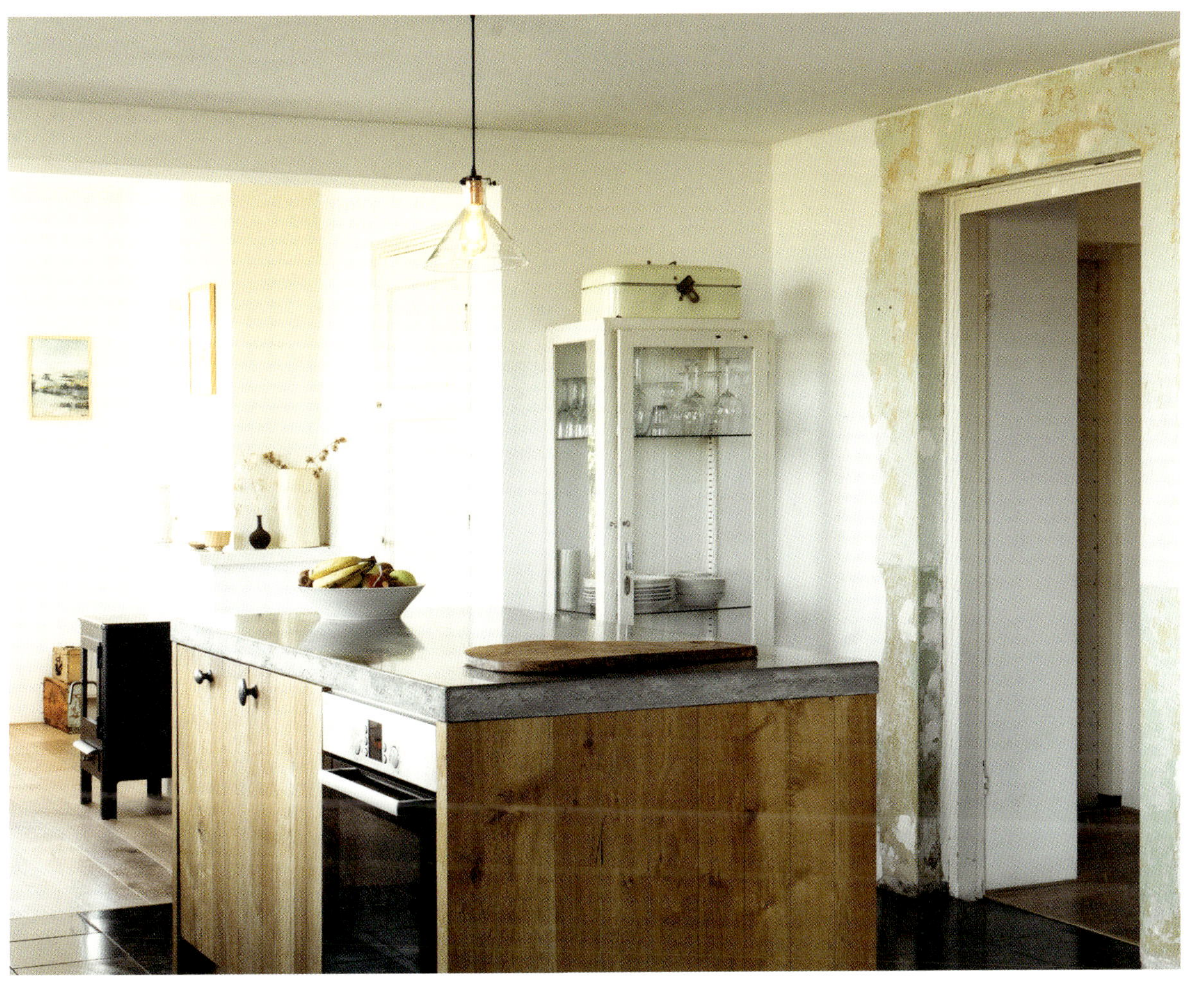

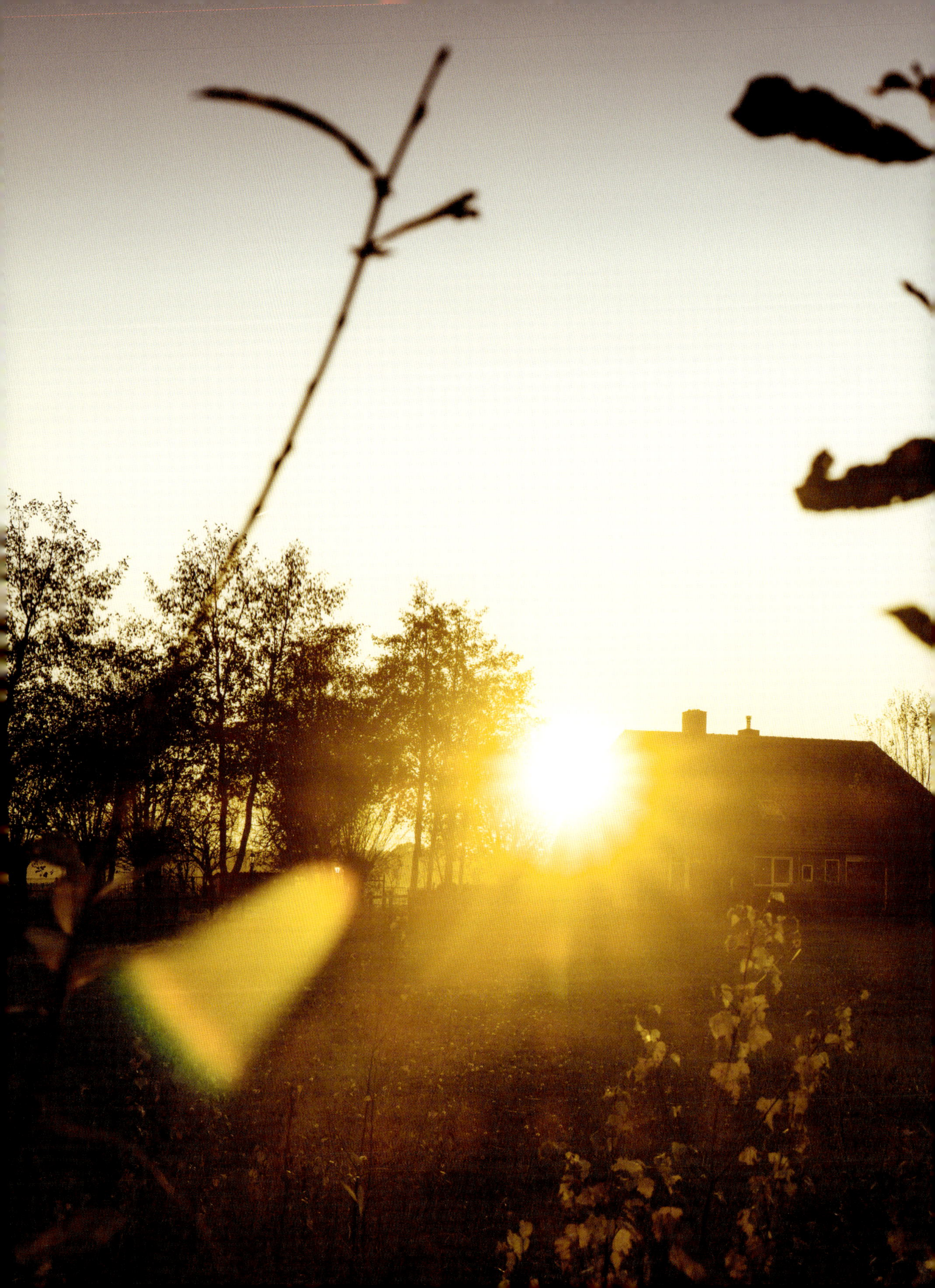

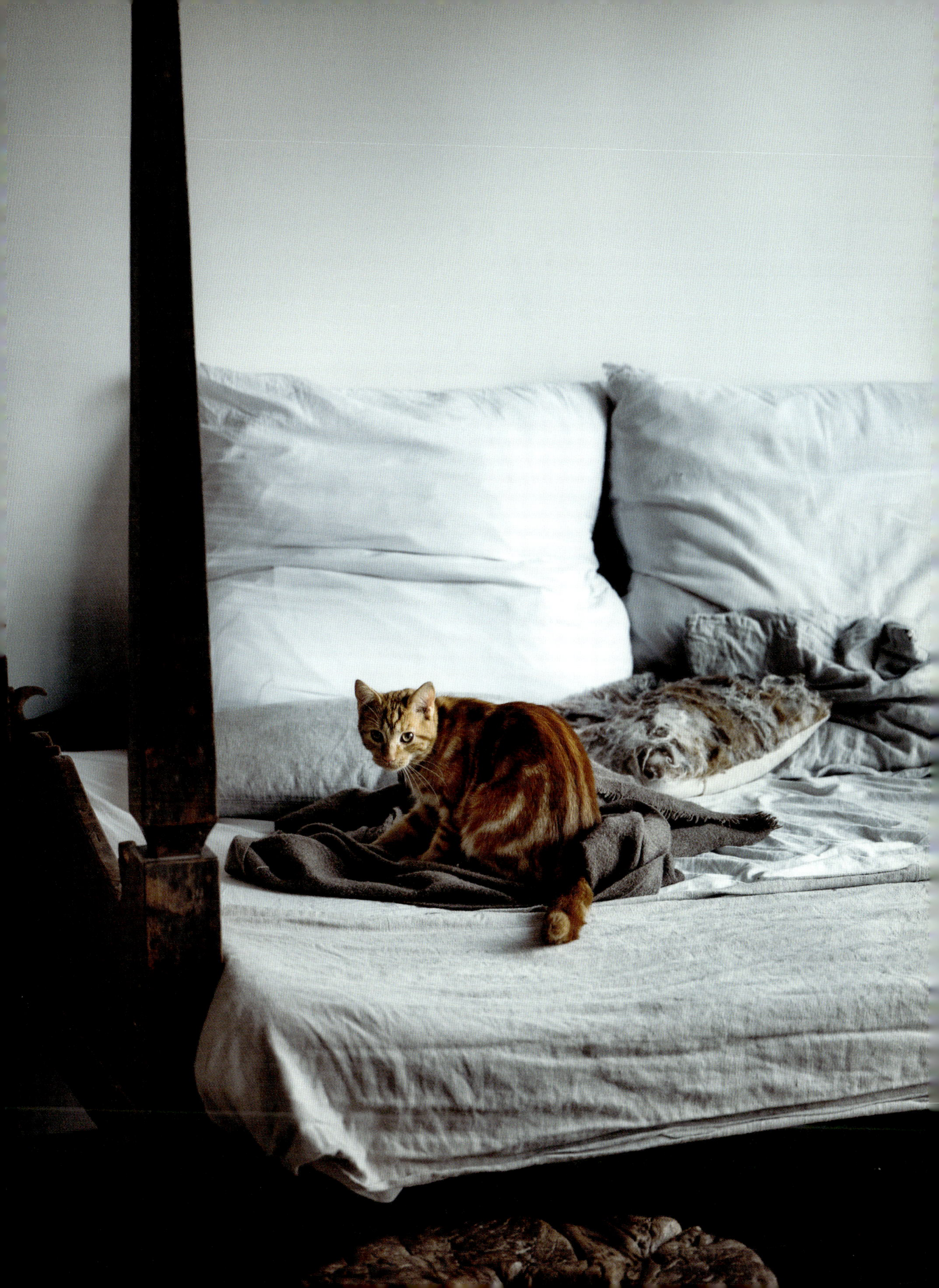

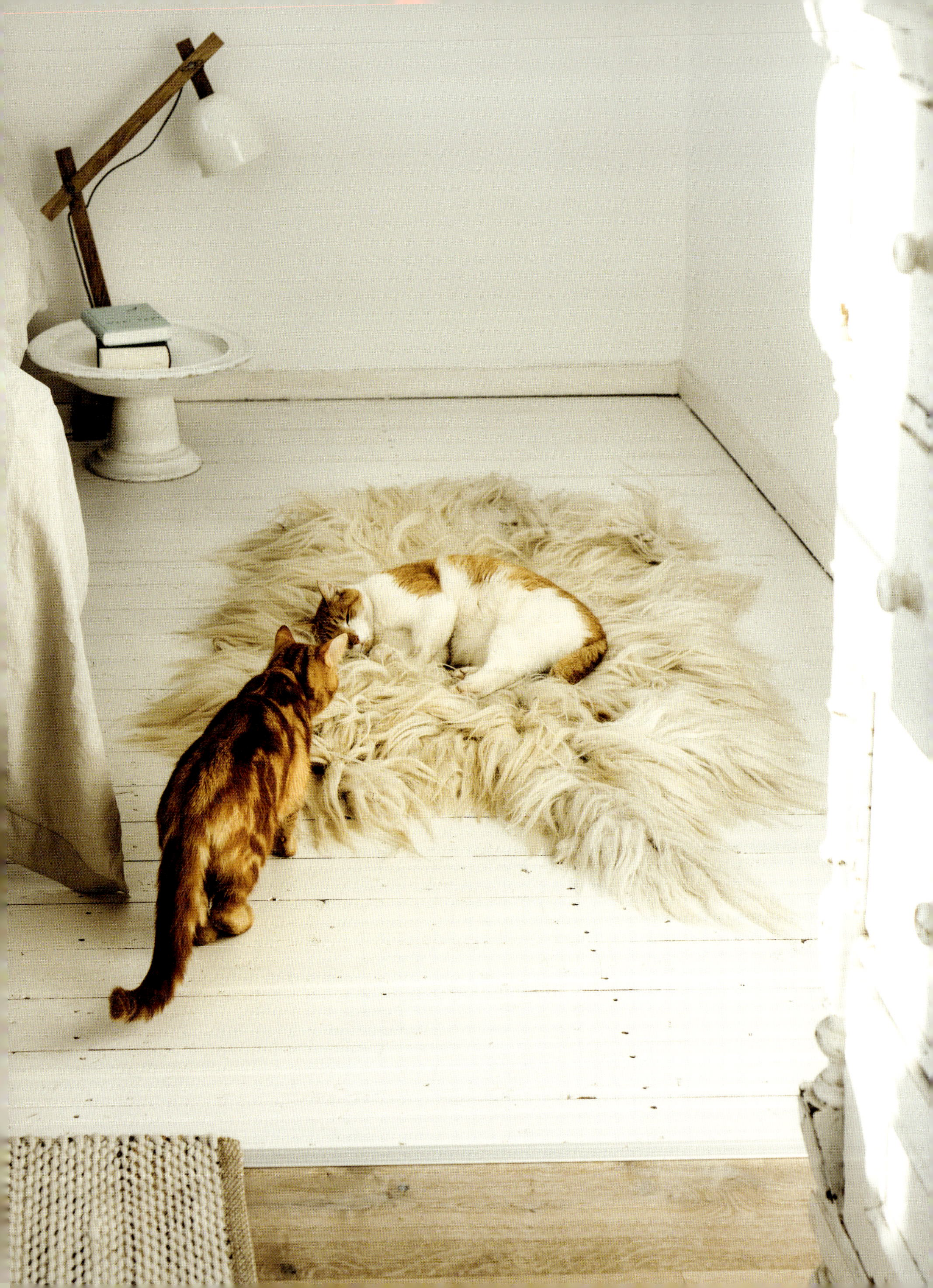

Lana and Ives said they would only move to the country if they could have more pets. In addition to the animals they already had, a saint bernard joined the family, as well as chickens and a kitten.

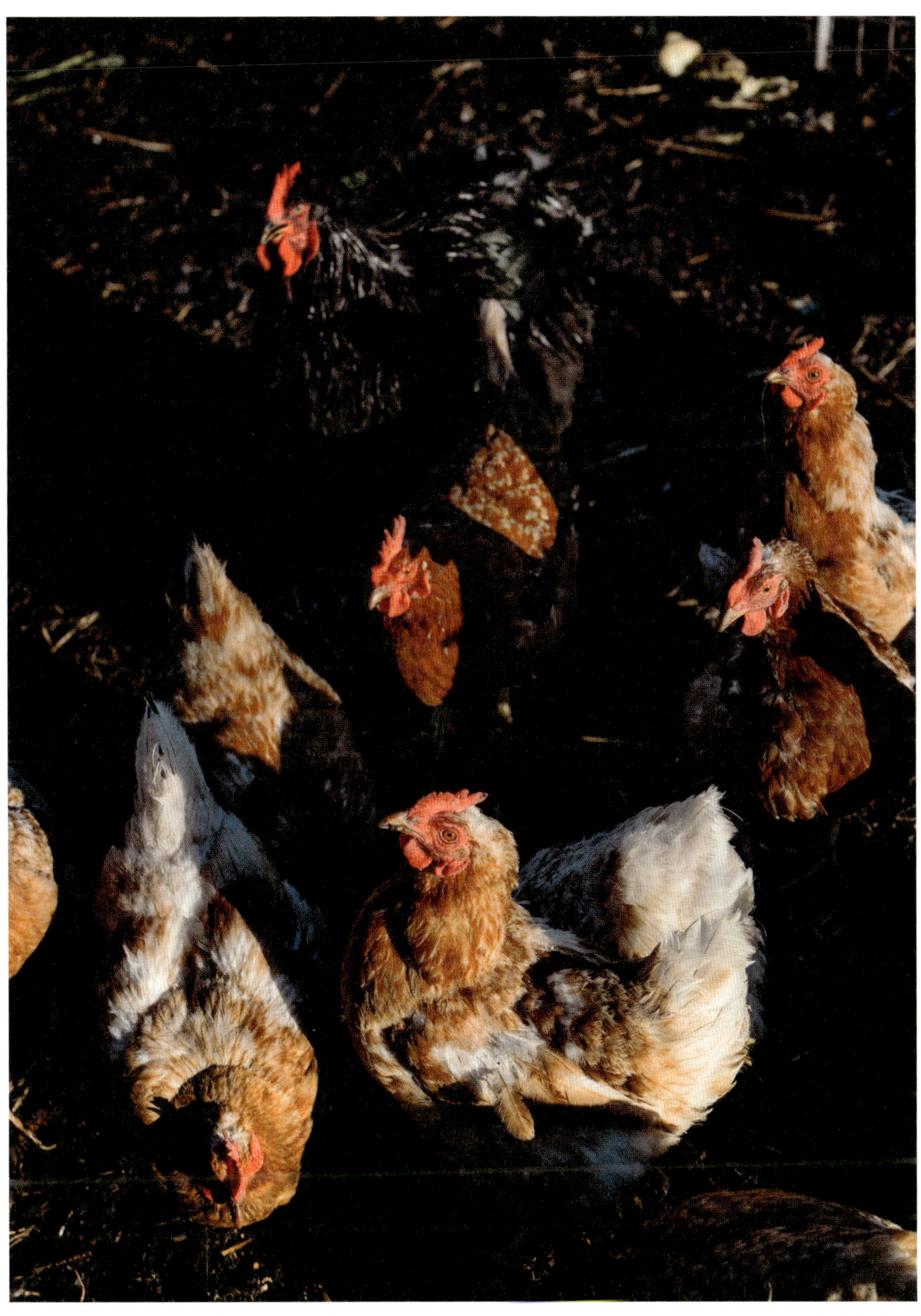

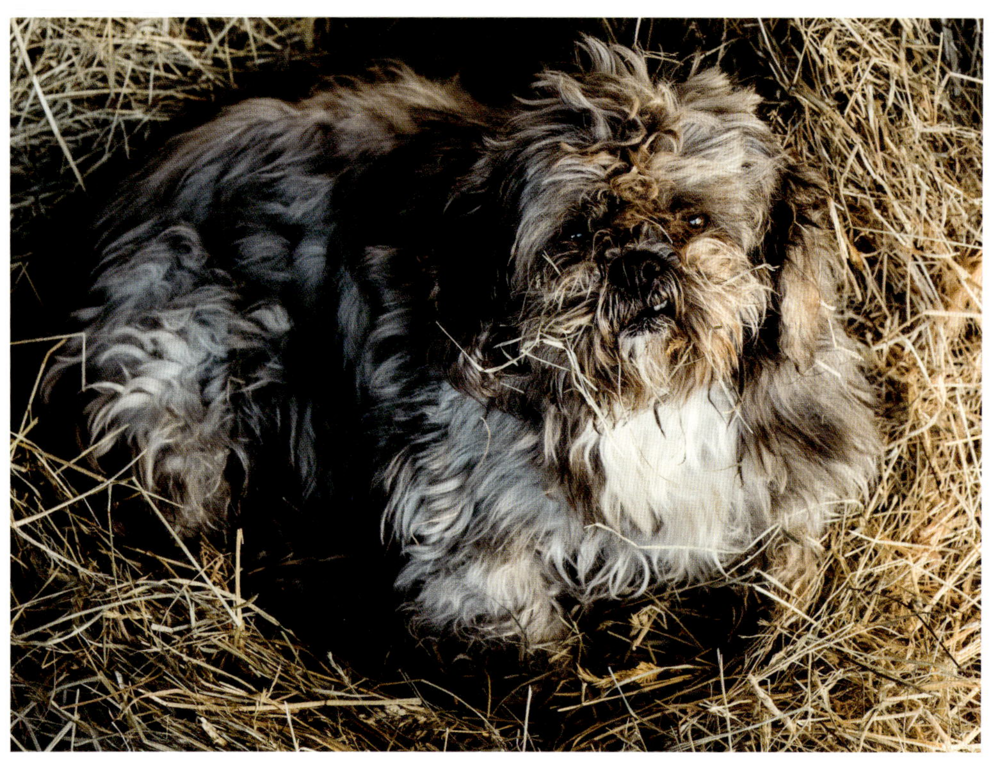

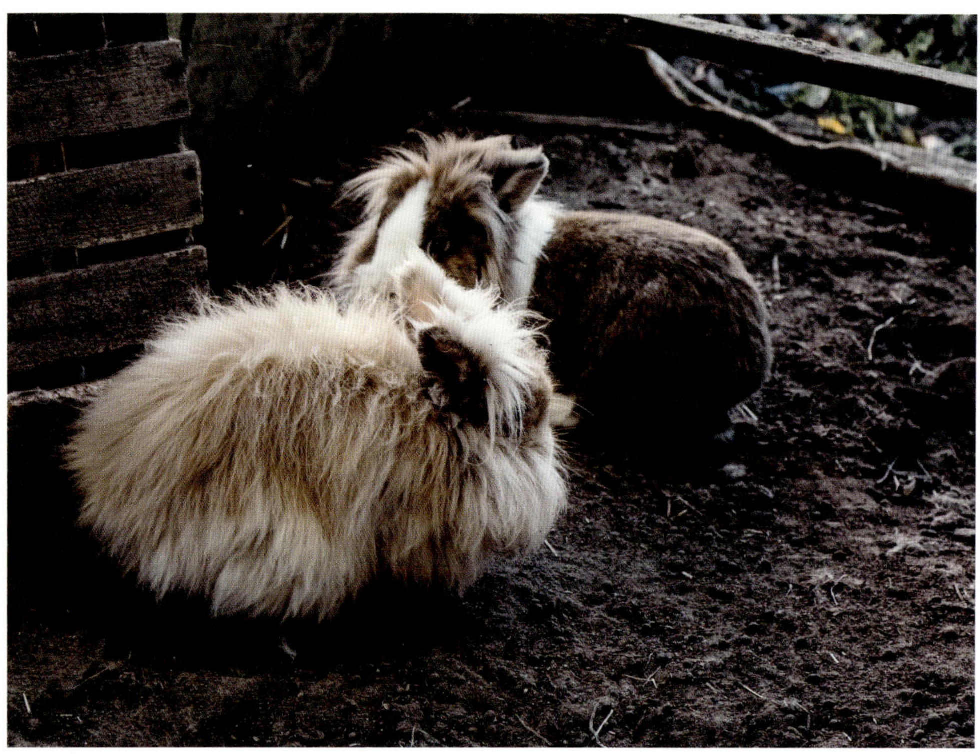

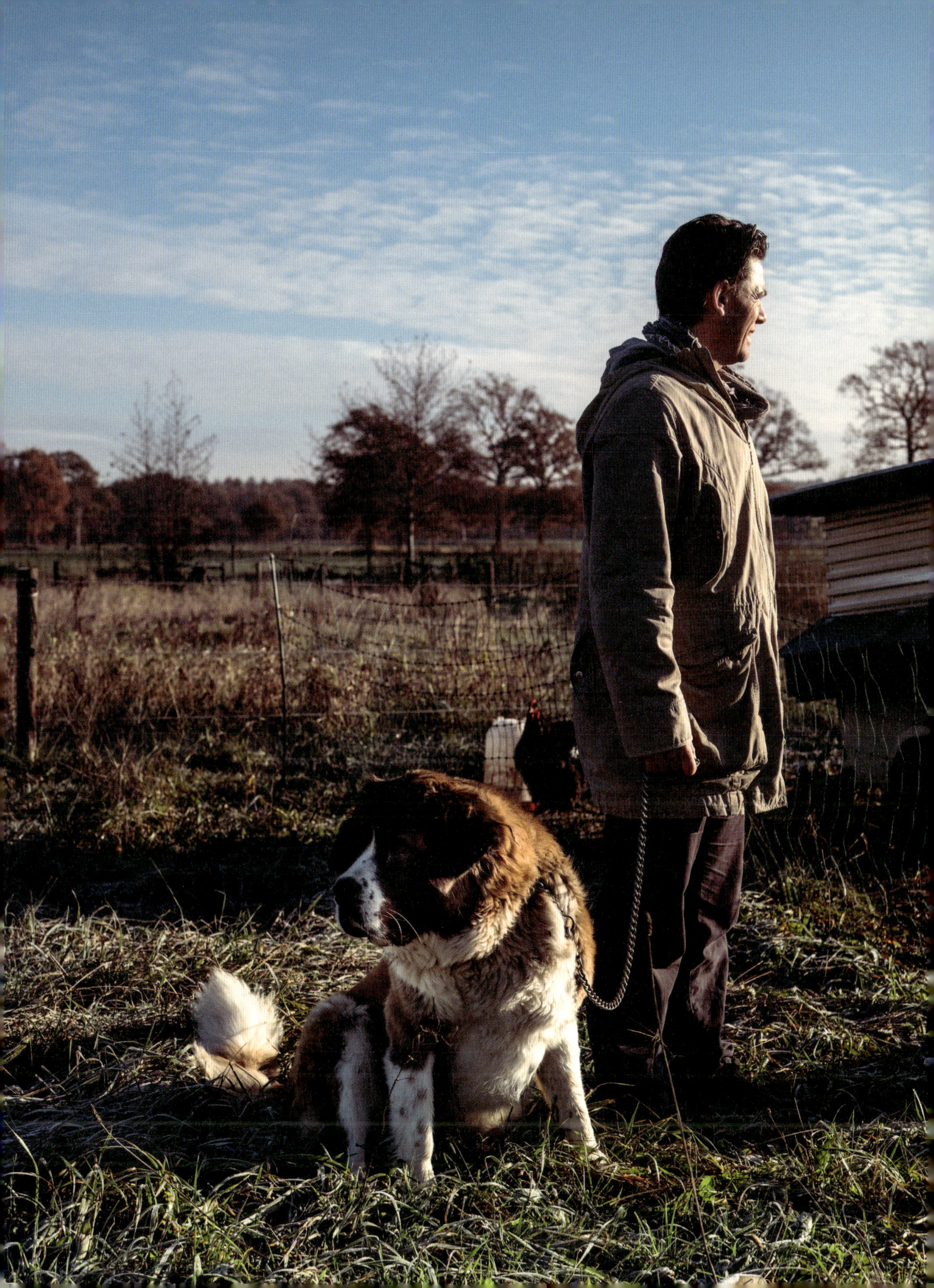

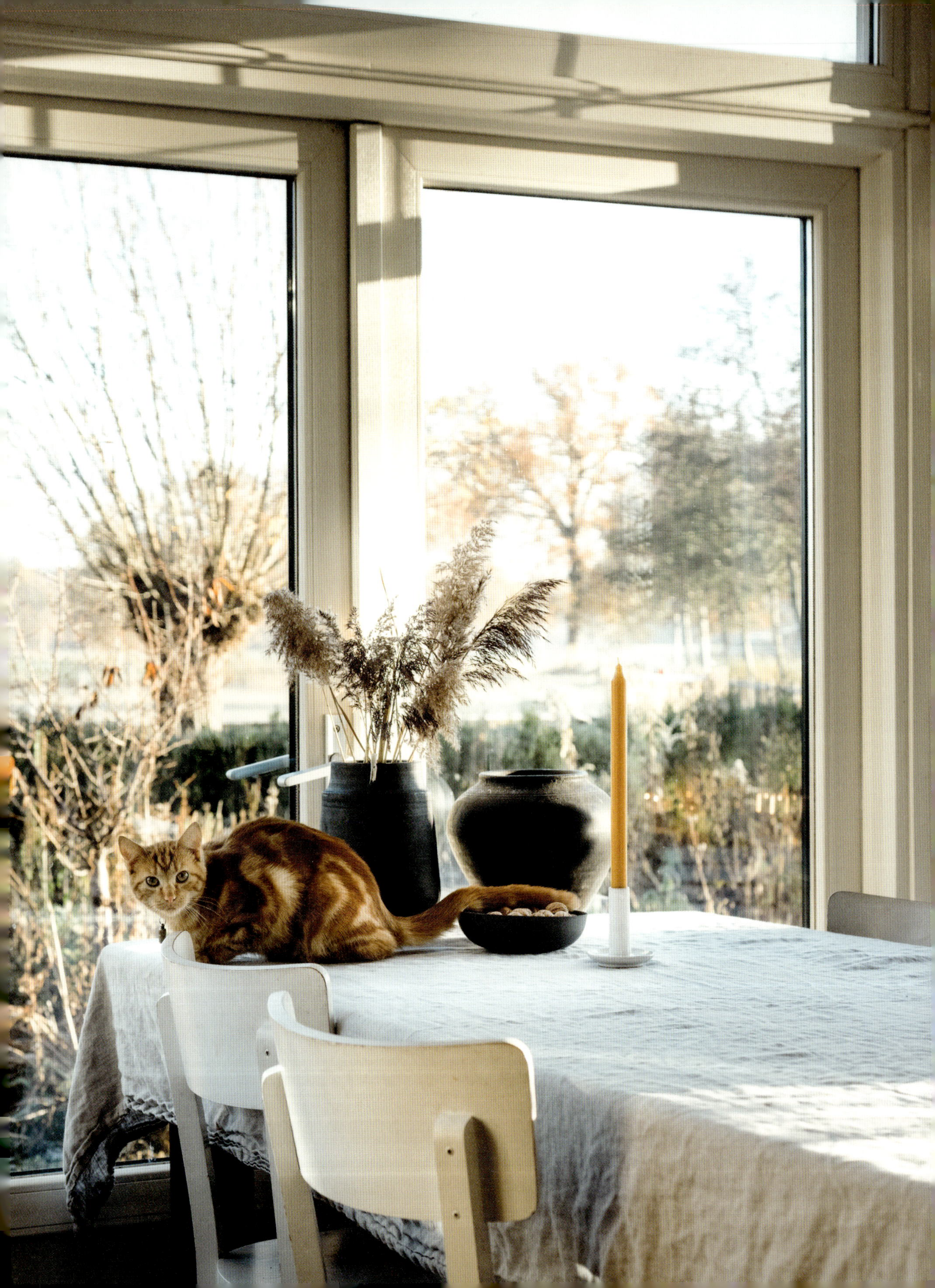

Mera runs the shop Stilleven. She displays many of the objects
at home. Niek is in charge of the Tiny House, a nature cabin on
the farm.

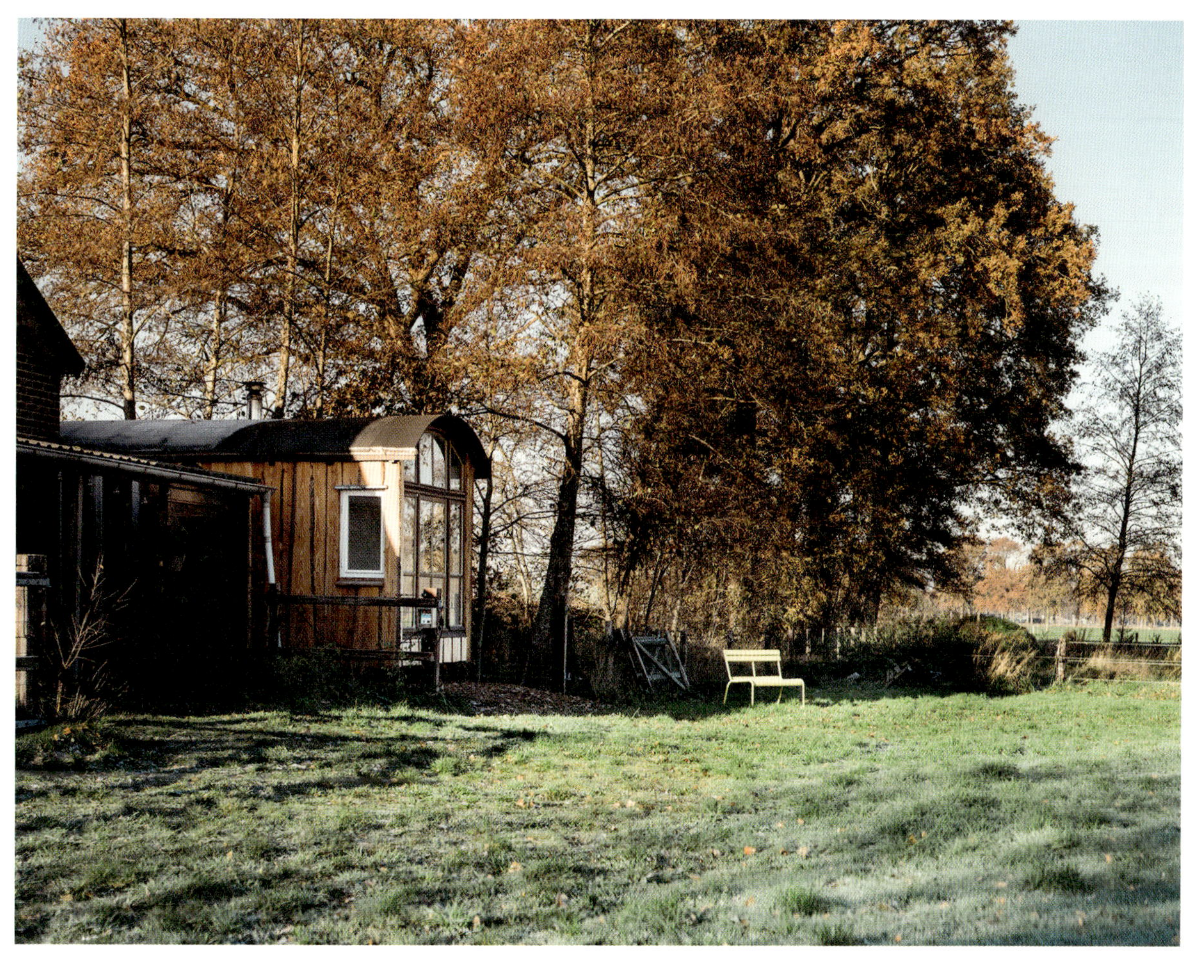

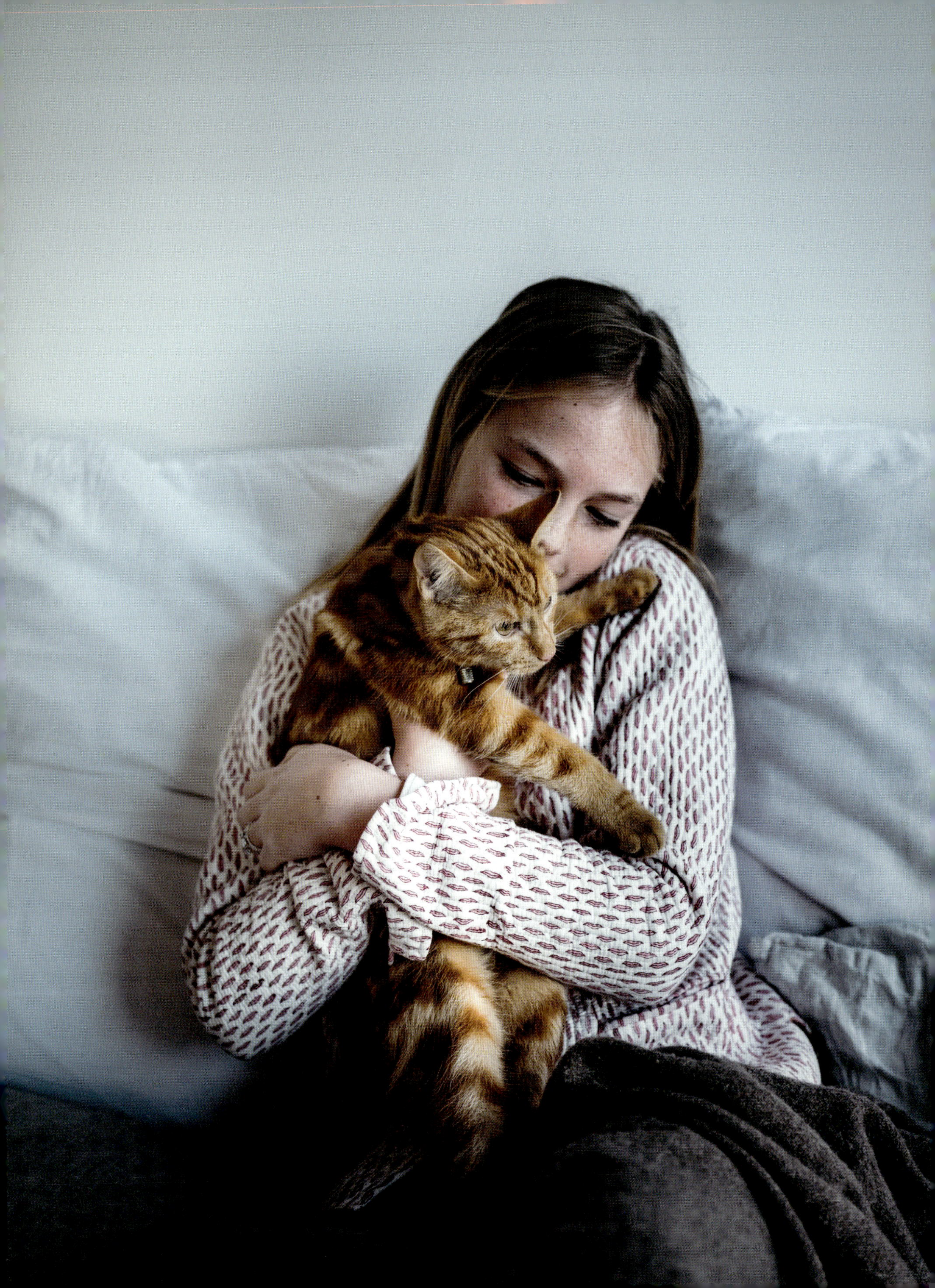

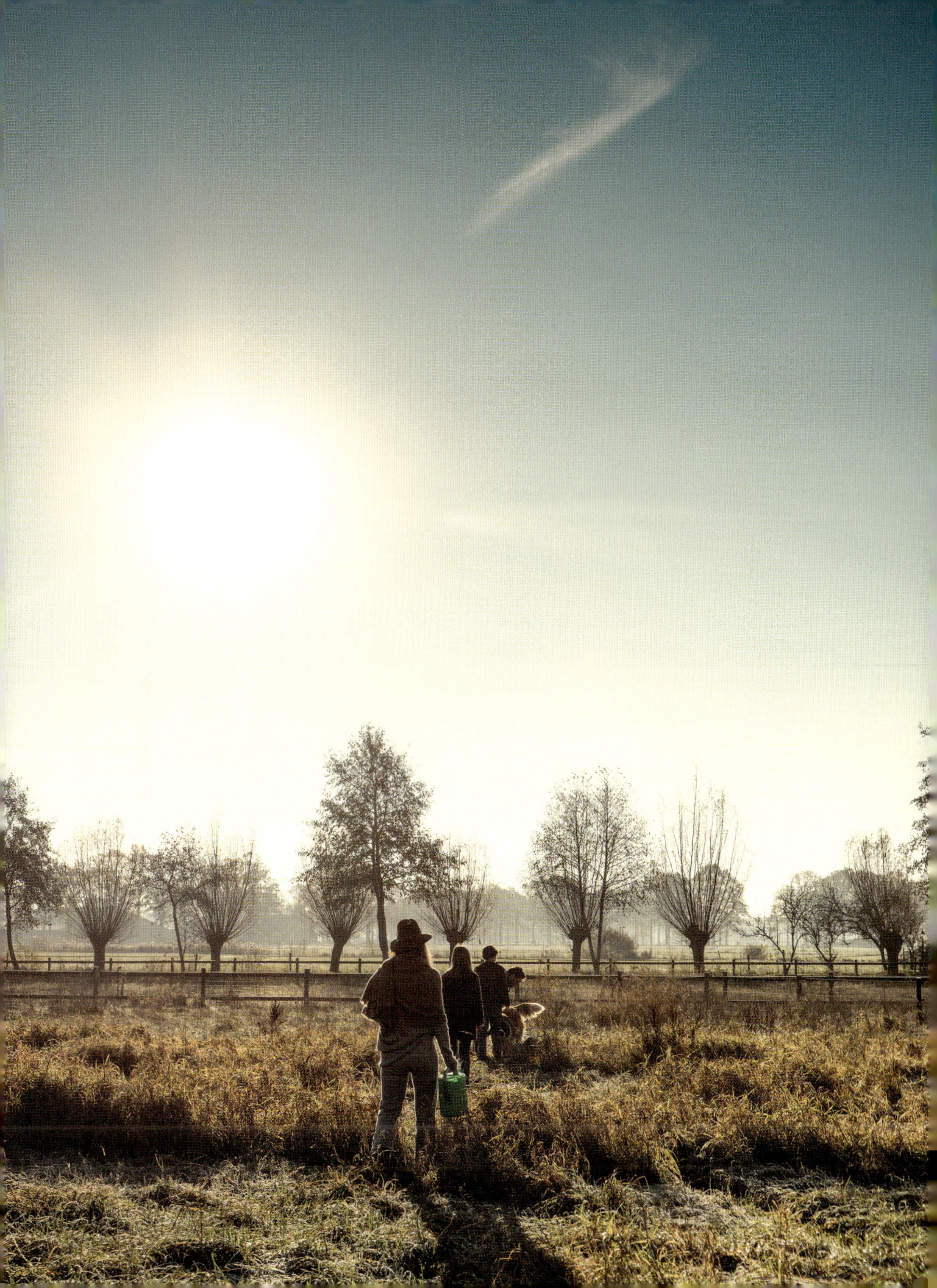

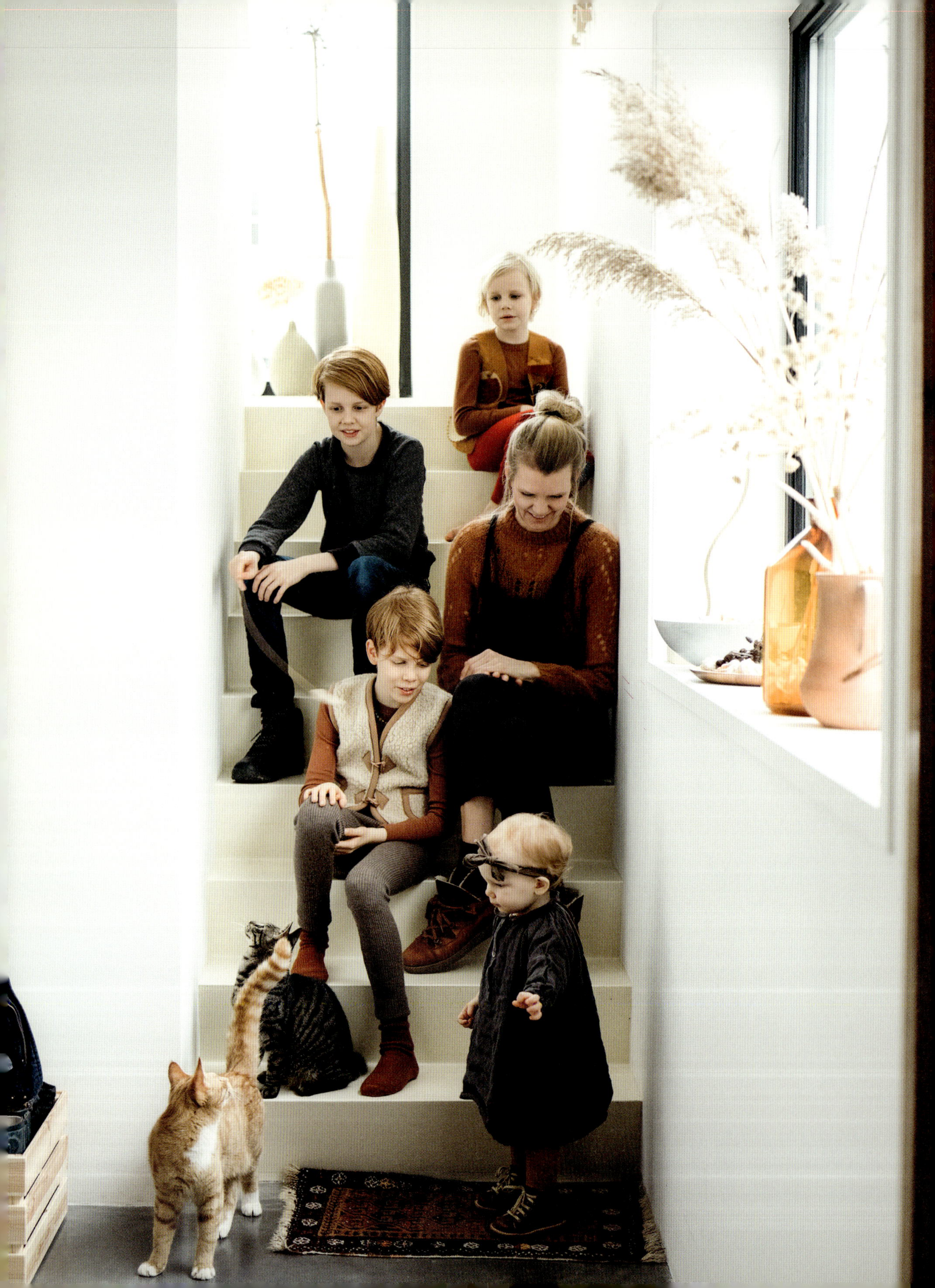

Tessa and Menno, who have four children, were looking for a new place, where they could be close as a family and close to nature. They designed their sustainable and liveable house themselves. A large living room where everyone could meet, while having a space of their own, was one of the most essential items on their wish list. The kids feel at home in the serene and stylish spaces, and so do their cat siblings, Pluis and Muis. They take possession of the house, while the children are at school.

Together at home

A wooden box is probably the most accurate description of the home of Tessa Hop and Menno 't Hoen. Four years ago, the couple bought land in a new residential area. Unusually for the Netherlands, there were no building restrictions in place. Items on the couple's wish list included peace and quiet, light and space. The new-build is made entirely from wood with natural materials for the interior. You can't help but notice the ample open space on the ground floor, which combines several functions, including cooking, eating, TV, playing, and working. The couple's four children, Mees (13 years), Polle (10 years), Guus (7 years) and Keetje (1.5 years) and the two young cats create a fun buzz. Large families sometimes tend to forget what it's really like to be together, which is why Tessa insisted on building one large living area, 'with plenty of corners where the kids can withdraw to read or play on their own.' Tessa, who is a full-time mum, succeeds in adding some structure to the daily chaos. A graduate of the Academy in Rotterdam, she made the choice to stay at home for her children.

Cat siblings

When we meet with Tessa, the boys are at home, and baby girl Keetje is sleeping upstairs. The family's ginger cat Pluis is lounging in the wooden rocker sleeping side by side with Muis, their black cat. They are siblings. Tessa found them online. They previously had cats, but they peed on everything, which is why they moved to a friend's farm. But the children convinced Tessa that they needed a pet, which is how she ended up getting not one, but two kittens. The owners of the nest also had a large family, meaning the animals were already used to a busy household. When they're not inside, the cats like to run around the field outside and play with the cows. 'It doesn't matter how far they run, they always come back,' Tessa says.

Sustainable cat care

All four kids love them. But Guus is the biggest cat fanatic. The first thing he does when he comes home is to seek out Muis and give him a cuddle. 'I have noticed that he really enjoys their time together,' says Tessa, who stresses the importance of thoughtfulness in children and the close relationship between people and animals. The kids like living with and caring for the pets. They always make sure there is sufficient water and food in the house. Every day, the cats get a mix of vegetable and animal food – without preservatives. Their cat litter is biodegradable and compostable. Tessa and Menno are convinced that animal care products can also be sustainable.

A serene interior for a busy family

Menno was in charge of the house's sustainable architecture, including a heat pump and solar panels. Tessa took care of the interior, which feels very tranquil and serene. 'It has to be,' she explains, 'to counteract the buzz of a large family.' The calm atmosphere was obtained by combining white walls and concrete floors with built-in cupboards. The wood accents and furniture create unity throughout the dwelling. Tessa's innate sense of style prompts us to ask if she has any ambitions to work as an interior designer. She avoids the question shyly. 'I don't think it looks that special, you know. I spend a lot of time indoors because I'm a housewife, which is why I like to surround myself with beautiful objects that I love.' She sees a home as a safe haven for her family and the two pets, who are also part of it. They blend in nicely in the interior with the warm colours of their fur. And there is a reason for this.

Ginger hair, ginger cat

Originally Tessa wanted calicos, but she ended up bringing home a black and a ginger kitten, 'because the children have such lovely red hair.' Muis, the black cat, is the more active one. During our visit, he sniffs our son and hops on to the sideboard to swat at the grasses in the vase. He loves dried flowers. Muis also loves to play with the children's toys. He can even pull a wooden toy truck by a string. For the time being, the cats are relegated to the ground floor. Soon they will be allowed up the stairs and into the bedrooms. There are plenty of beds and corners where they can lounge so they can follow the sunlight as it works its way through the house. Until the kids come home from school, of course. Because then it's time for cuddles.

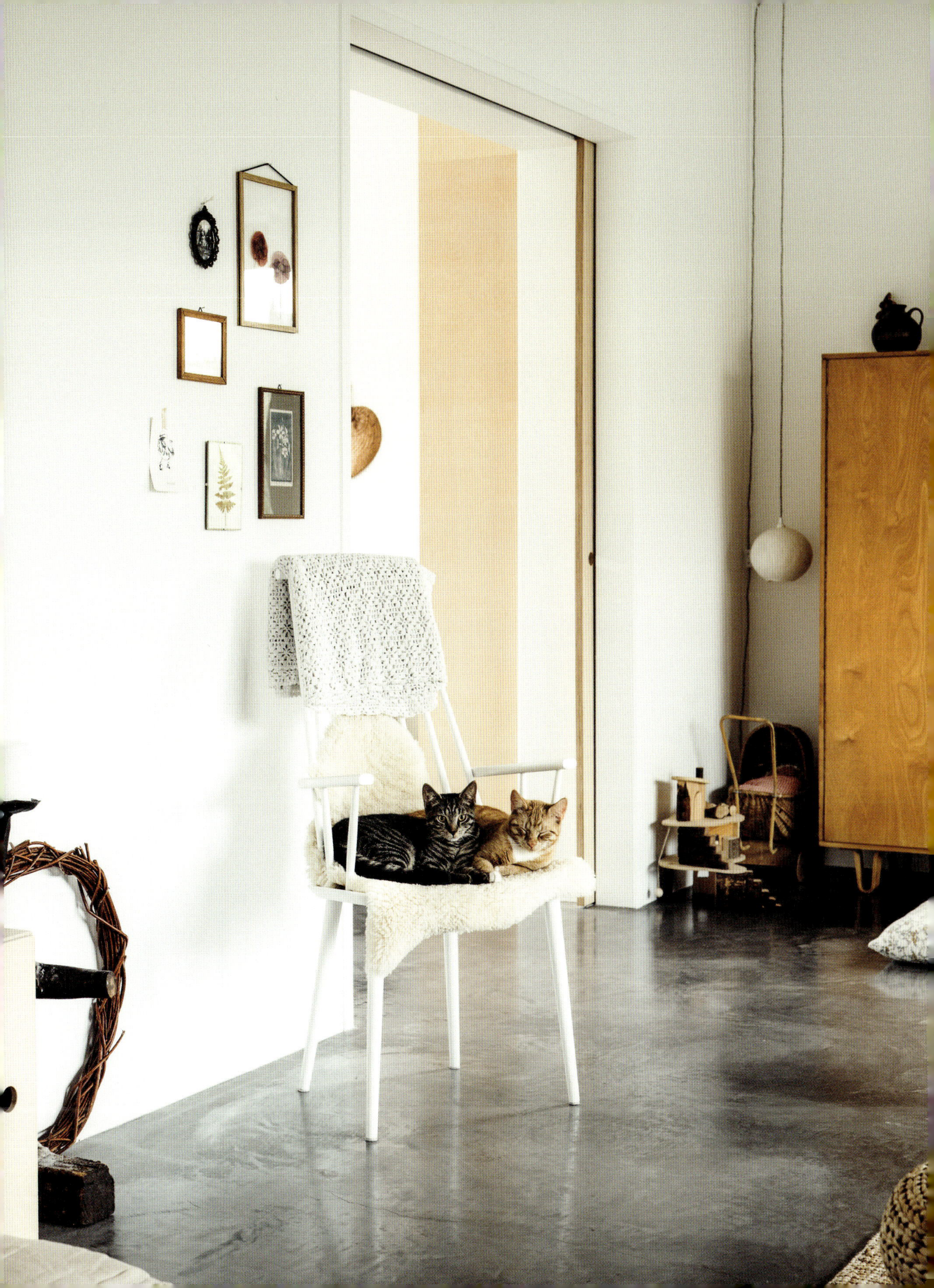

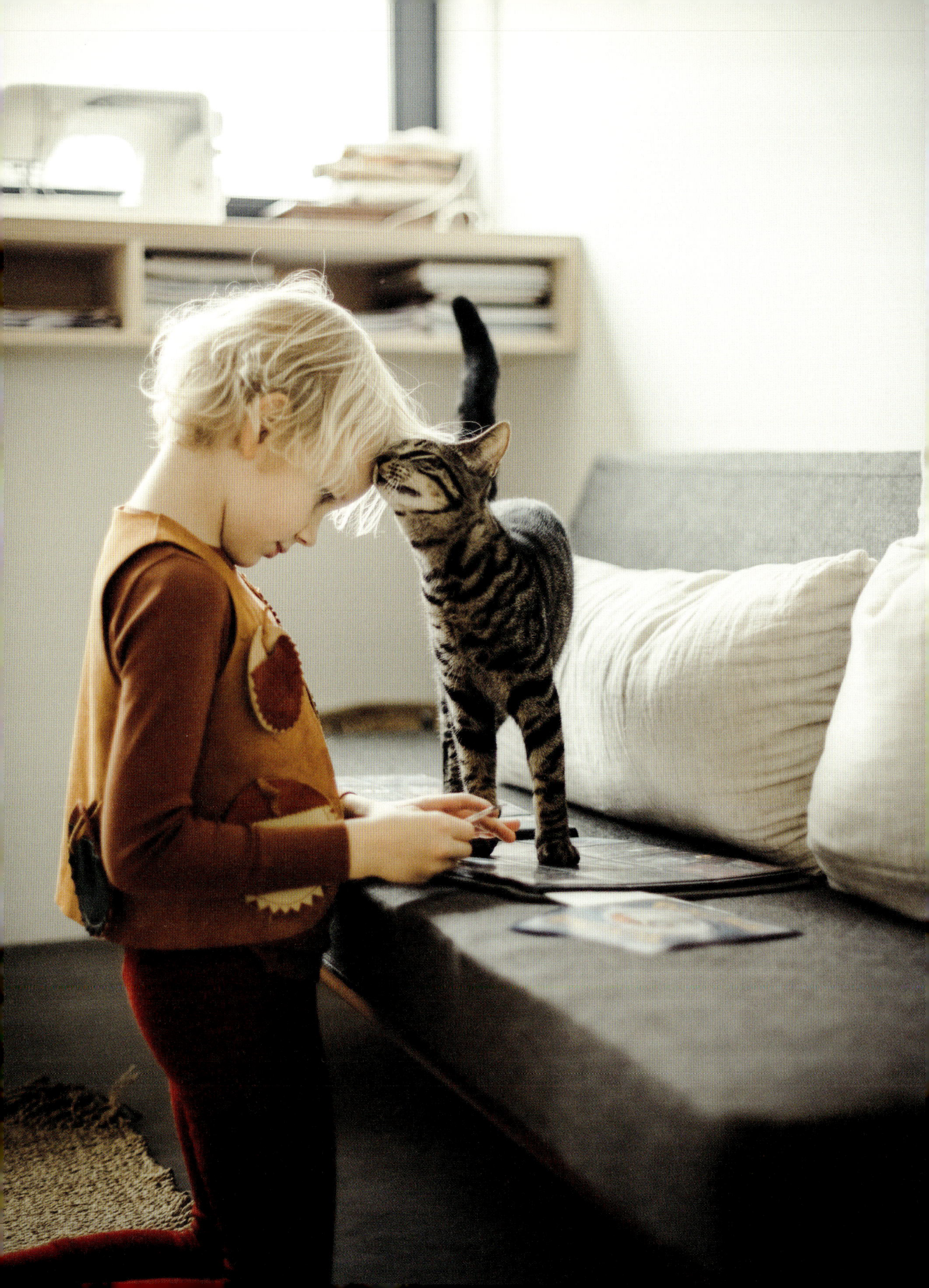

Tessa likes to surround herself with personal objects, light colours, and natural materials. She decided to keep things pure and clean to counteract the buzz around the house.

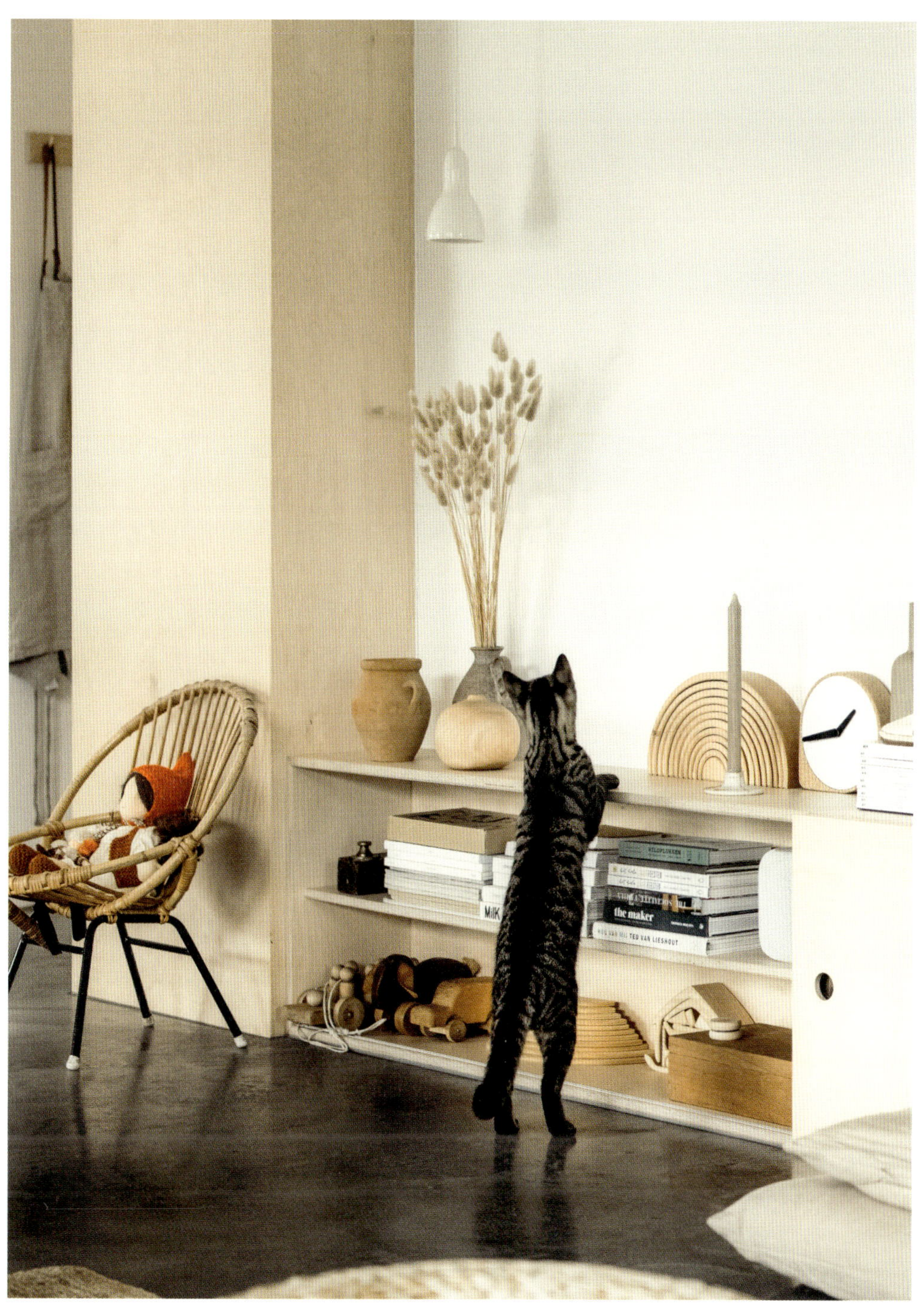

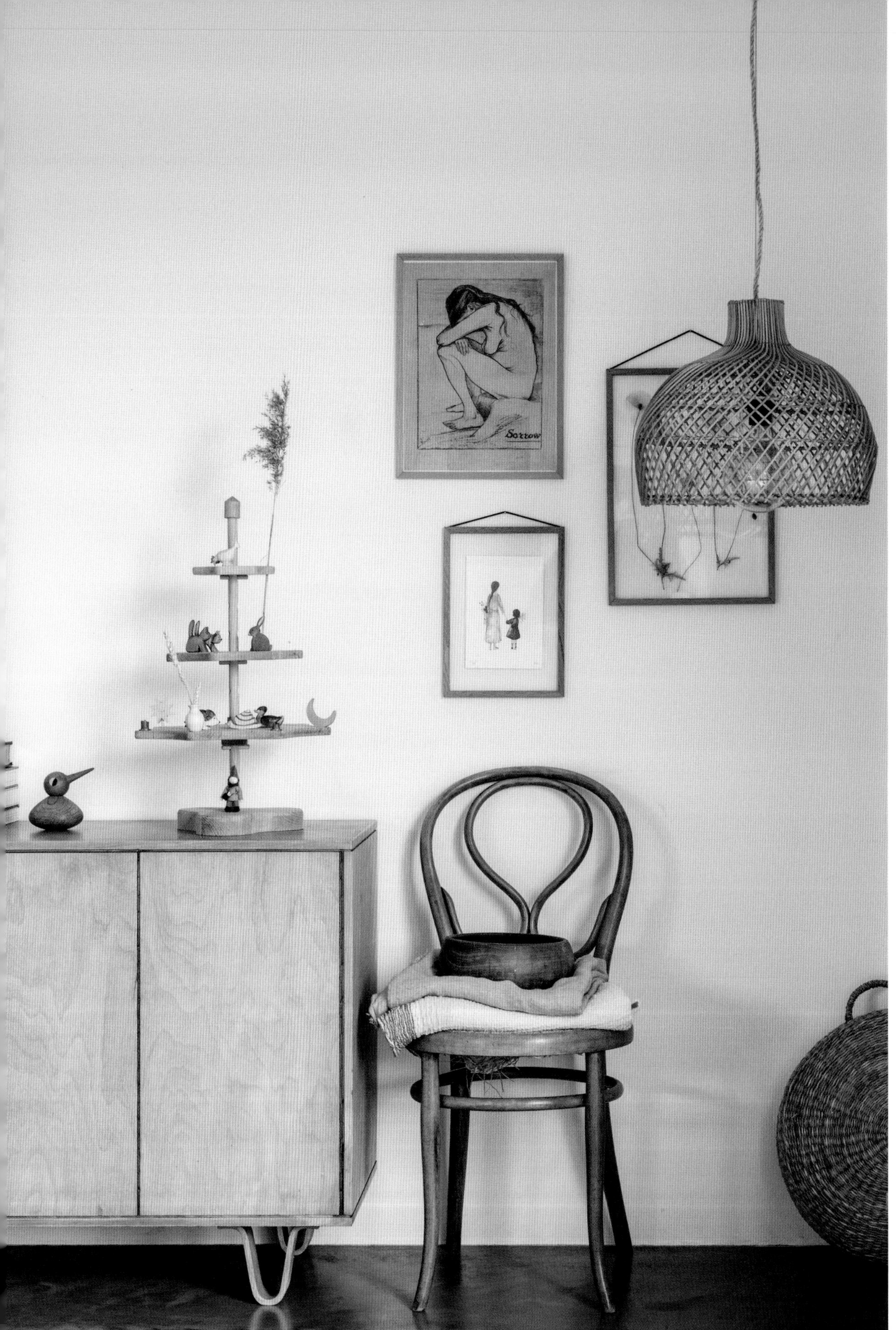
Sorrow

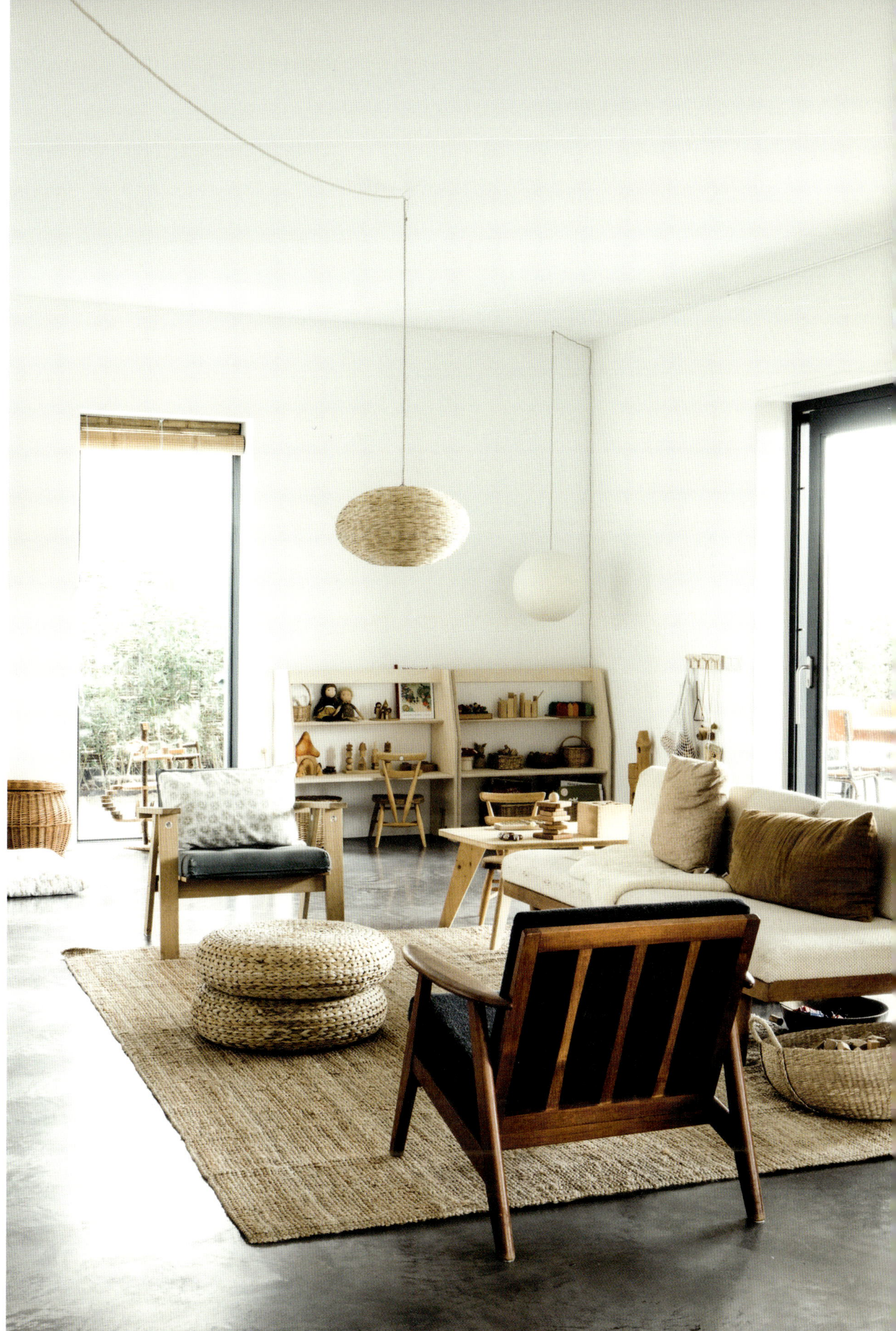

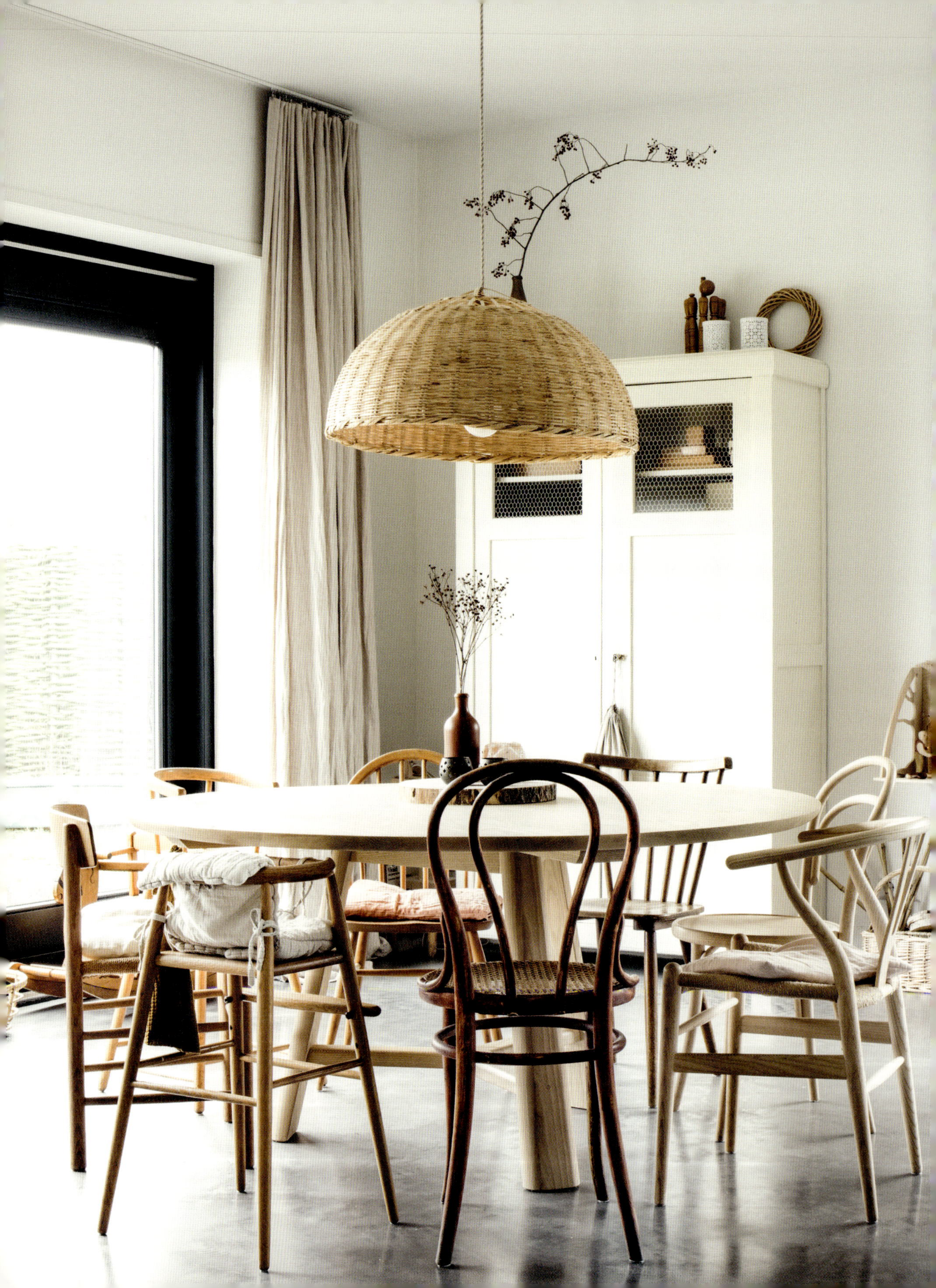

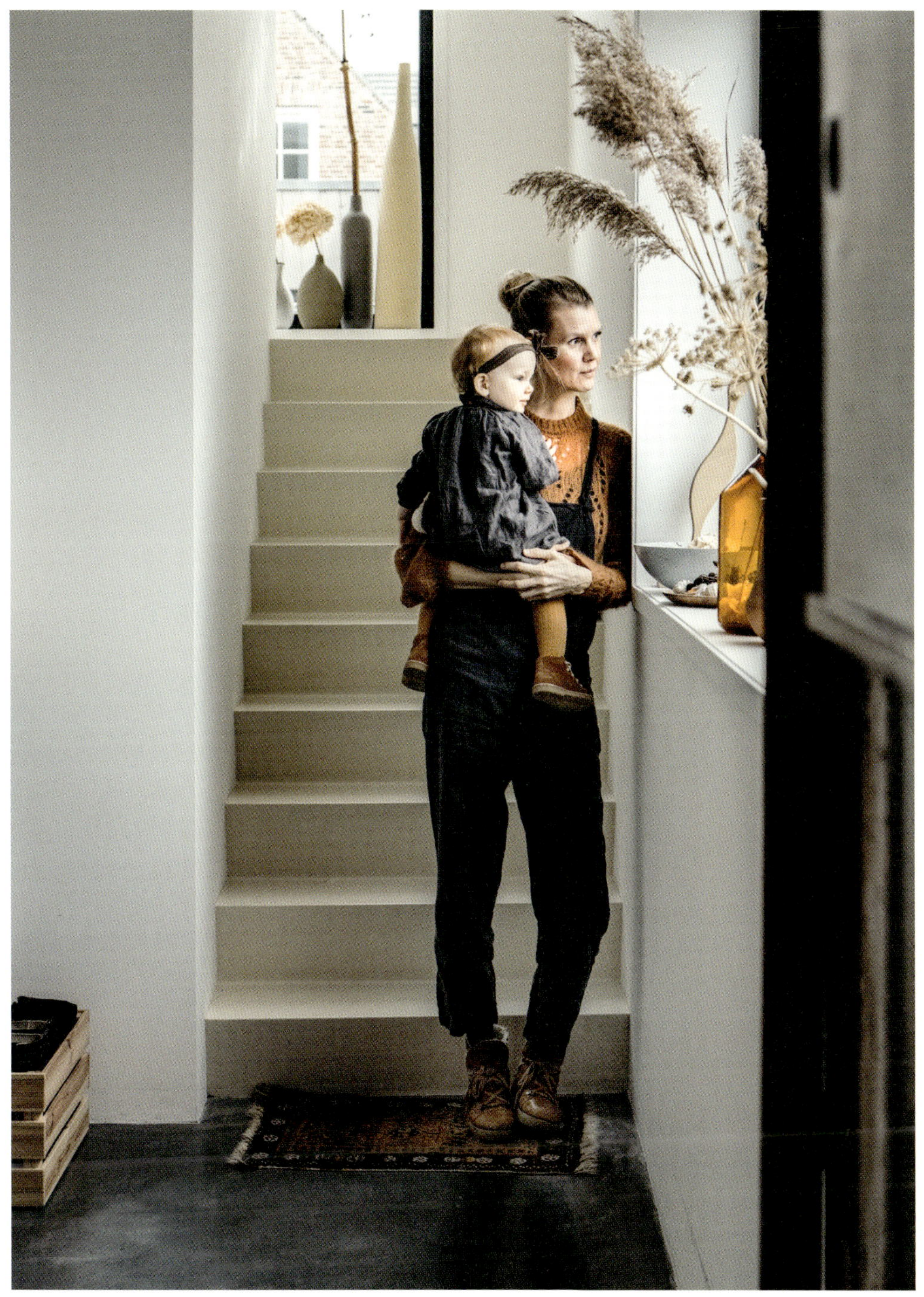

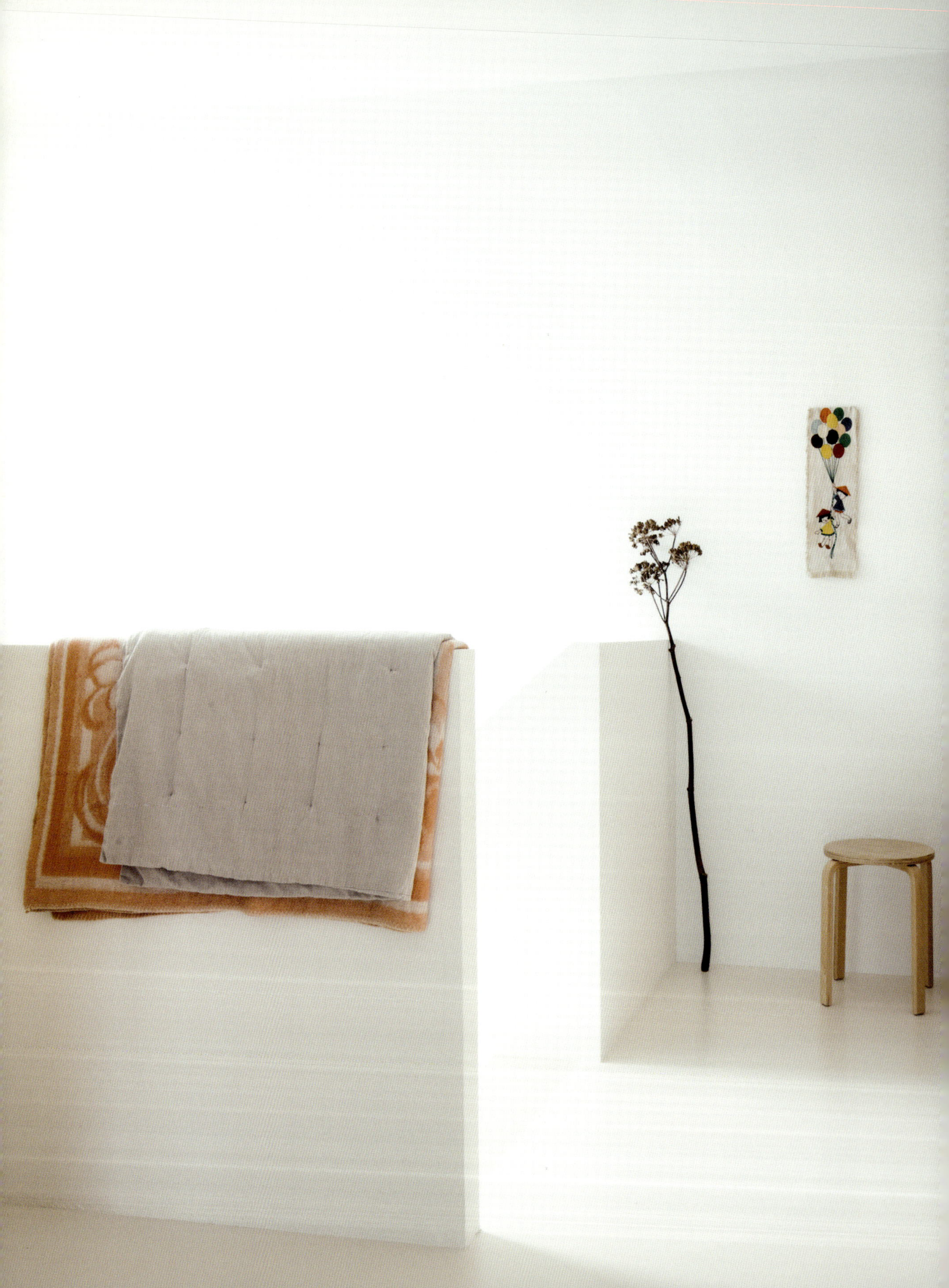

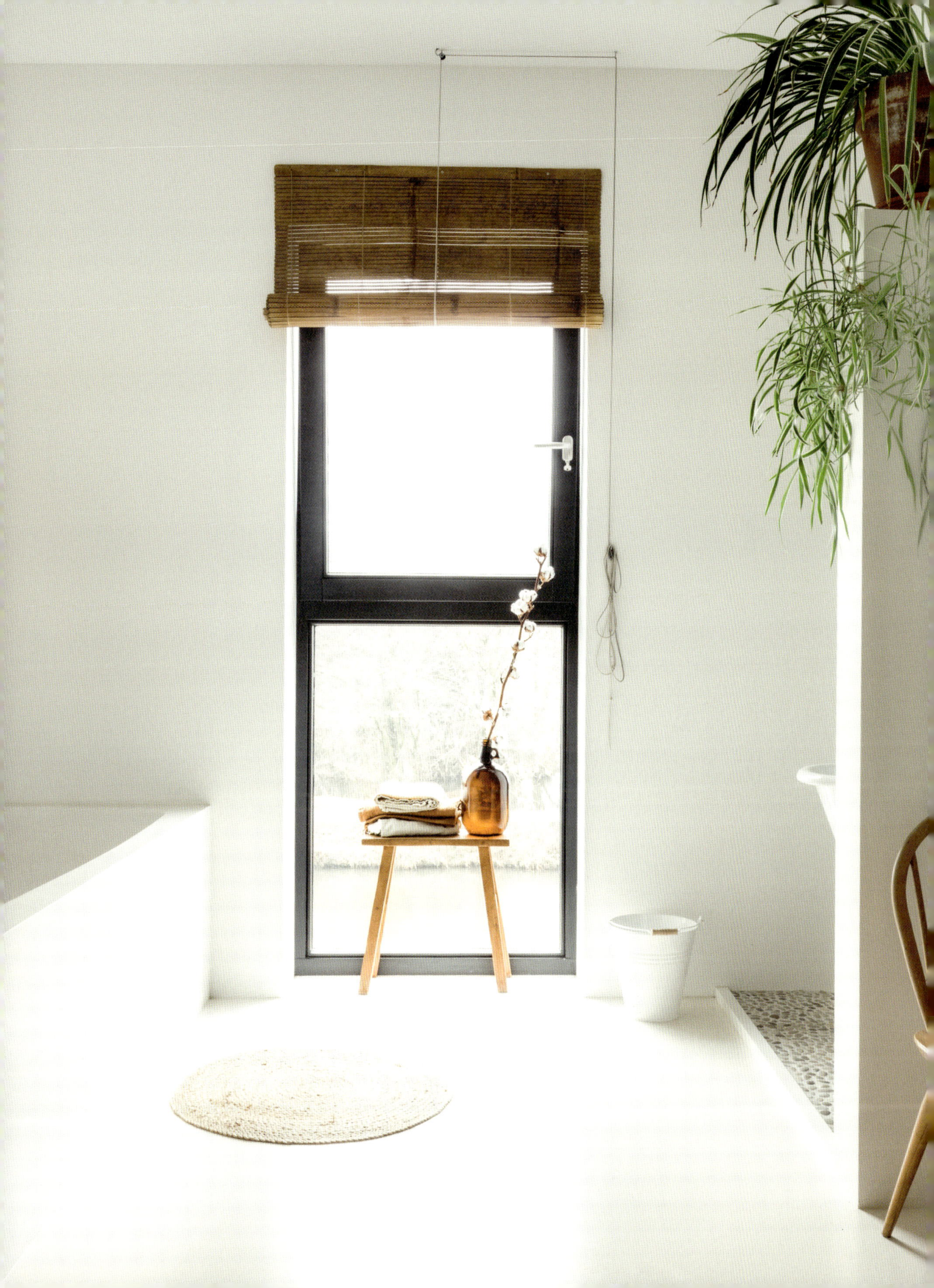

The warm tone of the fur of the two kittens blends in with the
interior. The animals like to lounge in an armchair or romp
around with the boys' toys.

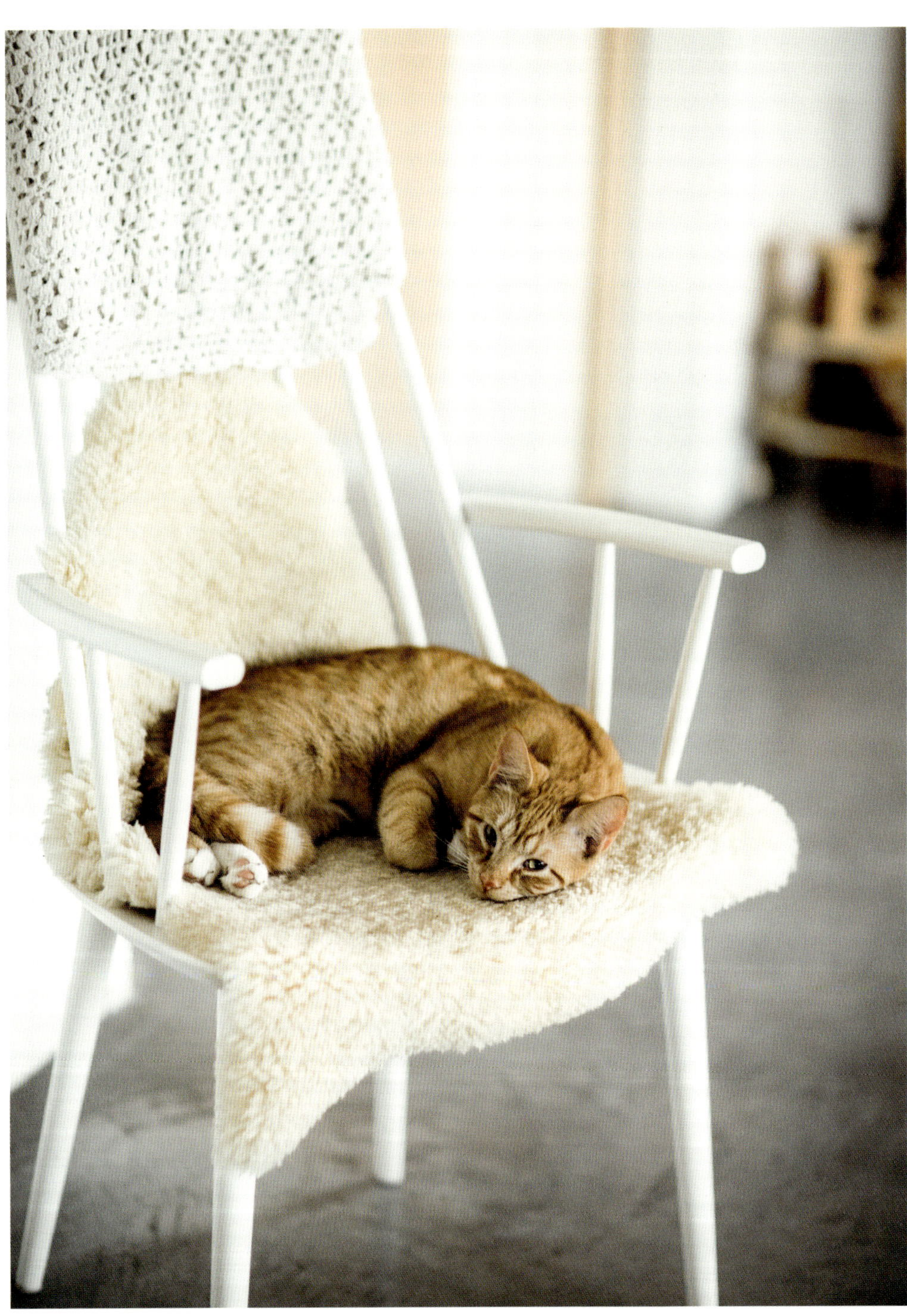

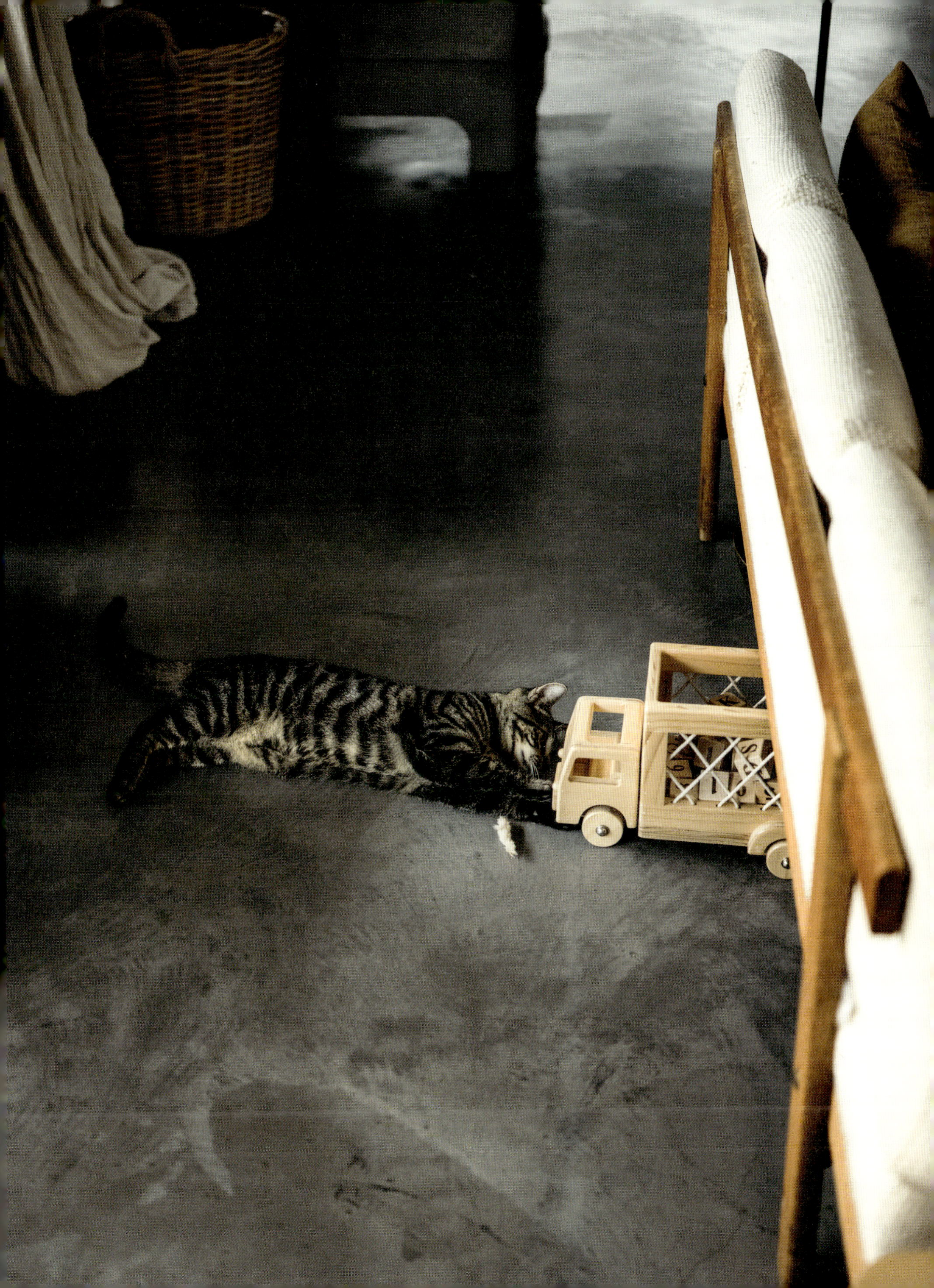

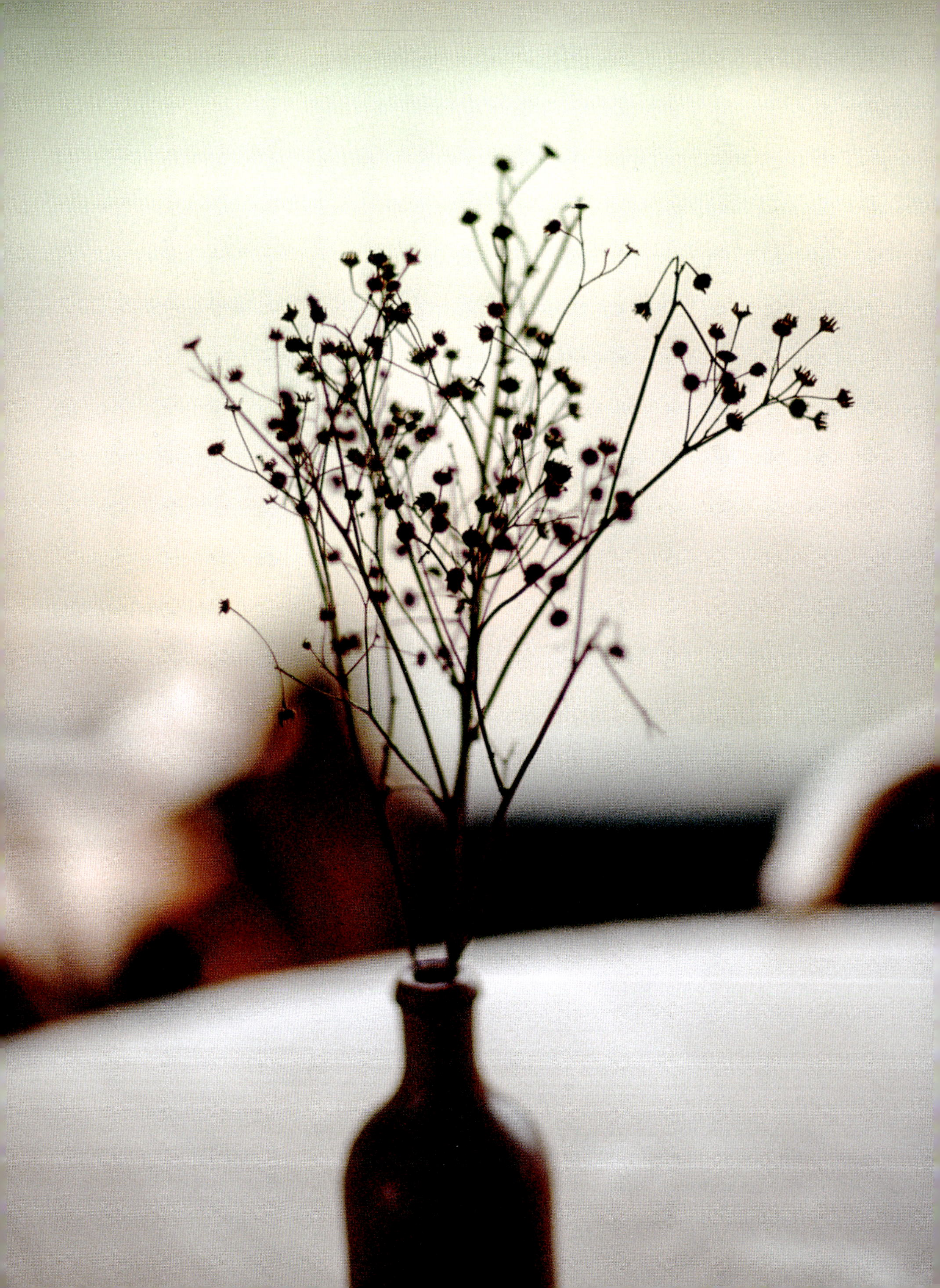

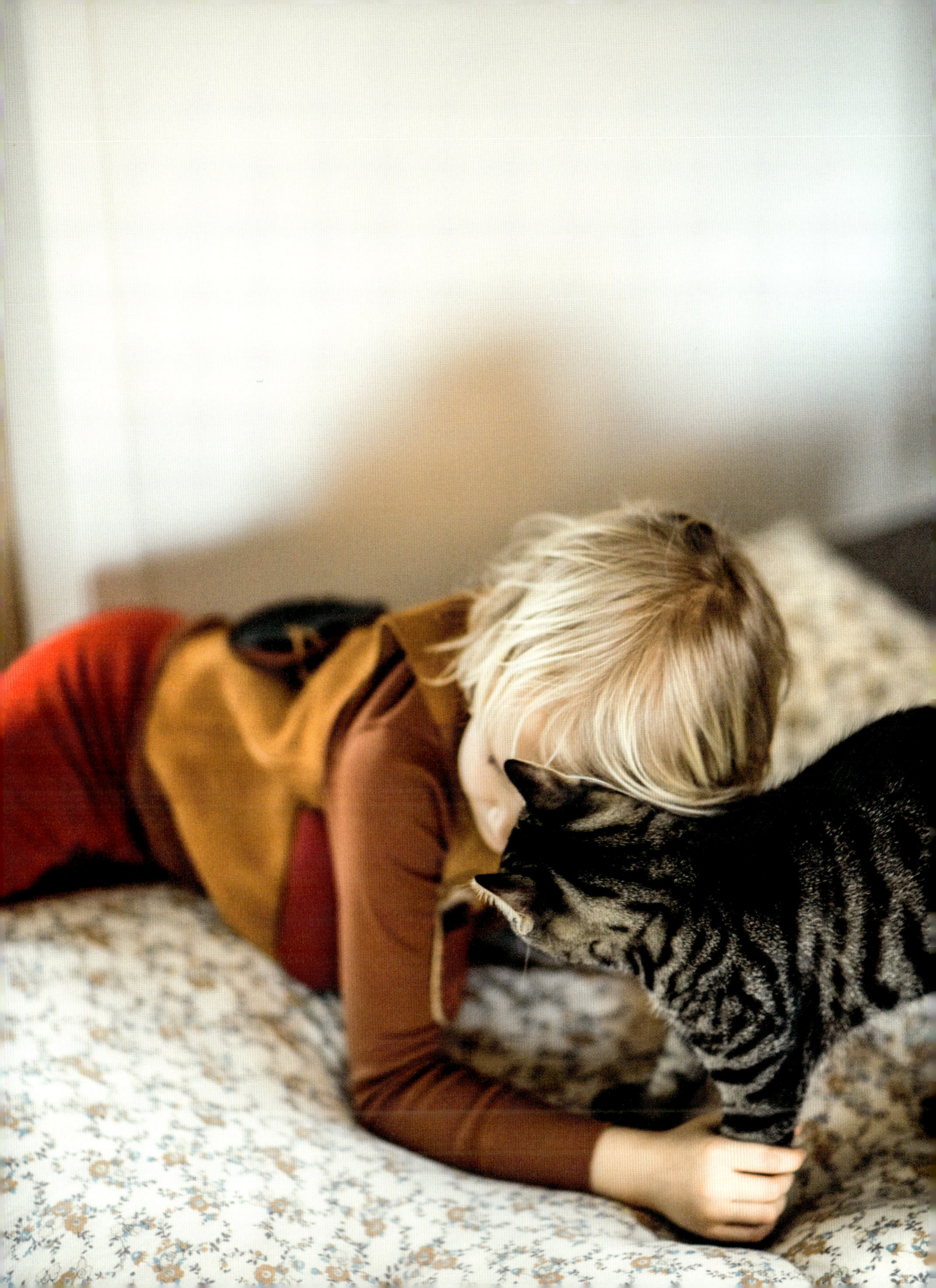

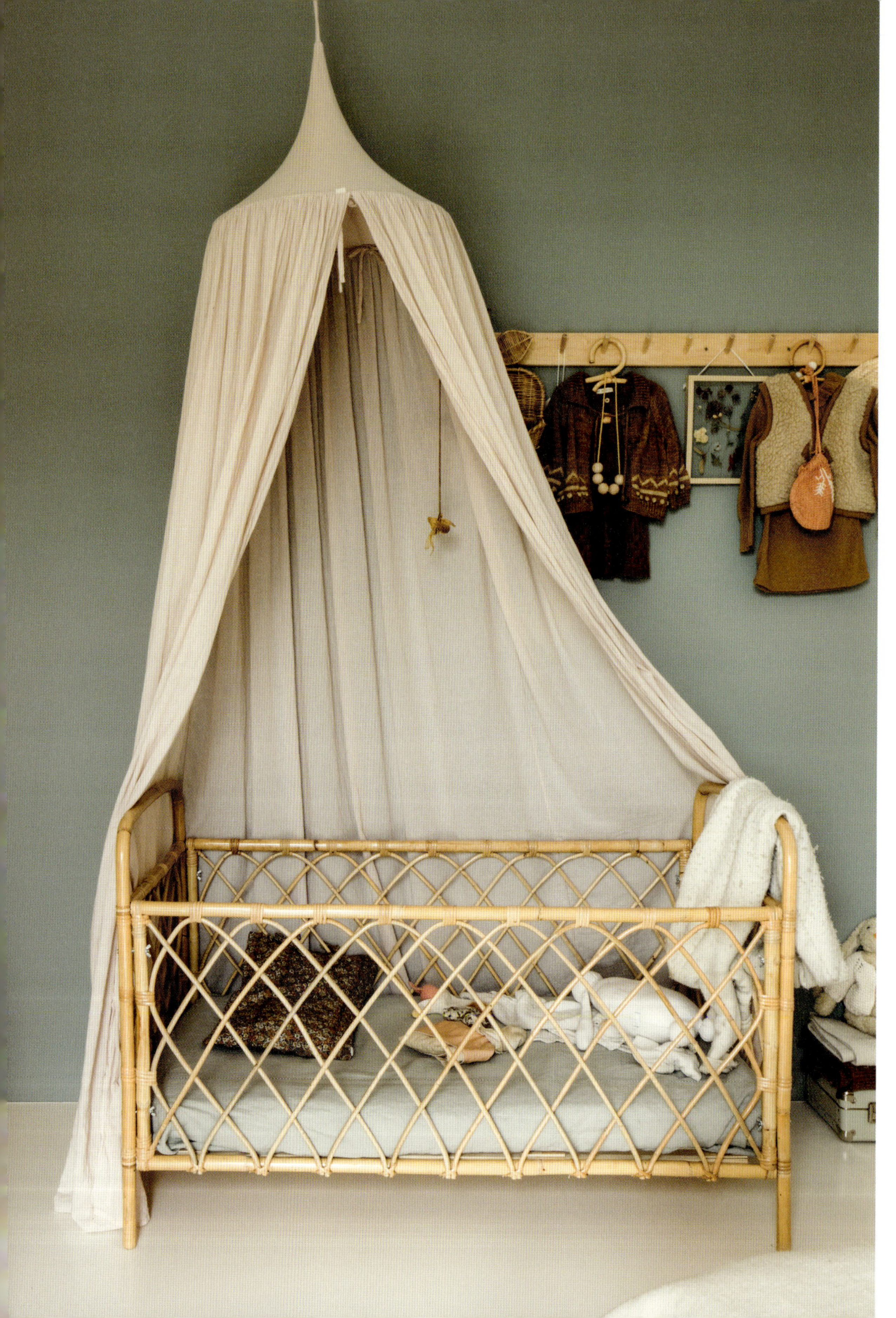

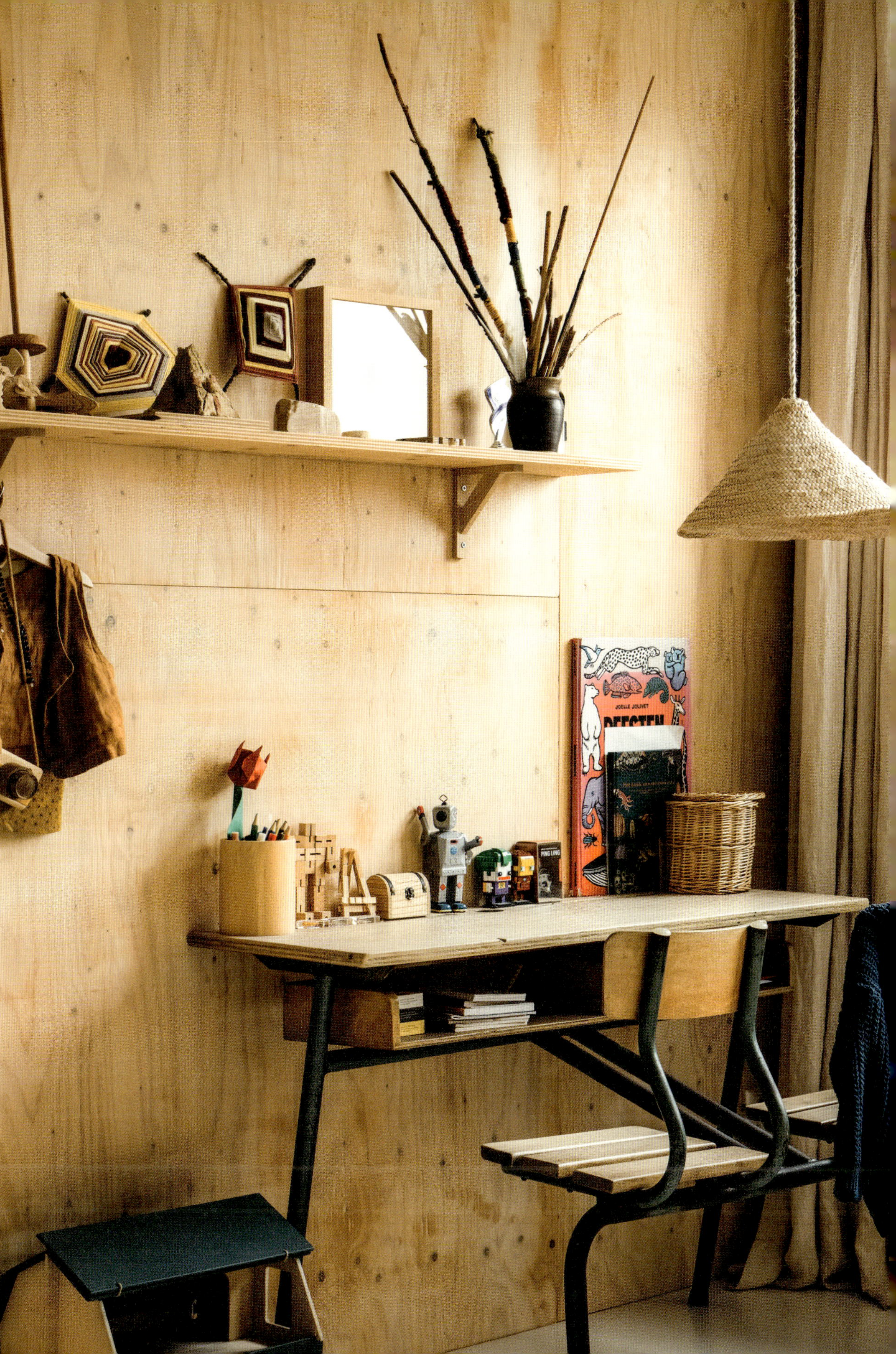

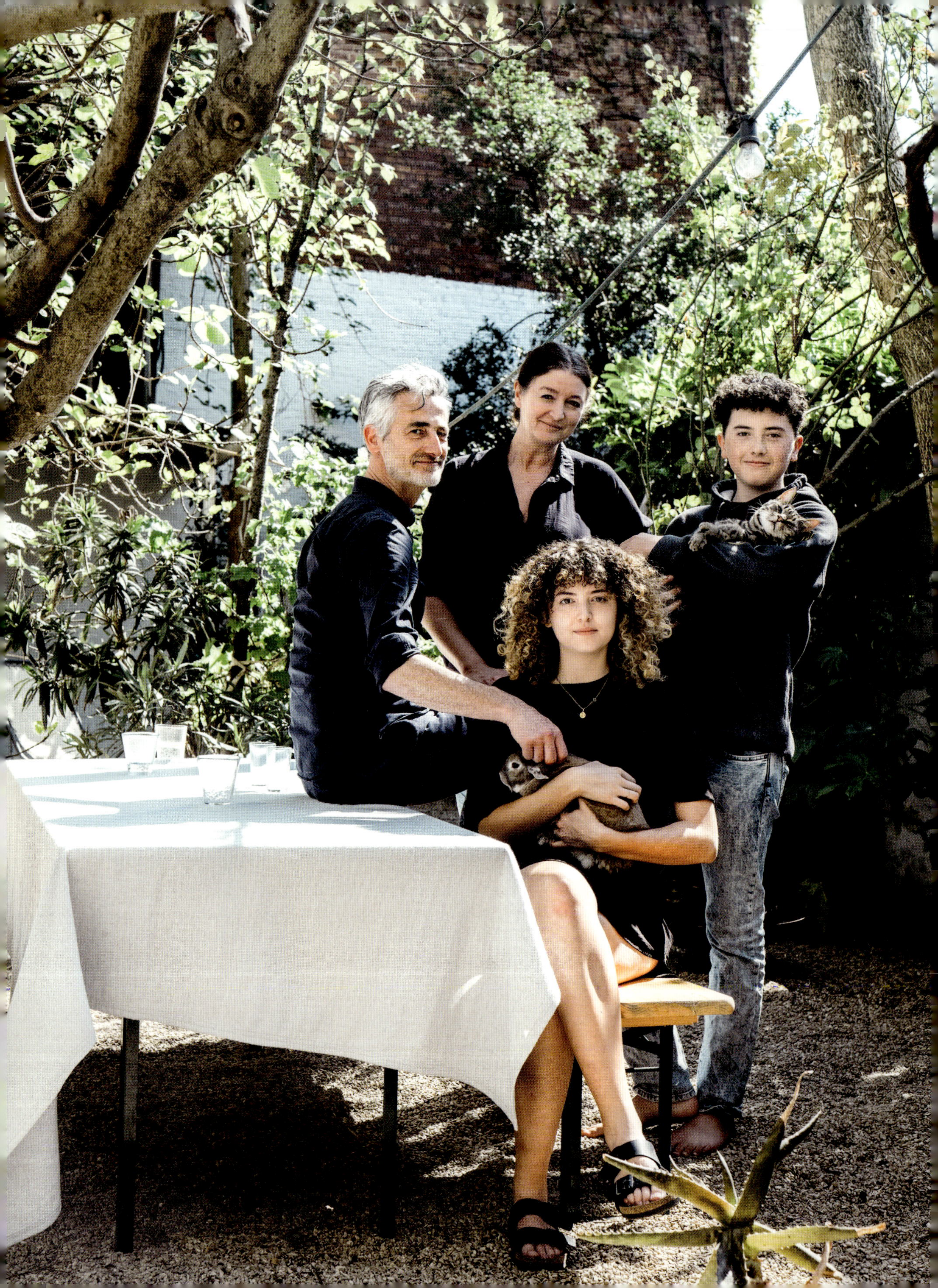

The art deco townhouse in which Ann, Koen and their two children live is a unique gem with plenty of contrasts and surprises. The classic ornamentation is paired with industrial elements and modern art to create a bold mix. But also with furniture, they made themselves, which the cute bunny and the tomcat love to jump on and off. The pets create plenty of chaos and are a favourite conversation topic. Despite their small stature, they have a significant impact on their owners and life in the city.

A passion for pets

Ann Van der Auwera is a food stylist, Koen De Ceuleneer, an artist. Together they run a restaurant called September. 'We share a passion for good food and animals,' says Ann. They got the bunny and the cat at the request of their children, Pilar (22 years) and Voss (12 years). 'We all love pets. The children find them very important, and so do we. And they are a fun conversation starter and topic. They are our common ground as a family. When we're on holiday, we wonder how our little friends are doing, and we exchange holiday snaps with our pet carer.' Both Ann and Koen grew up with animals. And the pets they have now perfectly suit their busy agenda and lifestyle. 'They require a minimum of care and commitment, but you get a lot in return.' During the interview, the cat and the rabbit contend for our attention and show why they deserve it.

Respect for the house's history

The surroundings in which the pets live are magical and atypical. Twenty years ago, the couple discovered this classic art deco house. They bought it from an elderly lady, whose father, a colonel, had built it in 1885. The top floors had been converted into different apartments, but fortunately, the ground floor had been conserved intact. It featured several original art deco elements, such as wooden wainscoting with mirrors and paintings, velvet wallpaper, marble mantelpieces, and glass. Ann and Koen describe the ornaments as 'whipping cream' because they are so in your face and over the top. Koen confesses that he has thought of painting everything white, but 'if we really want a different style, then we should move so somebody else can enjoy all this beauty.' The kids yell 'no way' in the background.

Italian bistro

The house's historic assets made it quite difficult for the occupants to add a personal and contemporary twist to it. And yet, they succeeded beautifully in their endeavour by incorporating furniture they built themselves, as well as artwork and industrial elements. They don't mind that it clashes here and there. 'That is exactly what makes this house so unique,' says Koen. The abode is teeming with contrasts. The extension with a kitchen and dining room is the latest addition. The round tables and long bench against the tiled wall are reminiscent of an Italian bistro. Poot, the rabbit, feels entirely at home here. He observes the neighbourhood cats that visit the garden and chases them. While he looks all fuzzy and sweet, he's still the boss. He gets on very well with Streep, their cat. The two always seek each other out and rub noses. But they also exchange blows in their competition for attention.

A rabbit with sore hocks

The bunny was a consolation prize because Voss initially had his heart set on a dog. 'And one day we returned from the market with a rabbit,' Ann remembers. The two are firm friends. When Voss lays on the floor, the bunny jumps on top of him. He is free to roam the house, which causes plenty of problems: 'When we put ourselves at his height, we realise the damage he has caused throughout the dwelling. He nibbles the cables, the sofa, and floor paint. But we really can't get angry at him. He's too adorable,' Ann laughs. The rabbit is currently contending with sore hocks, which is a typical skin problem in bunnies and is caused by flooring. The roughness of the tiles and the gravel impacts the way he puts down his feet. This creates friction and wounds. Soft blankies, hay, and soil help treat it.

A playful studio cat

Streep, the tomcat, happened to find them one day. He had accompanied their old cat into the garden and joined her for dinner. Instead of running off, he rolled over with his paws in the air. Pilar knew he was here to stay: 'He's the cuddly pet we've always wanted.' The creature is much more playful and active than the rabbit. He horses around with twine and the strips of the milk carton. Streep is the family's fourth feline. 'I find pets more appealing than people,' Ann confesses. 'They make you instantly happy,' Koen adds. Pilar points out that animals can communicate and stresses the importance of interaction. 'Coming home to a pet is such fun. They wait for you and welcome you enthusiastically. You're never alone.'
 Unlike the cat, the rabbit cannot make it up the stairs. Streep meows his way to Voss's room. Now and then he also visits Koen's studio, which looks out onto the nearby park. Pilar tells us that he secretly hides among her father's paintings, drawings, and fragile sculptures. Streep is a stubborn cat who will not be deterred by anyone or anything.

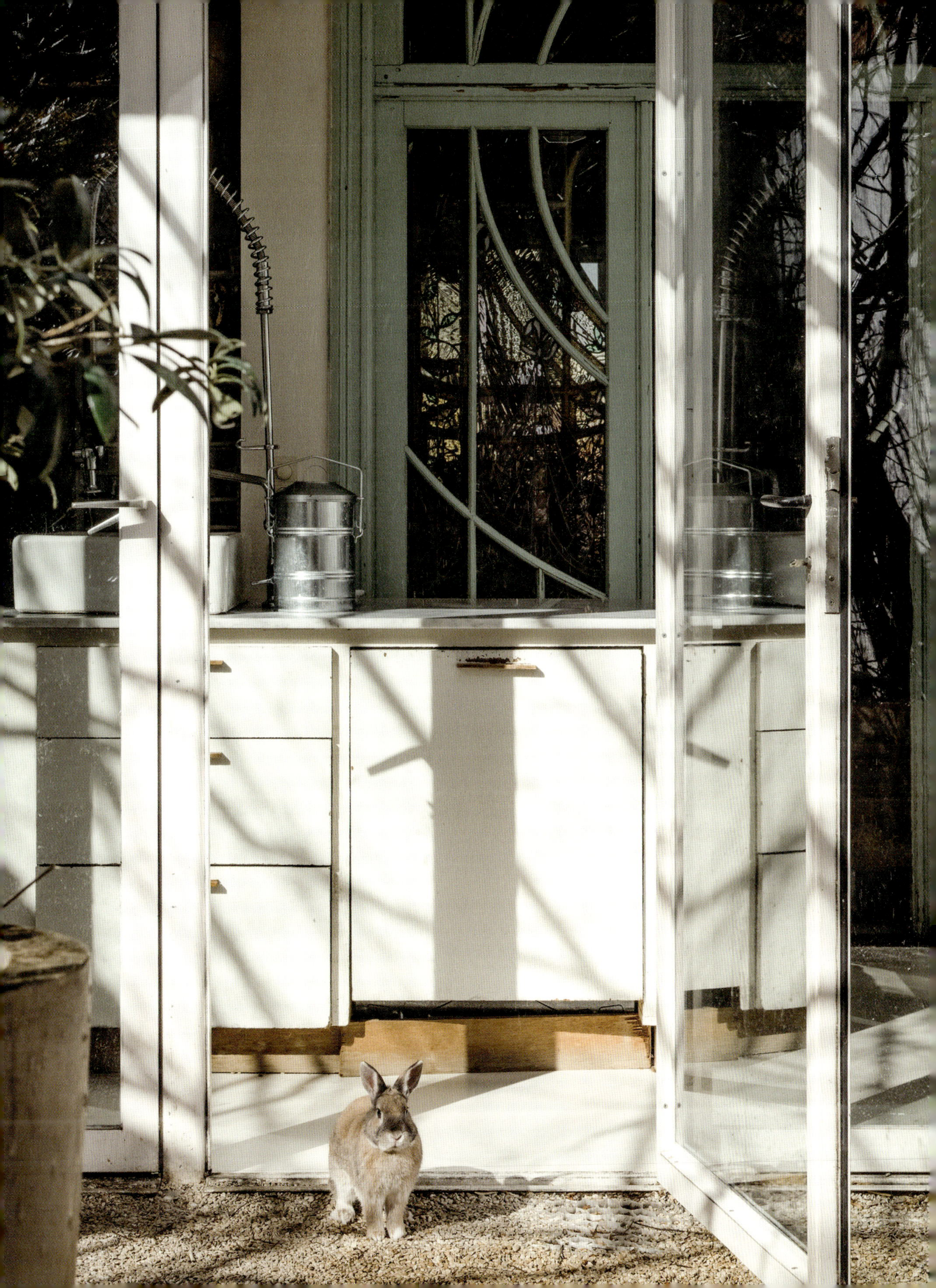

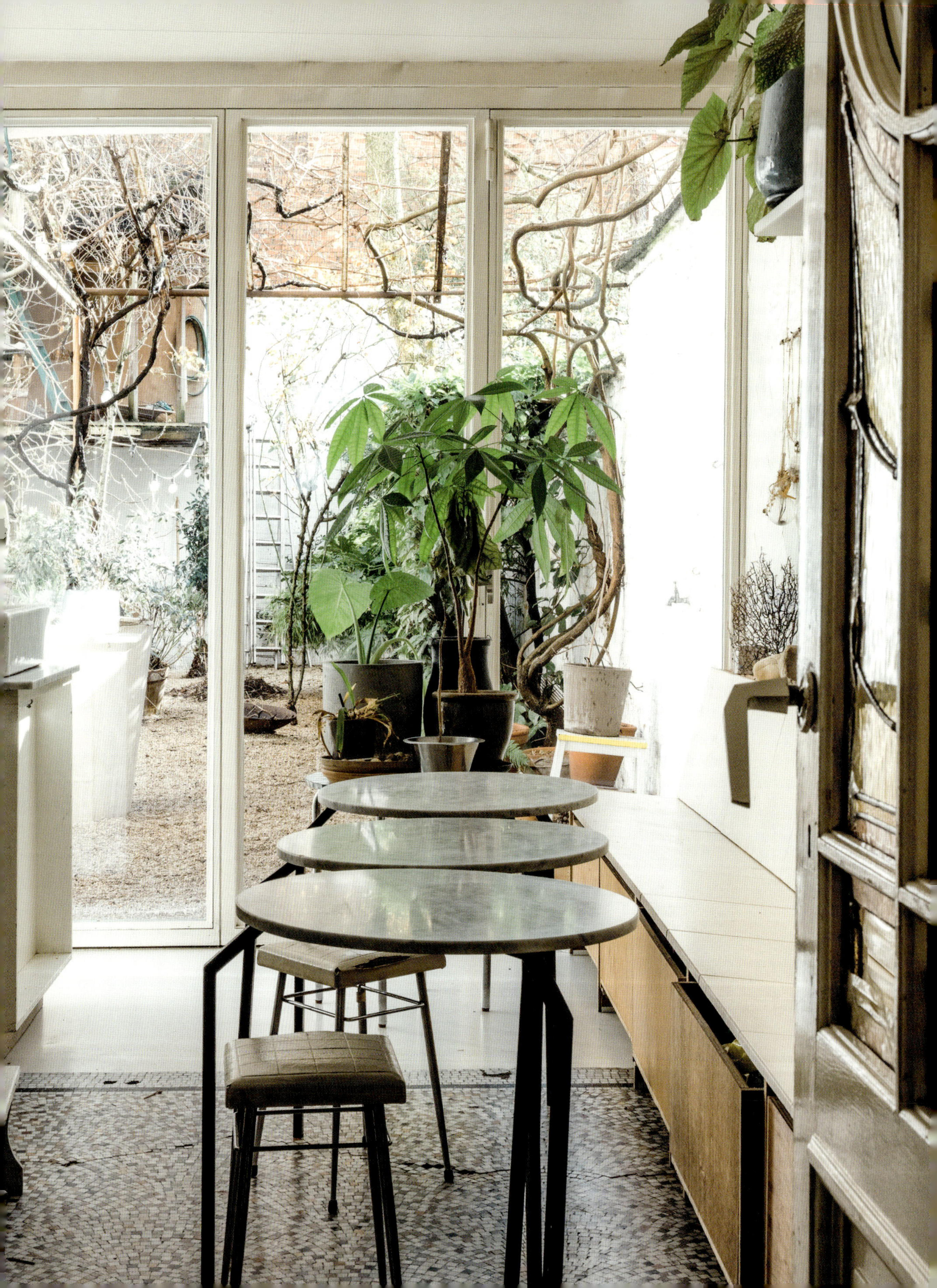

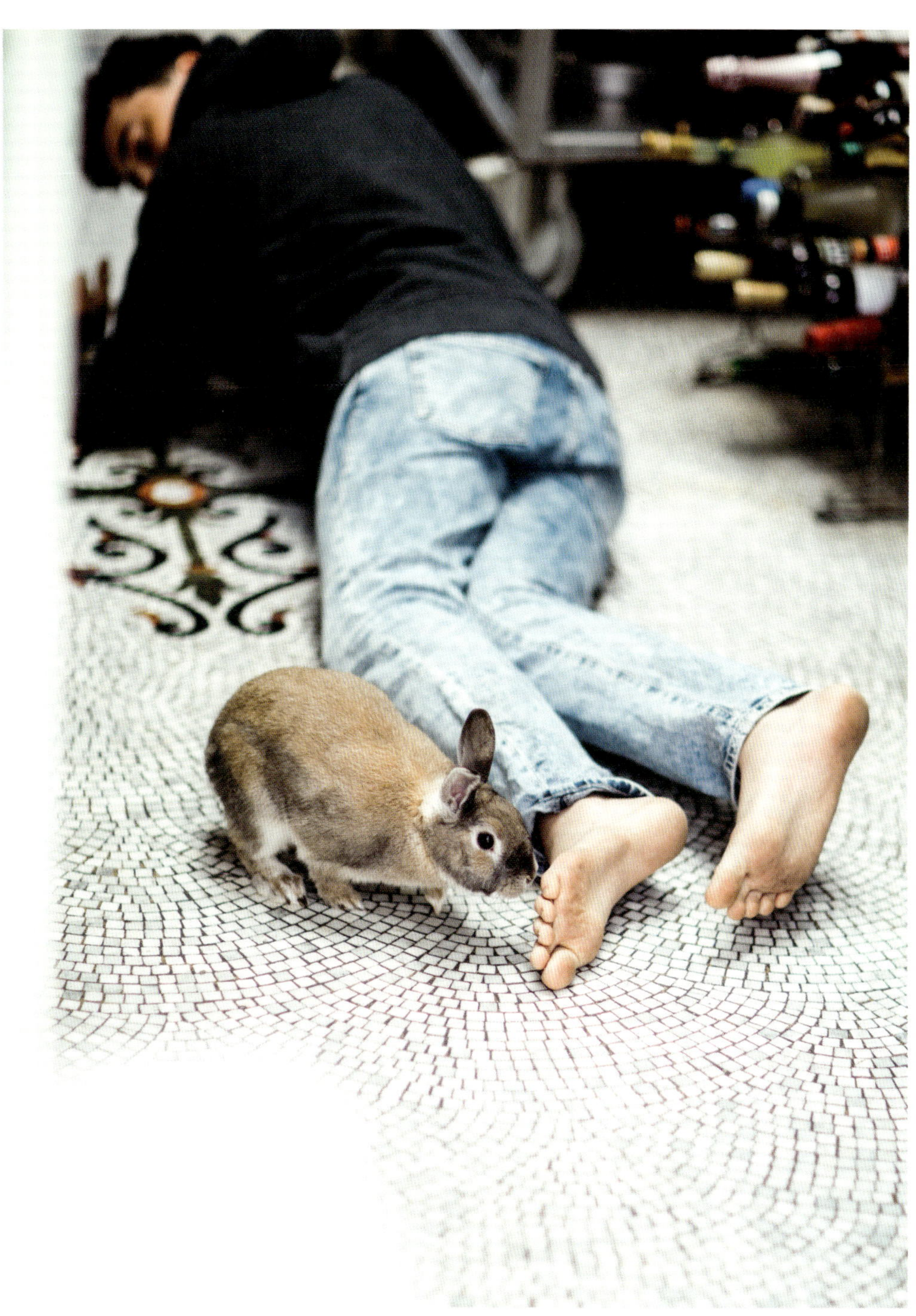

The dining area has all the allure of a cosy, Italian bistro.
The rabbit likes to sit under the table or on top of Voss when
he's lounging on the floor.

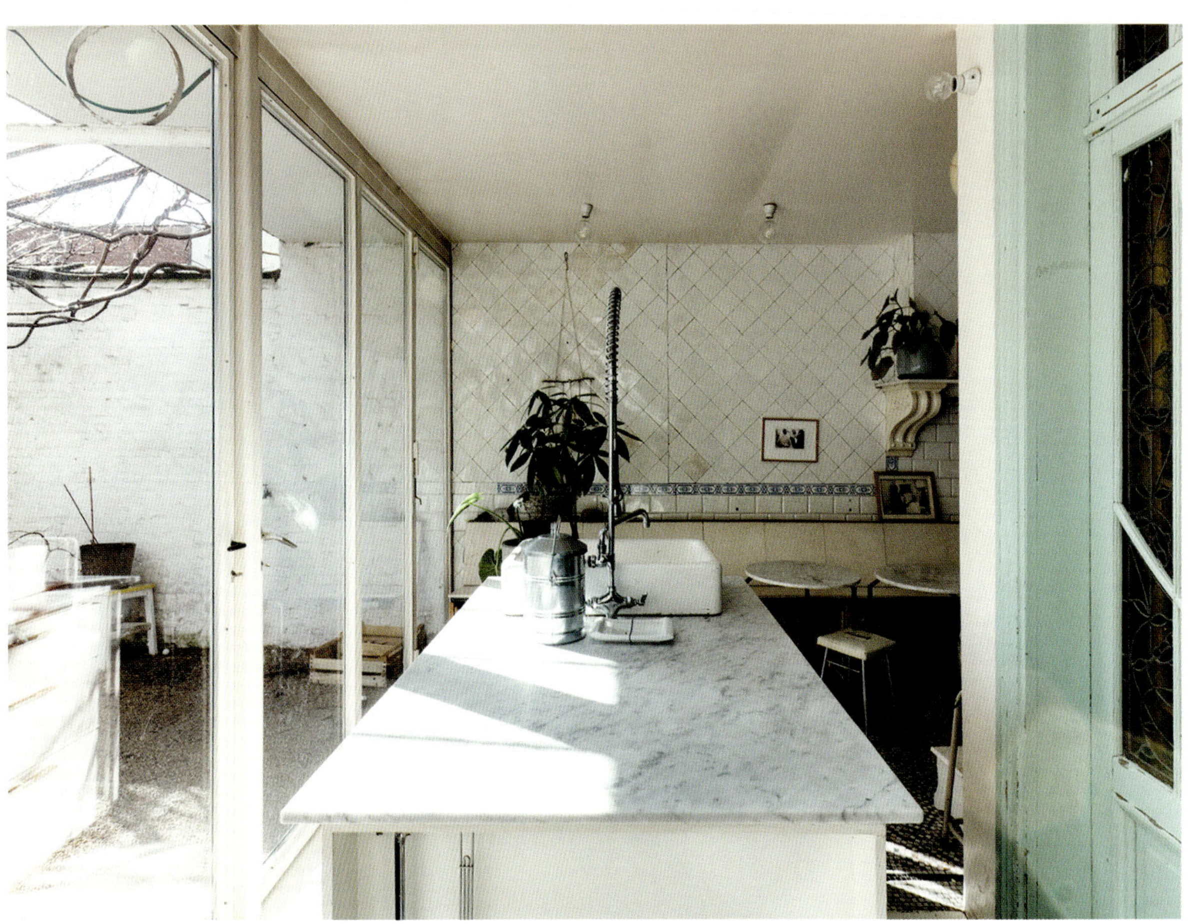

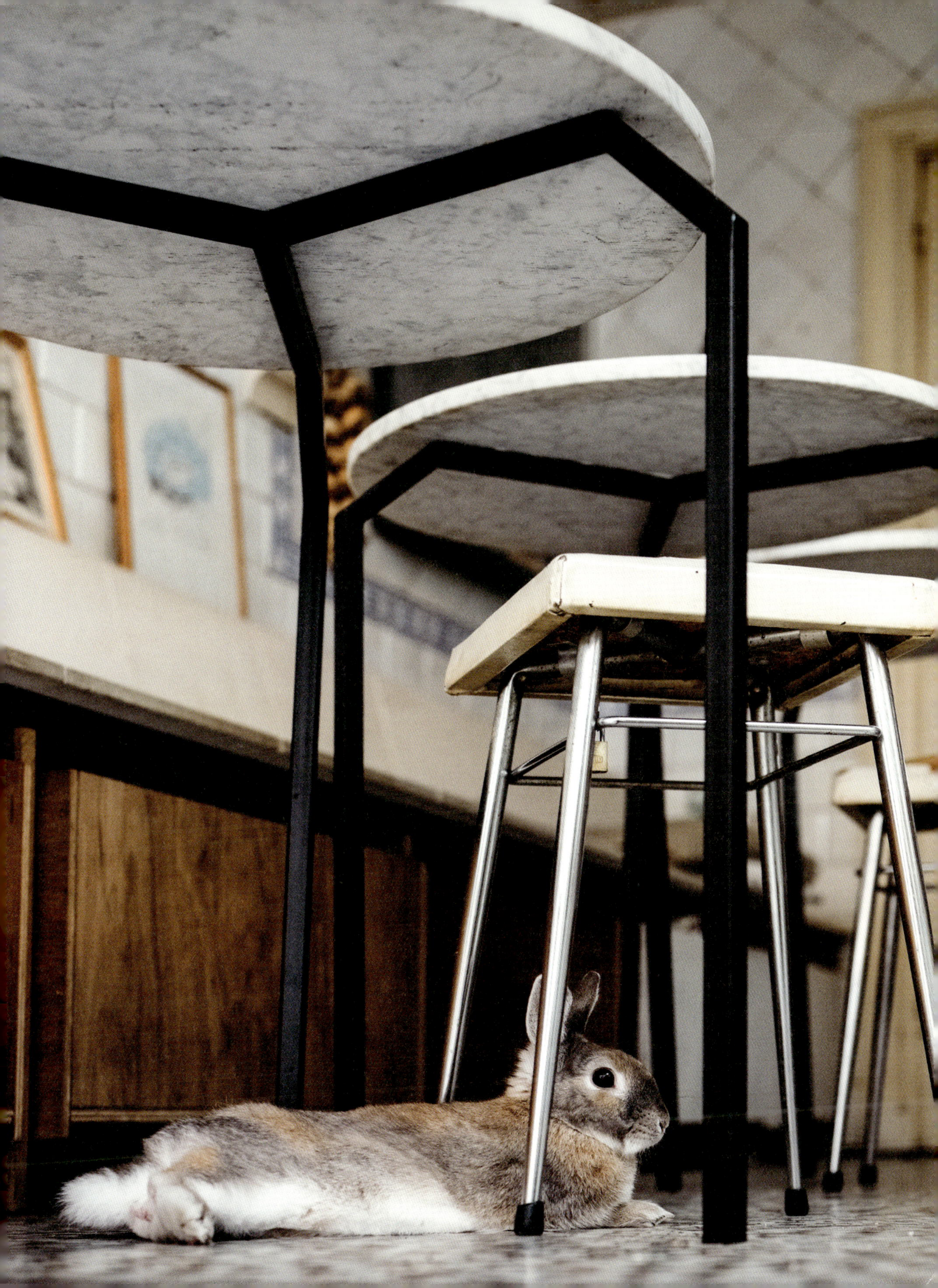

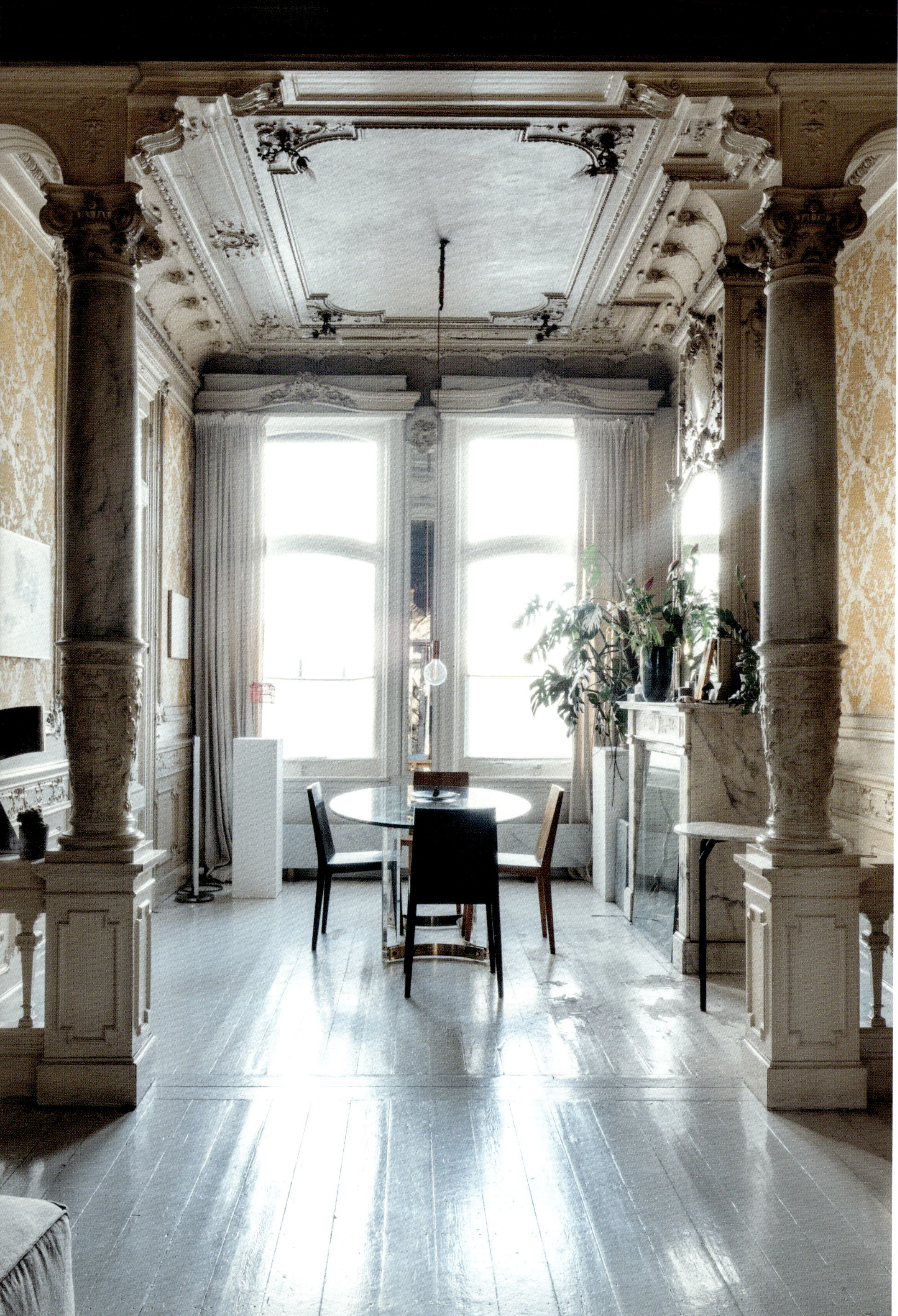

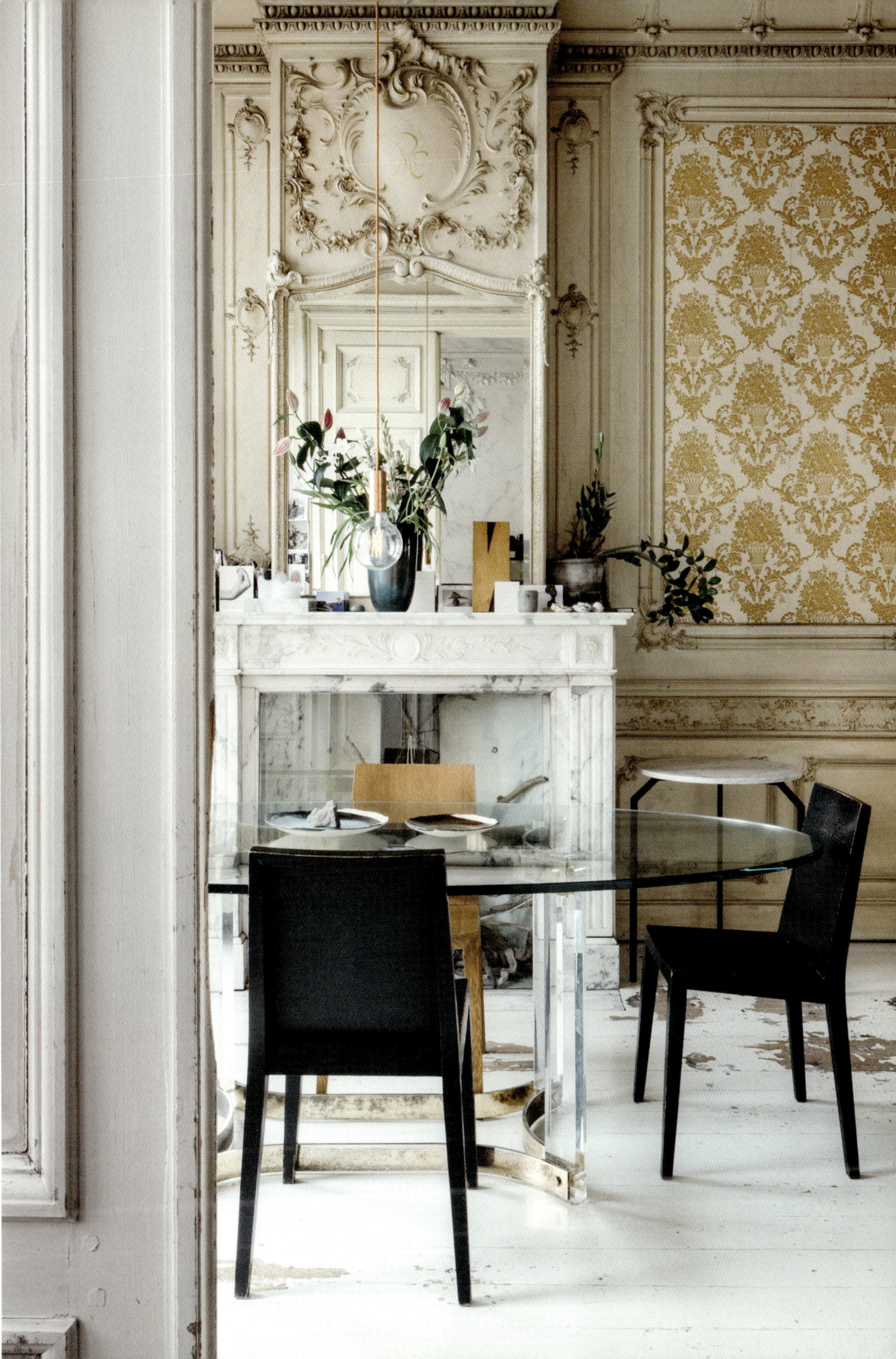

In addition to running a restaurant, Koen De Ceuleneer is
also an artist. He transposes line drawings into paintings and
sculptures in his studio.

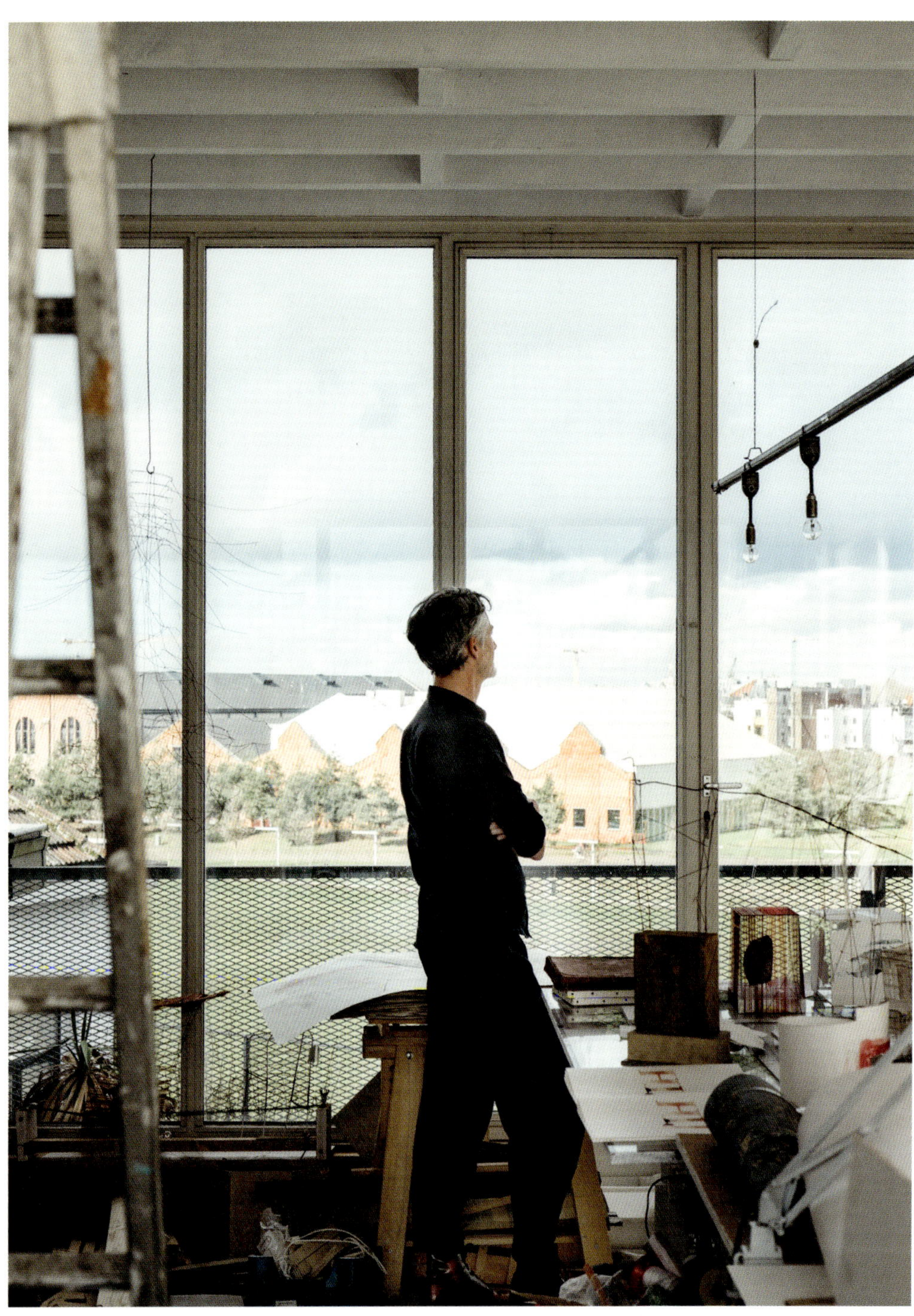

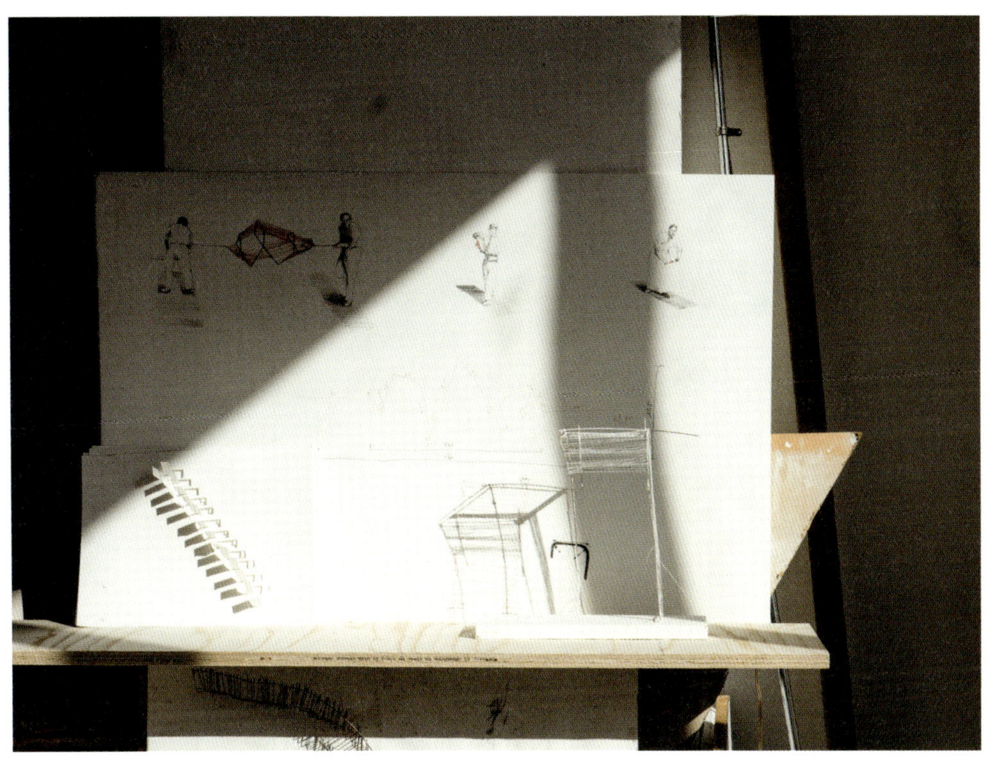

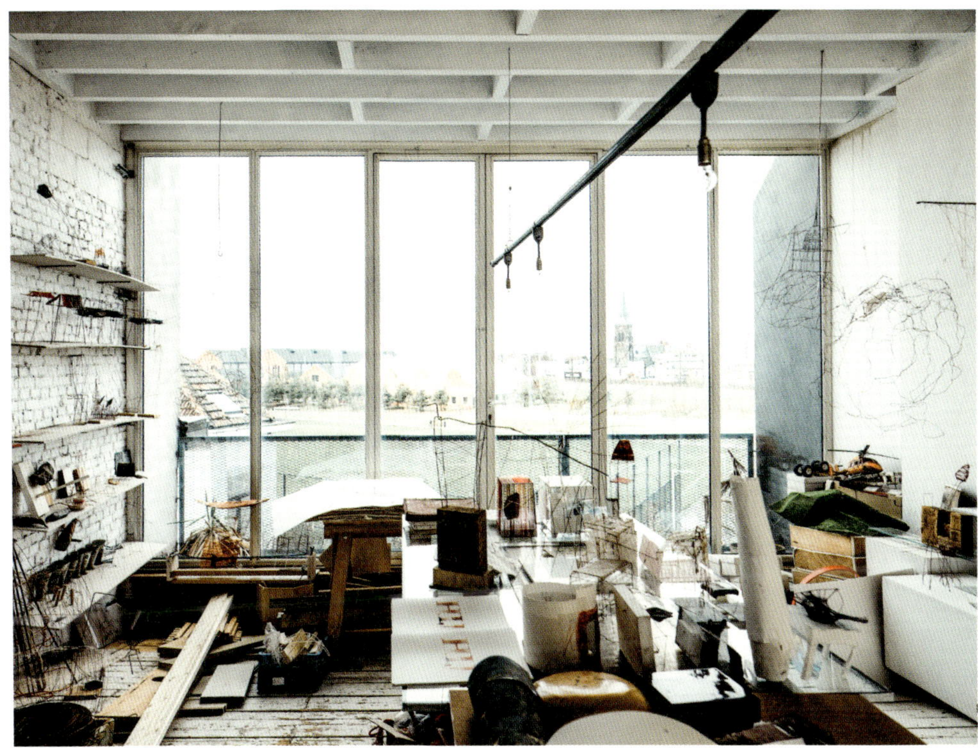

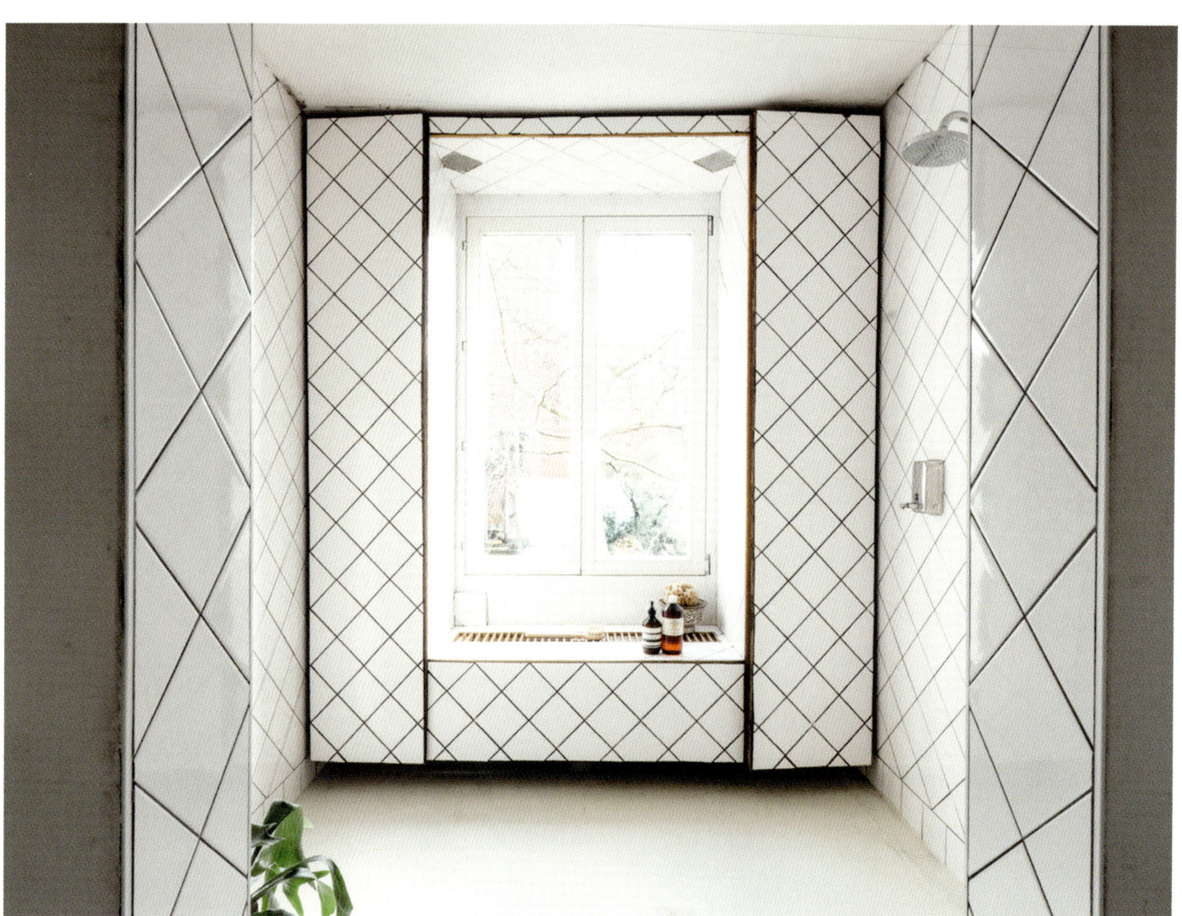

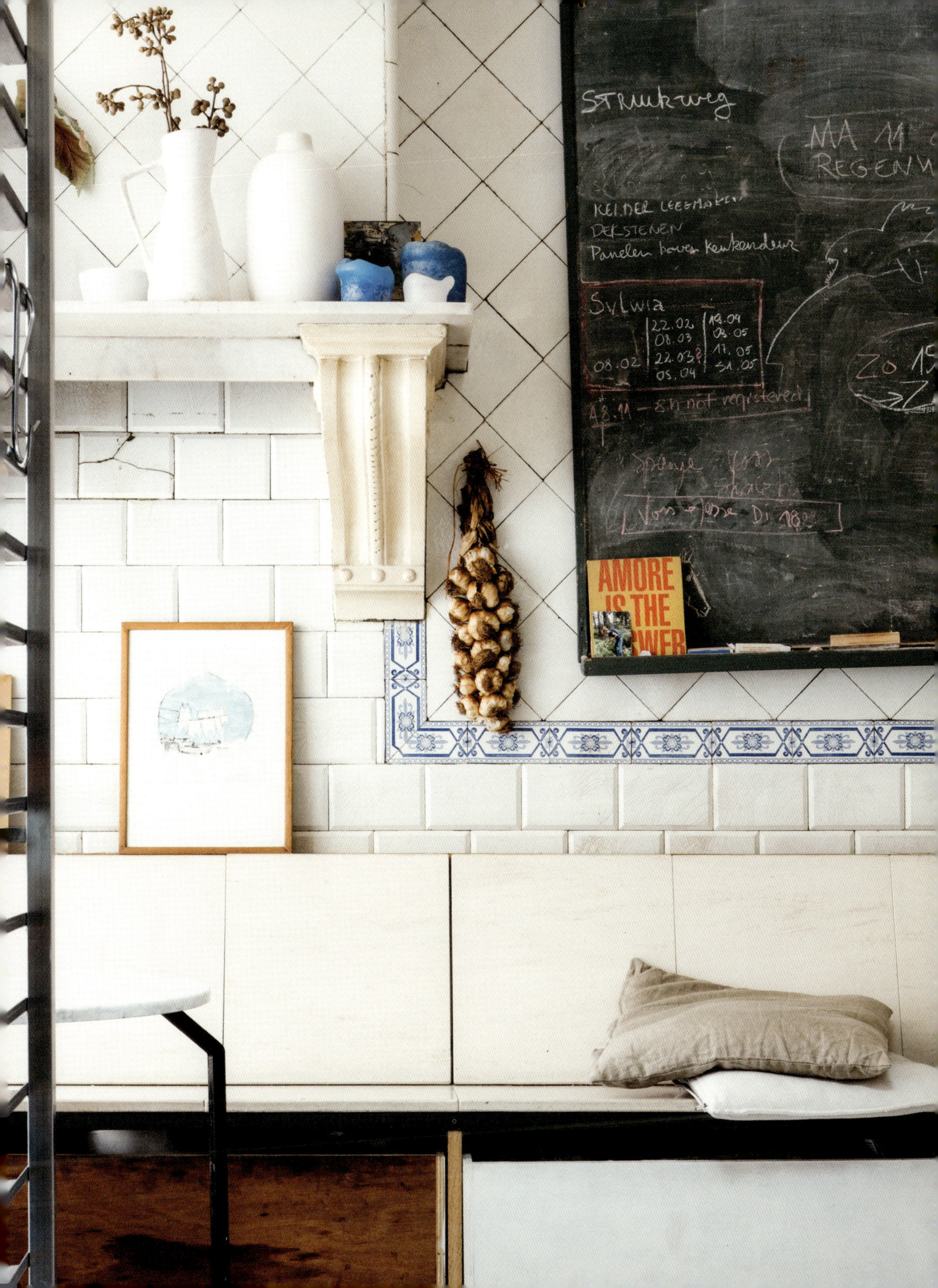
Struikweg
MA M
REGENW
KELDER LEEGMAKEN
DEKSTENEN
Panelen boven keukendeur
Sylwia
22.02   19.04
08.03   08.05
08.02   22.03   17.05
05.04   31.05
48.11 — 8h not registered
AMORE
IS THE
WER

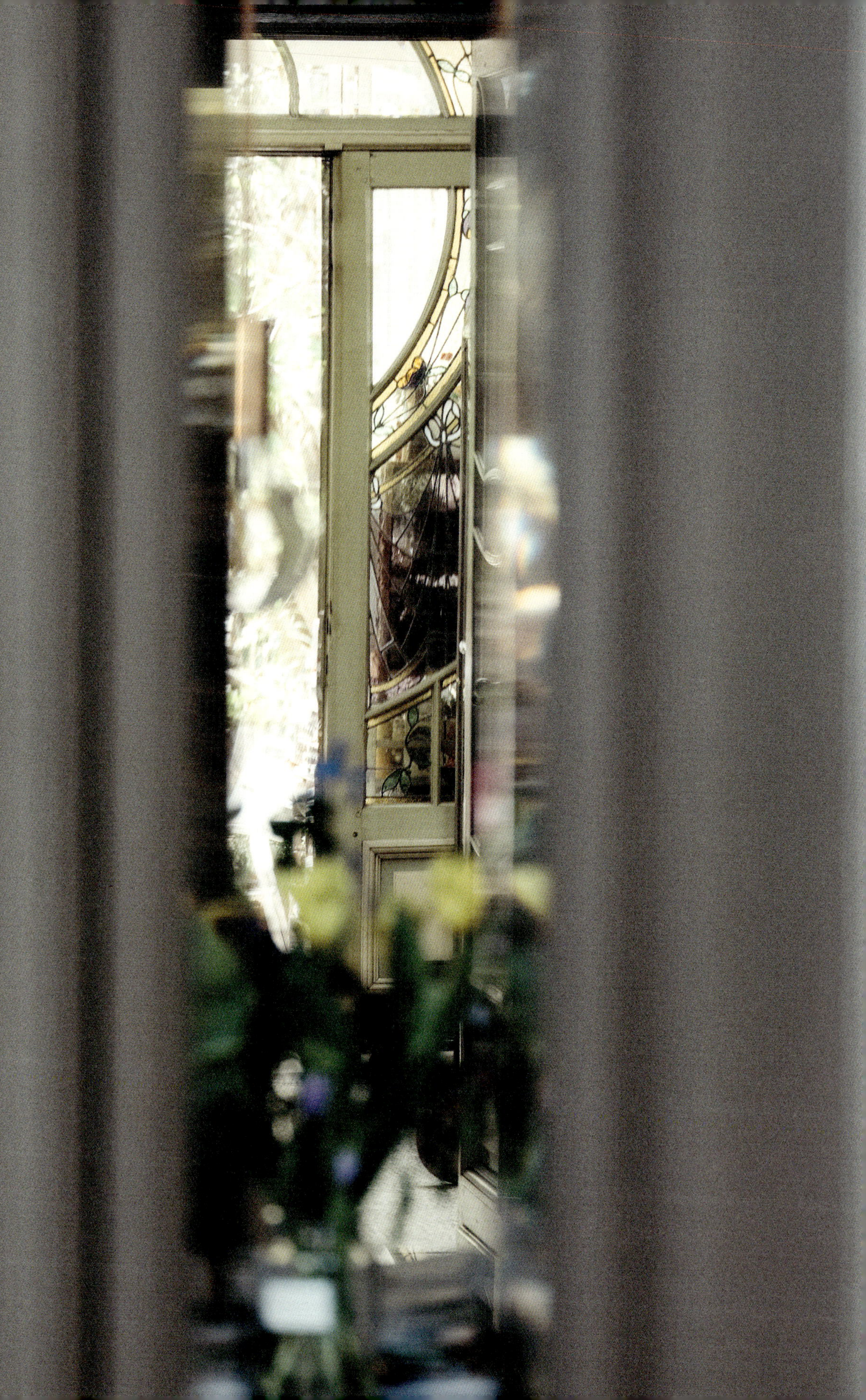

The pets are one of the family's favourite conversation topics.
'The children find them important, and so do we,' says Ann.

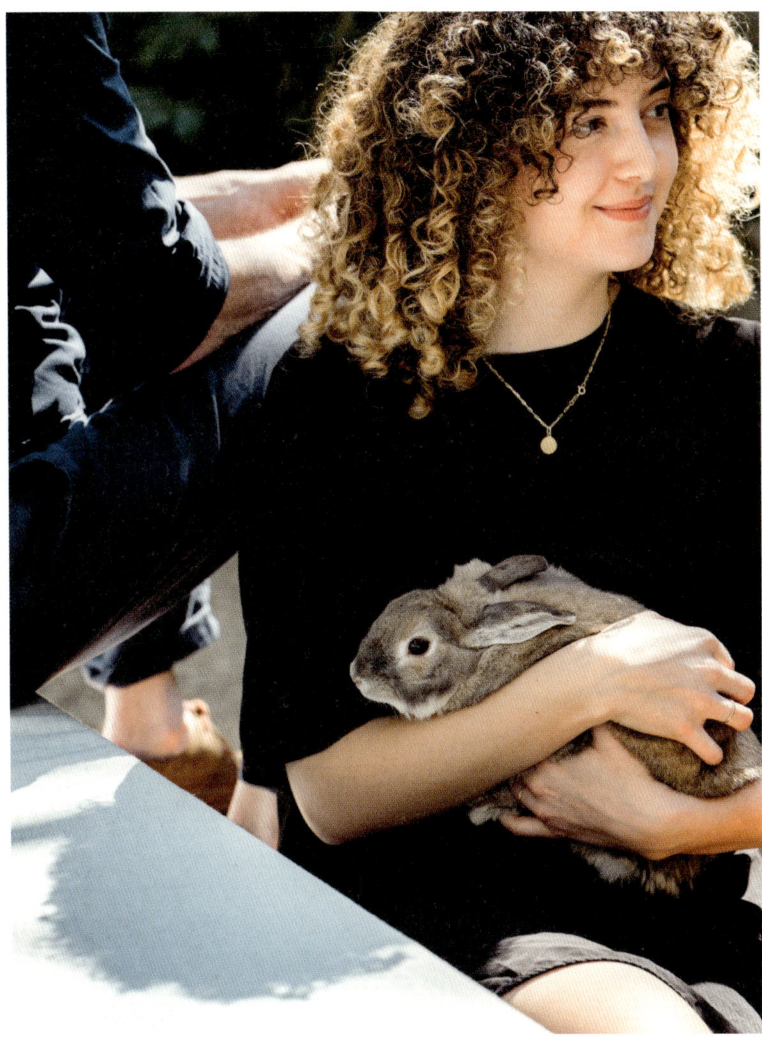

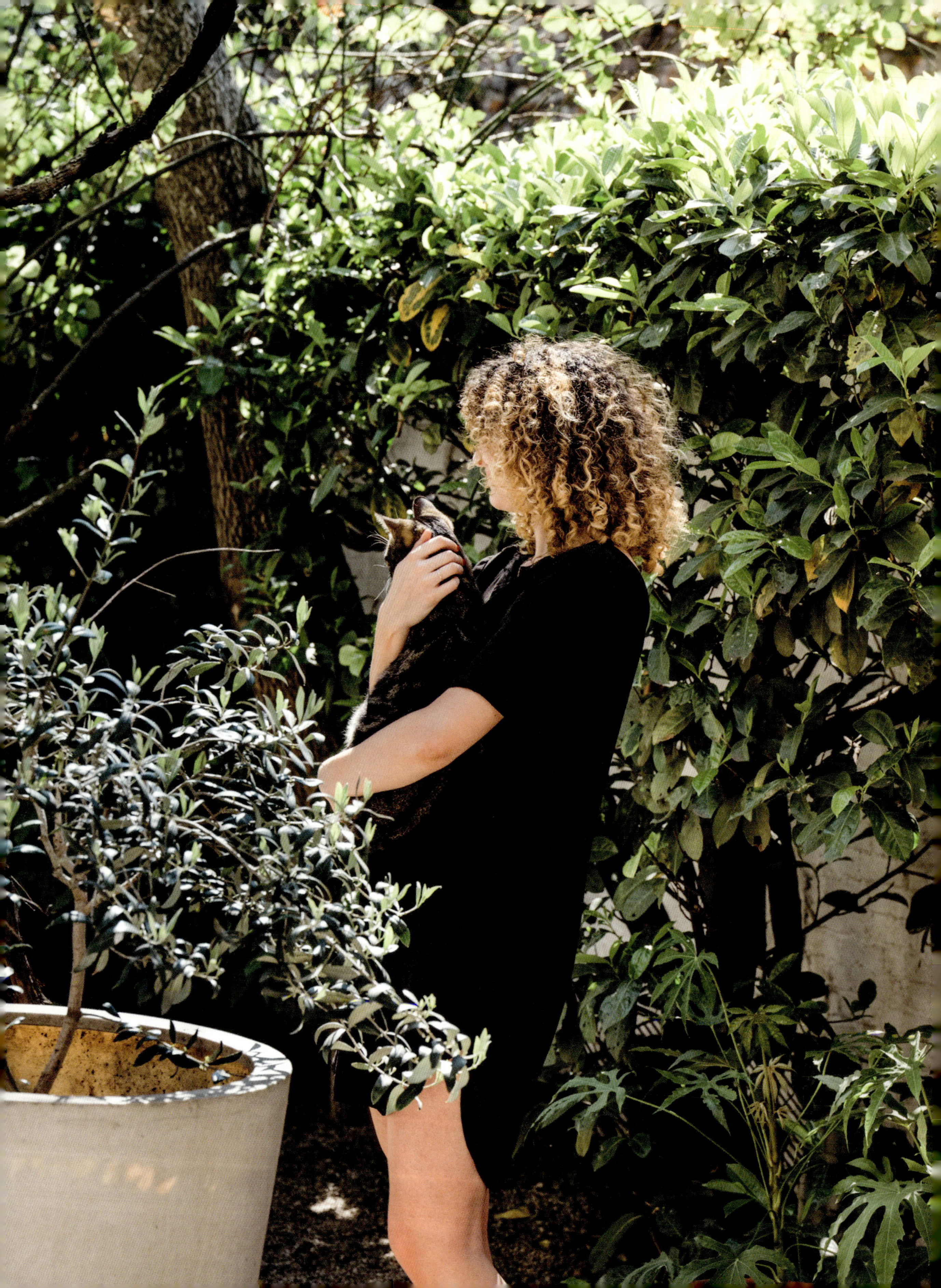

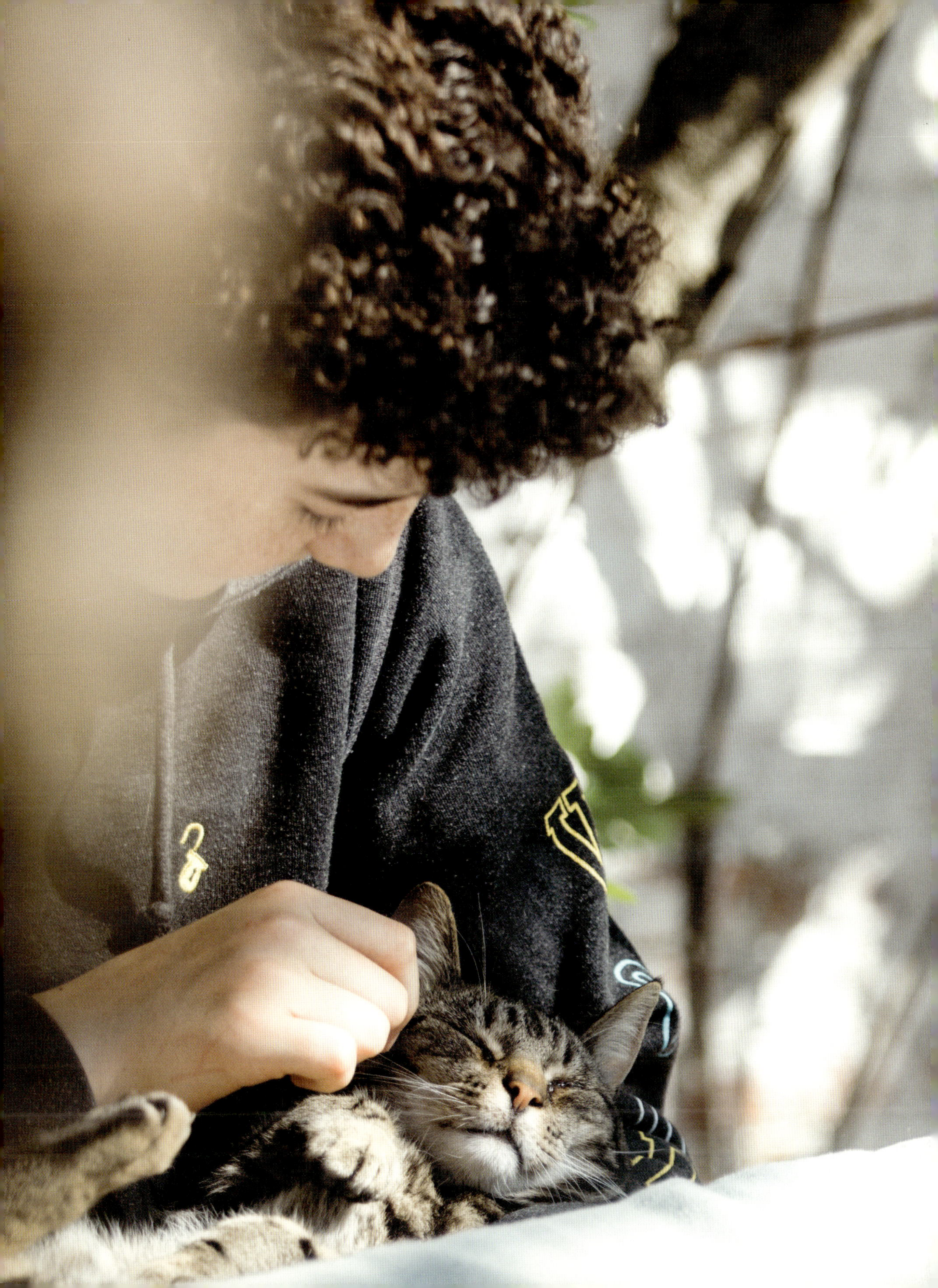

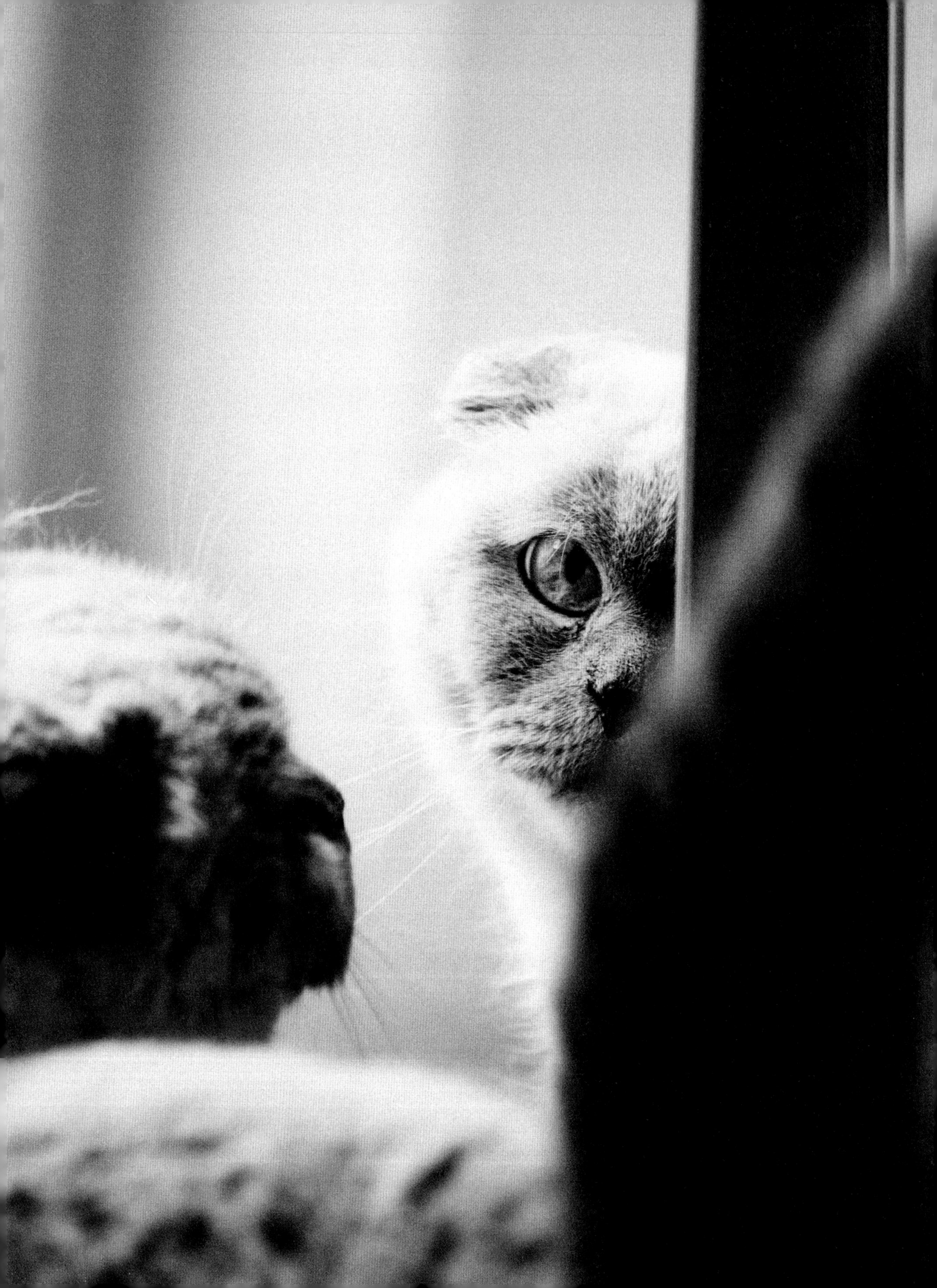

Word of thanks

We would like to thank Marc Verhagen of Luster Publishing for believing in us. For giving us the time and space, we needed to create this book. Karoline Neujens, Dettie Luyten and Sandy Logan for the fantastic teamwork. All the families and friends who opened their homes and hearts to us. All the pets and our own cats, who inspired and moved us. And finally, our baby son, Nolan Ayo, who was born while we were working on this book and who came with us everywhere we went. Thank you for loving animals just as much as we do.

Wild at Heart
For the Love of Pets
and Beautiful Homes

Concept: Bart Kiggen & Magali Elali
Research & text: Magali Elali
Photography & graphic design: Bart Kiggen
D/2019/12.005/8
ISBN 9789460582455
NUR 454, 431
© 2019 Luster, Antwerp (Belgium)
www.lusterweb.com
www.coffeeklatch.be

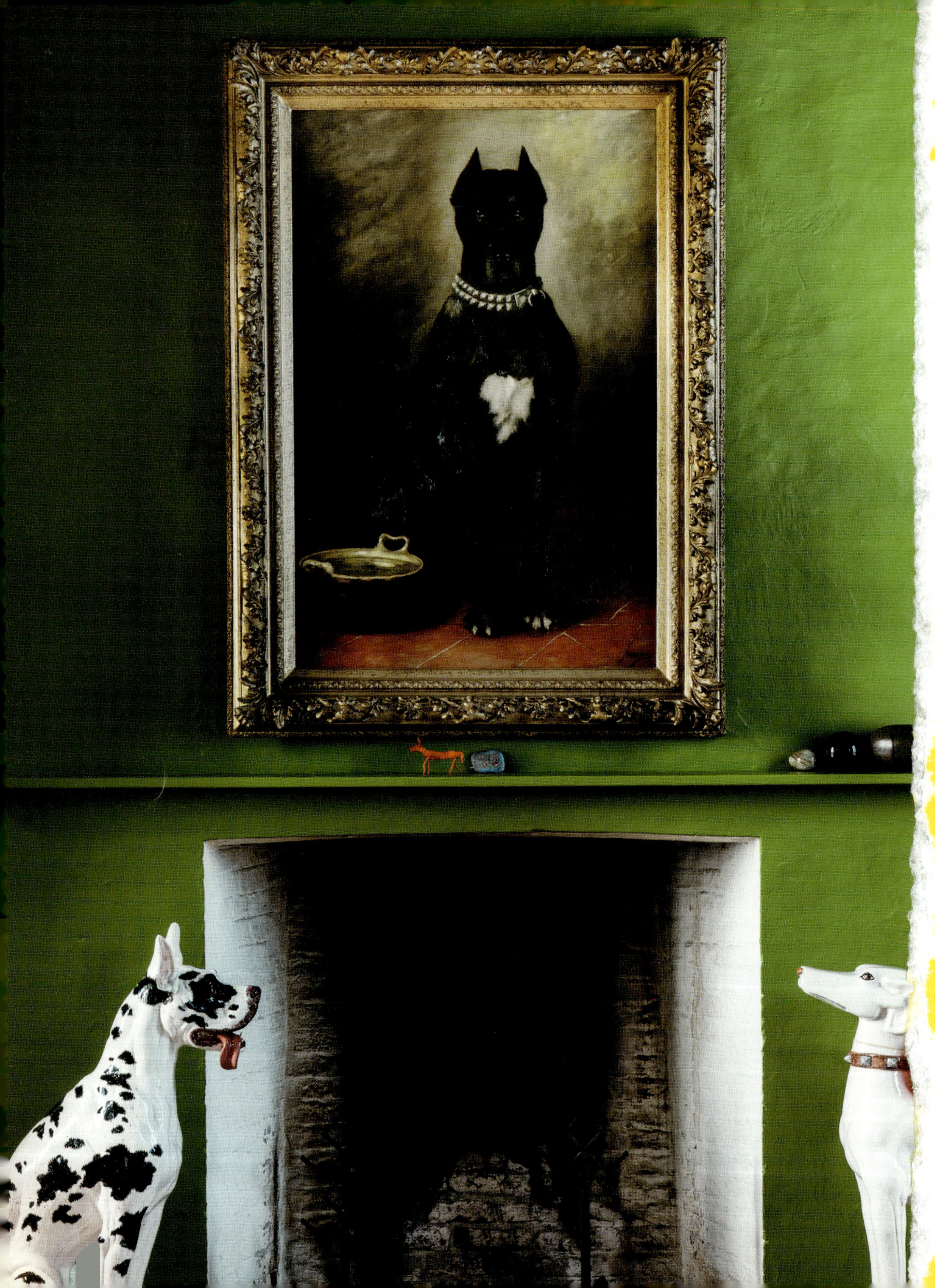